Fear Thy Neighbor as Thyself

Paul Parin
Fritz Morgenthaler
Goldy Parin-Matthèy

Fear Thy Neighbor as Thyself

Psychoanalysis and Society among the Anyi
of West Africa

Translated by Patricia Klamerth

The University of Chicago Press · Chicago and London

The University of Chicago Press, Chicago 60637
The University of Chicago Press, Ltd., London

PAUL PARIN, FRITZ MORGENTHALER, and
GOLDY PARIN-MATTHEY are Swiss psycho-
analysts from Zurich. Together they have also
written *Die Weissen denken zuviel,* a psychoanalytic study of the Dogon people of West
Africa, as well as numerous scholarly articles.

Library of Congress Cataloging in Publication Data

Parin, Paul.
  Fear thy neighbor as thyself.

  Abridged translation of Fürchte deinen Nächsten wie
dich selbst.
  Includes bibliographical references and index.
  1. Agni (African tribe)—Psychology.
2. Personality and culture—Case studies. 3. Psychoanalysis. I. Morgenthaler, Fritz, joint author.
II. Parin-Matthey, Goldy, joint author. III. Title.
DT545.42.P37213   301.29′666′8   79–24360
ISBN 0–226–64583–5

Originally published as *Fürchte deinen Nächsten
wie dich selbst: Psychoanalyse und Gesellschaft am
Modell der Agni in Westafrika,* © Suhrkamp Verlag,
Frankfurt am Main, 1971, all rights reserved.

Contents

Preface

The publishers of this American edition of our book have suggested that we introduce ourselves to our readers in a preface, and that we present a retrospective evaluation of our work. We welcome this suggestion, since only a few of our earlier, short papers in this field (75, 81, 82) have appeared in English. The book (80) that grew out of the first large-scale ethnopsychoanalytic field research project carried out by our team, among the Dogon in the Republic of Mali, was translated only into French and is no longer available. Moreover, the field research leading to the present book was done in 1966, thirteen years ago. The material we gathered during a later visit to the Anyi, in 1971, could no longer be incorporated, and the papers dealing with our later research have for the most part not yet been translated into English (see appendix to the list of references).

At the end of 1965, when we left for our fifth field research project in West Africa, we had been practicing full time as analysts in Zurich for thirteen years, and the youngest of us was forty-six years old. We had arranged our private practice so that we could be free for about six months every two or three years to pursue our psychoanalytic investigations of various West African peoples. The geographical area for our studies was more or less chosen for us during our first trip (1954/55), when we got to know the school system in effect in the colonies in West Africa, which had been retained by the nations in that region that had gained their independence in 1960. This meant we would be able to conduct psychoanalytic interviews in French with the men and women of tradition-directed cultures; a superficial knowledge of their languages and the occasional help of an interpreter to be trained by us would be the only supplementary tools we would need. All our trips were financed from the proceeds of our practice in Zurich; only for the third and fifth (1965/66 to Anyiland) had we applied for and received grants from the Swiss National Foundation for the Promotion of Scientific Research.

During our first two trips we used a simple interview technique; only in the subsequent evaluation of our findings did we apply the genetic and dynamic viewpoints of psychoanalysis to explain character traits and behavior that differed conspicuously from those occurring in our own culture. In 1960, after we had broadened our originally quite rudimentary knowledge of ethnology, we selected as the subjects of a field research project the Dogon, about whom there exists a considerable body of anthropological and sociological literature. We hoped that by studying the available literature we could narrow the cultural gap from the very beginning so that we would be able to dispense with the usual ethnological exploration and apply our psychoanalytic technique with the fewest possible modifications.

The course of psychoanalysis is frequently compared to a journey into the innermost realms of the soul. Our eagerness to acquaint ourselves with the peoples of alien lands came from the same source as our interest in our profession. We were interested primarily in learning something about the inner life of a small number of normal adults belonging to a people whose life-style was totally different from that of the Europeans and Americans with whom psychoanalysis has been chiefly concerned. Above all, we assumed that different child-rearing practices would lead to different psychological development and to different personality structures. We did not want to change both the subjects and the methods of our investigation at the same time; thus in the beginning we adhered as closely as we could to the psychoanalytic techniques we were used to. The briefness of the individual psychoanalytic studies (whose goal, naturally, was not therapeutic) was compensated for in part by the fact that there were three of us, each working with different subjects at the same time, and that we regularly checked each other's work and discussed it together.

Very soon we discovered, to our surprise, that it was not at all difficult to motivate our partners to talk with us for an hour each day, in keeping with the basic rule of psychoanalysis. We found that the minor modifications in psychoanalytic techniques that had to be accepted (such as paying some of our subjects for the time they spent with us) did not distort the course of the interviews in any way, and that their effects could be identified and discounted. The interpretation of resistance to a continuation of the interviews or to an intensification of transference prepared the way for more searching interpretations, which—with the help of additional information provided by our subjects on their memories, dreams, fantasies, and sometimes through their acting out—enabled us to make quite plausible reconstructions of their psychic development and the dynamics of their unconscious. Naturally, in dealing with their resistance, we had to take into consideration how alien we were to them and what specific disturbance factors our presence and our life in the village had introduced. In contrast to other ethnological techniques, our method made it unnecessary for us to ask questions, and this proved to be an enormous advantage. The more comprehensive our knowledge of economic conditions, social institutions, and traditions was to begin with, the more clearly the mental and emotional life of our interview partners could emerge. Our own psychoanalytic manner of thinking was not a problem. Insights developed in much the same fashion as with Europeans, as long as we were constantly prepared to question this, that, or the other aspect of our theoretical expectations and, if necessary, to modify or abandon it. And this approach is no different from the one that ought to be used with any new subject, European or otherwise. One specific difficulty was that our life in the village could be observed by all; this meant we were forced to maintain the psychoanalytic reserve and restraint required during therapy twenty-four hours a day in order to confine emotion-laden contacts to the interviews. At least this was so in the beginning, until all our interviews had gotten off to a good start. What we found much more distracting than any European prejudices were certain expectations that we had set up in connection with one African people and then unconsciously transferred to another; this was troublesome until we were able to make ourselves conscious of these "counter-transferences."

Using psychoanalytically oriented interviews as the main tool of ethnological investigation is a kind of action research, governed by tried and tested rules.

One result of our ethnopsychoanalytic research was our early recognition of the need for certain modifications in psychoanalytic theory, modifications required to reconcile it with our observations. The phases of libido development, for example, were retained as a genetic concept but had to be redescribed in many details to take into account the effects of different child-rearing practices. Ego development in the Dogon and in the Anyi results in hitherto unfamiliar structural patterns, necessitating a description of typical defense organizations, of the "group ego" and the "clan conscience." We have found that individuals belonging to other peoples are capable of entering into normal love and social relations even though their preoedipal fixations and the outcome of the oedipal conflict differ greatly from the Western pattern.

It is clear from the discussion above that we have followed the psychoanalytic theory of personality and have made no attempt to elaborate a new one. For in the last analysis this is the only school of psychology today that can claim to integrate other viewpoints (such as learning theory or Piaget's theory of cognitive development) into a developmental and adaptive model and to give due consideration to the dynamics of psychological life. There were two inevitable disadvantages to our decision to retain the psychoanalytic model. First, psychoanalytic terms may be misunderstood as referring to pathological conditions by readers oriented to the early beginnings of psychoanalysis, when it was primarily a medical discipline and when it had not yet been generally accepted that there is no fundamental difference between the psychology of normal, healthy individuals and that of ailing, disturbed persons. Second, our descriptions invariably appear clumsy when social factors play a role in shaping psychic life. We are gradually trying to develop new concepts that will be easier to deal with; we began with this in the present book and have been continuing in our recent papers (157, 158, 160, 161, 162, 165, 166, 168, 169).

In our opinion, the most significant insights gained lie in our recognition of the way historical, economic, religious, and all sorts of social factors, with all the interrelationships and contradictions inherent in any cultural setting, penetrate deeply into psychological development—into conscious and unconscious mental life—and can still be assessed there. This book constitutes an attempt to apply the psychoanalytic method not only as psychology, but also, at the same time, as a social science. This called for supplementary investigative techniques (pp. 12–14).

Today the ethnologist is in the same position as the historian. Within a few short years after he has completed his field research, the living conditions, the political and economic situations of "his" people or tribe may have undergone changes. Even in what Lévi-Strauss calls the "cold cultures" of Africa, violent transformations have been brought about by the economic forces of the world market, by political upheavals, and by the influence of Western and Islamic ideas on the traditional order of things and thought.

Nevertheless, when we visited Bébou for the second time, in 1971, we found the old order more or less unchanged. The sale of the precious woods from the country's forests, whose proceeds the government hoped to use to finance a modernization of the economic structure, had changed the landscape but had as yet had no effect on the fertility of the soil or on the climate. The adjustment to the demands of the world market through an expansion of the plantation economy and the increased employment of immigrant workers was proceeding very slowly. We have no information on what the situation is today.

But we had a continuing interest in the Anyi we had known and in the further course of their lives; furthermore, our stay in the village had also left its marks. To illustrate this, we shall summarize here some of the impressions we gained in 1971, though the reader will understand our remarks on the later fate of our interviewees only after he has read the book.

In the village itself, the chief, who had aged rapidly after the deaths of his older sister and his last wife (in 1971 he was eighty-three years of age), still retained his power and continued to exercise his role as a structuring force. There was only one correction we had to make in our earlier observations and conclusions. When we first arrived, without having announced our visits to Bébou, Yosso, and M'Basso in advance, we were greeted with spontaneous cordiality. Even people we had hardly known during our first visit embraced us affectionately. There were laughter and tears, and many people begged us to visit them without standing on ceremony. We had not expected such a spontaneous expression of emotion on the part of the Anyi, though we were almost certain that they recalled our sojourn in their villages with pleasure. After the first three or four days, however, the spontaneity subsided entirely. All the interpersonal relations in the village once more seemed to be dominated by the familiar complicated and brittle rules of ceremony, by undercurrents of tension, projective anxieties, and disguised distrust—just as we had found them to be five years before.

We met almost all of our interview partners once more. Thomas Assoua had left the court in Bébou that he had inherited from his father—in contradiction to the matrilineal rules of inheritance—and had moved to Yosso to take over the court of his mother's brother, who had died in the meantime. His first wife, the girl from a distinguished family, had gone back to him so that he now had two wives, as befits the head of a family of renown. Anoh Michel's wife Jacqueline had decided to stay with him and had borne him a second child, but he was still struggling to consolidate his marriage by taking a second wife and to improve at long last his economic and social position as a planter. He was still being helped by his maternal family and, because of its strong influence on his professional and psychic life, he was still finding it difficult to assert himself. Jean-Pierre had written to me and asked me to bring him a transistor radio. Unfortunately his ambivalence toward me was still so great that I was unable to see him. He failed to appear for the appointments I arranged with him through his friends. On the last day of our visit he sent me a message through a younger brother (cousin) to the effect that he was filled with longing to see me but was lying intoxicated in a "cabaret"—a place out in the jungle where they tap the oil palms for wine, some ten kilometers from the village. I had neither the time nor the desire to go out there to meet him.

Suzanne was no longer in Bébou. They told us she had married and moved away. The information they gave us about her husband and her new address was so vague and contradictory that we had a hard time finding her in Agnibilekrou. She was living there as the first wife of an Anyi of distinguished family, who was not only unusually handsome, but also successful. He had his own business as a gunsmith, being one of the very few Anyi who work at a skilled trade. Our visit was the occasion for a ceremonial banquet that lasted six hours, including preparations. Suzanne was now the focal point of a large court with an extensive family; she had kept her oldest son Syrien with her and had had two more children in the meantime. Her new life was that of a distinguished and elegant first wife—exactly what she had always dreamed of and exactly in keeping with tradition. Her unhappy love affair with Paul, which had seemed to be the dominant factor in her life at the time of our interviews, was apparently forgotten—in fact had been undone. She made no mention of it.

That our psychoanalytic interviews had also had therapeutic effects was even more obvious in the case of Elisa than in that of Suzanne. Elisa was well on the way to achieving what her analyst (Madame Parin) had predicted as a potential favorable development for her more advanced years. In spite of her low birth, she was a first wife in the court of the chief, who had lost his two closest female relatives. Her oldest son, whom she had been carrying during our first visit, was with her, and she also had a newborn baby. With her mother, her sister, her sister's little son, and three youngsters who had been "given" to her, she had established a new maternal lineage, for whose welfare she felt responsible. She no longer spoke of the father of her first child and in fact was not interested in any man. She was unwilling to speak with

Madame alone but would talk only in the presence of her retinue. She had leased fields from the chief, enough to guarantee the subsistence of all her lineage, and was about to open a tailor shop, which she wanted to equip with a Swiss sewing machine. Sewing is considered a male profession among the Anyi. Thus Elisa was trying to perpetuate the ideal pattern of an Anyi lineage economically both in accordance with the ancient tradition and at the same time in the "European" manner.

When we examine our book with critical eyes, we cannot help being aware of how much is missing. We were unable to reach sufficiently convincing conclusions from the 130 Rorschach tests we administered. We were unable to deal with symbolism in the Anyi culture and language or with a number of other ethnologically important matters. An intensive discussion of certain problems seemed more important to us than an extensive presentation, which in any case could not have been exhaustive. Even at the outset we had not expected to find simple, easily defined recurrent phenomena that would "explain" the life-style and culture of the Anyi.

In this book, as in our book on the Dogon (80), we have tried to illustrate our method by including as many detailed case reports as possible. Three of these had to be sacrificed because of the need to abridge the American edition (which constitutes 63 percent of the original). We have also had to omit a fairly exhaustive discussion of the history of the Akan peoples and a biography of our friend Ahoussi de Bernard, village chief and king of Alangouan, both designed to illuminate the influences of earlier ways of life and the impact of the colonial period on present conditions. And finally we had to leave out a discussion of some aspects of comparative psychiatry (the transcultural psychiatric viewpoint) as well as a psychological analysis of the messianic healer Edjro Josué, to whom many Anyi had turned in hope of salvation and healing.

On the other hand, it is quite possible that the abridgement may have made the book more readable without altering its underlying message in any way. For what we wanted to demonstrate with our study of the Anyi was the usefulness of the psychoanalytic method for the social sciences. Ethnologists whose interest goes beyond the institutions of a "culture" to the individual, whether his life-style is exotic or European/American, will find that we consider our method an indispensable tool of anthropology. If we have succeeded in communicating this conviction, we shall be content.

Quotations from French sources appearing in the text were translated from French to German by the authors and from German to English by the translator; quotations from German sources were translated into

English by the translator. Translations from the Akan languages were taken from the original sources cited (e.g., Abraham [1], Busia [6], Delafosse [13]), or rendered into English by the translator. All translations from the Anyi language for which no source is cited were prepared in French by François Kakou and other assistants in Bébou, then translated into German by the authors and into English by the translator.

Except when English spellings could be documented (cf. Agni = Anyi), all Anyi proper and geographical names have been retained in the spelling used by the Anyi themselves, that is, in French orthography.

The names and identities of persons appearing in the text have been dealt with in two ways. Most of the people we worked with expressed the wish to appear in our book in recognizable form, that is, to be quoted and referred to by their real names. Those who did not want this and those we were unable to ask have been given fictitious names and their identities disguised to make them unrecognizable.

Most of the Akan sayings and proverbs quoted in the text were taken from published sources such as Abraham (1), Christensen (8), Danquah (11), Debrunner (12), Rattray (31), Riis (37), and Wilks (43). Many of them had appeared for the first time—without translations or commentaries, however—in J. G. Christaller's collection of 3,600 "Tshi proverbs" (Basel 1879).

Unless otherwise indicated in the text, the dancing and mourning songs were recorded on tape by the authors, most of the mourning songs at the funeral festivities for Thomas Assoua's father in Bébou. The translations into French were done by one group of interpreters, whose renditions were then retranslated line by line into the original Anyi by another group and submitted to the singers themselves for verification.

In kinship patterns, the term "maternal lineage" refers to all living persons belonging to the maternal kin, whether or not they live together. We use the terms "matrilineal" and "according to the maternal line" to describe the practice of determining kinship ties by descent from the mother as opposed to descent from the father, as is done in a patrilineal family system. The word "lineage" used in connection with the Anyi, however, refers not to a unidimensional line (grandmother-mother-daughter-granddaughter), but rather to a "bundle of lines" (grandmother-all her daughters-all their daughters, etc.). Figuratively, maternal line or lineage includes all the living *and* deceased members of the kin concerned.

In Anyi kinship designations, there is little point in trying to differentiate between "genuine" biological and "merely" symbolic membership in the maternal lineage, since the two categories are treated identically as far as organization is concerned. Many families, particularly the distinguished ones, trace their descent from a mythical ancestress, from whom biological descent is patently impossible, while other individuals go back only as far as a grandmother whose daughter was really their biological mother. Associated daughters (given to or adopted by the kin as children) have the same status as those with direct blood ties. When we use the term "clan," we refer specifically to that particular family membership or form of kinship that, among the Akan, is derived from mythological descent and associated with a totem animal. (In the metapsychological phrase "clan conscience," however, "clan" is synonymous with "group.")

We translate the French *féticheur, féticheuse* as "(male) shaman, female shaman." Although this term is generally not applied in African ethnology, its functional connotations correspond exactly to the *féticheuses* of the Anyi. Other available terms such as magician, sorcerer, healer, witch doctor, and medicine man are not in accordance with that institution.

Our study makes no claim to ethnological completeness. We have devoted no space to the significance of the Ashanti gold weights, since they do not play an important role in Anyi culture, nor have we mentioned the Anyi grave figures of Sanwi, which are unknown today in Alangouan.

Amounts of money mentioned in the text are given in cfa francs, the currency of the area. In 1979, the exchange rate was two hundred cfa francs to one United States dollar.

1 Launching the Investigation

Caligula Africanus

They remind us of the Romans in the declining years of the Empire—proud of the fading memory of half-forgotten warriors long since turned to dust, looking down in their arrogance from the pinnacle of a long-vanished power whose afterglow makes their decline seem even shabbier and sadder. With sophistication and artistry they drape the tattered purple toga of social etiquette to cover the barrenness of depravity and poverty; in extravagant, financially ruinous funeral festivities, following the rituals of alien, imported gods, they bring sacrifice to the shades, which take revenge on their children—and rightly so. They would die of hunger if their despised foreign workers were to depart from their cities. Yet the weary display of the remnants of a superiority they enjoyed for centuries suffices to prolong their noble decadence. If one day the last noble gentlemen, the last lovely ladies, intoxicated with palm wine, should be slain by their servants and left to the encroaching rain forests, we would realize how much intelligence and charm, how

much skeptical common sense and melancholy wisdom had been lost
with them. Not one of their kings, not one of their female shamans
could exorcize the avenging furies of their passions. Thus they bear the
splendor of their fathers and their treasure of gold through the nocturnal terror of their fears, through never-ending downpours, over rapidly
disappearing paths through the jungle—"d'avant'hier jusqu'aaah"—
from the day before yesterday into eternity.

The absurdity of the title—assigning the proud epithet "Africanus"
to that vicious weakling Caligula—is not merely a cruel jest born of our
imagination. When we left their kingdom after spending four months
there, it seemed to us that Albert Camus (142) had captured the essence
of the Anyi far better than we ever could:

> *Caligula:* Yes. I want the moon . . . . Do you think I'm mad? . . . Yes.
> All right. But I'm not mad, as a matter of fact I've never been saner
> than I am right now. That's just the way it was. I suddenly had the
> feeling that I had to have the impossible . . . .
> *Cherea:* . . . Let's not do anything to stop Caligula. In fact, let's
> encourage him to go on along that path. Let's introduce some method
> to his madness. Someday the time will come when he'll stand alone
> before a realm of the dead and the dead kin of his dead.

What have we just done? We have insulted, falsified, distorted,
exaggerated, whitewashed, generalized—and we shall continue to do
so. Because it is the only possible way. When we simply describe
people, we do not do them justice. We may be strangers to them, or we
may be acquainted with them. If we recount everything we know about
them, the affront remains; how can anyone dare to study people, to lay
bare their innermost feelings, and to describe them coldly and sci-
entifically? In doing so, we subject, not the person described, but the
reader of the description to the same mortification so painfully experienced as narcissistic injury during psychoanalysis—a reaction that must
be gradually overcome if we are to discover what manner of persons we
are. How reprehensible, then, to apply this procedure not to ourselves,
but to our black brothers. Only our naive belief in the usefulness of
knowledge thus acquired can justify our undertaking.

The Anyi have an ancient custom. When an Anyi has done or said
something bad to someone else, he asks an "elder" to convey his request for forgiveness. The "elder" is then obliged to carry out this
unpleasant errand on behalf of the evildoer. He does not find this difficult. After all, he was not the culprit. The injured party accepts the
apology. His own magnanimity compensates him for the wrong he has
suffered and enhances his stature in the eyes of his fellows. The matter
is settled. But is the injury really forgotten?

We call upon the nonexistent spirit of scientific veracity to convey our apologies. They will certainly be accepted. But will our penetrating Western impertinence be forgotten?

More than this—the fact remains that we have falsified, distorted, and so on. And we have done so deliberately. A statement such as "the Anyi are like the Romans before the fall of the Empire; their soul is like that of Camus's Caligula, and they are doomed to share his fate" is absolutely false, and it is impossible not to make such false statements.

We need a picture of our past—more precisely, not of ours, but rather a picture such as is normally handed down by tradition in our culture. We need a picture that we recognize because it has something to say to us, even though it may have little to do with the past reality of our people, and even though it is extremely doubtful that it corresponds to any past reality at all. Our language and our mental processes are made up of such inaccurate pictures—especially inaccurate when we try to apply them to peoples of an alien social structure, with an entirely different history, culture, and psychology. It is the purpose of scientific investigation and description to reduce the number of these in-accuracies.

We are convinced that we have found an appropriate tool in the psychoanalytic method, but it is a tool that originates exclusively in our culture, in our manner of thinking. Thus we shall go on making errors that stem from the dissimilarity of the cultures involved, and go on trying to correct them in the light of criticism and observation. Anyone who rejects Freudian psychoanalysis as a means of exploring and describing the personality is advised at this point to read no further. But those who are merely skeptical of its application to peoples of another culture, or specifically to Africans, may appreciate, as we do, previous experiments of this kind (61, 80, 133); we regard the present book as a continuation of these.

During psychoanalytically oriented interviews, the attempt is made to eliminate barriers and obstacles by talking about them—by interpreting resistance, making the subject aware of it, and thus helping him master it. This obviates the need to ask questions that reflect our curiosity, our way of thinking; *their* way of thinking and feeling can be observed more clearly. Empathy and intellectual reconstruction take the place of a direct recording or statistical evaluation of data.

Which People?

We were looking for a people we could compare with the Dogon, whom we had studied in 1960; in other words, a people as different from the

Dogon as possible. We also wanted to work with a social group that had remained true to its traditions but with whom we—as psychologists—could communicate in a European language.

In 1960 nine independent states were established in that vast region of West Africa that had been united during the French colonial period under the name French West Africa. Each of these nine states possesses a school system, taken over by African teachers long before independence, that offers a unique prerequisite for our type of investigation. For the education offered in these schools has promoted a superficial adaptation of the pupils to the borrowed civilization without inculcating a genuine acceptance of its values. This is one of the reasons school attendance usually has comparatively little influence on the traditional identity of French-speaking West Africans—a circumstance that was all to the good as far as our study was concerned.

Five-year primary schools were established in this region beginning in the first decade of our century and increasing in number during the twenties and up to World War II. Their distribution throughout the area was independent of the natural resources available in a given region or a given town's access to the transport network. In many villages and settlements remote from the centers of civilization some of the population—primarily the men, of course—speak French.

These, then, were the factors that determined the geographical area where we set out to find "our" people. We knew from experience that in Europe and America it is possible to psychoanalyze patients who cannot use their mother tongue in talking with the analyst, and this has been confirmed in Africa as well (61, 80). The inevitable disadvantages inherent in carrying out psychoanalytic interviews with Africans in a European language simply had to be accepted, because in practice it was impossible for us to acquire the necessary fluency in the language of the people selected.

The right people for our purposes was one that would represent an antithesis to the Dogon within the framework of the realities common to all West Africa, and such a people could best be found in a region characterized by the political history—and, consequently, by the school system—described above.

Since the psychological factors were still to be determined, we hoped above all to find a family structure contrasting with that of the Dogon. The latter are organized in patriarchal, patrilineal extended families; in other words, descent from the paternal line determines membership in the family, place of residence, and thus many other institutions such as the laws governing the inheritance of property and honors. In the contrasting matrilineal organization, the maternal line determines parentage.

We assumed that, in contrast to the patrilineal structure, which is the structure prevailing in the Western world as well, emphasis on the maternal line and on the membership of the individual in the lineage of the mother would be bound to have vastly different effects on the smallest social unit, the nuclear family into which the child is born and in which he often experiences the most decisive period of psychological development. Thus our challenge to the direct application of the psychoanalytic method was this: Can it help us understand members of a matrilineal social structure in spite of its origin in the psychology of a patrilineal society and in spite of the fact that one of its fundamental concepts, the oedipal conflict—allegedly or genuinely—is exclusively a product of patrilineal family organization?

In Africa there are a great many large, and innumerable small, ethnic groups living in close proximity, and many of them intermingle and overlap. On the Ivory Coast alone there are approximately fifty-three of them. Within the confines of the area shaped like a V, its left arm extending north to the Ivory Coast and its right reaching as far as Zambia, there are some peoples with patrilineal family structures, but most of them are organized according to the matrilineal pattern; outside this area no matrilineal organization is found. We know of no plausible theory that might explain this geographical distribution historically or on any other basis, but it did make it easy for us to define the geographical area for our study as that part of the Ivory Coast bordering on Ghana, where the territory of the former French West Africa coincides with the area inhabited by peoples organized according to the matrilineal principle (fig. 1).

Consulting the ethnological literature available for this area, we came upon the Anyi people, in the southeastern corner of the Ivory Coast, near the Ghanaian border, a people living next door to the famed Ashanti—who had defied the British Empire in no fewer than four wars—related to them, and resembling them.

Quite apart from the fact that the Anyi have a matrilineal clan system while Dogon society is based on the patriarchal extended family, there are many points of contrast between the two peoples. The Anyi live in the damp rain forests, the Dogon in the arid savannas. The Anyi grow crops for the world market, primarily coffee and cocoa, and are dependent upon imports of foreign goods (some from Europe) and upon artisans and foreign workers from poorer areas, whereas the Dogon grow millet to meet their own needs, export very little—and only to African markets—and are economically self-sufficient, sometimes exporting workers to wealthier areas. The Dogon are heathens with a social system that is complex, singular, and firmly rooted in myth, religion, and the structure of their economy. The Anyi call themselves

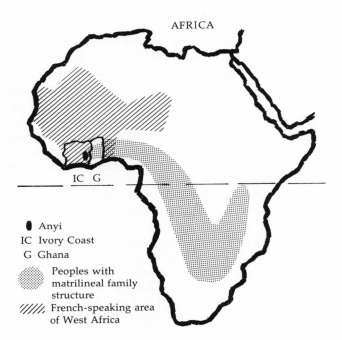

AFRICA

IC G

● Anyi
IC Ivory Coast
G Ghana

Peoples with
matrilineal family
structure

////, French-speaking area
of West Africa

Fig. 1. The territory inhabited by the Anyi in the rain forest in the southeastern corner of the Ivory Coast, near the border of Ghana.

Christians, and their religion is a syncretic mixture of native and alien, old and new elements. Their social structure must reconcile elements rooted in the traditions of an ancient warrior people and in the life-style of hunters and gatherers with a "European" system of production—without the support of a comprehensive religious or political order. Nevertheless, stubbornly and conservatively, the Anyi seem to have preserved their identity as a separate people. The insight into African psychology that we had acquired during our study of the Dogon frequently got in our way in dealing with the Anyi. The Dogon never resort to constraint in politics or pedagogy; the Anyi, by contrast, achieve their social goals almost exclusively by constraint, fear, and punishment. We never heard a child crying for any length of time in a Dogon village; someone always hurried to comfort it. Our stay in Bébou, on the other hand, was an ordeal simply because of the incessant, heartrending sobbing of the children, day and night.

Which Village?

We established our headquarters in Abengourou, the seat of the préfecture and souspréfecture, and set out to look for "our" village, the "primary social unit" in which we intended to live and work.

The territory inhabited by the Anyi was formerly divided into three provinces or regions, called Sanwi, N'denié, and Bongouanou. For our investigation, we wanted an area where life was relatively stable—where traditions were not entirely unchanged but were still alive. Political unrest, catastrophic economic depression, or any too comprehensive or rapid changes in the demographic structure as a result of emigration or immigration would make our work impossible. An equally important prerequisite was the availability of enough French-speaking inhabitants in the village we selected. Access by fairly well-kept roads was desirable, but at the same time "our" village needed to be far enough away from the main traffic arteries to have preserved a fairly quiet style of life.

On the basis of these criteria, we were soon able to narrow the choice to the region of N'denié. Here we visited approximately twenty-five villages and finally decided on Bébou, with its two neighboring villages Ehouessan (commonly referred to as Yosso) and M'Basso. Only later did we learn that these three villages, and the small settlement of Blékoum (situated, like M'Basso, on the Comoë River), had originally constituted a single kingdom, Alangouan, with Bébou as its capital (fig. 2).

In the beginning we had no idea that our choice, by virtue of its history, was so uniquely suited to be the "social unit" of our investigation. What attracted us was its location off the main traffic artery, the ease of communication among the three villages, so obviously similar and evidently belonging together, via a good road, and—most of all—our first impression of life in the village and our meeting with its chief.

The roads and paths, paved with crushed red laterite, led through the "rain forest" to our village. In 1911 Chéruy (7) described the area as follows:

> The soil of Indénié is covered by dense forest everywhere, an impenetrable curtain broken only by the rare artificial clearings where there are villages and plantations. Extremely narrow paths, and some fairly wide ones, lead through the forest, connecting the villages with

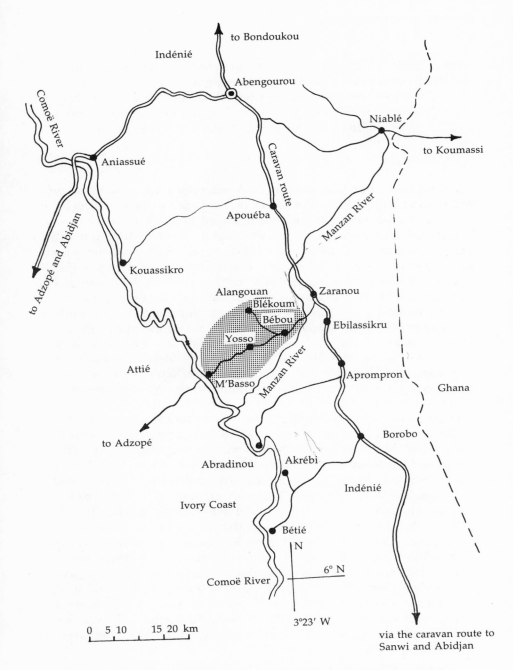

Fig. 2. The "Kingdom" of Alangouan lies between the Comoë and Manzan rivers and is surrounded on three sides by the Anyi territory of Indénié. Alangouan borders on the area inhabited by the Attié in the west, and Indénié borders on Ghana in the east.

one another. . . . The weariness that plagues one during these long marches is due chiefly to the unrelieved monotony of the landscape. What wears one down in this forest is its eternal sameness. After marching along for a few hours, one tries desperately to see what lies ahead; but one's eyes are stopped by the never-ending curtain of green that hides the horizon.

The landscape has changed very little since that time. Chéruy's description would still fit the belt of jungle that curves around the entire Gulf of Guinea, from Guinea to Togo. And yet we know that this is Anyi territory as soon as we see the inhabitants. The Anyi are fairly tall for Africans, dark brown in color, and slender; both men and women wear bright-colored togas. Proud and stately, their eyes fixed on us strangers in distrust and contempt, they could never be mistaken for any of the neighboring peoples, and certainly not for their foreign workers. Their facial expression is depressive or reserved. Their women frequently are beautiful. The old people sit on low stools in the dark shadows at the rear of their courts. The children, naked or dressed only in shorts, play in small groups in the courtyards or in the side streets. There is no marketplace, no community center to serve as a focus for life in the village. If one equates the inner courtyard of a compound with an apartment, the villages resemble Western cities in which the streets are used exclusively for traffic and the inhabitants must go visit each other when they want to meet.

When we first came into a village, we would start a conversation with children or teenagers. As soon as a number of older boys and girls joined the group, the conversation was continued in French. We asked to be taken to the "chief."[1]

The preliminary arrangements were always reminiscent of those preceding an audience with royalty. First, the young people introduce us to a number of dignitaries, one of whom welcomes us and conducts us to a court, either his own or that of the chief. In the meantime the chief has changed into the toga reserved for official receptions. Accompanied by his dignitaries and perhaps by a favorite small son, he enters and invites us to sit down on his terrace. A nephew of the chief, or sometimes another young man, the village schoolmaster, for example, is assigned the role of interpreter—or rather spokesman, since most of the chiefs are able to speak French. After the opening words of welcome, the conversation seems to languish. Drinks have been brought in—beer, lemonade, or wine. Before we drink, the chief spills a few drops on the ground for the spirits of his ancestors. Then, through the spokesman, he asks for our "first news"—"il dit qu'il attend vos premières nouvelles." The answer is expected to be brief, to mention where we come from and what we want to do, and to conclude with a compliment for the chief.

After this he may ask a few questions. In the more remote villages our visits are sensational events. In those villages the chief may suddenly turn to the crowd that has gathered to see us and, addressing a fairly lengthy speech to his dignitaries, may explain what he considers to be of interest in our "first news." When the conversation begins to lag, it is time for us to take our departure. Sometimes we are invited to visit another, less noble court, where the whole procedure is repeated.

When we return a second time to a village, we have to go through the same ceremony once more. This time we can bring a bottle of gin as a present for the chief. The second visit lasts longer. The chief now asks for our "second news," which is expected to be more personal and more concrete. We explain that—circumstances, villagers, and especially the chief permitting—we might want to carry out our investigations in the village. Usually we have no way of telling whether he understands just what we intend to do. No questions are asked. In any case, everyone thinks that what we say is merely a pretext, that we will reveal our true intentions later on. In spite of this, they invite us to stay in the village. As a rule, a live chicken is deposited in our car as a first gift from our hosts.

As far as we know, of the twenty-five villages we visited, twenty-four were permanently and deeply offended that we did not decide to remain; the inhabitants made this clear to us during subsequent visits. They might say, for example, that their sick people needed our help. We realized only little by little what we had really done to offend them; it was not that we had done nothing to benefit the village, but simply that we had deprived it of its "right of possession" over our persons. The prestige associated with the presence of wealthy foreign guests would have lent the village an unprecedented aura of glory. The chief of one of the villages we visited presented us with a thousand-franc bill as we were leaving and refused to take it back. He explained that it was a pledge to guarantee that we would—indeed must—remain in his village. This more or less reduced us to the status of debtor slaves, who in olden times were obligated to serve a king from whom their kin had accepted money.

This attitude is not merely a relic of the colonial period, during which African peoples quickly learned that the power and influence of the white masters were so great that only friendship with them could bring genuine advantages to the lives of the villagers. Treich-Laplène, the first authorized representative sent by France and one of the first Europeans to travel in this part of the continent, reports similar experiences (30). Marcel Monnier, one of the members of the Crozat-Binger mission, who spent four days (from 17 to 20 July 1892) in one of the villages we inspected, wrote the following about King Bénié Kwame in the village of Bétié: "He received us with the genial air of an aristocratic host welcoming his guests, and immediately expressed his ardent desire that we should remain under his roof for many days. His Majesty will have to be content with forty-eight hours of our presence."

Finally we made up our minds to establish our headquarters in Bébou, carrying out supplementary research in Yosso and M'Basso as well. Our decision was made rather suddenly—we suspect as a result of weariness and indecisiveness, and because we realized that there was no way of predicting the course of our investigations no matter which village we chose. At that time we were not yet aware of the historical cohesion of the three villages, with Bébou as the main settlement. Without knowing it, we were about to take our places in the traditional order, still very much alive in the person of the chief, Ahoussi de Bernard.

Before our second visit, approximately ten days after the first, we had sent notice of our coming. We found Ahoussi in his court, attired in a plain dark-colored toga and accompanied by only a few younger people and a small boy of about six. He was obviously delighted to see us and immediately waived all ceremony. "I knew that you would be back. Bébou is just the right village for you. You will be able to work here as you want. I know what white people need." It would be easy to find a house for us, he said. His own niece had a house that she would be glad to lend to any friends of his.

Is is strange that we never had any difficulty in connection with payment for our stay in Bébou—or payment for anything else—either with Ahoussi or with any of his subjects. We never had anything stolen, and no one ever tried to cheat us—in a country that is wealthier than its neighbors, to be sure, but in which there is also a good deal of poverty and in which both men and women are obsessed with the ideas of money, property, indebtedness, and stealing. The gold the Anyi so ardently desire is buried in the land of their dreams, in their past, in their dreams of a better future, and in their envy of the more fortunate, the richer, who are better off than they and whom Mother Earth has showered with gold without any work or effort on their part. There is no gold; not in reality. Only the tiny heaps of gold dust that the old women carry knotted in a corner of their togas. Sometimes they pour it into the palm of their hand and show it to the whites, a smile playing on their lips. Otherwise they are sad. For them the age of gold is past.

In the eighteenth century, when the Anyi first fled to the rain forests to escape their victorious cousins, they found gold in the sand of the rivers. In the vicinity of the present village of Bébou, the warriors once brought their king a gold nugget as large as a man's forearm. Since it was too heavy to take along on their raids, they asked him what to do with it. "Break it into pieces!" was his reply—"*Bébou!*" in the language of the Anyi.

Not until we were just about to leave was there an end to the rumors that we had come to the Anyi country only to find out where there might still be gold. Our psychological studies, our treatment of the sick, everything that we had said and done was intended only to conceal our true intentions—to return one day and steal the gold from the earth, the gold of the Anyi.

The Techniques We Employed

Ethnopsychoanalysis makes use of a wide variety of investigative techniques. Figure 3 summarizes graphically those we employed. The focal point is represented by psychoanalytical interviews repeated over a fairly long period—a method we had used successfully with other African peoples to attain a proper psychological understanding; radiating out from the center are the shorter exploratory interviews with both normal and mentally disturbed individuals.

Our further investigations were intended primarily to help us understand our discussion partners better. These are indicated in the chart by the converging lines. The other lines point to fields of observation providing data that were particularly important to an understanding of some other field. The chart does not include data obtained through study of the pertinent literature.[2]

It was in Bétié, a large village without a chief, that we found our interpreter, François Kakou. Fortunately, François was a capable interpreter and was intelligent and well-mannered. Nevertheless, he did not seem to be quite happy. He had found friends in the village and usually came to work more or less willingly when we needed him—though sometimes he failed to appear. He was often disposed to chat with us and always understood immediately what was wanted of him; but he kept "forgetting" that he was only supposed to interpret and would either give us his own comments on what people said or simply say nothing at all. Sometimes he was an indispensable help to us, sometimes a source of helpless annoyance.

Living in the village was in itself a valuable source of information. Quite probably, no white people had ever lived there before for any length of time. Just what did "living in the village" involve? First of all, it meant being the constant objects of a suspicious watchfulness, the defenseless recipients of ceremonial visits by people to whom we were

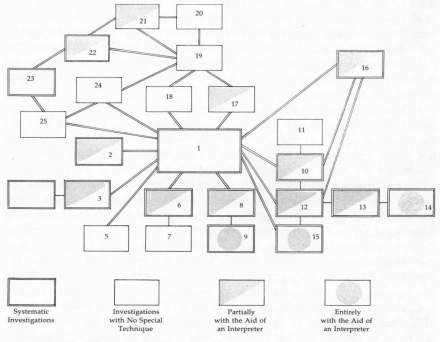

Systematic Investigations	Investigations with No Special Technique	Partially with the Aid of an Interpreter	Entirely with the Aid of an Interpreter

1. Psychoanalytic interviews with five men and two women (totaling 279 hours)
2. 130 Rorschach tests
3. Direct observation of children
4. Films: infant care
5. Observation: school in Bébou
6. Family sociology: courts and courtyards
7. Topographical survey of the village of Bébou
8. Interviews: value systems
9. Recordings and translations: songs, myths
10. Exploratory interviews with normal individuals
11. Criminological survey
12. Exploratory interviews with mentally disturbed individuals
13. Female shamans and healers
14. Edjro, the healer, and his patients
15. Exploratory interviews with mentally disturbed individuals in Bingerville asylum
16. The bodily sick; daily office hours
17. Contacts with foreign laborers, shopkeepers
18. Political contacts
19. The economy
20. The Ivory Coast; other African countries
21. Neighboring Anyi villages
22. Selection of the primary social unit
23. Contacts with the chief
24. Life in the village of Bébou
25. Social events; funeral ceremonies, soccer

Fig. 3. The structure of our investigations.

expected to offer refreshments and with whom courtesy demanded that we exchange hours of empty "first talking." On the other hand, we were shielded by the ritual network of etiquette, so that we "belonged" not just as distinguished foreigners, but as Anyi—for they themselves tend to entangle each other in similarly distrustful social contacts. We "belonged," yet we remained outsiders—it was an atmosphere of alienness curiously mingled with close intimacy. The private interviews with the inhabitants, which took place in tents we had set up on the outskirts of the village, were satisfactorily set apart from our other social contacts by our choice of site and by the different ceremonial patterns we established for them.

Whenever there was a funeral ceremony, we—like all the others—contributed our share to the expenses involved. This was one way we escaped the odium of the whites, "who never do that because they do not believe in celebrating a funeral"; nevertheless, we were never accepted on the same basis as the Anyi in this respect.

Several times each day sick people would appear in our courtyard to ask for medical treatment; we found it best to establish a regular hour for such visits in the evening three times a week. Only very rarely and after lengthy persuasion would a patient we had helped agree to "repay" us by submitting to a Rorschach test. We found it impossible to use questionnaires or even individual direct interviews to elicit answers to our questions regarding the attitudes of the Anyi, especially on the rearing of children, but also on various social institutions. In general, neither the men nor the women seemed capable of providing reliable data in response to direct questions. They either made no reply at all, tried to change the subject, or casually gave contradictory answers obviously dictated by the fancy of the moment. On the other hand, not infrequently we were able to find energetic older women who had no compunction about telling us confidently just what they thought. When we wanted to question them, they would call together a circle of younger women and girls. In four villages we succeeded in getting together a total of six such groups, consisting of six to eight women each. Then the question-and-answer procedure became a fascinating game. The oldest woman present spoke first, expressing her opinion briefly and clearly. After each such answer, the younger women would speak up, freely and without shyness, each indicating her agreement with what had been said or pointing out her differing views on the matter. This method brought us a wealth of material in the form of individual statements. It seems that, with the Anyi, what one thinks and what one feels one ought to do are very different from how one really acts. This is even truer of the Anyi than of our own culture. There are matters, however, in which no such dichotomy exists.

A simple compilation of the various investigative methods employed cannot, of course, reveal the most important factor of the entire procedure, the emotional climate—acceptance and rejection, the feelings of affection and the tensions of animosity, in short the patterns of emotional motivation according to which a psychoanalytic investigation is and must be carried out. Until the very end of our stay, we found ourselves still trying to define and clarify the development of these emotional relationships, as the following example will show.

Our living in the village conferred a certain prestige upon it, but at the same time it made our own status enigmatic. The king was our host, his niece our landlady. This lent us prestige in turn, and earned us the respect of the inhabitants; but it also gave us an aura of awe, fear, and subservient intimacy such as is the prerogative of the chief. That we had chosen our friends from among the traditional ruling class did not, as one might assume, bring us the political opposition or enmity of the "youth faction," but rather brought its envious acceptance. Our treatment of the sick evoked neither the gratitude nor the cooperation of the inhabitants, but in the beginning made us seem uncanny beings, able to disguise our genuine, potentially dangerous intentions with particular deviousness. Later, however, our medical activity brought us recognition as performers of a social role, as beings who are so inhumanly good that they do things for others with no expectation of repayment, who thus obviously need nothing for themselves. This in turn was an advantage to our status as psychologists in the village. In other words, our friendship with the king and his family and our free treatment of the sick brought us prestige. Our social role as foreigners, as friends of the chief, and as physicians created fear and suspicion. A shift in this attitude came about first among the supporters of the king, then among his political opponents, and finally among our patients and their families—but without any change in our social role. We became objects of jealous acceptance. Psychoanalysis speaks of a shift in transference. Here the initial terrifying transference, with the object representation of a phallic, violating mother, gave way to a gentle, siblinglike affection not unmixed with jealousy and—parallel to this—to an emotionally positive mother transference. The emotions transferred to an individual can change without any accompanying change in his social role.

It was only toward the end of our stay that old Denda, the king's sister and thus "first lady" of the village, assigned us a new role. She lived next door, in the same court as we did, and we had gotten into the habit of bringing her a bottle of Coca Cola every day, which she would pour into a gourd cup and sip slowly. At six o'clock each morning she came to thank us, taking each of us by both hands and curtseying to us. One day she asked her brother to tell us that she had finally realized who we were and what we were doing in Bébou! According to her, we were not really whites at all; we were her departed ancestors, come back to watch over the living. There was no other explanation! For the living were not like us, and whites least of all. In May 1968, two years after our departure from Bébou, Denda died. Ahoussi wrote us a short, sad letter to let us know.

1. Ahoussi de Bernard

2. Denda, the sister of King Ahoussi

3. Thomas Assoua

4. The Assoua kin

5. Suzanne

6. Anoh Michel

7. An unhappy toddler

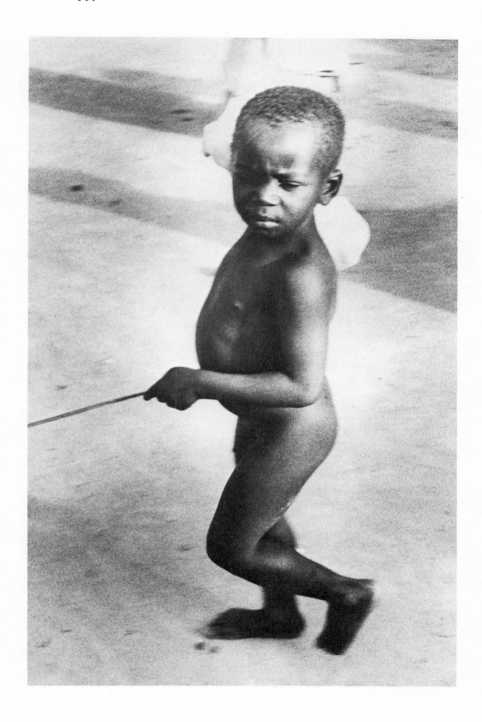

8. Young Anyi girl

9. Young Anyi men from M'Basso

10. Elisa

11. Woman from Aprompron

12. Brou Koffi

13. Mother and child

15. Distrust

16. Melancholy and wisdom

2 History, Political Organization, and Value Systems

The Anyi, an Akan People

"The Anyi number more than 100,000," wrote Köbben (25) in 1956; it is very probable that this figure has increased in the meantime. (In 1950 the total population of the Ivory Coast was estimated at 2,520,000 and in 1965 at 3,338,000 [22].)

It seems to us appropriate to speak of the Anyi "people" and not, as one might expect, of the Anyi "tribe" (140). They are speakers of "Twi," a term that comprises a number of languages spoken by the "Akan" in Ghana and in the eastern part of the Ivory Coast. Whether these are to be regarded as dialects (Berry, as cited in Manoukian [28]) or as different but related languages (22) has not yet been determined. Six of the Akan peoples (the Ashanti, Fanti, N'zima, Akim, Kwah, and Akwapim) (16) live in Ghana, and three (the Anyi, Baoulé, and Abron) live in the Ivory Coast Republic. All Akan peoples live in societies characterized by the maternal lineage system; that is, descent is determined

by the maternal line. The same system is the foundation of their traditional political and social orders. As far as the Anyi are concerned, the
turbulent history of the past 250 years has awakened in them the feeling
of a separate identity as a people. They often use the term "our cousins"
in referring to the Ashanti, and they call the Baoulé "those who have cut
themselves off from us."

Psychological experience invariably has a historical dimension. And
psychoanalysis, based on exploration of the past of the adult, cannot
afford to dispense with a knowledge of the traditions of the persons
who reared its subjects or the traditions with which these subjects live.
Family and clan structures, themselves a part of these traditions, constitute the subject's environment, which in turn determines the psychic
development of each people in a way specific to it. Myths, religions,
and traditional value systems will help determine the behavior of coming generations as components of the superego or clan conscience. The
same economic and social laws that had validity in the past continue to
influence much of modern life, to dictate the criteria for "reasonable"
and "unreasonable" behavior. They continue to influence cognitive
processes and emotions, the events of the secondary process. It would
be inexcusable for us not to make use of the history of the Akan peoples
as a basis for our ethnopsychological investigation, since we are fortunate enough to be able to consult the works of a number of European
and African historians, all of them attracted by the glory of the Ashanti
past. Precolonial and colonial biases, however, often obscure the course
of events. The time has come when the Africans will be writing their
own history.

These remarks apply to the Anyi to a particularly high degree. In the
words of Dupire (14), it is "extraordinarily difficult to understand the
simplest behavior on the part of an individual outside its historical
context, which begins with the exodus of the Anyi people" (approximately 150 years ago).

A full account of the historical and mythical past of the Anyi, to which
we shall be referring constantly, would go beyond the scope of this
abridged edition of our book. Nevertheless, we hope the reader will be
able to interpret the experiences we chronicle here against the background of historical analysis as the product of historical development.
The remarks that follow, brief as they must be, will give some idea of
the most important historical facts.

Beginning with the end of the seventeenth century, when the Ashanti
Federation of Kumasi was founded, the history of the precolonial
period is the history of all the Akan peoples, but especially of the
Ashanti. Since their exodus to their present territory at the beginning of

the nineteenth century, the Anyi have developed a history of their own, under French colonial administration, during the period extending from the foundation of the "autonomous Ivory Coast colony" in 1893 to the granting of independence in 1960, and since then as an independent people living in the Ivory Coast Republic.

The earliest federation, held together by matrilineal ties, was headed by King Obiri Yeboa, who invaded the Kumasi area as a conqueror. It was expanded into a powerful empire by his nephew, King Osei (Koffi) Tutu (1695?–1731) and the latter's successors. This expansion was possible primarily because Portuguese traders had introduced domestic plants whose cultivation made it feasible for larger numbers of people to live in permanent settlements in the damp rain forests. This was the prerequisite for the transition of the Akan from a hunter-gatherer economy to a way of life based on villages and towns. In like manner, the military superiority of one tribe over another was made possible by the importation of firearms. At the same time, the young political structure was offered a new source of revenue in the form of predatory wars to capture slaves, and in the commerce in slaves and gold.

The founder king Osei Tutu has become a legendary hero. It was Sigmund Freud (109) who recognized the Oedipus legend as the typical heroic tale of our culture and who interpreted it as a reflection of the most incisive emotional relationships and conflicts of the child—in short, as a "family romance." In his words, "A hero is someone who has had the courage to rebel against his father and has in the end victoriously overcome him." This particular sentence, transplanted to the Anyi myth of Osei Tutu, would have to read as follows: "A hero is anyone who first manages to evade his 'oedipal' conflict and then succeeds in mastering it outside the maternal family, for anyone capable of this feat can return out of exile to the kin of his mother, like the nephew to the throne of his uncle, and can identify with the nurturing and authoritarian traits of both his father and his mother."

The political organization of the Anyi follows the same structural principle as the maternal lineage. The cohesion of the kin depends upon the mothers and daughters; in the political structure, the family's community of material interests and its emotional ties are embodied in the queen mother, who—together with the other women—is generally responsible for upholding the constitution and the laws, while the king, as a prestige figure, as commander-in-chief of his warriors, as custodian of the treasury, and as guardian of the legal system, fulfills the function of the executive, namely, the embodiment of power in domestic and foreign affairs. From the point of view of sociopsychology, the numerous wars and feuds that took place among the individual Akan nations might well be explained by saying that the integrative forces of the matrilineal society failed to prevail over the destructive rivalries and conflicting claims to power of the men—and kings.

It was feuds of this kind that were responsible for the exodus of the Anyi and for the seizure of their present homeland by conquest at the turn of the eighteenth century. In retrospect, the French, who annexed the territory as a colony first by means of protectorate agreements concluded with individual Anyi princes and finally by force of arms, found themselves confronted by a development that can best be described in the words of Chéruy (7):

> At the time of the migrations, the leader was a chief who exerted real power over his followers, a man whose reputation was such that he was able to gather several families about him, to persuade them to seek a new home, to share with him the precarious fate of emigrants, to wrest a new land from its often reluctant inhabitants. Such a man—by virtue of these facts alone—was the absolute master of his people, at least as long as they had not settled anywhere. And, even once the conquest was over and the invaders established in their new home, the successors of the chief who had led the immigrants enjoyed a certain amount of prestige, and their families were considered more distinguished than the rest. But this development marks the end of the "kingship" of these rulers; their realms were now "kingdoms" in name only.

During the period of the "autonomous colony" of the Ivory Coast (established in 1893), the colonial administration did everything in its power to develop the economy into a profitable source of revenue for the home country. The first coffee plantation was established in 1881, and this marked the introduction of forced labor. This was followed in 1900 by the head tax. In 1887 the French began to exploit the precious woods of the region, and the export of rubber was introduced in 1903. In 1908 the first cocoa was imported. Wherever it was necessary in order to achieve these economic ends, the old social and political structures had to be destroyed and replaced by a centralized, bureaucratic administration and hegemony. The area was divided into administrative districts (cercles) under the "chefs de canton" (regional administration officers), with total disregard for traditional hereditary claims (1910) and a good deal else besides.

The life story of Ahoussi de Bernard (born in 1888), king and chief of Bébou, which we cannot recount in full here, makes it clear that the colonial powers did not succeed in their efforts to destroy the structures of Anyi society. In World War I, the most the French could congratulate themselves on was that their colonial empire did not entirely disintegrate; the Anyi rulers, on the other hand, were able to consolidate their positions. During the twenties, Ahoussi even reestablished the long-abolished and nearly forgotten Kingdom of Alangouan and organized its capital, Bébou, in accordance with the principles of an Akan state. In 1942, when the Pétain regime tried to reintroduce forced labor, abolished in the meantime, it ran into effective opposition on the part of the traditional lineages, whose position had become much stronger. And at every attempt to reinstate the patriarchal family organization with inheritance from father to son—which would clearly have been in the interests of both the colonial and the native plantation owners—the maternal lineages made their power felt; and, instead of being abolished, the system of matrilineal inheritance was strengthened and, with it, the legal system and the power structures associated with it. Thus it comes as no surprise to learn that traditional chiefs, whose power base is their lineage, frequently became rallying points for political power in the struggles of the parties that have taken place since the introduction of civil rights and universal suffrage in 1945. The status of Chief Ahoussi in "our" village of Bébou brought it home to us that the independence of the Republic (since 1960) has led to no significant changes in this respect. When we were there in 1966, the "king in the republic" was still a genuine Akan king.

Why Not Join the Green Elephant?

"Stop! Police inspection!" We are confronted with this sign on a road some miles south of Abengourou in January 1966. I pull out our "gray card" and wait for the policeman in uniform to issue the usual warning: "Drive slowly, sound your horn before a curve, help to reduce the accident statistics of the Republic." But this time the policeman is not concerned with inspecting anything. He withdraws and a young man in civilian clothes bends down to talk to us in the car: "Have you already paid your annual party dues? Two hundred cfa francs per person. Yes? But of course, everyone has to pay. You *are* registered in the souspréfecture?" I nod and reply cautiously, "Yes. I've been living here for the past few weeks and intend to remain for some months. In the village of Bébou. But I don't think I have to pay any party dues. I'll be glad to contribute voluntarily, though, because I am in agreement with the platform of the RDA." I am about to hand him 400 francs for myself and my wife, but the young party man has suddenly disappeared; he has gone over to the police car parked down the road from us. The cashier, a short man in the white Moslem shirt affected by the Arabs and with an iron cashbox in his hand, looks down at the money I have placed on the hood of the car, undecided whether to take it. "Go ahead, take it—it's the annual dues for my wife and me." Without a word he hands me a membership card with a picture of a green elephant and the letters "RDA"[1] printed in red underneath. It takes me quite a while to persuade him to accept our money, and he finally does so only after checking once more with his supervisor; then he enters our names and even membership numbers on the cards. At this moment a truck loaded with workers on their way to a construction site is flagged to a stop. The passengers are lined up, and as we drive off we hear: "You have to pay. No excuses now!" The uniformed policeman reappears and waves us on.

We are in a country that is in the process of change. The party, which by definition unites all the citizens of the Ivory Coast Republic under its banner, must somehow manage to contact all its members. What could be more logical than that the police, whose task it is to serve the common good, should be asked to take over this job for the party of all citizens?

Where there is no bureaucratic apparatus such as we have in Europe to integrate every citizen automatically into the structure of the state, one fact soon becomes clear: force is the most effective means of ensuring the individual's obedience. In the Ivory Coast Republic, the head tax levied during the colonial period has been abolished. There is no income tax, in fact no direct tax at all. Many public service functions that in Europe are carried out by government authorities are here delegated to the party. In addition, it has assumed responsibility for the enormous task of replacing traditional and outmoded ways of life with new and better ones, of replacing the law of the jungle with the values of a modern communal structure.

In Bébou we have become the friends of the chief—owing in part to our own efforts. We begin to wonder whether this development may not turn out to be counterproductive for what we want to accomplish. People may say that researchers who ally themselves with the old order, with the custodians of tradition, are incapable of appreciating modern problems and thus the "new Africa"; their standpoint would be one-sided, to say the least, and their receptiveness for the present impaired, attuned to the past. And how could they expect the youthful representatives of the independent, postcolonial Africa to feel any confidence in the friends of the elderly chief, a man who had cooperated with the French!

We realized that the opinion the villagers formed about us strangers would depend first of all on what the ruling class thought of us, and that we would be assigned our social role in keeping with this opinion. In time, the impression we made on our subjects by displaying tolerance and neutrality (both indispensable qualities for a psychoanalyst) would gradually come to contrast with this role. From the very beginning we would have to try to establish ourselves in the good graces of the strongest and most active forces in the village, to avoid becoming entangled in political controversies, and to make certain we would not be associated with the colonial period of the past.

During our visits to other villages, we observed that those with traditional chiefs seemed to function better as social organisms than those in which elected bodies of the modern type had taken over the task of administration. On the one hand, every single village seemed to have developed an atmosphere of political tension between the older dignitaries and the young, modern-minded leaders; on the other hand, our visits were so short that this tension had no effect on the village's relations with us. Sometimes a young schoolteacher, who apparently represented the village and whose use of RDA slogans identified him as representing the new order as well, would guide us immediately to the chief; or a chief—with whom we could very well have talked alone—would have a younger party member summoned to take part in the conversation. The circumstances of the moment, the determination to get along somehow or other with the visitors, or the feeling for etiquette were quite sufficient to bridge political differences, at least temporarily.

In Bébou we adopted an attitude of active neutrality. We took advantage of every opportunity to become acquainted with one of the leading groups, and gradually this led to our integration into the social structure of the village. In this way we became good friends of the chief and his family, and it soon became apparent to us that none of the inhabitants was capable of comprehending our truly "modern" project in any terms but those established by the old order. It became equally clear just what political effects the new order has in an Anyi village and how pointless it is to ask whether a stranger should or can join a political party. The representatives of the progressive left in our village showed no resentment of our friendship with the chief. On the contrary, it was only after Ahoussi had confirmed that we belonged to the village that they found themselves able to work with us effectively.

Our work in the neighboring village of Yosso began under an evil star. For a long time we were not sure whether the reason was distrust based on political factors. After the first ceremonial contacts, the youthful deputy of the absent village chief became extremely reserved in his behavior toward us and referred us to Erneste, the "chief of the young men."

Erneste was a member of the young left. His face plainly expressed his distrust; his behavior was at the same time servile, assiduous, and hostile. As soon as he had heard of our plans, he ordered all the young men between eighteen and twenty to register for an interview with the

"doctor," and there was nothing we could do to persuade him to re-
scind his command. As a result, of course, all those young men (only a
few of whom spoke French well enough for our purposes anyway) were
lost to future cooperation. We suspected Erneste of trying to sabotage
our project with his pretended willingness to help, though this is by no
means certain. Perhaps he simply wanted to enhance his own importance as "chief of the young men." In accordance with tradition, the
young people can be ordered to perform certain services by their com-
manders.

The political situation between the two villages was extremely complex. Two years before, Ahoussi, who traditionally ought to have been
in charge of Yosso as well as Bébou, had spoken out against the election
of the new chief, a half-caste, and had supported the candidacy of the
young man who had received us as the chief's deputy. With the help of
the modern faction, the half-caste had won the election in spite of
Ahoussi's intervention, and since that time there had been no official
contact between Ahoussi and Yosso. Nonetheless, in some mysterious
fashion Ahoussi always seemed to be well informed about everything
that happened in the neighboring village.

In reality, however, the tension between Bébou and Yosso had
existed longer than two years, going back to party controversies that
had taken place before the granting of independence and the victory of
the state party, the RDA. At the time of these controversies, a majority
in favor of the Progressives had formed in Bébou, and the families of
some RDA supporters—yielding to massive pressure—had moved
away to live with their relatives in Yosso. Ahoussi himself was regarded
as nonpartisan. All those who still remember that period are full of
admiration for his shrewdness. "He saw right away that the RDA
would emerge as the stronger party and stuck with it from the very
beginning, whereas almost all his people were shortsighted and supported the Progressives."

Our position in Yosso improved slowly. We made friends with a
number of dignitaries and gained the goodwill of the old women we
treated in our medical office hours. As a result we were soon able to
begin our investigations there, too. Even so, the atmosphere was often
disrupted by Erneste's intrigues against us.

It was not until two and a half months later that we realized it was not
political factors that had made our work in Yosso almost impossible.
From purely personal, neurotic motives, Erneste had turned against us;
as soon as the villagers had gotten to know us better, he stood there alone
with his distrust.

One evening a kind of party delegation from Yosso came to call upon
us in Bébou. When Ahoussi came in for his regular evening visit, he

joined in our conversation with the guests. A second meeting was arranged, and during the weeks that followed the old conflict between Ahoussi and the people of Yosso was amicably settled.

Our friendship with the chief had not compromised our position in the least; in fact, it had contributed to settling political differences between the traditional ruler and the governing party of the neighboring village. The Anyi first assigned us the status proper for unusual phenomena in a society ruled by tradition. If we had espoused an ideology in this environment instead of basing our behavior on the exigencies of human needs, our effect on the local society would have been akin to that of a high explosive—instead of studying them as they were, we would have changed them.

The far-reaching effects of the new political order on the lives of individuals was one of the most frequent topics in all our interviews. The new order exerts its influence by altering the economy and the administrative system as well as through the specifically "postcolonial" attitudes of those who hold political office. Attempts at direct state intervention in the life of the village were usually ineffective and—viewed from the point of view of the inhabitants—ludicrous. In January, functionaries of the state party went through the villages to collect the annual dues. When the energetic young party representative arrived in Bébou, it was two o'clock in the afternoon. The inhabitants were still out on the plantations. He began by calling upon the dignitaries. At about eight o'clock that evening he came to see us, accompanied by the chief. He was quite drunk and had not yet collected party dues from a single person. The following morning the schoolchildren ran about collecting the membership cards that the guest from the city had scattered all over the village. The guest himself was distraught and morning-afterish, scared to death to go home without having finished his job. Shortly before the official car was to pick him up, he asked to see Ahoussi and begged him for help. Ahoussi rounded up a few young men, went in person to the compounds belonging to his own clan, and within an hour was able to turn over the dues he had collected from all his relatives and foreign workers, accounting together for about a quarter of the village population. Very probably he had dipped into his own pockets to make up the dues of those who were unwilling or unable to pay. Full of gratitude and with his self-assurance restored, the party man now demanded that Ahoussi go out and collect the money due from the rest of the inhabitants. The chief replied, "That's all I can do for you. Go back and explain matters to the party as best you can. You can tell the bigwigs at headquarters that Ahoussi is no longer a king. Kings have been abolished. I now wish you good day and goodbye. And I intend to remain in my house. The money I have collected from my people will be used for the common good. Long live the Republic."

The sousprefet in Abengourou, in kindly condescension, sent his greetings to the old king. In Zaranou, the former seat of the "chef de canton," a party member had been installed as chief, with the assignment of administering the surrounding region, including Alangouan. This area, the smallest administrative unit, comprises about thirty villages.

The young gentleman in Zaranou was apparently well-to-do. He dressed elegantly, in European clothes, and owned two automobiles. During all the months we spent in Bébou, we noticed not a single trace of his influence. When he goes to the city, Ahoussi lends him his golden rings, chains of office, and ceremonial robes. The young man is convinced that these turn him into an imposing figure. The gentlemen in Abidjan receive him in friendly fashion and smile behind his back. The Akan kings have always lent their jewelry to their ambassadors going abroad so that the latter could bear witness to the splendor of their rulers. Without realizing it, or because he feels the need of an authority figure to lean on, the naive party member was playing the role of a hired messenger for his political adversary. Ahoussi said with a smile, "I myself am no longer in politics, but my golden rings still are. Gold determines politics nowadays just as it always has. If that young man manages to accomplish anything, in reality it will be the old man who did it. If he fails, people will say, 'Things were different when the king himself used to come down to the coast'."

It looks as though the independence of the republic has had no influence at all on the village. In reality, though, economic development and political renewal are making themselves felt here to a greater extent than in some neighboring countries that became independent at the same time.

All revolutionary changes come from above and are introduced centrally, just as they were under the colonial administration. On the other hand, the Anyi have developed methods for steering these forces without overtly opposing them—which, of course, would be useless. They go along with innovations only up to the point where they begin to contradict their customs and life-style. They refrain from placing obstacles in the way of the state- and party-ordained renewal, intended to create a uniform society, but as a group and as individuals they manage to evade it so successfully that their old, ostensibly superseded instances finally have to intervene. As a result, each Anyi is confirmed in his identity and—if he is forced to or if he wants to—can again accept a portion of the new order. The slow agony of their vanishing religion and philosophy, their lineage organization and chiefship, help to temper the impact of the renewal process. Instead of adjusting or protesting, the Anyi have chosen the path of syncretic incorporation of certain innovations into the decadent equanimity that marks their way of life.

Value Systems and Cognitive Patterns

Abraham (1) has this to say about the ideology of Africa:

> In periods of political transition, . . . in which African countries already find themselves, . . . many events are liable to appear bizarre. Their underlying rationales . . . and those silent adjustments which decide what are preserved and what are discarded, can only be brought to the surface by a clear exposition of the theoretical complex which sustains the culture involved. There is always such a complex, and it evinces itself in the interplay of cultural values and cultural discrimination; but of course, participation in the theory, as distinct from the practice, of the culture is made their preoccupation by only a minority of the people.
>
> In Africa, there is a wealth of traditional general ideas, which make themselves felt both in the present-day theories of politics and society in that continent, and also, to the extent of independent countries at least, in their practice. It is important to carry out investigations into the theories of these cultures.

There can be no doubt that such fundamental ideas exist in every culture; they can be abstracted from social conditions and they find expression in the body of thought of the culture concerned, in its philosophical or religious systems; often they can be recognized in specifically developed forms as the ideologies of certain social classes. One example of such an idea in our Western culture is the conviction that the individual behaves, or should behave, in a sensible and reasonable manner, which—applied to society—leads, or should lead, to an improvement of conditions, to progress. The Anyi, in contrast, believe that the individual is behaving appropriately when he observes certain rules that determine his own nature as well as that of society as a whole. In this context the nature of the individual and the nature of society are different aspects of the same structural system.

Empirical-logical thought processes—existing side by side with magical ones—are common to both cultural groups. The European is quite capable of behaving unreasonably and inappropriately, even evilly or sinfully, and in fact he does so when he directs his efforts against the interests (defined as ethical principles) of his fellowmen.

Among the Akan, any violation of the rules (which apply equally to the nature of the individual and to that of society) is bad, because such behavior disrupts an order that is assumed and accepted as existent. Error and sin are synonymous. Pragmatic behavior must be directed at eliminating the harm done to this order, not at repairing the damage by the application of reason.

By and large, it has been the French-speaking ethnologists (among others, Griaule, Dieterlen, and Tempels in Africa) who have tried to center their accounts on the thought structure of African societies, a structure from which the particular institutions and functions of that society could be plausibly derived. Their conclusions regarding this structure were based both on data gathered from the culturally aware elite and also on their own reconstructions made by abstracting from existing institutions. This approach was a particularly rewarding one in cases where a system of correlations among material, social, and mental phenomena could be clearly demonstrated. In keeping with the linguistic theory of phonemes, Lévi-Strauss went even further and vowed to find a structure he could then derive from the existing institutions solely by applying the process of logical abstraction.

African scholar Abraham's advice, that "it is important to carry out investigations into the theories of these cultures," comes very close to the approach employed by these ethnologists. Abraham specifically warns against attaching too much importance to the social institutions themselves—that is, against attributing to them laws of their own (as Western ethnologists frequently do) instead of viewing them as the temporal and spatial manifestations of a more general ordering principle, of an idea, as would be more appropriate in Africa.

We see no way of following this advice, however; we have no choice but to describe the value systems and cognitive patterns of the Anyi in terms of the cognitive processes of our own culture, thus risking a misinterpretation based on prejudices conditioned by this culture. For closed intellectual systems, that is, the more or less abstract structures of a human community, whether based on Western or on African thought patterns, do not permit the researcher to adjust continually to the facts as they emerge, to achieve understanding in all those areas where it is just barely possible. From a certain point in their development, the "theoretical complexes" on which a culture is based—and the theories concerning these complexes—are determined by logical-abstract cognitive processes. Further observations (with a biological or psychological method, for example) made in an organizational system other than the one that gave rise to the once-established theory must be integrated into the postulated structure. Either the entire theoretical structure is called into question, or the facts must be recorded for the time being as isolated phenomena, and the researcher must wait until an explanation can be elaborated to permit their inclusion in the ideology or structure concerned. Our goal, on the other hand, is to present the facts in a comprehensive context with all other phenomena. Consequently we must center our study on any established ideology that cannot be reconciled with the facts; in the process, the ideology itself may be questioned or modified.

As an example, the psychological studies we proposed to undertake would have to disregard what is already known in the fields of biological maturation and psychological development during childhood, since these aspects are not a part of the cognitive system of the Akan; they are irrelevant, incidentally, to a great deal of Lévi-Strauss's structural theory as well.[2]

In other words, in order to understand, we follow a materialistic-scientific approach; we observe and describe value systems and cognitive patterns in combination with other forms of human expression and with social institutions; we alter our working hypothesis and our theory (which can be regarded as the "structural elements" of our research activity) when they no longer appear to make sense; and we try to bear in mind that our description will inevitably be one elaborated by alien observers attempting to explain their observations in terms of their own cognitive processes. It cannot be the same as a description elaborated by a member of that small minority among the Akan themselves that even today may still be making a deliberate effort to participate "in the theory, as distinct from the practice, of the culture."

Nor would it even have been possible for us to evolve a metaphysical system for the Agni in the abstract, that is, without reference to their institutions. The picture we have of their cognitive processes and value system is not consistent enough, probably not because of a lack of data (either from personal interviews or from the available literature), but because these systems themselves are not consistent. Thus we would have had to restrict ourselves to describing isolated ideas having little or no relation to one another or, as some authors have done, to sketching a picture that would conform to the requirements of Western philosophy but that would hardly reflect the realities of Anyi life—and would certainly not be recognized by the Anyi themselves.

Chiefship

When the king's breasts are full of milk,
it is his people who drink.

One would assume that the political ideology of the Anyi could best be derived from the rules that govern the uterine lineage, since the latter, by its ties and the commitments it imposes on its members, shapes the life of the community and of the individual. An example will make it clear, however, that the researcher must turn to the world of the men for information concerning the ideas that define the public life of the community.

Every Ashanti king bequeathed his stool to posterity; blackened from burnt offerings, it was supposed to have the magic power to protect the surviving members of his clan. The clan sacrificed to the stool and directed its prayers to it; in short, it was the foundation of an ancestor cult. The first stool was the property of Osei Tutu, the founder of the dynasty. It was called the "golden" stool and—metaphorically—the seat of the soul of the Ashanti people. Together with the original one, the blackened stools of later kings, arranged in hierarchical order, were preserved in a place of worship (26, 33). A schematic representation of the origin of the stool, the groups to whom it belongs, and its spiritual significance appears in figure 4.

The ancestor and his—later—sacred stool are the property of the maternal lineage, which, as the living community, owns it, reveres it, and needs it. But the spirit that embodies and perpetuates the effective principle is masculine and derived from the paternal line. To acquaint oneself with these ideas, one must examine above all the activities of the men, and one might as well begin with the institution of chiefship.

As chief and king, Ahoussi has created his own symbol to express his principle of government. The staff that his son and chief dignitary, Dibi, bears in front of his father during official ceremonies is ornamented with a wooden figurine inlaid with gold, representing a small boy whose hand rests trustingly on the back of a lion. The chief explains: "The little boy thinks to himself, 'This is my father's sheep'; the lion thinks to himself 'If you knew who I am, you wouldn't do that.'"

This symbol is not Ahoussi's invention, despite what he says. Consciously or unconsciously, he selected it from among the symbols making up the body of thought of the Akan. In one of Rattray's books (33) there is a reproduction of an almost identical figure, symbolizing the Ashanti proverb "There is always someone who doesn't yet know the lion."

Only a child can be deceived about the power and menace of a lion; everyone knows and fears the chief; the children of the community can rely upon him; anyone who offends him should remember that though he may seem harmless to the weak, his nature is wild and dangerous.

The symbolic figure and its explanation express the function and position of the chief as Ahoussi conceives of them within the larger framework of Akan ideas. His personal conception stresses certain aspects of chiefship and disregards others. But the figure is not merely a representation (symbolization). Even the choice of a symbol and its ceremonial use embody one important function; the institution of

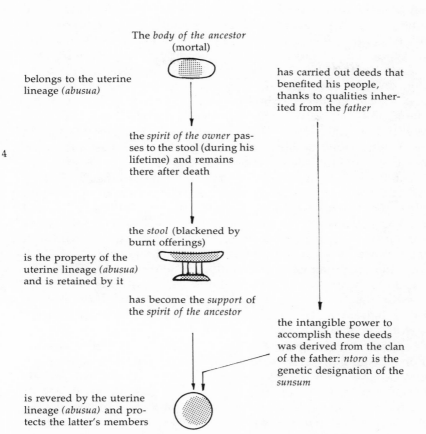

The *body of the ancestor*
(mortal)

belongs to the uterine
lineage *(abusua)*

has carried out deeds that
benefited his people,
thanks to qualities inherited from the *father*

the *spirit of the owner* passes to the stool (during his
lifetime) and remains
there after death

the *stool* (blackened by
burnt offerings)

is the property of the
uterine lineage *(abusua)*
and is retained by it

has become the *support* of
the *spirit of the ancestor*

the intangible power to
accomplish these deeds
was derived from the clan
of the father: *ntoro* is the
genetic designation of the
sunsum

is revered by the uterine
lineage *(abusua)* and protects the latter's members

the *spirit of the ancestor* is
called *sunsum* and is nonmaterial and immortal

Fig. 4. The stool of the ancestors.

4

chiefship announces itself to the village, takes up its functions, and demands respect. The ceremonial manifestation of power stresses the masculinity of the chief's role; his public functions give expression to phallic-aggressive attitudes (staff, lion, exhibitionistic attitude). The staff-bearer leans on his staff, the king on his dignitaries; this is the function of the hierarchical structure—which, incidentally, is so inadequate in Bébou that the chief complains of the inefficiency of his dignitaries and has to appoint his own son to this role. Brou Koffi, chief of the village of M'Basso, also laments: "I don't even have an elder to turn to when I need advice." The role of chief is by no means an autocratic one—he too needs someone to lean on.

The child resting its hand on the lion's back stresses the chief's concern for his subjects, for the members of his clan, and assigns him a maternal role. The psychological impact of the symbol is concentrated in the sinister warning, "If you knew...!" The threat and the latent savagery of the lion are difficult for the Western mind to reconcile with either the power of a king or the nurturing function of a mother. With the Anyi the annihilation of an enemy is a "masculine" act, reserved exclusively to the chief. In the symbol it is linked with the "maternal" aspect, with the sadoanal aggression that many Anyi mothers direct— parallel to their loving concern—to their own helpless offspring, sometimes with a good deal of malice.

One of the taboos imposed by Chief Ahoussi on the village throws additional light on his conception of his role. The visitor is soon struck by the fact that there is not a single dog in Bébou. In other villages one sees numerous spotted mongrels, and even in the huts in the fields around Bébou some families keep dogs that they use for hunting. The people say that the chief would order any dog straying into the village shot on the spot. They add that the chief paid a great deal of money for a charm he bought up north, and that one of the prerequisites for its proper functioning is that there must be no dogs in the village. Ahoussi himself tells us that when the village was new there were only two compounds, hardly larger than field huts. The rest of the site had not yet been cleared and really belonged to the spirits of the forest. To settle matters, Ahoussi had summoned a mighty sorcerer from the land of the Baoulé. The sorcerer waged war on the spirits, killing three of them, and buried his charm where the village was to be built. But he warned that the charm could protect the village only if certain conditions were fulfilled, and the most important one was that no dogs should enter the village. The spirits of the forest kept leopards as dogs, and the dogs of the spirits would come into the village and devour the dogs of the inhabitants, thus destroying the power of the charm. The chief was to be responsible for seeing that the ban was maintained so that the charm could do its work. Ahoussi had objected at the time that if one of the white people who ruled the country should happen to visit Bébou with his dog, there would be nothing he could do about it. The sorcerer had replied that, provided the dog remained only a day or two and was kept tied up all the time, it would not matter. But if the dog were to stay in the village two weeks or longer and leave his calling card all over, then the spirits of the forest would not keep their bargain with the sorcerer, the leopards would come, and the charm would be powerless.

The chief has introduced other taboos as well, and he keeps a careful watch on their observance. For example, it is forbidden in Bébou to mash food of any kind after nightfall. Ahoussi explains that this arrangement is just the same as a written treaty; as long as he keeps his part of the bargain, his treaty partners—the spirits—will keep theirs. This was the reason he had forbidden his dignitaries—the idiots had disobeyed his orders more than once—to bring dogs into the village and had threatened to shoot the dogs himself if they did. So far the taboo has been observed, and the charm has proved effective. Bébou has had no deaths due to measles, for instance, though many children have died in the surrounding villages. When soldiers were being recruited during World War II, the authorities took twelve men from Bébou but sent them all back as unfit for military service, while those recruited from other villages in the neighborhood all had to serve as soldiers.

That the population of Bébou, in spite of the high birthrate, has decreased during the past few years, and that the recruits were presumably sent back only because—like all the village inhabitants—they were suffering from chronic ailments, does nothing to shake Ahoussi's conviction.

For the chief, the charm and the right and duty of ensuring observance of the treaty concluded with the spirits of the forest, in other words, of the taboo, is primarily a means of achieving his objectives—indirectly by protecting the village from dangers threatening from spirits that cannot be warded off any other way, and directly by supervising the observance of the taboo rules. The villagers concede his right to do so, since he has substantiated his own authority by that of the mighty sorcerer from the north and, by paying the latter, has contributed to the common welfare.

The history of the taboo on dogs was recounted to us by many of the villagers—each time in a slightly different version. Our interpreter François stresses the relationship of the taboo to the property of the village, pointing out that the sorcerer's services were exceedingly expensive; thus, even if the charm did not work the treaty ought to be honored for economic reasons. Thomas tells us that dogs and gold are incompatible. When a villager is prospecting for gold in a drill-hole and a dog happens to appear on the scene, the gold—which the prospector has just seen gleaming before his eyes—suddenly disappears. Elisa's version is the most concise: the gold is transformed into the dog (and thus vanishes).

In all these versions, dogs, or more precisely the excrement they leave behind, are related to gold and wealth. For the Anyi, and often in Western legends as well, the dog is a dirty, anal animal whose scorned filth contrasts magically with that highly prized anal product, the ownership of gold.

Closer study reveals that the objectives of the chief are not very different—psychologically—from those of his subjects. His main concern is to increase his wealth, that is, his village and its inhabitants, and to guard it against loss. Naturally this statement has validity only if one regards people as property. As we shall see, the Anyi's relationship to other people, above all to his own children, is identical to his relationship to material possessions. "They belong to me, and so I can do whatever I like with them"—and this, in our opinion, is why the begetting of children is a defense against loss anxiety and why the loss of a relative is a dreadful experience, one that conjures up anxieties that must be combated with denial and magic.

Naturally the chief has also employed other means (which seem more normal from our point of view) to achieve his purpose of augmenting and safeguarding his property—his subjects. At the moment, for example, he is engaged in building a larger school to make village life more attractive to modern-minded parents.

In reality the ban on dogs, which to us seems exotic and reminiscent of magic, has the status of a political ideology. The basic features of the institution of rule are reflected in the observance of the taboo. As long as it is obeyed, the authority figure feels secure in its intentions and its power—even though the reality may be quite different; the villagers continue to practice the ritual because they participate emotionally in the ideology it reflects. In similar fashion, the citizens of many Western countries feel themselves at one with their democratic form of government as long as it adheres to the ritual of parliamentary procedure; the ritual perpetuates the ideology even when it has long since become obvious that the intentions that led to the establishment of democratic institutions in the first place are no longer being carried out.

In the opinion of many scholars, the Akan ideology of royal power corresponds very closely to the ideology of an absolute monarchy of the European type. Brou Koffi, the village chief in M'Basso, voices the same complaint as a dethroned European ruler when he says, "Nowadays you must be clever, very clever in fact, if you want to be chief.... It used to be much better. The chief could give orders and sentence people to forced labor. He could give orders to a young man.... It's not that way any more. Now, when you order him to do something, he answers 'Are you the one who feeds me?... you have no right to order me around!' You can give all the commands you like, they pay no attention.... Even your son won't obey you any more. That all comes from being independent. They don't yet understand what that means. They think it means freedom—just like that. As if they could do whatever they liked and didn't have to work any longer.... Everybody distrusts everybody else. They get into fights. Then they come to me with their stories.... I've no more to say."

In summary, it is possible to derive a psychosocial organization from the ideology of chiefship. The king stands at the apex of a social structure based on an aristocratic hierarchy. He ensures observance of the taboo rules that he has imposed in the interests of social organization. His subjects obey these rules because they identify themselves with myth and ritual (i.e., with the projective system and its conjuring procedures); the fear of the consequences of violating a taboo binds both them and their ruler to the traditional system. The practice and display of male aggressive power makes the king the object of passive wishes on the part of his subjects. They identify with him because he represents and portrays the aggressive masculinity they need in order to counter the possessive claims of the maternal lineage with a modicum of independence. As a result, they inevitably submit to a new possessor, the king, who embodies the claims of the most distinguished maternal lineage, the one that rules over all the rest.

In the foregoing section we have described the exercise of authority, but we still have not clearly explained just what its power is based on. The days when the chiefs had political and economic instruments at their disposal are long over. Nowadays their power has its roots in a balanced system for the exchange of material values (149), of rights, and of duties.

In Africa it is a basic fact of life that an authority figure is expected to give to those who are dependent upon him; the "power to give" is then supplemented by the "right to take" (65). The relevant Akan saying is the one quoted earlier: "When the king's breasts are full of milk, it is his people who drink."

Ahoussi characterizes the more or less maternal aspects of rule as his duties—concern for the physical and mental well-being of his subjects, the function of ceremonial representation, and the offering of hospitality. These are balanced by the duties of his subjects—to show him respect, to obey him, and to perform certain services for him (he receives one-third of the hunters' booty and of any gold that may be discovered), a relic of the early hunting and gathering days. Economically, this exchange is meaningless. The king has no way of forcing his subjects to obey him. His economic position as one of the "rich men" of the village enables him to perform certain financial services for the inhabitants without compensation. As a matter of fact, Ahoussi is an entrepreneur; he employs a number of day laborers, who are not yet integrated into his family, and he rents out a coffee-husking machine complete with operator. But his status as a member of the very rudimentary class of small-scale businessmen—and he is by no means the most successful among them—still does not explain how his power as chief has managed to survive the abolishment of political power.

Psychologically, the act of giving in itself is the most important basis of power. The villagers have an irresistible urge to turn to their chief in case of need—"The chief is there for all of us, and he has everything." His personality, his behavior, and his attitudes all have a seductive effect. The process is similar to what happens to European youth today; the overabundance of consumer goods and luxury products is felt to be a form of repression, a constraint imposed by society—for young people are all too easily tempted to fulfill their urgent desires. And the chief, whose function it is to give, is just as little able to suppress his desire for power; by means of his generosity and his contributions to their material welfare, he forces the subjects who belong to him to be satisfied with him. He is not in a position to deny his subjects funds or influence. No matter how much Ahoussi sighs and complains that he has to take care of everybody, though he has no power, he still gives his Mobilette motorcycle to a stonemason who wrecks it, lends his hypodermic set to a healer who never returns it, gives his dignitaries money to pay for funerals or other ceremonies to which they do not even always invite him.

What the sociologist terms the "power to give" and Ahoussi describes as his "duty to satisfy everyone" is still a durable foundation of the institution of chiefship. The conception of the chief as the mother who nourishes, upheld by the oral needs of his subjects, embodies—from the sociological standpoint—the principle of dependence upon him. In this way he exercises a power that in other social systems is anchored in material dependence on the authorities.

As far as the king is concerned, the formula can be reduced to this: They ask me for things; therefore they need me, and thus I can rule them. While in earlier times the Ashanti kings could be deposed by the dignitaries acting as a group, today an Anyi king can be deprived of his throne even more easily—and, psychologically, more effectively. People stop coming to his court; no one asks him for anything; thus he is no longer a king. He succumbs—so people told us, anyway—to depression and is no longer capable of carrying out his office.

A Justice Based on Balance

The attitude of many African peoples toward law is dominated by the concept of balance. When someone has committed an offense, it is up to his family to put things right in his behalf, to replace the loss incurred by the victim, or (after a murder, for instance) to compensate the kin of the victim for the loss of one of its members. Thus there is no division of the law into civil and criminal codes; there is only a civil code. The "judges" (family elders, priests, chiefs, council of elders) are not official judges, but rather arbitrators and experts; as Field (15) puts it, they "administer not law, but what they deem to be justice." They are members of the existing social and political establishment and thus identical with the officials of this establishment. There is no separation of powers. The "oral justice" of balance has been done as soon as the belligerent tension between the offender and the injured party (i.e., between their families or lineages) is eliminated.

This African view of the law probably does not exist in its pure form anywhere today—certainly not among the Anyi. There are other principles as well, whose role is of greater or lesser importance—for example, qualifying certain behavior as socially undesirable by branding the offender (social ostracism), restoring the spiritual equilibrium of society, and finally reintegrating the offender (through purification). The retaliatory principle, "an eye for an eye, a tooth for a tooth," according to which the penalty must be commensurate with the guilt incurred, can be found only in rudimentary form. As with us, too, the deterrent effect in reality depends more on the degree of ostracism imposed than on fear of the immediate effects of punishment. The very slight importance attached to the guilt-punishment principle in the Anyi legal system is not surprising when we consider the relatively insignificant role played by lasting reaction formations to sadoanal strivings in the evolution of the Anyi personality.

Certain peculiarities of the Anyi conception of the law can be brought to light by comparing their earlier legal institutions with the present ones. This may seem an idle undertaking, since the government no longer concedes the Anyi a juridical system of their own devising. Instead, they fall under the jurisdiction of an independent court that applies modern norms of civil and criminal law based on the French model. On the other hand, their thinking is so evidently dominated by legal considerations and their daily life so frequently disrupted by disputes that cry out first of all for traditional juridical settlement that such considerations mark broad areas of their culture and their personality. There is hardly any interpersonal relationship—including that between parents and children—and hardly any action in economic and communal life that, sooner or later, does not require a ruling by the court. In 46 of the 146 fantasies related to us by Jean-Pierre there was at least one court sequence. One can either admire the high level of development that the Akan have achieved in their legal system or deplore their almost uncontrollable inclination to become involved in belligerent tensions that require such frequent recourse to the courts. In a psychological investigation both points of view have a certain validity—the first in terms of the strengthening of ego functions through participation in the thought structures of legal processes and the support of the ego through juridical institutions, and the second in terms of the disruption of interpersonal relations by the assault of hostile impulses.

Field (15) believes that the "whole system of justice is merely an elaboration of the system of calling upon a senior and asking him to decide upon the right and wrong of a dispute. Two young brothers call in their father. If they have different fathers they call in both. If the quarrel is more serious, the fathers call in grandfathers and uncles to assist. If a man quarrels with his wife, they call in elders from both families. If a man quarrels with his neighbour, *any* distinguished elders may be called in."

This impression, acquired by Field during her study of the Akim just before World War II, corresponds exactly to what we saw in Bébou in 1966. The administration of justice occupies family courts at a number of levels. As an Anyi proverb has it, "When a family elder settles it [a dispute], there is peace." The king is the head of the lineage; serious cases are referred to him.

The seemingly simple principle that a dispute should be settled between the members of the families concerned is found among many African peoples. It does not explain, however, when and in what circumstances a quarrel becomes a matter for the courts, nor does it shed any light on the underlying philosophy of justice. These aspects can best be elucidated by reference to one of the institutions typical of legal administration among the Akan, the so-called Ashanti oath. This "oath" guarantees justice, gives shape to the procedures involved, and determines the stage of appeal within the jurisdiction of the family courts.

The oath consists of a fixed formula and alludes to a tragic event that happened to the ancestors of the judge. The defendant himself determines the level of the court by appealing to a man of recognized reputation to judge his case. He may say to him, "If I did commit the offense I am accused of, then it is true that a certain misfortune once befell your family and will befall it again." The judge, as the custodian of his family taboo, must ensure that the taboo is not violated. If he discovers that the accused is innocent, then the taboo has not been broken. If, on the other hand, he turns out to be guilty, then the accused has violated the taboo and must accept the penalty for having done so (not for the crime itself!). The plaintiff also has the right to swear such an oath, thus proving the veracity of his statements "under the taboo rule." If he should be exposed as a liar, he would have to expect the same penalty for violating the taboo.

The judge is not guided by an abstract code of laws. He is defending a taboo of his lineage. The criminal case has become a civil one. Busia (6) interprets the same situation in the opposite way—that a private quarrel, by virtue of the appeal to a high-ranking dignitary and to the king, who are representatives of the political system, becomes a case for the public courts. The two interpretations coincide if one bears in mind that there is no distinction between civil and criminal law or between public and private injustice.[3] True, the king ensures that his family taboos are observed by the entire community, but this merely reflects a highly personal duty toward his own lineage.

The stubbornness with which the opposing parties defend their respective cases is decisive for the choice of the court and thus for the importance attached to the taboo in question. The defendant who chooses his own judge determines through his choice just how serious the offense is to be considered in the eyes of society and helps to determine the degree of social ostracism that will be meted out in the judge's ruling to atone for it. The extent to which the existing order has been violated is reflected in the amount of the fine to be paid. Important taboos of high-ranking dignitaries are expensive. Such payments correspond neither to what the criminal code regards as fines nor to what the civil code describes as damages. In the Akan conception of the law, the original offense is less important than the intensity with which the quarrel is pursued. The ultimate goal is to counter a stubborn dispute with a correspondingly high degree of authority and—more explicitly—with a correspondingly stiff fine to be paid by the culprit. The idea of adequate compensation for damages inflicted influences the amount fixed by the judge only secondarily. After he has handed down his ruling, the amount of compensation is agreed upon with the family of the injured party. The most serious offenses are murder, acts regarded as incestuous, and adultery with the wife of a high-ranking personage.

All direct mention of the events alluded to in the "oath," all the tragic or shameful deaths of revered ancestors, the defeats, and the plagues, is forbidden, for this might have disastrous consequences. Busia (6) explains this by saying that the departed ancestors would be angry or sad to be reminded of them. In the psychology of the individual, self-protection against the reemergence of repressed events, avoidance of giving verbal expression to unhappy memories and thereby conjuring them away with the help of magic are regarded as defense mechanisms. In the form of taboos, they acquire the purpose and the validity of a social institution. The taboo has undergone a change in function in that it has been pressed into the service of the legal system and thus diverted from its original purpose.

It is characteristic of the Akan legal system that, although it is based on a publicly effective system of balance, it has more or less incorporated existing family taboos. It is as if the lack of an abstract legal code, the lack of a stable individual superego capable of distinguishing clearly between innocence and guilt, had been recognized—as if Akan society had become aware of a gap in its ideology. As if the Akan had said to themselves, "We have no such thing as a rigid code of laws, but we have a highly differentiated society that is threatened by frequent controversies among its members. Let us borrow valid prohibitions from our family structures, where they already exist, from the magic-inspired anxiety about a recurrence of family misfortunes, from the taboos of our noble families. Let us incorporate these tried and tested laws of private emotional homeostasis, the basis of our clan conscience, into a system of justice that guarantees balance and the settlement of conflicts and at the same time permits the social condemnation of pugnacity and—ultimately—a definition of the degree of reprehensibleness inherent in a given offense."[4]

Erikson (101) contrasts the "moral self-observation" that develops in early childhood with the "supra-individual formulation of behavior rules," in other words, the juridical system. He writes as follows: "In its mature evolutionary form in the world of adults, this evaluating element is reconfirmed at a higher level in the form of a legal system and represents publicly what has developed in each individual through an inner process." The supraindividual rules of behavior of the Anyi are bound to be different from ours, not only because their society has different living conditions, a different history, and a different organizational form; the inner process is different as well. Individual circumstances, on which the public community is based, are very different from those in our culture, as becomes drastically clear whenever European legal codes impinge directly upon Anyi life, whenever two systems of legal thought come into confrontation.

During the early years of the colonial period, French courts were concerned above all with witchcraft trials, cases in which witches were alleged to have "eaten or sold the flesh of another person." Such trials have long since become a thing of the past; today this problem is left up to the female shamans and the healers. During the early years, though, every witchcraft trial contained scenes that might have been taken from the present-day theater of the absurd. The witches of the Anyi were descended from the maternal lineage of the plaintiff. Helpless old women were accused of having caused disease and death. Naturally the French judge was wholly incapable of believing in the truth of such accusations, but sometimes he was inclined to leave open the question whether the death involved might not have been the result of poisoning. The court was unable to prove material damage, though it was regarded as a fact by the plaintiff and often admitted by the defendant. The Anyi were not the least interested in seeing the deed punished or the disease and resulting death annulled—they were the results of witchcraft, and so nothing could be done about them anyway; all they cared about was reestablishing spiritual order and social peace. This could be achieved first by the public confirmation of witchcraft and second by the imposition of commensurate fines. However, since the European judges had no choice but to relegate the "facts" of the case to the realm of superstition, the stubborn bargaining for compensation was bound to strike them as an extortionist swindle. While the court set all its machinery in motion to unmask the blackmailing culprits, the Anyi fought with still more witnesses and still more oaths for official recognition of the unbelievable. For them witchcraft was the most immediate and most tangible expression of anxieties and injuries that were of endopsychic origin and had little connection with the material world and that they wanted to delegate to the public sector for handling—in the form of a witchcraft trial. The outcome of such trials was invariably absurd. Sometimes the judge might allow himself to be persuaded of the reality of the accusation, resorting, presumably, to the European legacy of fear of poisoning and belief in witches that he had revived by identification in these dreary tropics. This, of course, turned the European order upside down. Usually, however, "reason" triumphed, and the plaintiff, already frightened and helpless and thus truly an injured party, was sentenced to jail for slander or for attempted extortion.

In the Anyi ideology, the purpose of law is primarily to eliminate social tensions by healing mental anguish; whether a new injustice is committed in the process is totally irrelevant. The poor old witches had no choice but to bring forward accusations of their own or to incite new strife some other way. If they were unable to do so, they were the losers. They were no longer important to society. And the French court had served no purpose whatsoever except to affirm its own existence and with it a legal system that was meaningful to the judges and their superiors; it had ordered the atonement of a guilt that had never existed and established an order that permitted the continued existence of the original disorder.

Not only the French officers and civil servants who sat in judgment in the courts of Zaranou or Abengourou at the turn of the century, but anyone, at any time, may find himself confronted with the subjective aspects of his culture-specific conception of the administration of justice.

In January 1966 an edict was published in Bébou prohibiting any hunting beyond what was necessary to meet the needs of each family; a few days later a minor functionary of the forestry department caught a poor planter violating the new ban. The planter had gone hunting at the request of an "employer" who was not a member of his own family and, according to the edict, would be penalized by having the "employer's" rifle confiscated and by a relatively modest fine. The culprit and his family were seized with despair and fear. How great was their relief and how eloquent their praises of the functionary when he finally allowed himself to be persuaded to accept a generous bribe and to content himself with confiscating the rifle rather than charging the planter officially. The forestry official promised to tell his superior that he had surprised an illegal hunter, but that the latter had thrown down his rifle and fled unrecognized. In this way he would be commended for his zeal. The villagers had the satisfaction of having settled the matter by negotiations conducted by the elders of the planter's family. The fact that the bribe amounted to several times the expected fine was quite irrelevant. No one was able to understand how I could find the bribery business worse than recourse to normal legal channels. The functionary had shown himself receptive to human influences; he had accepted apologies and material compensation for his magnanimity. The initial feeling of helplessness before the cold, "objective" letter of the law had been replaced by a feeling of relief that an acceptable balance between the power of the functionary and the powerlessness of the surprised culprit had been achieved with the help of "normal," traditional forms of behavior.

Taboos

One might say that taboos, handed down by society to protect interpersonal relations from dangerous aggressive or anxiety-evoking libidinal tensions, are the precursors of the superego. The buttocks of an Anyi chief must never come into contact with the earth, for this would bring misfortune. The skirts of the queen of England must cover her knees, otherwise . . . well, certainly something dreadful would happen.

We have seen how Ahoussi exploited the taboo on dogs for the purposes of chiefship, and how the legal system makes use of taboos by incorporating the sanctions against their violation. Perhaps the decisive distinction between a legal norm and a taboo is that the latter punishes automatically, while the former requires a court trial in order to be enforced. The penalty for violating the rules of etiquette—the queen's skirts—derives much more clearly from human beings than from transcendental instances whose effective energies the analyst thinks he has located in the unconscious.

Be that as it may, one has the impression that the Anyi have just about reached the low point with their taboos, most of which must serve to enforce other rules of behavior.

One evening, Morgenthaler is playing a popular twelve-hole game with the young Baoulé, Joseph. Thomas Assoua joins them, obviously jealous. He informs them that it is forbidden to play games in Bébou after sunset; otherwise the spirits of the forest will descend upon the village (and bring misfortune with them). Joseph stops playing. Morgenthaler asks why. "Well, naturally—if the chief finds out, we'll have to pay a hefty fine." The chief comes in and remains alone with Morgenthaler. "That business about the spirits is nonsense," he says. "I made that rule because I don't want people to go on playing all night so that they're too tired to go to work the next day." Is this to be regarded as a reasonable rule, a superstition, or a taboo? The villagers' fear of the spirits, built into the taboo, serves a sensible purpose and supplements the power of the chief. Although—quite rightly—he considers drinking palm wine more harmful than playing an innocuous game, he has no taboos at his disposal to protect the inhabitants of Bébou from alcoholism.

The Anyi taboo on incest reinforces the acknowledged rules of exogamy, as it does in our culture. The taboos on working the land on a Wednesday and venturing into the forest on a Thursday (because on a Thursday one is bound to encounter the restless spirits of the dead) have become just as much a part of the rhythm of work as the Christian custom of observing the Sabbath. People go to work only four days a week; no one objects, because there are no exceptions. Jean-Pierre's father dies unexpectedly one Thursday in the forest. The son maintains that he committed suicide. An explanation has been found for the suddenness of his death; the taboo has been revived in its consequences. According to Field (15), the strict taboos imposed by the Akim on contact with menstruating women may well be the reason man and wife often live in separate households till they reach old age. In Bébou, where there is no such taboo and where the men have no particular fears regarding menstruation, the institution of separate households must be explained some other way. But even in Bébou hardly any man would dare to have sexual intercourse with a girl whose first menstrual period had not yet taken place and been publicly announced.

The multiple application of taboos can be explained by the fact that more comprehensive rule systems are more effective in the complicated social order of the Anyi than are separate, unrelated bans on single acts. And, in fact, nowadays the only effective taboos prohibiting only one specific action are those related to certain magic or ritual acts. Every healer and every female shaman has his or her own taboos, yet both place their rituals in the service of a larger order, contributing to the restoration of individual well-being or of family or village peace.

Our impression of a dearth of "pure" taboos, that is, taboos that forbid only a single expression of undesirable behavior, may be due to our own investigative approach, for we were concerned with Anyi ideology as a whole. We made no distinctions between religious and profane aspects, and only for description have we differentiated among individual institutions. In any case, the Anyi predisposition toward developing taboo anxiety is great; otherwise the taboos could not possibly be so effective in the manifold areas they cover. In a classic study, Freud (105) compared this anxiety with anxiety of conscience and characterized the latter as the more social formation. And the ambivalence that Freud regards as the reason for the development of taboos does, indeed, color all interpersonal relations among the Anyi. Where the ambivalence comes from is another matter. No matter how necessary, reasonable, or unreasonable a given prohibition may be, it is hard to conceive of a taboo whose ultimate purpose is not to help suppress mobilized rage.

Their difficulty in controlling anxiety-evoking instinctual conflicts is probably the reason the Anyi develop taboo anxiety, and also the reason this instrument of social regulation is so effective; their wavering feeling of identity, on the other hand, probably explains the strong tendency of many Anyi to establish new taboos and their fondness for reviving others that have fallen into neglect or oblivion. There is hardly anything more conducive to making an individual feel himself part of a group and to distinguishing between his own and other groups than sharing the same taboos. The individual's feeling of identity relies upon social markers, that is, upon clearly perceptible signs of acceptance from his fellow group members. In the individual's ego, the feeling of identity has the function of reconciling contradictory impulses and of resolving anxieties and conflicts in such a way that he remains in harmony with the group. This ego-plus-social aspect of taboo observance does not exclude the inner dynamics of instinctual ambivalence that are covered by the taboo; these two factors are mutually supplementary.

Among the Anyi, and presumably in most social structures that have taboos, confirmation of the feeling of identity has the higher priority.

Modern ethnologists (148) have pointed out that totemism, coupled with a taboo on killing the totem animal of the clan, originates from a need for self-definition, a need to be different from other groups and to organize into groups. In Bébou the taboo is just about all that is left of the ephemeral clan structure of the Anyi.

In addition to the uterine lineage, which was the most influential unit, the Ashanti had a hierarchy of eight great clans, each with its own totem animal. According to tradition, this hierarchy could be traced back to the original, often mythological, blood relationship of several maternal lines, whose descendants were scattered over a wide area (17, 23). Members of the same great clan regarded themselves as distant relatives and were not permitted to marry. All Akan peoples are supposed to have had the same clans (11); among the Anyi they played only a minor role (25). Many Anyi today do not even know which great clan they belong to and which totem animal is taboo for them. On the other hand, there are also taboos linked with the paternal line (ntoro), though the latter has practically no significance in determining clan membership, and the paternal line, too, has a totem animal. Like other Akan peoples, the Anyi usually teach their children the taboo but do not reveal the name of the paternal clan; the taboo the father was brought up to observe is passed on to the son.

Thomas Assoua tells us: "I don't eat turtle. It's very good to eat, but I refuse to eat it. The turtle is my father's totem animal." He goes on to explain that neither the father of his father, nor in fact anybody of the Assoua family, has ever eaten turtle, and that his son will never eat it either. Thomas lacks the strength to carry out the ancient rituals that, for his father, may have confirmed his feeling for his origins (on the banks of the Tano River) and his membership in the group. But as long as he refuses to eat turtle and thus observes the taboo of his paternal clan, he feels like a man, a worthy son of his father. Like the other men of Bébou, Thomas himself is a member of his mother's family. His self-confidence is shaky and his feeling of identity uncertain. The introject of an overpowerful mother, to whom he submitted, and the lack of any real chance to identify with his father, whom he recalls only as a remote and ineffective figure in his childhood environment, are obstacles to the active, masculine role he is called upon to play in the community.

The Anyi do not observe all taboos handed down by tradition, but only those that help bolster their feeling of identity where it may be defective. The men of Bébou, bound by hundreds of strong ties to the mother and her lineage, have a particular need for confirmation and consolidation in their roles as males and fathers.

Etiquette

They're of noble house, that's very clear:
Haughty and discontented they appear.
                                    Goethe, Faust I

Everywhere in Africa etiquette and ceremony used to play an important role, especially in the more highly developed kingdoms, where there was a need to stress the gulf existing between persons of different status even though their living standards might be more or less the same. The ceremonial acts that are obligatory in the presence of persons of high rank seem to help to deny feelings of envy and rebelliousness, to provide both groups with clearly defined boundaries and the resultant security, and to preserve the power structure (65). But such acts are typical not only of the great men of the ancient kingdoms; all the Anyi in Bébou and in the shabby jungle villages base their daily lives on forms of behavior that can be compared in their strictness, intricacy, and subtlety with the ceremonies observed at the court of Louis XIV. The briefest description we have of Anyi protocol, by Mouëzy (30), covers ten pages. One might conclude that their social system, having lost so many of the taboos that regulate interpersonal relations among other peoples living in the tropical zone, has set up an elaborate framework of etiquette, or that the almost total usurpation of the administration of justice by the colonial authorities had robbed Anyi society of its system of regulation, forcing it to devise a substitute that needed neither public institutions nor power to be effective. Neither conclusion can be verified on the basis of history. We can, however, attest that tensions are apt to develop among all Anyi when they are confronted with others, and these tensions are just as acute as—and very similar in character to—the tensions that can be expected to arise anywhere in the world between the powerful and the weak, the rich and the poor.

The system of etiquette is based on the individual's need to demonstrate his own prestige, to differentiate between his own status and that of others, and to see confirmed his own identity and his own assessment of his worth. Violations of protocol lead to annoyance and insult; the injured party reacts to these violations with feelings of narcissistic mortification, of shame, and ultimately with a loss of self-esteem and with impotence. All these reactions are equalized as soon as the partner begins to behave in accordance with the rules of etiquette; the system functions automatically. But, since the underlying tensions are often too strong and etiquette—simply because of its complexity—may fail to function as it should, the individual usually has an anxious, unhappy feeling that others may commit some unpardonable offense in spite of the built-in safeguards. But for this, too, there is an established remedy. The party at fault offers his apologies. The injured party replies "Yakyi"—"never mind, it's all right." The matter is settled and the superficial affront erased. Once again the individuals concerned have succeeded in denying their deeper emotions and in avoiding an open controversy.

Frequently, however, the whole ritual proves ineffective, and an open quarrel cannot be averted. The parties appeal to an arbitrator, fail to settle their differences, and continue their appeal to higher and higher echelons of arbitration until they finally appear before a genuine court. It would probably be difficult to find another system of justice anywhere that is forced to concern itself primarily with "quarrels arising out of personal abuse" (6). Today the task of a judge among the Anyi is largely that of restoring the psychological equilibrium of the contending parties after it has been upset by their dispute.

After exchanging the prescribed greetings, the host—or when individuals happen to meet on the street, the more distinguished of the two, that is, the one who was greeted first—asks for the "first news." High-ranking personages address this request through a spokesman. There follows an exchange of commonplaces that define the encounter in time and space—such remarks as "I have just arrived here," "It is noon," "I've laid aside my luggage." Only then do the two proceed to more important matters, to the purpose of the meeting. When one wants to leave, one requests "permission to depart." Even a brief absence demands an oral apology and, when one returns, formal notification. As if it were necessary to resort to words to establish the proper distance between individuals who are not quite certain just how they stand with one another. For the psychoanalyst this is obviously not the best way to establish contact with people; everything seems to be directed to avoiding any closer contact, to concealing one's inner life behind the screen of etiquette.

But one of the most characteristic abilities of the Anyi is precisely this mastery of ceremonial behavior, which gives especially persons from distinguished families enormous self-esteem and the confidence that they can cope with any eventuality, from the problems of daily life to the more dramatic vicissitudes of fate. It seems one of the goals of the ideal self to be able to apply the proper formula on every occasion and thus to guard oneself against others' rudeness. As a consequence, the individual enjoys a kind of secondary narcissistic security denied those Anyi who, because of their low birth or their youth, are not able to comply with the requirements of ceremonial etiquette. Suzanne, for example, is capable of informing us with a smile that her beloved husband has already bought the poison he needs to commit suicide. And

Dibi, the dignitary, can forgive us the fact that he is excluded from all the advantages and prestige our presence brings to the village when we exchange polite, thoroughly noncommittal visits. Arrogant, indifferent, and just a bit nervous, the stately lords and ladies move through their village. Though their bodies are weakened by tormenting parasites and their souls are full of irreconcilable conflicts, they manage to conceal their weak points. The Djoula farmhands, who pose a real threat to their economic existence, look like their slaves. We ourselves, half-reluctant, half-admiring, capitulated before their etiquette, as did the victorious French officers and governors who had come to conquer their land. The rituals center the feeling of identity on a conception of self in which every Anyi claims the right to be regarded as a first among equals. As a matter of fact, the Anyi people as a whole have the manners of a courtly society and an arrogance otherwise found only among privileged classes.

Religion
No one needs to teach God to a child.

The Akan religion can be described as syncretic and animistic in character. This means that the Anyi tend to borrow religious concepts and rituals from other cultures without integrating them into a homogeneous religion. For example, an Anyi may call himself a Catholic by baptism, wear Islamic amulets, sacrifice to the spirit of the Manzan River, and—on occasion—even consult the female shamans of Yosso about the intentions and demands of the spirits. Furthermore, it is quite possible for a large variety of living and nonliving media—animals, trees, water—to be invested with noncorporeal spirits, and for these spirits sometimes to become the objects of rituals.

It is difficult to comprehend the religion, or rather the *Weltbild*, of the Akan when one is used to thinking in terms of concepts developed from the Christian or pre-Christian religions of the Western world. The countless, mutually contradictory, and frequently hopeless attempts of scholars to define Nyame, the all-embracing god of the Akan heavens, bear witness to the truth of this statement. Some have interpreted Nyame as a typical sole deity and have celebrated the Akan as the inventors of a pre-Judaic monotheistic system (11). This hypothesis, like the ones that follow, has found support in meticulous—and sometimes rather questionable—etymological analyses of the name Nyame and the epithets conferred upon the deity. Others have also regarded Nyame as a sole deity and tried to prove—in long scholarly treatises—that he had been brought to the west coast of Africa in prehistoric times through cultural contact with the inhabitants of the Semitic-Egyptian area and subsequently "Africanized" (29). Still others have seen in him a naively personified god of the Negroes, a kind of village chief assigned to heaven, responsible for administering justice and providing for his subjects, the children of earth (7). A number of scholars have assumed that Nyame, in response to syncretic needs, had been imported into the heathen pantheon of the Akan as a somewhat modified Allah from the Islamic regions to the north, or even that he had been borrowed from the Christians living on the west coast. Those thoroughly familiar with the Akan culture (33), however, were convinced that Nyame had originated as an Akan god, while others, who were of the same opinion, considered him relatively unimportant because he had no cult of his own. And finally there were those who—in keeping with the animistic tendencies of the Akan "to invest everything with life"— regarded him as a typical nature spirit, as the manifestation of a desire to enliven the heavens with a deity to correspond to the spirits of rivers and trees and to the numerous other gods who are consulted by priests and have cults dedicated to them. In the last analysis these scholars were no better off than the Baoulé when Delafosse (13) asked them about the god Nyame. Their reply: "He is too far above us and too different from us; he doesn't understand us, and we don't understand him."

In an attempt to do justice to Nyame—and the other religious manifestations of the Anyi—in spite of this plethora of theories, we decided to follow the path indicated by Africa philosopher Abraham and to try to comprehend the *Weltbild* of the Anyi and to contrast their religious thought as a whole (and not as an accumulation of isolated phenomena) with that of Europe. As early as 1912 Chéruy (7) had pointed out that the Anyi regard all natural phenomena as successive transformations or manifestations of the supreme being; this, of course, accounts for the large number of spirits and gods. And Field (15) states that all Akim ritual "is intended to multiply life."

For the Akan the world with all its natural phenomena—and this includes human society—is above all a spiritual structure. It is not that nature is made animate (this is of secondary importance), but that nature was felt from the very beginning to be spiritual, supernatural. Material phenomena are merely the expression, the manifestation, or the vehicle of the spirit. And this spirit is Nyame ("spirit" in the sense in which it is used in Gen. 1:1: "And the spirit of God moved upon the face of the waters").

In his essence, however, man participates in the all-embracing spirit to a considerable extent; the living being is spirit in essence, even though this spirit may be temporarily enveloped in flesh. Nevertheless, it is spirit that has been dispatched to the visible world to fulfill a specific mission. The spirit owes only its supplementary existence to God; in its true essence, it is not a created entity. Men are not God's creatures, but his messengers. For this reason man's relationship to Nyame and to the gods, demons, and spirits in which the spiritual principle manifests itself is not one of estrangement or awe in the same sense as our relationship to the transcendental, the supernatural. There is no unbridgeable gap between two worlds, the transitory and the eternal. Man's cults and rituals are not dedicated to the worship of authorities that are, in principle, different from or loftier than man himself, but rather of authorities existing within the order of which he himself is a part, in which they simply happen to be more powerful than he. The prosaic casualness and irreverence with which the Anyi perform their cult rituals are immediately apparent to anyone who compares these rituals with those practiced by Christians or Jews.

The earth is regarded as a principle similar to that of Nyame, that is, as spirit in which man participates, except that the earth is more material, more motherly, more tangible. There is no cult dedicated to it, but it does have one day on which man is not permitted to disturb it by going out and working in the fields; in Bébou this is Wednesday. Every adult Anyi spills a few drops on the ground before he drinks—"for the earth," some say, "because we live on it"; "for the ancestors," say others, "because in the end the earth will receive all of us." Shall we call this a cult or a sign of closeness? A habit or a superstition?

The saying at the head of this section can be amplified to express the idea that the child already possesses God, that his essence is spiritual even though he is not yet aware of it.

The Anyi in Bébou invest man not only with a mortal body, but also with an invisible, immortal, and indestructible soul—and with an invisible double of the body for good measure. The soul is attributed only to human beings, the double to all objects, animate and inanimate. Other Akan peoples have more complex and more comprehensive concepts in this respect.[5] But the inhabitants of Bébou are convinced that conflicts can arise between two components of the soul and make the individual ill; bodily illness is always the result of disturbances in the person's spiritual components. During dreams, a part of the soul leaves the body and can cause trouble or commit adultery (sexual dreams). After death, the immortal component returns to God and the ancestors of the maternal line, while the body's double wanders about as a discontented spirit.

The invisible world surrounding man is populated by an infinite number of gods and spirits that help one another, wage war on one another, take an interest in human life—or do all or none of these. When they wish to appear, they assume the form of a plant, an animal, or an inanimate object. Smaller gods—also components of the spirit—have established shrines for themselves and chosen priests as the custodians through whom alone they will act and help. Such a priest has managed to capture a flash of the divine spirit and has built it a shrine, which is considered to be holy as long as the spirit dwells there. When the god is addressed through the proper ritual, he is more or less forced to respond. He has no choice but to place his wisdom at the disposal of the suppliant. In this respect the gods are rather like kings, whose duty it is to help their subjects financially. The "power to give," on which the institution of chiefship is based, is derived from the same psychological laws as the power attributed to gods and spirits.

The question whether everything in fact is or can be endowed with animistic life never arises in the thinking of the Anyi. In terms of psychoanalytic theory, this would correspond to a general projective tendency, but a rather special one—the boundaries between the projecting individual and the field of projection (human or not) are blurred; "both belong to the same spiritual world." One might speak of participative projection. In case of need, however, when anxieties must be soothed or, in the Anyi way of thinking, a disequilibrium set right, sacrifice and other magic-related acts are required to ensure the sympathy of the spirit. For the latter is by no means viewed as always benevolent; in fact, when one needs to turn to him, one usually expects to find him angry or out of sorts. As a result, the strongest cults are those dedicated to gods that manifest themselves frequently because they are discontent and to those that rarely or never respond effectively to ritual ceremonies or prayers—for example, the spirit of a river that is always full of fish, but whose waters are dangerously turbulent.

According to Anyi belief, the god alone is active; he chooses his own shrine and priest, issues his prophecies, and demands his sacrifices. A god differs from an ordinary spirit only in having taken these active steps independently. The human suppliant remains passive. This passive mode of experience can easily be maintained with the help of participative projection. It is our impression that active appeals for help are made only when external dangers threaten or under the pressure of inner anxieties. This would explain the regressive mechanism, but not the constant preoccupation with individual gods, and not the inordinately large number of gods. Several other factors are of importance in this connection.

Rattray (33) gives an account of the sacrifice offered to the spirit of the Akata tree to induce it to cure an illness: "A string had been tied round the trunk of the Akata tree. This had been given as a token 'that the donor wished the god to bear him upon his back as a mother carries her child.'" This makes it abundantly clear how the god is expected to behave—like a loving mother during the child's early infancy. Other gods are supposed to have other qualities. This eagerness to treat "everything" animistically reflects a yearning for objects capable of coming to the aid of the individual's own unstable ego functions. There is no contradiction inherent in the fact that many gods impose strict rules and threaten drastic punishment—usually death—for breaking them. After all, is there anything that can give a timorous, indecisive person firmer support than a bargain sealed with a cruel and merciless almighty figure, the likeness of the phallic mother of early childhood, right after weaning? This is the period of anal and phallic libido development, during which the pattern for later object relations, most skills, and moral instances (superego) must evolve out of the individual's conflicts with the persons of his environment (oedipal conflicts). If the moral instances prove inadequate, then religion can provide a substitute.

Actually, the fundamental idea of the Akan religion resembles the religious views held by many Western intellectuals ever since the Age of Enlightenment. It is a kind of nonmystical natural philosophy, a participation in the spirit of creation but without primitive anthropomorphism, based on an ethical concept but without a moral code. Religion is understood as a feeling of union with other people, with one's ancestors, and with the world—not with a transcendental being. On this basis the Anyi are living beyond their means, religiously speaking. They do not possess the social poise—let alone the individual autonomy—needed to enable them to associate with their fellows as equals. A yearning for objects, an urgent need for guiding figures emerges—a need for gods and priests.

Priests, sorcerers, and female shamans are needed to mitigate, with their prophecies, the individual's anxiety and impotence in the face of a threatening fate and to interpret and enforce, with their rules and regulations, the will of the gods—in other words, ethical demands. Following orders helps to overcome both anxiety and guilt feelings. Here the moral precepts other religions provide automatically must be worked out anew or at least reformulated from case to case.

The actual objects, or rather object representations of the powerful imagoes, are spirits and gods. Spirits are a source of terror until they have selected a material medium, a priest, and a ritual for appeals. Gods, however, exist in many forms; in accordance with the laws of participative projection, their number is potentially infinite. They can be divided into two categories: the original, natural gods who have always had their shrines, cults, and priests in the land of the Anyi (for example, the god of the Manzan River, with Ahoussi as his priest), and the "purchased" gods who have been brought in deliberately with their benevolent or destructive powers, usually from other geographical regions, in order to place a village, a group, or all petitioners under their protection (e.g., Bébou's spirits of the forest, with the taboo on dogs).

The demarcation line between these two types of god is by no means rigid. Both types need tangible shrines. The most obvious difference is perhaps that the "imported" gods need an artificial, man-made support—for example, a clay jar—whose contents, however, are usually natural products such as soil from . . . , water from . . . , and so on. When an individual has procured a god of this type, by paying for him or performing certain services in return for him (undertaking long journeys, for instance), he usually remains the god's priest. Often the priest's original purpose was merely to acquire the god's power to do evil so as to harm his enemies. In this case it may happen that the rituals or artifacts that induce the god to do good are not acquired and that therefore the god and his priest can do only evil from that time on.

Since "everything" can be animated with the divine spirit, it is ridiculous to state that the land of the Anyi harbors "too few" indigenous gods and that the Anyi therefore must import their holy relics and gods from other cultures. The Anyi tendency toward syncretism, toward assimilation of concepts alien to their own culture, is not something that developed only after the decline of the great Akan empires, as a product of cultural disintegration. One external factor is certainly the political openness of the Akan states. From the very beginning, these states integrated foreign slaves into the most sacred echelon of the social organization, the uterine lineages, and they were able to consolidate their power in great part because of the production methods, weapons, and organizational systems they took over from their neighbors whenever they were superior to their own. The mythical origins of their kings "from alien lands" reflects the same principle as can be seen in the laws of inheritance that are still in effect today. The new chief of a court or family comes from another village; for the uterine nephew inherits from the brother of his mother, not from the father in whose household he has grown up.

Still more striking is the psychological aspect, which might be summarized as follows: We need alien gods, our own are not powerful enough to help us; besides, they are too evil; surely alien gods are more powerful and more kindly—we sense unconsciously that they have not been shaped by the unhappy experiences of *our* childhood. But, once established among the Anyi, these gods take on the characteristics of Anyi gods; they become cruel and lose whatever power they may have had to banish misery. This tragedy is what keeps alive the syncretic need for ever new gods. The unconquerable fear of the adults of early childhood and the feelings of impotence that are projected to "evil" witches and spirits whom one cannot hope to influence make Islam in particular seem attractive as "good" magic in comparison with the Anyi pantheon. The rigid rules of the Koran (as compared with the paucity of rules in the Akan tradition) and the written symbols that are unfamiliar to the Akan (which—better than any other symbolization—make power tangible and thus controllable) play an important role in the hope for religious help.

In every Anyi village there is a church. Everyone has a Christian name in addition to the first and second names he has received from his father. Many Anyi have been baptized as Catholics or Methodists. Once a year the Catholic priest visits Bébou to collect church dues from all the inhabitants "who do not wish to be known as fetishists doomed to go to hell." Each one is given a holy picture in return. Almost everyone pays, even young people who have to borrow the money; it is about the same as when the chief orders a collection taken up to pay for a sacrifice to one of the local gods.

The opinion expressed by a Ghanaian African on the question "why people become Christians" (16) might well be applied to Bébou— "Some people . . . become Christians when they have practised bad *suman* (an evil spell) and they found out that their sins are coming out, they run and make Christians. Some people be highway-men, then later they repent and become Christians. Some one may be a murderer and then he become a Christian he has repent from his sins. Some one may be a thief, he repent from stealing and become a Christian. Some one may have lorry accident." The God of the Christians is not so strict, He is able to forgive; the Anyi gods are interested only in sin, and that often costs a lot of money. Naturally it can be assumed that such Christians—perhaps all Christians, in fact—are guilty of something or other; otherwise why did they have to become Christians? For even the aggressive gods of the Anyi leave a blameless person alone.

There is a striking difference in the attitudes toward Islam and toward Christianity. One has, one possesses Mohammedan amulets and *marabus* (priests); one becomes, one *is* a Christian. The first can be compared to an alien, purchased god; the second to a suit of clothes one has acquired from the world of the whites. The first, nowadays, brings little in the way of social prestige—Islam is the religion of the Djoula, the foreign workers; Christians are whites or modern-minded Africans, people of importance—one wants to be like them.

Genuine, lasting conversions are rare. Of the approximately one thousand Anyi living in the three villages of Alangouan, not a single one is exclusively Mohammedan or exclusively Christian, with no other religious ties. The social system of the Anyi, which seems so permissive when observed from without, does not really liberate the individual.

The elderly dignitary Kwame came to consult us about his sexual impotence. In typical Anyi fashion, he had been neglected as a boy by his father, a Methodist preacher, and had been given away to relatives who did not want him. All he received from his father was a knowledge of a few Christian prayers and the conviction, which he still has, that if he does not recite these prayers and confess his sins to God every single day, he will be on his way to hell. His first wife put a curse on him when he took a second wife and all three of them were infected with venereal disease. The burden of the curse was this: If the sickness comes from the second wife, then you will become impotent with her; if it comes from me, may such and such a spirit take me. Kwame did become impotent. Years ago, in a panic, he abandoned both wives, leaving them his worldy goods, and obeyed a summons to Bébou to take over the inheritance and—in accordance with the laws of the levirate—the wife of his dead brother. Everything ought to have been all right; after all, the curse had nothing to do with her. But now the Christian curse reemerged from the past—if your new, third wife does not become a Methodist, if she does not pray with you, you will both go to hell. Kwame is impotent with her, too, and thus cannot marry her. This is a neurotic conflict, of course. Christian dogma has become an article of faith for Kwame, as for so many other Anyi people. And thus Kwame has something he can hold fast to, a measure of security he was not able to acquire from his father and his family.

All the great religions, of course, have taken over many foreign elements. Our Christian Christmas, for example, absorbed and replaced the heathen yuletide celebration. The difference between this type of borrowing and syncretism seems to be not—or at least not solely—that the former takes place at a higher level of cultural adaptation. The discreteness of the various gods of the Anyi is in itself an extremely culture-specific element, reflecting as it does the aggressive tensions existing among various introjected part objects. The greater depersonalization of Christian dogma and ethical doctrines makes an amalgamation of culture-alien elements into a uniform doctrine easier, but at the same time it alienates this doctrine from immediate human needs. The religious needs of the Anyi force them to operate with a large, constantly renewed number of gods; in compensation, they are spared the "double standard" of Christianity, which makes demands that its adherents are incapable of fulfilling.

Almost all Anyi religious rituals are performed in some sort of community group. At the very least, a priest or a male shaman must be present. And yet, when one compares the Anyi with other West Africans, one is struck by the fact that there is a definite restoration of

disturbed ego functions, a mitigation of personal (not collective) anxieties, and a confirmation of *individual* identity. Whereas all Dogon
rituals—regardless of the occasion or their mythical content—contribute
to the process of confirmation of identificatory unity with the group,
this is not so with the Anyi. In fact, in this respect the latter stand
midway between Europeans and the Dogon. Their rituals are almost
invariably carried out in the presence of mediators. Solitary sacrifice or
prayer is a rare exception to the rule. What the cult gives, on the other
hand, can hardly be shared by the community. The female shaman
gives Elisa certain rules to help her to adjust to the family and the
community, but she has to accomplish the act of adjusting by herself.
As far as her self-esteem is concerned, she gains an awareness of having
acted like a true daughter of her people at a critical moment, as when
she was compelled to accept the fact that her identification with the
whites was not sufficient to enable her to resolve her urgent conflicts
with her environment or to master the anxieties arising out of her inner
life.

The only exceptions—that is, occasions when the Anyi enter directly
into the community of their fellows with cult and ritual acts—are their
funeral ceremonies and their participation in messianic movements.
Once the spiritual link with the environment has been broken, their
inner resources are insufficient to restore the balance between the needs
of the individual and those of the community. The religion of the Anyi
is typically that of a conflict-ridden culture.

3 Family Organization and the Economy

Thomas Assoua (Fritz Morgenthaler—A Summary of Forty-six Psychoanalytic Interviews)

Thomas Assoua,[1] like most of the Anyi we met, has an ambivalent attitude toward us whites. He is suspicious and at the same time curious. During our talks together, he proves easily distracted. He says very little of his own accord. Frequently he simply sits there, staring at nothing and looking unhappy, but this contemplative behavior changes suddenly the moment he sees an opportunity to enhance his prestige. For prestige is about the only thing with which he can hope to influence a fate so dependent upon the whims of chance. During the first three weeks, Thomas very often fails to show up for his interviews. My feelings toward him are characterized by the same impotence and helplessness that mark his feelings toward the society in which he lives. My failure to follow the traditional rules of ceremonial politeness when I refuse to accept the fish he sends me as a gift of hospitality brings about a turning point. Thomas and I talk things out. For him, my behavior means that I can do what I like, that I am not compelled to do what society thinks it has the right to demand of me. Thomas invariably has to do what is demanded of him, but at the same time would like to have more autonomy; thus he is now able to identify with me. From this time on he appears regularly for our sessions and begins to talk about what really concerns him.

Thomas's father was an influential man in Bébou and had been involved in a somewhat obscure rivalry with King Ahoussi, for the latter had taken it upon himself to guide the destinies of the four founding families. One of these was the Assoua family, whose own claims to leadership and property conflicted with those of Ahoussi. The senior Assoua had had three wives and nine children. He died some months before our arrival in Bébou. Thomas expects to be appointed his father's successor and head of the kin. He has no enemies; everybody thinks well of him. Nevertheless, he is not confident of the outcome. No one can predict just how the family elders will decide at the final funeral festivities. According to the traditional matrilineal rules of succession, the son of Assoua's sister would be the legal heir, but according to the laws valid in the Ivory Coast today, the oldest son of the deceased inherits.

The final funeral rites for Thomas's dead father are to take place soon; they had been postponed until after the coffee and cocoa harvests. It is customary to wait until people have enough money on hand to be able to pay the high contributions levied for the ceremonies. Thomas has long since accustomed himself to the idea that all the momentous decisions affecting his life are made by some powerful person and that he can never tell in advance what they will be. His life is dominated by tension, doubt, and uncertainty. In anticipation of the funeral ceremonies, our talks take on a rather solemn character. In the eyes of the villagers, Thomas has acquired a special status because he talks regularly with me. His prestige is increasing. It is not the external aspects of our power—the material, medical, and social aspects—but rather the omnipotence of the whites in general with which Thomas has invested me that makes him able to identify with me. When he comes to my tent for his evening sessions, he wears his ceremonial toga, while I hasten to arrange for electric lighting, wiring a lamp to my car battery. Thomas has now reached the point where he speaks in detail about his life. Old feelings of resentment toward his father emerge. When he was a child, his father gave him away to an uncle. But because he was treated unfairly in the uncle's household he returned home. Since then there has been bad blood between the two families. Later his father selected a bride for him, but Thomas refused to obey his father's wishes and instead married a girl who was more closely related to his maternal lineage. Subsequently his wife left him, and he married a second wife from the court of one of the founding families of Bébou (fig. 5). Whenever he tried to escape the tutelage of others, he found himself caught fast in the course determined by the family. His apprehensions concerning the coming funeral ceremonies crop up more and more frequently in our talks. In reality, however, these fears are largely irrational. What Thomas is afraid of at bottom is the blind rage that might overcome him and lead to his humiliating himself if there should be a serious quarrel during the ceremonies and his repressed hatred of his revered father should break through.

When the funeral festivities take place on 20 February 1966, Thomas is appointed successor to his father. He had taken it upon himself to risk temporary estrangement from one of his best friends in order to comply with his father's orders that this friend should be made to contribute a specified sum for the final rites. The repression of his aggressive urges compels him to carry out his father's commands. He must continue to be an obedient son; otherwise his father will punish him from the next world. In his new capacity as chief, Thomas intends to assume responsibility for his kin in all respects. He comments on the quarrel with his friend: "Friends are like tongue and teeth. They are

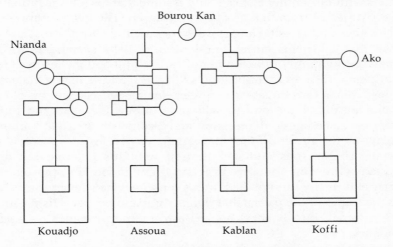

Fig. 5. A mythical ancestral mother, Bourou Kan, had two sons who came to Bébou as conquerors and took Nianda and Ako as wives. The four courts of Kouadjo, Assoua, Kablan, and Koffi (with one subsidiary court) are derived in matrilineal descent from these two women. The inhabitants of these four courts regard themselves as belonging to the same family, although the first generation did not follow the maternal line. Now Thomas Assoua, breaking through the maternal lineage once more, is to take over temporarily the court of his deceased father.

always together and yet always opposed. But both are needed to form the words we speak."

In this connection, he begins to talk about the succession of the king, who is already a very old man. According to Thomas, when the king dies there are only two families from which his successor could come. One of these is the Assoua family. But Thomas declares that he will never be village chief in Bébou. He is destined to fulfill a different task. His mother was his father's second wife. She was a member of a dignitary family in the neighboring village of Yosso and had left the court of the Assouas many years ago. Thomas will be the heir of his uncle in Yosso, becoming the head of his maternal kin and probably village chief in Yosso as well. In his fantasies Thomas already sees himself as the respected, powerful chief of the neighboring village, safe in the bosom of his maternal family. Though it is the matriarchal society that has predetermined the course of Thomas's life, he still avoids a situation of rivalry with his father, for in reality he lives with his father's kin, in which he was brought up and in which he has become a leading personality. Thomas often complains about the difficulties he has with the women of the Assoua court in his capacity as chief. The confrontation with these female figures also places a particular strain on Thomas's adult love life. We have no information concerning his early childhood relations with his mother and can only assume that his lot was probably not very different from that of all Anyi children. The deep disappointment in the mother left Thomas, even as a child, with a distrust of women that colors his entire emotional life. If he surrenders to his feelings, the longing for the mother of early childhood makes itself felt and brings with it an identification with the interests of the maternal families. This in turn threatens to undermine his self-esteem; his object relations are disrupted, and he falls prey to bewilderment and inner emptiness. Listlessness, depression, and alcoholism are found among the Anyi as the result of such developments. To avoid just such an outcome, Thomas has affiliated himself with his paternal kin and identified with their interests ever since childhood, in spite of the jealousy and rivalry this entailed. In his conscious view, everything that bears the stamp of the patriarchal clan is right and proper. His position in the paternal court bolsters his self-esteem and promotes his social ascendancy.

To preserve his psychological equilibrium Thomas needs both the identification with the maternal lineage, to be able to achieve libidinal cathexis, and the identification with the father, to maintain his self-esteem. He oscillates constantly between these two possible identifications, neither of which would suffice alone to protect him from severe conflicts. In Anyi society, the gender-determined lineages can be compared with unpredictable and inconsistent power structures, in whose tangled network the individual is trapped and made helpless, but at the same time prevented from falling and kept safe.

Because young Thomas possesses the qualities of a born leader, he is bound to find ways and means of mitigating the unpredictable and the inconsistent.

Kinship Patterns

A society that is organized in families based on matrilineal descent carries within it seeds of internal conflicts and tensions that do not exist in families and clans based on the patrilineal system. In keeping with existing theories (150), this is only to be expected. Is it not surprising, then, that the Anyi still cling to their traditional system even though it led to serious tensions in earlier times among other Akan peoples, and though the economic developments of the modern period seem almost to demand a change in family organization?

Since a wife and her children, as long as they live, are members of a family group to which the husband is not admitted, group interests are bound to conflict with the solidarity of husband and wife. The establishment of a common household becomes a problem, marriages are unstable, and the ties that develop between the father and his children compete directly with the authority of the matrilineal group. The disruptive effect on the matrilineal system of the father's emotional interest in his children has no exact counterpart in the mother's love for her children in patrilineal families. Since the wife usually changes her family allegiance with marriage, leaving her own family for that of her husband, she is naturally also able to identify more or less with the plans and goals of her new family.

Another source of tension is that a brother is bound to have an intense interest in the offspring of his sister and—logically—in her sexual activity, because it is her children that increase his kin, not those of his own wife. A brother's ties—both family and emotional—to his sister are extremely close; as a sex object, however, she is taboo. Frequently a strong rivalry develops between a man's wife and his sister. And often, even after years of marriage, he is apt to find that his only escape from this area of tension—which, of course, will recur with every new wife he takes—is divorce.

Social rules and the laws of inheritance make a male Anyi more dependent upon the brother of his mother than on any other relative. When this uncle dies, he will be his heir and—in accordance with the levirate system—is supposed to inherit the uncle's wives as well. In most cases, however, the heir—as the son of a different family—has grown up in a different village from that of his uncle and has been subject to the uncle's authority only in theory. In reality he has been brought up by his father, he has worked for his father, and he has augmented his father's property. Now that the plantation economy requires long-range planning for years ahead, the sons find it particularly unjust to be deprived of the fruits of their labor when the fathers die and the inheritance goes to a "stranger." Nor can the nephews be sure that their uncles will really provide for them instead of finding ways of leaving their property to their own sons. The matrilineal law of inheritance is still firmly entrenched. But it is only rarely that an uncle feels a genuine responsibility to provide for his nephew or—conversely—that a nephew feels an obligation to take over the family of his uncle along with the inheritance. The result is an atmosphere of suspicion and distrust—many uncles are afraid of being poisoned by their nephews so that they can inherit sooner; and many nephews hopefully await the death of their uncles and are afraid the latter may have found a way of cheating them of their inheritance.[2]

These and other family tensions are reflected in a steadily increasing fear of witchcraft. In every corner lurks a witch (invariably of the maternal lineage) who has already secretly sold your flesh, and you are condemned to perish—persecution anxieties in the traditional form, which threaten to inundate the functioning of society. "Can you sell a dress that doesn't belong to you?—All right! Then you can't sell the soul of anyone who doesn't belong to you and yours, who is not of your own family."

The family, the most important social institution, the institution that holds the Anyi together as a people, is sick, disintegrating, and decadent. The enormous contradictions and tensions inherent in any matrilineal system have become so acute that there is no longer any hope. The entire social structure is bound to collapse. The Anyi are a sick and miserable people.

One can arrive all too easily at this conclusion, and most Europeans who are acquainted with the Anyi would probably agree. Nor would the Anyi in Bébou disagree; they would stress the conflicts even more—they hate and fear their uncles, whom by rights they ought to love and revere, whom they ought to regard as second—and better—fathers. They are unable to conceive of a world without a family organization. They speak of their mothers, their fathers, their brothers, and these are the only people they want to have anything to do with. They cling to the family, but the family is no longer a functioning institution.

Even though we have just adduced—in general terms—arguments supporting this view, we do not believe it is correct; we believe we started with the wrong premise; namely, that the Anyi have a family organization similar to our own.

For the sake of argument, let us now adopt a different premise. Let us discard the concept of family as it appears in the Anyi culture and in ours, and instead let us state our premise as follows: The Anyi live in a social structure that assigns the individual simultaneously to several social systems or functional units. Each of these systems has certain functions that are familiar to us within the framework of "family" in other peoples. No single area of functions exactly matches the others; different rules are valid in each area; and in each area the members have common interests as well as conflicts arising out of contradictory interests.

This is rather difficult to visualize. We are used to dealing with forms of organization in which an individual belongs to different areas of social functioning or social systems; a worker has a family and belongs to it, he belongs to his place of employment, to a political party, to a specific district in his community. Each of these functional areas is governed by different rules. And the members of each area have quite different interests. When two areas overlap, the situation becomes difficult. For example, if many workers employed in a certain factory belong to the same party and, in their capacity as party members, agree to strike, they are acting in two different functional areas. The result will be controversies between the members of the two areas and inner conflicts in the individuals concerned. The worker wants to continue receiving his pay; at the same time, however, he wants to renounce his wages temporarily in order to join his party comrades in pushing through certain demands.

The Anyi are in a very similar situation, except that they refer to seven or eight of the most important areas of function to which they belong as their family—sometimes just one, sometimes several, and sometimes all seven or eight at once. Naturally, they know exactly which system they mean in any given instance; they never confuse their mother with an aunt of the maternal or paternal line of descent whom they also call mother. They know that their obligations toward the elder of the compound in which they live are not the same as toward the elder who is head of their kin and lives in a different village.

What we mean when we think of family is pretty much the same as what the Anyi means by the same term, namely the following: A family is a group of people characterized by a feeling of belonging together, belonging together by virtue of descent, marriage ties, or other forms of affiliation. One important purpose of the family is procreation; sexual needs play a role in and are regulated by the family. In addition, there are usually other common interests, particularly economic ones and those arising out of the circumstance of living together. Moreover, to a greater or lesser degree, there are also conflicting interests among family members.

But it is another aspect included in our concept of family—that each individual belongs to only one family at a time—that led to the erroneous conclusion that the Anyi family must be on the way to disintegration because of inner tensions. If we forget about the term "family" in connection with the Anyi and speak instead of functional areas that complement and overlap each other, then the tensions appear "normal" to us, and the survival—indeed the vitality and strength—of the traditional form of social organization becomes understandable. This form does not negate the special conflicts within the society or the personal problems of individuals, but the significance attributed to them is different. Tensions that would rupture the family circle we know may even strengthen cohesion in a different family system.

In each of the family systems of the Anyi, an individual has ties to persons with whom he is closely associated in another or in several other systems as well as to persons who join the system "from outside"; and each system has a hierarchy of its own, characterized by its own prerogatives, obligations, and dependencies. Any sociology of the Anyi people would have to begin with a description of these overlapping groups and could only then proceed to derive from them the various social roles assigned to each member. The various single family systems would provide the chapters in an overall work on the structure of society.

The most important entity is the *maternal lineage,* to which an individual belongs till the day he dies. This group decides the fate of individuals—for generations to come—and determines to a large extent the institutions we call the state, the economy, and the society. In addition, each Anyi also belongs to one of the eight great original *clans* and is thereby related to every other Anyi for whom the same totem animal is protected by taboo. Thomas Assoua, like many other Anyi, has been taught the rituals of his clan by his father; when he became chief of the Assoua court, he continued to practice them because he felt a need to confirm his identity. And it bothers neither him nor the other people of Bébou that the original clans are in reality derived from an amalgamation of the uterine lines of descent (with the relevant exogamy rules and obligations!). More important for Thomas, who has taken over his father's court, is confirmation that he has succeeded his own father and is not merely the hireling of a powerful maternal family in which his opinion counts for nothing.

Anyi fathers have a habit of behaving so importantly in public that some European observers have concluded that *descent through the father* (*ntoro*) alone is decisive, that Anyi society is purely patriarchal, and that the maternal lineage is at most a relic of the past and plays no role today except in the discussions of the ethnologists and in the conversations of a few old men—or rather old women. As a matter of fact, it is quite possible that some Anyi may think so too. This is the modern, French, Christian idea; besides, it would mean a better law of inheritance, more in keeping with modern trends, and above all would gloss over the fact that the men, though they have the prestige and power roles, are in reality totally dependent on their mothers and sisters. In fact, there is also an exogamy rule applicable to a certain category of paternal relatives. The father is responsible for supporting his children, paying for their education, finding marriage partners for them, punishing them when necessary, and ensuring their good behavior—all of them perfectly justifiable obligations, even though many fathers evade them. The subordination of the paternal kin to the maternal lineage is illustrated in the example of Thomas Assoua. He has just achieved his ambitious goal of taking over his father's court (after his older brother had waived his claim), but he declares without a moment's hesitation: "This is only temporary; I hope to inherit in Yosso later on, and then I'll leave here, because my mothers live in Yosso." Köbben (25) describes numerous examples of fathers who were genuinely concerned over the welfare of their sons and were willing to leave their property to them via deeds of gift or inheritance contracts set up during their lifetimes—but tradition was too strong for them; involuntarily they ended up by reinstating the maternal families as their heirs. As late as 1966 the situation was just the same in Bébou; a father would "forget" to legalize a deed of gift in favor of his son, or he would make over to his son a large plantation that had not been worked for years and would let the matrilineal inheritance system take its course for a small but highly profitable plantation. On one occasion the assembled elders of Krinjabo, after long discussion, had even agreed to a proposal made by the French governor (who wanted to see the coffee and cocoa plantations in the hands of families that followed the system of direct linear inheritance) and—in a jointly drafted law—had gone so far as to introduce inheritance through the paternal line, only to recant the following day and return to the old system. Christian baptism—in the name of the Father, the Son, and the Holy Ghost—not only confirms the people of Bébou in their belief that they are different, better, and more up-to-date than the heathens and Moslems who work on their plantations; it also proves that they have at least received *something* from a father... even if it is only the name Charles or Degaulle—still another father figure who is remote, who takes no interest in them, of whom they know and expect just as little as of God the Father in heaven or (all too frequently) of their own fathers.

One would expect that language usage, words as the classifying symbols for various relatives, would bring some measure of order into family structure. Amon d'Aby (3) was positively indignant to hear the term "cousin" used in connection with the Anyi; they have only brothers and sisters, mothers and fathers, grandmothers and grandfathers, each term embodying the specific genealogical knowledge needed by the individual if he is to feel secure in his use of etiquette in the complex system of kinship. (Only the father's sister may sometimes be called "female father.") Despite its strict separation of generations, the *classificatory family* comprises much more than just the families of the two parents. It also includes the families-in-law, collateral lines, and stepparents and their families, as well as distant relatives who were divorced and have remarried. This multidimensional system is open at both ends—at the top, to include the dead, and at the bottom, to take in the as yet unborn. Within the system's coordinates, the Anyi go about their daily lives, constantly occupied with meeting obligations, evading commitments, consolidating ties, and entering into dependency relations only to dissolve them once again.

When Jean-Pierre moved to Bébou at the order of his older brother Thomas (the oldest son of his mother's older sister) to work with me, he had to request permission to leave from his older brother (from the same parents). The latter answered neither yes nor no, which meant that Jean-Pierre's mother had no objections. But when he spoke admiringly of his "big brother," he was referring either to one of the two distant cousins (one on his mother's side, the other presumably on the father's side) who had money and prestige down on the coast and who had done a great deal for him, or to the husband of his youngest sister, a Moslem from the north, whom he loved devotedly because he possessed his dearly beloved sister, but whom he also hated and despised—for precisely the same reason.

One might stay in an Anyi village for quite some time without becoming aware of the family systems described above; yet one would know exactly what "the" family looks like, namely, an *extended family organized in a court* (fig. 6). A court community of this kind is an impressive structure; it provides living space and boundaries, and it gives the observer the feeling that he has discovered the fundamental functional unit of Anyi life. A court in Bébou or Yosso looks exactly the same today as it did seventy years ago when the first Europeans arrived. The only differences are that now the roofs are covered with corrugated iron instead of palm fronds and that many courts now have concrete wells from which the women draw water for their households in plastic buckets on long fiber ropes.

In 1906 Clozel (10) reported the following:

The houses of the Anyi are quite small, often consisting of only one room, and some are no more than sheds. Every compound is made

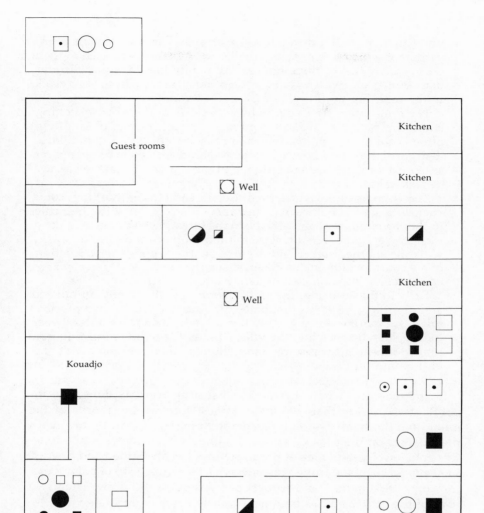

Fig. 6. Kouadjo's court. Thirty-three persons live in the court, only twelve of whom belong to the kin of the owner.

up of perhaps half a dozen houses, arranged around a main courtyard onto which two or three smaller courtyards open, each of them
bordered by two or three houses. All family life takes place in the
main courtyard, which is the scene of busy activity from six o'clock
in the morning until it gets dark in the evening.

The four or five wives of my host take care of their housekeeping
chores in this courtyard, some going out to fetch water or kindling,
others cooking plantains, which are made into *futu*. The national
dish consists of a meat or fish stew prepared with palm or peanut oil,
seasoned with pepper and onion, and eaten with plantain or cassava
(ignam) cakes.

The young people, who leave the court early in the morning, come
back with several bottles of palm wine. Others go out with their rifles
to shoot a monkey or an antelope in the forest. The younger children,
who stay at home, remain close to their mothers and wrestle noisily
with one another in the sand. Apart from the people, the population
of my court includes half a dozen sheep, two or three dozen chickens,
and three or four somewhat mangy dogs.

Early in the morning, the oldest member of the family, unhurried
and dignified, takes his first bath, rubbing his body with a precious
salve . . . examines his togas and decides which one he wants to wear
today. Then he goes into the village for a little while, returning from
time to time to discuss some transaction or other in privacy with one
of the dignitaries.

In the evening, when the day's exhausting work is done, the inhabitants lay aside their working clothes, torn by the thorns of the
jungle and the symbol of their contempt for manual labor. Women with
their babies on their backs, adorned with silk head scarves and attractive gold jewelry, and men of proud stature, freshly bathed and dressed
in neatly washed and ironed togas, pay visits, drink a sip of palm wine,
exchange "first news," and request permission to withdraw. The lively
idyll of the courtyard has become a courtly cermonial ritual.

An attempt to determine just who lives in a court (fig. 7) shows
immediately how strong the tensions among the inhabitants must be,
quite apart from the personal problems of each individual. Even the
attempt encounters difficulties. Etiquette and value concepts stipulate
that only persons who "belong together" may live together. A statistical
study carried out by Field (15) among the Akim merely demonstrated
that a court is never inhabited by one family alone. Naturally the court
is "owned" by a family, and no institution could be more anxious to
maintain its property than the family—and none could possibly fail
more abysmally. The affiliated and associated persons and the foreign
laborers, of course, belong primarily to an outside group with which
they maintain their solidarity. Court people who were accepted volun-

tarily for the sake of the family's economic interests are easier to get along with than those who had to be taken in—as frequently happens—for reasons of etiquette or because of the family's dependence on a chief or on some powerful mother figure.

European sociology is to be congratulated on its very productive idea of classifying the living community of the past—the household consisting of a farmer with his farmhands or an artisan with his apprentices and journeymen—as an "extended family." The people of Bébou, however, important as their affiliation with a specific court is for them, would disagree: "No, it's not the persons who live in the court that belong together, but all those *persons for whom 'one woman cooks'*" (fig. 8). This system, which gives far greater consideration to inclination and origin, and in which marriage ties and a common childhood find expression to a certain extent, goes beyond the living community and is subject to control by the value hierarchy generally prevailing. One young woman in the Assoua court, who simply wants to follow the dictates of her heart and cook only for those persons she is really fond of, was nicknamed "the mean woman"; people say she begrudges others their food because she is envious. It ought to be so easy to adapt at least this one family system to individual needs. All a woman would have to do is to send food only to those who really "belong"—yet here too individual/private interests are subordinated to collective ones.

By definition, the family is the intersection at which the social order impinges upon individual wishes. We are all too prone to regard our own families as instruments to serve the interests of the autonomous individual. Quite possibly the prohibition of incest, regulated by exogamy rules of one kind or another and found in all social structures, is a consequence of this conflict. The child is physiologically and psychologically dependent on his environment, that is, on his parents, while his instinctual needs develop into oedipal desires. The society on which the child is dependent provides the exogamy rules and thereby channels "egotistical" desires in a direction that ensures physical and emotional survival (of the individual *and* the group), though only at the price of inevitable conflicts (in other words, the oedipal conflict).

Around the interior of the courtyard cluster the small square houses with their corrugated roofs, some built in a row, others standing apart. Here we expect to find what sociologists call the small, or *nuclear family*—father, mother, and children. Table 1 shows that there are a good many exceptions to the "prevailing opinion" of the Anyi, that when a woman marries she moves in with her husband and the two of them bring up their children together. In some cases no common household is established at all, and duolocality is by no means rare. Thomas explains this by saying that men and women would get on each

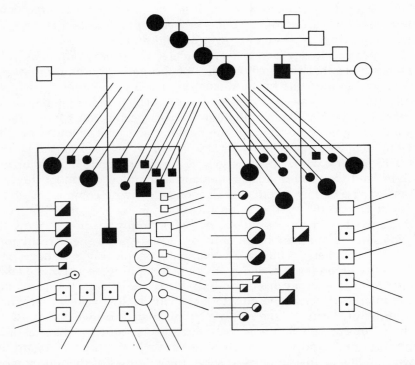

Fig. 7. Six courts in Bébou and their inhabitants. Each court is under the jurisdiction of a chief belonging to the maternal lineage that owns the compound.
Thomas Assoua is an exception in that he has taken over the court of his father.

The inhabitants of a court, however, are not all members of the maternal kin
that owns it; they also include persons associated or affiliated with the lineage
through marriage, as well as foreigners, both Anyi from other villages and
members of other ethnic groups.

The lines converging under the ancestors of the maternal lineage represent
the members of the maternal family that owns the court. The horizontal lines
emanating from the associated and affiliated persons indicate that they belong
to a family other than that of the owners. The diverging lines indicate those
inhabitants of the court who are not related in any way to the family that owns
it. The Anyi thus designated belong to other maternal lineages, while most of
the foreign laborers are members of paternal families.

Thus the living community includes persons whose family interests coincide
with those of the court, a second group whose family ties are not the same as
those of the relatives in whose court they live, and a third group who have no
kinship ties whatsoever with those in whose court they live.

The clearly delineated, unifying space of a compound is thus inhabited by
persons with ties and obligations to other groups, persons whose family interests may be in competition with the interests developing out of their membership in the living community itself.

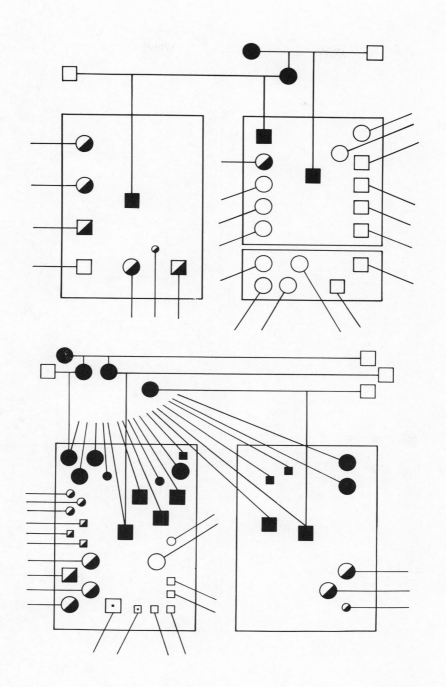

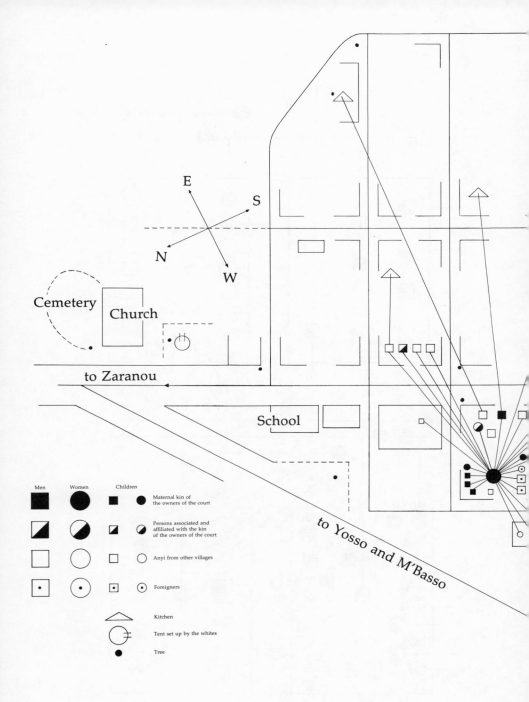

Cemetery

Church

to Zaranou

School

to Yosso and M'Basso

E

S

N

W

Men	Women	Children	
■	●	■ ●	Maternal kin of the owners of the court
◩	◑	◩ ◑	Persons associated and affiliated with the kin of the owners of the court
□	○	□ ○	Anyi from other villages
⊡	⊙	⊡ ⊙	Foreigners

△ Kitchen

⊖ Tent set up by the whites

● Tree

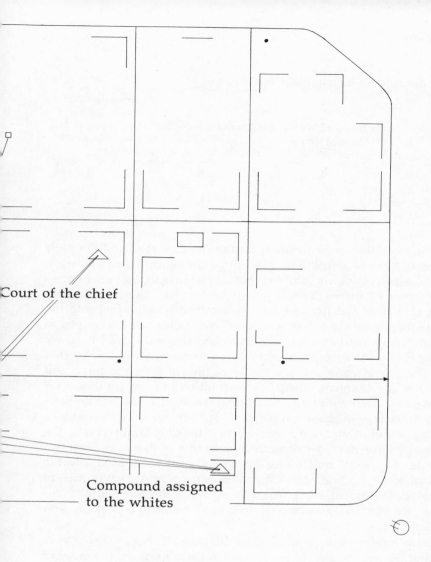

Court of the chief

Compound assigned
to the whites

Fig. 8. The persons for whom a woman cooks. This does not necessarily coincide with the inhabitants of a compound. In this sketch of the village of Bébou,
Kouadjo's court and its inhabitants have been singled out for detailed description. In the center, Kakou Bra, Thomas's wife, cooks for most of the inhabitants
of her compound as well as for several persons in other compounds to whom
she has special ties. Conversely, some of the people in her compound have their
meals prepared by women living in other compounds. The group of persons for
whom a woman cooks is determined by a combination of conventions, personal
obligations, and emotional ties.

Table 1 Incidence of Various Household Forms

	Common, with the Wife's Maternal Family	Common, with the Husband's Maternal Family	Separate (Duo-local), Each Spouse with His Own Maternal Family
Married men (N = 24)	4	11	9
Married women (N = 39)	7	14	18

other's nerves if they were together during the day, too. And the high incidence of divorce seems to confirm this. Here, within the framework of the smallest living units, the psychoanalytic investigator encounters the first familiar patterns. This is where the first love affairs take place, the first romances and dramas that transform the individual into the enigmatic being we are trying to understand. Rules and exceptions to rules that determine the social microcosm and shape the conditions we term the culture's average expectable environment (114)—in other words, the object world and the reality of the child during important years of his development. There is a temptation to compare this environment of the Anyi with rare or abnormal family milieus familiar to us through contacts with European patients. But here we are deceived by a kind of optical illusion; the nuclear family is the only family system the European patients have, whereas this is not true of the Anyi. Even so, the smaller the social unit under investigation, the more clearly the individual emerges, and with him those aspects and peculiarities of psychical development that, in spite of very different cultural influences, are ultimately subject to universal human, biological, and psychological laws.

One very fundamental psychological difference between the Anyi of Bébou and Europeans should be stressed at the outset: the character of their object relations.

The development of object relations in the Anyi child—like that of children all over the world—begins when the infant first starts to turn to a single person (the mother, or the person taking care of him), as soon as he has learned to differentiate this person from himself.

In the case of a child growing up in a Western family, the individual that emerges at the close of psychic development, after complex maturation processes and conflict resolutions, is capable of maintaining lasting object relations. If he is not to appear abnormal, the European must develop the ability to focus his emotions on those persons closest to him for a long period. This may not always guarantee monogamous family life in mature years, but it does permit the stable existence of a

relatively small, unchanging family with the requisite feeling of belonging together—above all, a family that need not compete with other,
similar systems.

In comparison, the Anyi would have to be viewed as immature and
pubescent throughout their lives, insecure in their personal ties, incapable of a stable focusing of emotion on any object—psychically abnormal, one and all.

There is another way of looking at it that may be more illuminating.
At the conclusion of psychological development, the child reared in the
Anyi environment retains the ability to give up object cathexis easily, to
keep his feelings toward love objects unstable and fluctuating, and
above all to avoid focusing his emotions consistently on only a few very
specific persons. When an Anyi cannot avoid binding himself to a
single individual, he begins to feel anxiety. He is afraid of becoming so
dependent that he will not be able to bear the loss of this individual
without injury to his physical or psychological integrity.

Such individuals are well suited to be part of many competing family
groups, since they find relief in precisely the same situation that would
call forth unbearable inner conflicts in a European. In the Anyi environment a European, with his mature, lasting object relations, would
appear abnormal and maladjusted and would find life intolerable.

Whereas in our Western culture it is only marriage that entails a
change in family affiliation (except for adoption), among the Anyi children are often given away, and their feeling of belonging to some of the
above-mentioned family circles undergoes a switch. The acceptance of
an inheritance, the frequent divorces, and the equally frequent moves
to the courts of other relatives in turn bring about change in respect to
various communities and provide new love objects, new ties.

To us, it often seemed to reflect unparalleled hardheartedness and
cruelty when an Anyi child was given away to some relative or other, or
sent to the compound of a female shaman (as was Suzanne) or somewhere else simply because this suited the commitments and interests of
its parents. We found it cold and calculating when a young man, ostensibly in love with his wife, informed her out of the blue, "My mother
wants me to take a second wife. Then I can be sure that you won't leave
me [because this would be tantamount to conceding her husband to a
rival]. If you don't like it, you can leave." There is no doubt that such
experiences cause severe pain to the person concerned, a pain that often
cannot be dealt with adequately; experiences of this kind are bound to
be traumatic. Who can say whether a Western child suffers more or less
intensely when he is compelled by our family structure to suppress his
hatred of his overly severe father or of an envied sibling, or whether a
wife who feels compelled to go on loving her husband simply because
she has always done so is not faced by a situation just as traumatic as

the Anyi wife whose husband has decided to experiment with polygyny.

Comparisons like this, based on emotional judgments and prejudices, do not make an investigation any easier. A tension-laden order prevails in the courts and villages of the Anyi. The inhabitants behave normally as long as we do not measure them with the yardstick of our own normality or try to explain their social structure arbitrarily as a distorted, abstract relic of itself. It is impossible to decide whether they have adjusted more or less satisfactorily to their society than we have to ours.

The Destruction of the Towns

While other African peoples have horizontal social structures, such as age groups of boys and young men initiated at the same time, that balance the vertical family structures, organized of necessity more or less hierarchically, the Anyi have only rudimentary horizontal structures. An "old man" is someone who has become chief of a court, a "young man"—whether married or single—anyone who is not yet in charge of a living area. This distinction refers exclusively to social status; it does not reflect social organization in any way.

The "society of the young men" does have an elected chief. People boast that in the Ashanti state this chief, who was also called the "speaker of the commoners," had a great deal of influence on the king and his decisions. Dibi, "chief of the young men" in Bébou, merely has the office of an arbitrator. The "young men" of Bébou have not been able to gain any public influence in spite of the fact that, in the beginning, the governing state party, the RDCI, was completely dependent upon their support. Erneste, the chief of the young men in Yosso, interprets his function in terms of using his authority to settle as best he can the constant disputes among the "young men," so that he can always be in a position to provide the village with a more or less efficient work party for urgent tasks, such as transporting a dead body. For one would not get very far if one relied solely on the social responsibility of the "young men." Without a chief to keep them in line, they would get out of work in any way they could. The chief of the young women has no other function than to organize the modest rites that commemorate a girl's first menstrual period. The two age groups of the girls and the young women have no inner ties that go beyond the general solidarity of the females against the males.

If one regarded the Anyi as farmers living in village communities like many other Africans, one would indeed be surprised to see them behave so proudly, casually, and freely despite their subjection to numerous hierarchical institutions that govern and discipline them. In reality, however, they are an urban people, as regards both their life-style and their mentality. We speak of "villages" because crowded dwelling areas with several hundred inhabitants simply are not towns in our terminology. The Anyi feel only contempt for people who go on living in the field huts they erect for themselves near the distant plantations where they work. A roof over one's head is a necessity because of the sudden showers that come in every season. Thus the huts are indispensable technical objects; they are not regarded as places to live.

The layout of Bébou (fig. 6) is typical; the only difference is that it is somewhat more geometrical than that of other Anyi towns, thanks to the surveying abilities of its founder, Ahoussi. In front, along the main road, are the courts of the dignitaries, that of the chief being especially large and elegant, and farther back from the road are the compounds of less distinguished citizens. The living areas assigned to the foreign laborers are called Djoulakrou, Baoulékrou (the town of the Djoula, of the Baoulé), and they are marked off clearly as separate town districts. Quite apart from the fact that most Anyi would be asolutely terrified of going into the forest at night, that is, out into the open country surrounding the towns, they derive the greater part of their sense of life from the awareness that they are townspeople—not anonymous, but promenading up and down the streets in the evening, visiting their friends, indulging in their love affairs just as they please. If I'm not interested in someone, I simply don't know him; if I'm fond of someone, I pay him a visit. If he insults me, he's no longer an acquaintance of mine, but reverts to the status of one villager among many. It would be no great exaggeration to say that the best part of Anyi life is devoted to the enjoyment of their urban civilization. When an Anyi leaves his rain forest, he goes to a city, to Abidjan or to some other really "French" city on the coast, or perhaps to the land of the Ashanti or the Attié—in short, to a place whose inhabitants enjoy an urban style of life, and never to a "real Negro village."

In these circumstances it is all the more astonishing that the Anyi themselves are destroying their towns. Admittedly, it is the government that provides incentives and issues decrees; the unhygienic old houses, without the comforts of civilization, are to be torn down, and the inhabitants are to build new ones that will meet the demands of modern life in every respect. The authorities provide the bulldozers to tear down the old buildings, but the owner of the premises has to pay the operating costs. And if he wants a new house he has to build it himself. While we were still looking for "our" village, we saw a number of villages that were destroyed and abandoned, as if they had been bombarded. In most cases only one or two courts were being rebuilt. Here and there people were still living in a house that had escaped destruction, while others had moved in with relatives in other villages or had found shelter in the field huts out at their plantations. During our stay in Bébou, half the famous old town of Zaranou, once an attractive African market town, was reduced to dust and rubble, and the inhabitants moved away. "They have more money hidden away than people think; they'll rebuild it." This suspicious speculation about concealed wealth, so typical of the Anyi, turns out to be unfounded. There is hardly any family that has enough money—or is a sufficiently good credit risk—to be able to replace its demolished house.

It would be premature to conclude that this reflects the disintegration of a society that is destroying its homes in an orgy of self-annihilation, a society that is committing material suicide. Long ago, when the Anyi first seized the land, they left the cities undisturbed and moved on. The cities were engulfed by the rain forest, and new towns were founded. Amélékia, which the French razed "in retaliation" during their brief colonial war of conquest (the inhabitants fled to their field huts, as the inhabitants of Zaranou are doing today), was founded anew and rebuilt on the same site. Ahoussi reestablished Bébou by the simple expedient of ordering his relatives to join him there and inducing families who were under obligation to him to turn their children over to him.

It may be precisely the high value placed on the town that causes the Anyi to be dissatisfied with theirs and to want something better—that leads them to discard what they havé, to let it go to ruin. They treat their own children as if they were commodities. They want a lot of them, simply to have them around. And then the children learn to walk; the adults no longer pay so much attention to them: "They're still too small, they can't run away whether we look after them or not." Do children have any value? It almost seems as if the protodiacritical faculty, the ability to distinguish between inanimate and animate, had never fully developed—as if the Anyi were able to confer the quality of "animate" upon things or people or to abandon them entirely as worthless objects, all according to the needs or the whims of the moment. For the benefits to be derived from both things and people lie in the future, in the gratification of a desire, in a blissful fantasy, and not in dreary reality. The houses in the hot and humid towns are full of stinging insects and dangerous disease germs. In the evening they echo with ghostly screams from the bush. The aroma—and intoxicating effect—of palm wine draws a pleasant veil over the compound. What we want is a nice new town, one that always has the atmosphere that this one has in the enchantment of evening and intoxication. Let's let the old town go—it never really fulfilled what it promised anyway.

In 1949, when Kouame Binzène first introduced the plan to promote building activity in the Ivory Coast by means of housing loans, he encountered a good deal of resistance. King Essey Bonzou of Alangouan, who had visited the impressively designed Ashanti cities of Fanti and N'Zima on the Gold Coast, was among the first to recognize the need to rebuild the Anyi towns. And not a few villages were sacrificed to this first modern building program. Boutillier (5) gives a detailed account of the fate of Abongoua, whose inhabitants decided in 1953, "under the leadership of a young and dynamic traditional chief," to create a modern city of concrete houses with three, four, or five rooms each. "The initial phase consisted of the establishment of a network of roads, necessitating the demolition of more than half the village. A total of 600 houses, which had made up 60 of the original 110 courts, were destroyed . . . . As a result of this preliminary work . . . life in the village underwent a complete upheaval." On the basis of several highly questionable sociological polls on what the villagers themselves really wanted, the author draws up a list of the positive and negative aspects of progress to be expected from the upheavals inevitably entailed in the demolition of an old village and the erection of a new one. For Boutillier, looking into the future with a feeling of helplessness akin to that of the Anyi themselves, believes that in spite of the financial and technical difficulties that will have to be overcome the end result is bound to be different and somehow better. Our impression of some of the modern villages built in the late fifties was that they are totally unfunctional as living areas and that the needs inherent in the social structure have proved stronger than the building loans, state subsidies, and urban construction plans based on the unfortunate model of French low-income housing settlements. Most of the Anyi have moved out of their dreary rows of gray concrete houses, leaving them to the Djoula, who—as immigrants—are socially uprooted anyway and thus can be expected to adjust to them more easily.

The Profession of the Planter

Whoever invented the profession of planter
ought to be caught and punished!
                                                Anoh Michel

In the Western world the development of cities has generally gone hand in hand with changes in the methods of production. The urban population devotes its energies to the skilled trades, to commerce and industry, and to political and military administration. The shift away from an agrarian subsistence economy brought with it a mentality and life-style totally different from those of the farmers.

In Africa, however, the traditional attitude toward the soil and toward agricultural labor is not necessarily coupled with a rural mentality. The value systems and the identity experiences have different contents and are differently distributed than in the West. The statement that the Anyi have an urban mentality is not really formulated correctly. One

ought to say "a mentality similar to that of Western urban dwellers."
Nevertheless, the fact remains that the Anyi devote themselves with
singular exclusiveness to agricultural production.

In Indénié and Alangouan there are only very few individuals who
have secondary occupations as skilled workers or artisans. Very few
Anyi are employed as teachers, civil servants, or judges. At present
there is not a single one who operates an independent commercial
enterprise in his own community. In our group of three villages,
which—after all—we had chosen precisely because they seemed to be
typical, not one person (not even the schoolmaster) earned his primary
livelihood in any branch other than agriculture.

Taking the contrast between an exclusively agrarian economy and an
urban-aristocratic mentality as a starting point, one can formulate the
most important questions concerning the links existing among the economy, the social structure, and the psychology of the Anyi—and one
can find the most misleading and the most sophisticated answers to
these questions.

N'da Assinien, for example, is convinced that "the Anyi would die if
they had to work as hard as the Djoula." This reflects his own
hypochondria, no more intense than that of many of his fellow citizens,
and a depressive feeling that he is physically without energy and inadequate; but it also reflects his arrogance and his contempt for those
uncouth foreign laborers who are content to perform menial work. At
the moment a large lumber camp is being built at Yosso to exploit the
industrial timber of the surrounding forests. In Alangouan alone, several hundred men regard themselves as unemployed; yet not one of
them would be willing to accept a relatively well-paid job as a
lumberman—N'da Assinien least of all.

The farmhands and artisans in the land of the Anyi are foreigners.
Anyi houses are built by seasonal workers from Dahomey (Benin); the
carpenters and locksmiths are usually Baoulé, and other construction
elements requiring skilled labor are sent across the border into Ghana
for completion. The textiles for Anyi togas are woven and dyed in
Manchester, Lyons, and Saint Gall. The Anyi still cling to the traditional
division of labor, in which they themselves are the aristocratic great
landowners who are neither willing nor able to perform manual work.
Their subjective timorous feeling that they are physically weak and the
resultant, all too necessary reactive need to bolster their self-esteem
with fantasies of megalomania that have only the most tenuous foundation in reality fit neatly into the framework of a sociohistorical
derivation.

Social facts are mutually dependent. One can proceed from the opposite derivation (25), according to which it was not the preservation of
tradition, but rather a violent change dictated by external circumstances

that forced the Anyi to live predominantly from a plantation economy for which they are not suited either physically or temperamentally. They have been compelled to shift from an agrarian subsistence economy to production for export to the world market—to the cultivation of coffee and cocoa. This has led to changes in three functional areas: economic life, the organization of society, and the legal structure as regards the ownership of land. A plantation economy requires large-scale production units and the steady investment of capital and labor over a period of years. The hierarchical social order is being replaced by a management-labor relationship that makes up for the relative shortage of native labor by importing economically weaker foreign laborers who are regarded as inferior from the standpoint of culture and traditional value systems. This reinforces the legal conception that the land itself is the property of native families. On the other hand, the latter must sell their land to their workers in order to be able to pay them, and—more important—they are forced to deviate from the previously valid principle that the land belongs to nobody, that is, that no one really owned land, but that anyone who asked for permission was entitled to use it.

Our description of this interdependency is extremely brief, but the conclusions are obviously the same. Both preservation of the old tradition and its violation as a result of the forced cultural transformation have turned the Anyi into aristocratic great landowners without the necessary labor force to enable them to work the land of their fathers themselves, into a group that must resort to the disintegrating legal system of its ancestors to compensate for its physical inadequacy and its lack of ability to adjust to new modes of living and working.

The Economy and Society

Marguerite Dupire (14), Boutillier (5), and above all Köbben (25) have published detailed studies of the way economic change has led to cultural change, of the circumstances under which hordes of foreign laborers have come into the country, of the problems they have brought with them, and of the changes wrought by their presence.

The proper approach here would be a careful reclassification and comparison of all the material so far compiled, both economic data and observations of gradual changes in customs and attitudes, in terms of the explanations given by the authors concerned, in order to work out the centers of gravity and lines of force that would ultimately reveal, here and there, the significance and role of psychological factors. For the influence of economic change on the psychical state of those exposed to it is not a one-way process; in other words, it is not merely that "the introduction of plantations operated on an industrial scale is bound to lead to a disruption of village life" (5), or that "such functional disturbances normally make themselves felt first of all in the psychological state of the individual, as vehicles of pathological forces in the collective mentality, and inevitably result in general moral malaise" (21). The already-existing psychological state is not a blank page; as a rule the psyche itself is laden with conflict. Functional changes are not in themselves disturbances; they are "pathological" only when they overtax the ability of the group and the individual to adjust. And as for the above-mentioned malaise, it can be safely assumed that it is not restricted to cultures that are exposed to accelerated change.

Since there is no clear causality, no cause-and-effect relationship involved in the dynamic interchange between the economy and society, let us select from among the totality of facts and supplementary data those that have the greatest influence on the present-day life of the Anyi and those that are largely determined by their psychological individuality or that affect the latter.

The land of the Anyi is extraordinarily rich, and until recently it was available in abundance. As a people they are wealthier than their neighbors. In their own land, it is not the individual's share in the means of production that decides whether he is rich or poor. When we say the land is rich, we mean that relatively less (quantitatively) labor creates greater increment in value; but the kind of labor required is unusually difficult and tedious (qualitatively and subjectively).

Total consumption requirements, that is, everything needed to sustain life, could be met in the country itself with a comparatively low investment of labor. In reality, however, only about 40 percent of the total requirements are met by domestic production; all the rest is imported. This would be a characteristic ratio for a population midway in its development from a self-sufficient agrarian economy to an industrial one. With the Anyi, the problem can be traced back to the traditional division of labor between the sexes. The women are responsible for producing the goods needed to sustain life. In former times the men were responsible for providing the "imports" in the form of hunting booty and the spoils of their marauding wars. Work on the industrialized plantations has taken the place of these activities. Advancing industrialization has to be integrated into traditional customs and value criteria into which it simply will not fit.

The collective and individual feeling of identity of a warrior/hunter-gatherer culture with its specific value systems is in harmony with the typical psychic attitudes and qualities of the Anyi and with the pattern of skills they have acquired through training, but it is at variance with the exigencies of agricultural and industrial production.

The right of ownership of the land is at present regulated in such a way that the land itself—as the only important, potentially profitable means of production—is the inalienable property of the families. Its usufruct, however, accrues to the individual who actually cultivates the soil.

The Anyi have no experience whatsoever in commerce, credit systems, or market economics—not even in the simple economics of barter; yet they must rely upon import and export to meet more than half their consumption requirements. The use of money as an economic instrument is greatly hampered by its manifold psychological associations and by the enormous emotional value attached to it.

The wealth of the Anyi is modest compared with that of the industrial nations. Their annual consumption is approximately half that of Greece or Turkey, but is twice that of India and two to ten times that of the African states in the adjacent savannas.

The fertility of the soil provides a realistic foundation for the ancient symbol of the gold country, Alangouan. When we arrived in Bébou, three old women were burning off a forest area at the edge of the village. It looked like a battlefield half ravaged by fire, where titans had engaged in strife with tree trunks as weapons. The women were sticking kernels of corn randomly into the soil or the ashes. The corn, which in Europe needs an entire season to mature, was harvested three months later. After another month the second crop was already beginning to mature. The same crop can be planted in the same field ten times running. No fertilizers are needed. There is hardly any seasonal interruption in the rate of productivity. The work needed for field crops consists in clearing the land, sowing, and harvesting. Coffee and cocoa plantations, admittedly, must be cleared twice a year, or the forest encroaches on the trees and smothers them. Clearing the land is extremely disagreeable and difficult work, even in the rather casual way it is generally carried out in Bébou.

At the time coffee and cocoa were introduced, the colonizers were of the opinion that "the ease of living makes the Anyi lazy . . . . Any effort demanded of them irritates them. It would never occur to them to praise the virtues of work" (7). A day's work on the plantations is so strenuous that the three (or four) days of rest observed by the people of Alangouan are physically necessary. The humid heat, the vertical rays of the scorching sun, the sudden cold rain showers, the sharp thorns and hordes of stinging insects of the rain forest would exhaust even workers not already weakened by chronic tropical diseases and anemia—as everyone in this area is. There are no proper tools available for the technical work, and there are problems in organization. A family could easily cultivate a coffee plantation that would guarantee it a yearly income approximately equivalent to that of a Swiss worker if it had the financial reserves or means of subsistence to hold out for the four years it takes a coffee tree to begin bearing. The present order is so unsuited to long-term planning, however, that enormous energy, intelligence, and organizational talent are required to carry out such a project successfully.

One person alone cannot do the necessary work. A team of at least three full-time workers is needed to lay out and care for a plantation. The team must be self-sufficient or depend upon alms from the cassava and plantain gardens of the women. Internal tensions are apt to break up the team during the long preliminary work or to necessitate regroupings that are less than ideal, either economically or from the point of view of the persons involved.

This is the reason so many poorer Anyi can claim that they own twenty, fifty, or one hundred hectares (1 hectare = approximately 2½ acres) in coffee and can tell you exactly where they are and when they were planted. When you try to find them, however, all you see is rank secondary jungle. The information you have been given is quite accurate in that the man really *has* cleared the land and planted trees on a number of occasions, given the whole thing up, started all over again somewhere else with other workers, and finally abandoned the new plantation, too, to the jungle before it could begin to bear fruit. The man counts up the number of abortive attempts and takes his initiative for economic achievement.

Brou Koffi, the village chief in M'Basso, is one of the most efficient planters in Alangouan. With a glance at the sky, he says: "If it were not going to rain tomorrow, I'd go out to my plantation and burn off a piece of land . . . . Clearing land with a hoe is too hard for me; I have workers to do that. I can do the job myself if I use fire. Then I'd like to plant the orange tree slips. The workers don't know how . . . . They'll start bearing in seven years. I want to plant oranges because you can pick them all year long. With coffee and cocoa there's only one harvest every year, and between harvests you don't have anything. That will be different with oranges . . . . I'll be the first man in this part of the country to plant a whole grove of orange trees. When the trees are grown, people will go by and ask who this beautiful orange grove belongs to. And they'll say it belongs to Brou Koffi, the chief of M'Basso. And the people will think how fine that is and hold my name in honor."

"You would enjoy having an orange grove?"

"I'm thinking of the money. Whenever I go out to the plantation, I think about how much money I'll make on the harvest. When I think about the money, I can find the energy to work." People who think about money as if it were comforting, nourishing food find long-range planning difficult.

It is probably more than just a metaphor to say that the Anyi experience the earth as the "nurturing mother" of early childhood. They know—from their experience during infancy—that a mother is capable of giving nourishment and affection in accordance with her child's needs. Instead, she refuses and remains adamant and hostile in spite of the submissive wooing of the growing child, just as the rich soil of the rain forest, in spite of its abundance, refuses to satisfy the needs of its children. Until recently it was possible everywhere in Alangouan and in the entire Indénié region to obtain land for new plantations from the chiefs. The new restrictions on the clearing of new forest areas do not apply to the abandoned plantations, which would be perfectly suitable sites for establishing new ones.

One might compare the fertile, still only sparsely settled land to a warehouse of highly efficient industrial machinery at the inhabitants' disposal. Already fueled, the machines are ready and waiting to be put to work. But the levers are too hard to operate, and the plagues turn the work site into a foretaste of hell. And if the fortunate producer dares to pause for a rest before trying again, his machines are promptly devoured by the jungle, and his helpers have departed in anger and discord.

Many Anyi are able to achieve gratification of their desires and even implementation of their plans in their fantasies. Either because failure forces them to, or because they are cowed by reality, they content themselves with imaginary success. It is not ownership of the means of production that makes a person wealthy, but very special and very rare personal qualities and a particularly fortunate concatenation of social circumstances. Anyone who is poor was simply not so fortunate. The Akan have always feared and despised poverty. According to them, "poverty makes a nobleman a slave" and "poverty is madness." They seem to realize that it is personal and family weaknesses that are apt to lead to poverty.

As in other countries, the introduction of better technological equipment and an up-to-date system of economic management will presumably reserve participation in the production process primarily to those who already control the means of production. Their loose ties with their fellowmen and their penchant for altering reality by means of fantasy-governed thought processes may predestine them just as easily to becoming large-scale industrial planners as eccentric outsiders. It is extremely unlikely that they will develop into dependable, industrious wage-earners within only a few generations.

The women take care of gardens planted in cassava root, plantains, other food fruits, and herbs. In addition, they prepare palm oil and vegetable fats from the fruits of the forest, gather snails, and catch fish. Since a woman cooks for "all persons who belong," all that is expected of the man is that he provide supplementary food, especially meat from the hunt. In earlier times the economic contribution of the man consisted of captured slaves, gold, and the tribute paid by a dependent or defeated tribe. He is still expected to make his contribution to the household, but nowadays it takes the form of clothing, shelter, luxury goods, safeguarding the moral and physical well-being of his family by means of sacrifices and tributes to shamans, priests, and chiefs, and money for the schooling of his children and for modern health services. In reality, though, the women often end up paying these costs. Above all, however, the men are responsible for financing the costly funeral and mourning ceremonies.

This division of labor between the sexes is by no means adhered to consistently. There are many men who cultivate plantains and cassava for their own use or for the market, who gather food and go fishing like the women; conversely, there are some women who start plantations and leave them to their daughters. But if one classifies productive achievement according to the purposes for which its profits are used, the fact remains that all the "extra" costs of living (which amount to more than 50 percent!) are supposed to be borne by the men. Though the material prerequisites of a plantation economy are vastly different from what the Anyi were accustomed to in olden times, their approach to a task is still that of the warrior, hunter, or food-gatherer—a brief, aggressive foray in a group formed temporarily to carry out the activity at hand. They hope for quick success, and for that one needs luck. Failure attests the disfavor of the spirits and the gods, who then have to be coaxed into a more benevolent mood the next time with the aid of magic. Psychic prerequisites and social rules have not yet become adapted to the new methods of production. On the one hand, the constant demand for revenue from industrialized agriculture and the open export market encourage the establishment of new plantations. On the other hand, the cultivation and care of these plantations offer the Anyi about the same degree of permanent financial security as regular visits to the casino in Monte Carlo would offer a European. In the real world of the Anyi, as in his perception of it, only his wife's garden has permanence, bringing forth its fruits as regularly as the women provide food for the tables of their fathers, husbands, and sons, evening after evening, routinely as a hotel kitchen, regardless of whether they prepare these meals gladly and with affection or grudgingly and with hatred.

Thomas intends to plant cocoa on the neglected plantation he has inherited from his father.

Thomas: Cocoa is difficult to cultivate. As soon as the trees are a few years old and just beginning to bear, they usually wither and die.
Morgenthaler: Well, then surely it's not really worthwhile!
Thomas: The chief of M'Basso has cocoa seeds from Ghana. They're much more resistant and don't die. Last year I went to him and bought twenty pods, there are forty to fifty seeds in each pod. For twenty-five francs each. The chief gave me more than twenty, but I

still only owe him five hundred francs for them. He gave them to me on credit. But sooner or later, of course, I'll have to pay him.
Morgenthaler: And what did you do with the seeds?
Thomas: I planted them in a frame in my uncle's field hut. Then the rats came and ate them, and that way I lost almost all the beans I'd bought. All I've got left are my debts—five hundred francs.
Morgenthaler: Isn't there anything you can do to keep the rats from eating the beans?
Thomas: You can set traps to catch the rats. Or if you soak the beans in petroleum before you plant them, the rats won't touch them.
Morgenthaler: Well?
Thomas: I forgot to.
Morgenthaler: Oh.
Thomas: Well, I didn't really forget. I took the beans out to the field hut. I had already split them. Then they have to be planted the same day. I sent the children to get some petroleum, but they didn't bring me any. So I just planted the beans without soaking them.
Morgenthaler: Now I understand how it happened.
Thomas: If I had soaked those beans in petroleum, by now I'd have about eight hundred little cocoa trees. As it is, I've lost everything.
Morgenthaler: Are you going to plant more?
Thomas: To do that I'd have to buy new pods. And to buy new ones, I'd have to pay what I already owe—five hundred francs for nothing. Because I'd need at least a thousand francs to buy new seeds. I can't afford that much right now. I'll have to wait till the coffee is sold.
Morgenthaler: You mean you don't have any money left from the last harvest?
Thomas [with an embarrassed laugh]: Well, no. I had too many expenses because both my father and my child died last year, and I had to spend all my money on the two funerals. It will be quite a while before I have my new cocoa plantation.

A glance at this story makes it clear that the traditional customs, though they once served a valid purpose, could not provide a very useful basis for industrial agricultural production. Coming as a stranger from a more technologically developed region of the world, one can perceive, as the colonizers (7) did, "behind their inertia, their refusal to undertake any effort demanded of them, their fondness for lying, bickering, and complaining, an alert intelligence that understands the situation perfectly—'If we obey them and start this new work, they'll demand more and more of us. So it's better for us to promise to do a thing and then wait till they force us to. In the long run, we'll have to go along with them. We can no more resist the pressure of their authority than we can resist the temptation to spend the profits to buy all those luxury goods like clothes and those enjoyments of life that mean so much to us.'" It is possible that these comments are more applicable to the situation of colonial exploiters confronted with passive resistance than to the culture-specific psychology of the Anyi. A knowledge of the childhood experiences of the Anyi reveals at least two factors that are anything but conducive to developing an ability to plan actively and to implement plans systematically. In the most decisive phase of the maturation and development of active behavior patterns, the Anyi child has an extremely one-sided relationship to adults. He is ordered about, is subject to constraint and suppression. He "learns" either abject submissiveness or passive withdrawal. As far as the exercise of physical skills is concerned, he not only is given no encouragement but also lacks the foundation of a positive relationship to his own body and its abilities. Not only do the Anyi despise the manual trades, they are also remarkably inept at them and often injure themselves. Their physical skills are just as poorly developed as their ability to cooperate with their fellows verbally.

Foreign Laborers

These are good workers from Volta. We call
them slaves. They'll eat us up in the end.
                    Ahoussi de Bernard

In view of the inadequate physical aptitudes and skills of the Anyi as well as of their mentality, the army of seasonal workers and resident foreign laborers from the north represents a welcome supplementary force in the economy. Most of them are people who are willing and able to do nothing but manual labor in order to raise the low, and steadily sinking, standard of living of their families. To begin with, they have just as little ambition to take the place of their employers as laborers coming from the south of Italy to work in Zurich or Detroit have to become managers in the factories where they earn much more as unskilled laborers than they could earn in their own country.

From 1923 on, more and more of these people began fleeing from the savannas to the rain forests to escape being recruited as forced labor. In 1966 the government of the Ivory Coast Republic offered common citizenship to naturals of Upper Volta, Guinea, and Mali. This was a tempting offer (one that was not accepted, however) when one stops to think how much wealthier the Ivory Coast is than the other three countries. The demographic pressure from the savannas to the north and east on the rain forest belt, which has existed for centuries and which has triggered a kind of West African migration, fluctuates with the ups and downs on the political and economic scenes.

In Alangouan the influx had slowed down a great deal by 1966, though it had not come to a standstill. According to tentative estimates (based on the name lists kept by the Epidemiological Service), approximately 20 percent of the inhabitants of Bébou were foreigners, about 30 percent in Yosso, and 40–50 percent in M'Basso. Most of these foreigners were Mossi or other Moslems from Upper Volta, with Baoulé from the northern part of the Ivory Coast in second place. Most came for several years; quite a few had settled down there with their families.

As far as we can tell, in view of the near impossibility of determining the weight of individual factors in such a complex problem, symbiosis with the foreigners seems to have had no primary adverse effects for the Anyi on either their psychological equilibrium or the functioning of their social structure. It was only economic integration, highly advantageous to both groups, that brought with it social tensions and—ultimately—emotional difficulties.

Not a single planter in Alangouan has sufficient working capital on hand to permit him to hire workers on a monthly basis. The usual practice is to pay a small team of foreign laborers one-third of the proceeds of the harvest, one-half if the plantation is an unprofitable one. The foreigners send their earnings home; if they intend to remain for a fairly long time, they send for their brothers. Recruitment of labor is not a problem unless the prospective employer has a reputation for mistreating his help or cheating them out of their wages.

Conflicts can arise for the natives when they want to develop new plantations and discover that the laborers are cultivating plantations of their own and sending for their families instead of sending their wages home. A newly established plantation makes no profits until the first harvest, after four years, and all this time the laborers have to be paid in cash. The employer borrows the money he needs. When his debts become too much for him, he has only three possible courses of action. He can give up the entire project after one or two years, thus losing the labor and capital he has already invested—and since he is often unable to pay his workers what he owes them, he will have difficulty in recruiting new ones. Or he can try to continue cultivating at least a part of the area he has cleared, either alone or with a son or brother, until the trees start bearing. Or he can make over a part of his land to his workers each year in lieu of wages; in this way—depending upon the size of the project—the workers may acquire a plantation larger than that of their employer. Then, of course, they are lost as laborers.

The traditional property laws of the Anyi are intended to guarantee that they will be able to gain a livelihood from the soil. In principle the land belongs to the lineage, the maternal family, and its usufruct is leased in return for token compensation paid to the head of the family. The right of utilization is inalienable. On the other hand, as long as the land is being cultivated it cannot be taken away from the one who holds the usufruct. If the latter should die or emigrate, the land reverts to the kin.

Foreigners who have come into money and foreign laborers who have received a share in a plantation instead of wages naturally try to purchase land under modern property law and have their title to it legally recorded in the property register. This is the only way they can achieve equal status with the natives and be sure of keeping their property in the family. And this is the point at which the Anyi begin to react. The same Anyi who were totally dependent upon the foreigners now feel threatened in the very basis of their existence. They are afraid that all the land will soon be in the possession of these efficient foreigners, whose birth rate is already higher than their own and who seem to have an inexhaustible supply of brothers they can send for. Whereas in earlier times good soil often lay fallow—for the virgin rain forest is not regarded as productive—now there is already a shortage of land in some villages.

We had the impression that these more or less realistic apprehensions are reinforced by irrational fears. The very fact of competition with the other group appears as a threat. For all the Anyi we know, to be exposed to rivalry between like and like is an intolerable situation that causes anxiety and releases regressive mechanisms. The Anyi have the feeling that the foreigners are inundating them, that there is nothing they can do to stop them. They are bound to perish.

The political and economic countermeasure consists in a return to tradition. It is precisely that younger generation who have worked actively to develop industrial production, whose economic thinking is more European, and who—politically—support the RDCI against the traditional order that are calling for the restoration of the old laws. The same people who feel hampered in their long-range planning by the hegemony of the maternal lineage and its inheritance laws, with their stipulation that at the death of the father with whom they have worked to develop their coffee plantations they will lose these plantations to the heirs of the maternal kin, see no other way than to appeal to the authority of the maternal lineage, which possesses an inalienable right to the land. The result is a historical paradox. The industrialization of the economy is leading not to a modernization or Europeanization of social rules, but rather to a regression to the same traditional matrilineal order that had been regarded as the greatest obstacle to economic development.

It has been suggested that this problem, resulting ultimately from the immigration of foreign laborers, is the cause of the Anyi's decadence and will be the cause of the eventual disintegration of their culture. We doubt it. We do not view decadence as a historical development. At most the term could be used here to describe sociopsychological phenomena. The decline of the Anyi has been predicted as imminent for a long time; at the end of the nineteenth century the cause was given as the disputes among the clans, about 1900 as the abolishment of the authority of the chiefs, at the time of World War I as the campaign to collect raw rubber, then successively as forced labor, the introduction of cocoa, the introduction of coffee, controversies within the political parties, the struggle for independence, and finally independence itself.

True, in Alangouan the presence of foreign laborers did lead to the conflict described above between two rival planter societies, but it neither disrupted social structures nor created serious political or psychological difficulties.

A class of wage-earners with no other source of income has not emerged—and not only because this type of class is alien to both the Anyi and the immigrants. The unpropertied laborers either return to their own countries or, when they do remain, become entrepreneurs themselves or at least the partners of employers who have not—or not yet—succeeded in amassing sufficient working capital and are thus compelled to turn over the means of production step by step to their workers.

In practice there are three possible modes of association between the Anyi and the foreigners. All that is needed to establish the initial contact is an informal agreement between, let us say, a planter and a picker. Once the foreign laborer is there, the employing family tries to integrate him by marrying him to an Anyi wife. When this is practicable, both parties are satisfied. The Anyi have augmented their kin, and the newcomer has been incorporated into the ruling group.

This is exactly the same procedure the Akan peoples used to employ to increase their economic power and the power of their families by integrating slaves into the clan, thereby augmenting it through a collateral line. As a matter of fact, the traditional value concepts concerning slave labor now seem to be generally applied to the Djoula. Workers are first and foremost commodities, economic assets. No sooner have they settled in an Anyi village than every one of them is looked upon as a potential family member with the same rights as any other individual considered suitable for the purpose of increasing a family's property in the form of kin. It is this attitude that prevents the immigrant worker from becoming the target of class or group hate projections.

Those foreign laborers who are not integrated into Anyi families elect a chief of their own—in accordance with the patriarchal customs of their native countries, of course—who serves as their spokesman in the host village. The chief of the Djoula living in Yosso, formerly a *tirailleur* (soldier in the French African military forces), is not only the wealthiest, but also the most highly respected man in the village. He enjoys a better reputation among the Anyi than their own elected chief, Monsieur N.

On the one hand, the native Anyi have good reason to fear the economic competition of the foreign laborers; but on the other hand, the latter allay these fears by appealing to the authority of the Anyi, thus evoking the paternalistic attitudes toward which their employers have a natural inclination. The inhabitants of the savannas, totally unfamiliar with the functioning of a plantation economy, have no desire to assume technical responsibility. Frequently an employer may be all too casual in supervising his workers, so that finally the workers themselves come to tear him away from his palm wine or his girl friends and ask him for instructions so that they cannot be blamed later on for having neglected their jobs. Also, to keep themselves from being tempted to spend their wages before they have managed to save a fairly large sum to send or take home, the workers usually request to be paid only at the end of the year. For this reason they naturally expect their employers to provide housing, food, and medical care. The Anyi need never fear that their workers will suddenly leave them. They feel perfectly at home in the role of large property owners, though it must be admitted that they are often negligent in meeting their nurturing obligations toward their laborers—and toward their children. Still, the system works tolerably well until the immigrant—thanks to his economic advancement— becomes independent and is suddenly transformed into a rival who is represented by a well-organized ethnic group and demands equal rights.

Money, Wealth, Thievery

It has often been stated that "the introduction of a money economy" among African peoples is bound to lead to identity change and cultural transformation because it "transforms traditional common goals of the extended kinship group to those of personal achievement and individual careers" (65). Of all the innovations imported from Europe, the use of money is the one that has been accepted most unreservedly in West Africa. The Anyi are no exception. In fact, because of their traditional emotional ties to gold and their extensive foreign trade, they were probably particularly eager innovators in this respect. In the preceding pages we have spoken of money as if it had the same significance for the people of Bébou as it has for us. This is not the case, however. Precisely because gold and wealth represent traditional values, the present money-based economy is more of a retarding factor than a stimulus to cultural change.

When Brou Koffi dreams of his future orange groves and says it is the thought of money that gives him the strength to work, he is referring indirectly to the prestige he hopes to gain from his wealth. For, as the proverbs proclaim, "A man of wealth is a man of importance"; "The misdeeds of rich men are always invisible"; "The fame of noble birth is a private thing, the fame of wealth is public knowledge"; and "When wealth has come and gone, there is nothing more to come."

During the season when the coffee harvest is being sold, the trucks of the purchasing agents go from village to village. Scales are set up. The planters have had their sacks of coffee beans brought to the village street. Each sack is weighed, and the agent checks its contents. Then he pays the price fixed by the government, irrespective of the quality of the beans. It is typical of the Anyi that they can never wait until all the sacks of a given planter have been weighed, the total weight entered in the ledger, and the price calculated. They demand that each sack (32 to 35 kilograms) be weighed, registered, and paid for separately. The agents submit with a sigh to this time-consuming custom. Many of the planters are very good at figures. It makes no difference whether they multiply the price per kilogram by a large or a small figure—hectic and apprehensive, they are sure they are going to be cheated. When the sacks have been loaded onto the trucks, even the richer planters crowd around the agent, clamoring for "a little something," a small extra payment of fifty or one hundred francs. Then the excitement gradually subsides. Most of the planters have rather odd ways of handling the money they have earned. Some lose it, others give it away or hide it so carefully that they can no longer find it or the bills are eaten by termites. It rarely occurs to any of them that they might pay their debts right away.

They seem to be possessed by a deep-seated conviction that money is something that cannot be kept; one ought to have it, but others invariably get hold of it or steal it, and in the end one has nothing left. No matter how high the regard for wealth—"Noble birth cannot be cooked and eaten; wealth fills a man's belly"—they will never be able to attain it.

At present, moneylending is very popular in Bébou. The lender demands either no interest at all, or an exorbitant rate; he expects the borrower to repay double the sum at the end of the year, double the new sum, and so forth. The results, naturally, are ruinous transactions and a great deal of strife, but hardly a viable credit system. No one can demand repayment of a loan unless he is in desperate straits himself, and no one can refuse to grant a loan. Occasionally someone may repay a loan granted to a friend or relative whose position as a debtor has become embarrassing because the lender has lost patience. The same rules then apply to the new creditor; that is, one never speaks of money until it can no longer be avoided. In reality the Anyi talk a great deal about money, but it is never allowed to become a factor in their inter-personal relations. They are afraid—and rightly so—that relationships may be poisoned by strife if money plays a role, or that the other person may ask for a loan. Husbands and wives never know how much their partners have, and the same secrecy prevails between father and son and even more between distant relatives and between friends. In short, it looks as if money had absolutely nothing to do with barter or trade, as if its only purpose were to confer prestige upon its possessor or to smooth the course of particularly difficult interpersonal relationships, as if custom demanded that a person keep it a secret even from himself how much property he owns, so that it will not diminish or so that he can always hope that there may be more there than he thought. And in fact no one seems to have the slightest idea how much cash he actually has on hand, how much he owes others, or how much others owe him; everyone, though, is preoccupied with daydreamlike fantasies about how much he would have, if . . . , and how rich this, that, or the other person is. As a result, all frustration over money is effectively avoided, but hardly anyone ever learns to handle money practically.

Loss anxiety, held in check but never entirely dispelled by strict rules of etiquette, undergoes a quite general displacement—to a fear of thieves. Everyone is afraid of being robbed. Despite their inner need to build themselves fine new houses, they make the windows so small that the rooms have practically no air—just so that thieves cannot get in. They squander their money so that there will be nothing to tempt a thief. They suspect everyone, no matter how fond they may be of him otherwise. According to the court records of Abengourou, theft, burglary, and robbery are extremely rare in the land of the Anyi.

This irrational fear of thieves does not extend to the stealing of food from the fields. It is by no means uncommon for poor people to take plantains and cassava roots from a neighbor's field. This leads to a dispute, and the culprit has to offer his apologies, but he does not have to return what he has stolen. Things taken to satisfy direct oral needs are not regarded as having been stolen; the fear of thieves is restricted to money and what it symbolizes.

For the Anyi, as for us, gold and money have anal significance. Money is the representation of anal instinctual urges. In Europeans anal cathexis includes a retentive component; money can be hoarded, saved, counted. In the Anyi, subjected as they are to daily enemas during this phase, anal strivings are never retentive, but are invariably associated with loss emotions, with a feeling of not being able to hold back, of being robbed.

Wealth is not only equated socially with prestige and authority; it also symbolizes the phallic ideal of the father—desired, longed for, and admired, but achieved only in the form of fantasies. Women long for a rich husband, are disappointed by a poor one.

We Europeans experience the anal phallus symbolized by wealth as a terrifying instrument of power. We have every reason to fear the anal sadistic employment of wealth. With the Anyi, on the other hand, it is clear that the aggressive misuse of money is hardly possible, since they have no retentive component (no resistance to relinquishing it). They are quite capable of demanding exorbitant interest rates but incapable of hoarding money or refusing it. Socially, their cruelty must make use of instruments other than a money-based economy.

Is Poor Coffee Better?

After the harvest during the coffee season (December, January), one can find in every courtyard a picturesque group of men, women, and children gathered around a drying rack. They are sorting the dried beans. Discolored beans and beans with wormholes are discarded, leaving only green beans of uniform size, the signs of high quality. Sorting is a pleasant, relaxing occupation. Visitors stop by, help the sorters for a while, and exchange the latest gossip. A little girl awkwardly tries her hand at her first serious work. People laugh and joke.

This gave us a wonderful opportunity for establishing informal contact with the villagers. Unhindered by ceremonial etiquette, the ethnologist squats down with the others, sorts his little pile of beans, and takes notes, with an occasional covert glance at his watch to record the minutes and seconds taken up by all the small happenings that interest him.

And during the sorting we made a remarkable discovery. Not only did our pile grow much faster than those of the Anyi—who, after all, might be expected to know their business—but our beans were all nice and green and of uniform size, while those sorted by the others were almost indistinguishable from the unsorted coffee on the rack. How could we, beginners and absorbed in our own observations to boot, do our work so much more efficiently than the Anyi?

That year the price fixed by the government did not depend upon the quality of the coffee. Nevertheless, the agents could—and often did—refuse to accept inferior coffee, which always led to deep disappointment and vehement protest. Also, the price for each souspréfecture for the following year was to be based on the quality of this year's coffee.

How is this possible? How can these people—who look forward so eagerly to selling their coffee, who financially are largely dependent upon the proceeds from their coffee crops, and whose whole country is tense with anticipation during the coffee season—how can these people so completely disregard their own interests that they perform in such sloppy fashion a simple, pleasant task that even a four-year-old can do?

Let us forget about such factors as the work ethic, group psychology, and the reality principle for the moment and look at what happens to the coffee. The private coffee market has been abolished; its price fluctuations and manipulations—reminiscent of the ups and downs on a stock exchange—had ruined generations of planters. A system of uniform prices, guaranteed purchase by the state, and state-regulated export was introduced. The Anyi themselves do not drink coffee. There are plans to build an instant-coffee plant in Abidjan, and maybe they will start drinking it then. This strange product accounts for by far the greatest share of the national income and of government revenues. Yet the authorities in charge of economic affairs have no more idea than the Anyi themselves what to do about this blessing, these thousands of tons of coffee beans piling up in bulging warehouses. Should they try to improve their—really very bad—coffee by processing it in some way? Should they force the population to drink it? The world market is glutted with good coffee from Brazil, the West Indies, and Kenya, and there is little demand for even the best qualities. The International Coffee Board may have a solution to offer. Poor-quality coffee could be destroyed, burned up, dumped into the ocean. The more fortunate producers in countries with better-suited soils could pay alms to the Anyi from their profits. Must the Anyi accept and starve? No! A miracle comes to their rescue. Or rather not a miracle, but a development decreed by stronger economic interests and more influential forces than the International Coffee Board. The French government, during its paternalistic colonial phase, had compelled the Ivory Coast, by force and by seductive promises, to turn its economy into a monoculture based on coffee. This was a drastic structural shift, one that cannot be reversed at this late date without years of privation for the inhabitants. In any case, no matter how it may affect the coffee-producing black nations, France is now eager to make itself independent of the western hemisphere as a world economic power and to maintain its political influence in Africa in order to be able to counter more effectively those powers that might be envious of its chances at economic hegemony in West Africa.

For this reason France buys and drinks the expensive, poor-quality coffee produced in Bébou, Yosso, and M'Basso. Does sorting coffee contradict the traditions, the concept of life of the Anyi? Are they too clumsy to sort their coffee better? Are they incapable, or unwilling? Or are they perhaps merely very wise, very human, and very intelligent in an alien, mad, world, when they refuse to spoil those pleasant hours spent chatting in the shade by insisting on accurate work and pointless efficiency?

Death and Funeral Ceremonies
This land has too many dead.
    Brou Koffi

In the course of every life there are characteristic events, significant phases, during which the individual withdraws into himself and tends to free himself of all social commitments, while society insists with all the means at its disposal—ritual, constraint, and seduction—on having its due. At birth an infant is centered on itself, and the mother feels the need to withdraw with her baby into the exclusive symbiosis of the infant/mother dyad; only the name-giving ceremony or baptism brings her back into public view. From the psychological standpoint, puberty—with its awakening desire for a sexual partner—then marriage, the onset of mental disease, and finally death are all phases of a narcissistic withdrawal from society or of libidinal sexual exclusiveness. And even our individualistic and anonymous Western society is incapable of allowing two people to live only for their love. The moment we marry, church, state, family, and fiscal authorities immediately descend upon us to call us back to our duties and to the obligations imposed upon us by personal ties; all we are permitted is the brief intimacy of a limited honeymoon—and even that is often granted grudgingly. The peace of the dying, the deeply private grief of the mourners are cause for mandatory intervention by the authorities.

Psychoanalysis, with its emphasis on emotional consequences, would define all the "rites of passage" to be found in all the various cultures of the world far more broadly than is usually the case and, as far as their effects are concerned, would equate the efforts of a technologically perfected medical science to prolong life with a ritual hallowed by faith. The next step would be to determine which of the two rituals imposes greater constraint, pain, and discomfort on the individual concerned, and which gives him greater release, joy, and pleasure. Different as the results would be for different cultures, the fact remains that "great" rites of this kind affect the entire structure of society, unite the mythical with the material, and bring about a confrontation between group and individual interests. Among the Anyi, the great, definitive ritual is the funeral ceremony.

The learned Anyi ethnologist Amon d'Aby (3), deeply bound by the traditions and future of his people, devotes some thirty pages to a careful, though by no means exhaustive, description of their traditional customs concerning the dead. He concludes as follows:

> The funeral festivities are killing us, ruining us, keeping us from doing any useful work.... It is...a commonplace to say that they are a potential source of grave disorganization for society; the strange thing is that although everyone recognizes this state of affairs, nobody is really trying to do anything about it.
>
> ...[this institution's]...extraordinary complexity is becoming less and less clear in the minds of the population, giving rise to contradictory views and interminable discussions.... Like the never-ending quarrels around the deathbed, the humiliating treatment meted out to the widow has very little to do with the peace of the soul in the other world. Certain customs, such as the public or semipublic confessions, the widow or widower being required to go about in rags, the long hours spent each day in weeping and wailing, and the mandatory fasting that goes on for weeks or months, seem to us to be totally superfluous....
>
> ...Actually, all the costs incurred by the funeral feasts [given for the mourners] are borne by the chiefs of the courts, whose main concern is to preserve their honor. Consequently, whenever there is a death and funeral festivities in a village, everyone is bound to go into debt in one way or another and to waste his time....
>
> In view of the graveness of this threat, which weighs heavily both on the life of the individual and on society, it is high time that we take energetic action to free our brothers of "what is killing and ruining them." This will be less a matter of condemning the religious foundations of the rites concerned than of combating, with the help of energetic measures, their present factual degeneration.

One European (Clozel) who had to bury a friend in the land of the Anyi reminds us that the European ritual can be almost as depressing: "The death of a fellow citizen is a painful thing. Not only is one left alone to take care of the numerous formalities that surround a death in France; one also has to assume, one after the other, the functions of a registry office clerk (to issue the death certificate), a notary public..., a priest."

The unequal importance attached to funeral festivities in the two cultures is not sufficient justification for deploring them or joining in the clamor for their abolishment. Whether they are really degenerate cannot be decided in any case. It depends upon the viewpoint of the observer.

It would be more accurate to speak of adaptation. The gold traditionally spent for funeral ceremonies and the gold dust sprinkled over the face and body of the corpse have been replaced by paper money. The long fasting of the widow or widower has been discontinued, but the drinking—which brings a measure of forgetfulness—has been retained. The sacrificing of slaves has long since been abolished. On the other hand, merely sacrificing a sheep can hardly be expected to bring the necessary relief; thus other methods must be devised.

Even the modified ritual in use today illuminates the typical problems of the Anyi in the prism of a focal situation. A fairly high degree of ostentation is required here to cope with the grief of the mourners, and death nevertheless tears a rent in the fabric of life and leaves bewilderment in its wake. The chief of M'Basso described the situation succinctly when he said, "There are too many deaths in our land. The government has prohibited our traditional forms of mourning. And still we pay. There are too many dead."

The financial aspects are easiest to understand. The more important the person who has died, in other words, the greater the power he is likely to exercise over the living from his abode after death, the more costly his burial and the funeral ceremonies and festivities will be. Children, who are considered to have no spiritual power of their own, can be buried quite inexpensively. An adult is more expensive, and a chief or the ancestress of a maternal lineage is most expensive of all.

Anyone who takes part in a funeral ceremony must pay a certain sum of money to the family of the deceased. Very close relatives (such as Thomas, when his father died) must have this sum fixed by a respected male member of the family (in Thomas's case, a distant uncle), while the sums due from distant relatives—brothers-in-law, for example—and from close friends are set by the immediate family of the deceased. Persons who are not related, such as the chief of the village and those from neighboring villages, can decide for themselves whether they wish to make a financial contribution. If they choose not to pay anything, this is tantamount to a declaration that they do not want to be included among the mourners; if they give more than is expected of them, they consolidate their ties with the family concerned and create mutual obligations.

We Europeans wanted to be a part of the village but to remain a group apart, not too closely allied with any family but that of the chief (which was thereby eliminated theoretically and practically as an object of research). Thus it was essential that we should make a joint contribution commensurate both with our real prestige in the village and with our wealth (the most important factor in prestige)—in other words, a sum much smaller than people expected of us, since they imagined us to be immeasurably wealthy, but larger than any contributed by the Africans. We gave much less for the funeral of a dignitary who had died in Zaranou and whom we had met only for a medical consultation in which we were forced to diagnose terminal stomach cancer than we did for Assoua (Thomas's father), whose family we knew well through our work with Thomas.

We soon discovered that each funeral contributed important factors for the defining of our social role and even more important ones for correcting fantasy projections. Ceremonial visits decreased in frequency and took on the character of calls paid on distinguished members of the village community instead of formal visits to strangers newly arrived. We noticed a relaxation in rules of etiquette; the obligatory "first news" was no longer so protracted, and people dared to ask us more personal questions and even to discuss village gossip with us. They often brought visitors along to meet us—passing rural policemen, for example.

Most of the guests attending a funeral ceremony are members of the family of the deceased (in the classificatory sense). A toga is spread out on the ground. A treasurer or master of ceremonies announces the sum of money contributed. Approving nods and murmurs indicate that the sum is larger than was expected, while silence signifies that the contribution was small, but adequate. Frequently, discussions ensue. The treasurer may say, "We refuse to accept this sum. If you want to belong to our family, you will have to contribute at least so and so much." During the heated haggling that follows, feelings are not spared. The mourner may protest that the deceased or a member of his family had once insulted him, cheated him, or behaved parsimoniously toward him. The others reply in kind, accusing him of always having been stingy, envious, and mean. Eventually the mourner yields, pays up, and tenders his apologies, whereupon he is officially once more a member of the family. The churned-up rancor waits for the next opportunity to break out anew. The next death in the village often provides this opportunity. Before his death, Assoua had admonished his son that Anoh Michel would have to pay one thousand francs for the next death; otherwise he would be expelled from the family. And what man would dare to disregard the expressed wish of his dead father, whose spirit might well take revenge? Without a qualm, Thomas was ready to sacrifice his friend to the interests of his family and to his own prestige. The fact that Etienne Lazare contributes nothing at all infuriates Thomas. Not because his contribution would make any real difference, but because Thomas and his clan thereby lose a supporter and—above all—the prestige reflected by a large contribution.

In this way the "family" is reorganized every time an important funeral takes place. Members on the outer fringe or members with whom the aggressive tensions have become too great withdraw voluntarily or are shut out. New alliances are formed. The order of importance shifts within the subgroups and among the persons concerned. Those who give more, thus contributing more toward the prestige of the ceremony as a whole, acquire the status of important family members, though naturally this does not change their place in the age, inheritance, or housing hierarchies, which are not affected by wealth or by generosity. The family's overall prestige has been augmented in the eyes of the outside world. All of this is particularly important when the chief of a court dies and a new universal heir must be chosen. The selection takes place immediately after the last and most important funeral rite, the one at which the contributions are collected. The new chief then finds himself faced with a family system that has been reorganized in its composition and newly endowed with prestige. Internally, however, it is seething with new emotional tensions, and its prestige is no longer backed by its property assets. For the group is in debt and impoverished.

At his father's last funeral rites, Thomas collected 96,000 francs from the mourners. He is relieved because this sum exceeds even the cash expenditures for the final ceremonies. In addition, he had to pay 16,000 francs for the transport of the body from Adzopé to Bébou and approximately 100,000 for the coffin, the preparation of the body, and the preliminary ceremonies—all together about 210,000 francs. The time lost through the ceremonies themselves and the disruption of all business activity throughout the year by constant negotiations and preparations and through the total loss of credit-worthiness considerably diminish the cash income from the plantations. Considering that Assoua was not a wealthy man but an average dignitary and planter in a medium-sized village, it is understandable that his death brought his family to the brink of ruin and that a second death was bound to be "too much," since it would lead to complete indebtedness and total financial disaster.

There is one aspect of the financial side of a death that the Anyi never mentioned to us in so many words—that the family, on this one occasion, functions as though there were still a family treasure (of gold) in the charge of the head of the family; in reality, nowadays the assets of the kin consist of land, while money is exclusively private property. Inasmuch as the size of one's personal fortune is a closely guarded secret—out of fear of theft or loss—obviously there is no prestige to be derived from it. The impressively large funeral contributions and the public announcement of the total sum collected lend an aura of affluence. There is little vestige left today of the original purpose of the mourners' gifts, which was to establish an economic balance within the group.

Naturally the Anyi are right when they complain that they—the family group concerned—are being ruined by traditional funeral customs. The custom of contributing to the final rites has about the same effect on the transition to industrialized agriculture as have the high inheritance taxes in Great Britain; it becomes impossible for a family to amass capital assets. Whether this is favorable or unfavorable for the overall economy in the long run, we are unable to say. In any case, as far as the future of the new state is concerned, the trend is detrimental to the private ownership of capital and to the formation of an entrepreneur class and a worker class. Even our studies of the Ashanti state and of the way the Anyi deal with their foreign laborers have revealed factors that work just as much against the development of a capitalist society as the traditional funeral ceremonies in their present form.

Prestige derives from money; money is power. The self-destructive extravagance practiced by the Anyi is reminiscent of the potlatch of the Indians of the Pacific Northwest. Is its purpose to enhance the prestige of one's own family at the expense of one's neighbors, to win the bitter struggle for the place at the top? Most observers would probably conclude that the human need to surpass one's rivals goes beyond the difficult questions of surplus and want.

The need may be there; the ability to comply with it is largely lacking in the Anyi. Despite all the hostile feelings, an increase in a neighbor's prestige is not a diminution, but rather an enhancement of one's own. Identification and the desire to participate in this prestige are stronger, so that aggression is directed not against one's living rivals, but against fate, against one's own self in the form of masochistic suffering—and, projectively, against the deceased.

This distinctly un-Western mode of experiencing is reflected in the customs of the Anyi. When a body is to be laid in state, it is placed on a bed covered by a thick layer of bright-colored togas. The dignitary of Zaranou, for example, lay on a bed of sixty-three togas. Some twenty of these had been provided by the members of his family, the rest by the guests attending the funeral. The togas are buried with the deceased, except for one that is torn to pieces when the body is lowered into its grave. Each funeral guest receives a small fragment of this toga, which he wets with his tears and takes home as a souvenir of the ceremonial garment, his link to the deceased. The ritual drinking festivities prescribed by custom are even more expensive. They have great significance in avoiding or smoothing over rivalry situations. A large percentage of the hundreds of thousands of francs spent on funerals is invested in beverages—palm wine, beer, wine, and above all gin. As Thomas points out, one can hardly offer palm wine to a guest who has expressed his sympathy in the form of a thousand francs. And Thomas himself invested a good deal of money in expensive European beverages, which are regarded as hallowed precisely by virtue of this ritual custom. May sweet intoxication envelop the mourners and seal their communion with the dead person and his grieving children, widows, and parents!

On the way to the cemetery, the master of ceremonies spills a few drops of gin on the soil with the murmured invocation "Today we spill a bit of gin for you. Please let no quarrels arise during the funeral ceremonies, and let death not visit the village again" (30). With this the funeral ceremonies are officially opened. They last one week and end only with the final rites, one year after death.

Just as death is bound to visit the village again, strife is certain to break out during the ceremonies; it flares up at the bier, at the grave, over trivialities and over those subtle ceremonial details that Amon d'Aby says have become degenerate and obscure with the course of time and are thus a frequent source of dispute.

It is highly unlikely that the disputes arising during the festivities are all based on disagreements regarding formal procedures. Thomas's father, for instance, expressly ordered his son to carry through to the end a feud that had been building up for years. Why precisely at that moment?

Was it because he wanted to help the family, united for the moment by the shock of his death, toward a more peaceful future, purged of dissenting elements? Or because he realized that his death would inevitably lead in any case to an outbreak of the hatred that overwhelms these people at a disappointment or loss? And did he hope, perhaps, that the fear of losing face and the fear of his spirit, which would never tolerate an undignified quarrel around the bier, might serve as a check to manslaughter and a definitive estrangement?

All over the world, the death of a relative gives rise to a feeling of loss in those left behind. Our term for the behavior of the bereaved is "mourning." The emotional state of mourning persists until the individual has been able to cope with his loss psychically. With the Anyi there are certain other emotional attitudes and views that have to be considered.

No dead person (with very few exceptions) has died a natural death; someone or other has invariably caused his or her death by magic.

The spirit of the deceased remains in the vicinity. Offended, embittered, and deeply frustrated, it wanders about waiting for someone to do something to reconcile it.

Since the spirits of the dead have the power to avenge themselves, their desires cannot be ignored.

No fond memories, no gentle, melancholy awareness of past pleasures shared, no belief or consolation is able to mitigate the pain of
barren loss. The mourners sing interminably:

When you are here,
I see you.
You're not here,
I can't see you.
When you're not here,
I can't see you.
When I can't see you,
You're not here.
You're not here,
I can't see you.
I can't see you—
You're not here.

This is more than merely an expression of grief; it also contains the
fearful plea that the dead person, having caused pain by his death,
should stay where he belongs, in his world of spirits, with the ancestors
who are awaiting him, in everlasting union with Nyame—anywhere
but here among the living, who are doing all they can to bury him.

The poeple of Bébou are adept at expressing their feelings, including
their grief, in song, and in earlier times they conjured away their sorrow in sophisticated lyrics like the following (3):

If I am not consumed by fire,
I am doomed to die of thirst.
I am the bird
That bewails the day,
The bird that bewails the night,
The bird that has no one to console it.

Our sympathy does not deceive us; we too would be capable of feeling the pain expressed in these lines. But at the same time we would
feel certain that these are the words of the mourners. The Anyi are not
sure whether the song is a lament sung by the living or by the dead.

Naturally one cannot draw any psychological conclusions from this
lack of certainty about an ancient song; it is simply a paraphrased
symptom of the relationship of the Anyi to their objects. A disruption
in object relations leads to narcissistic regression. The real object is
abandoned and replaced by a fantasy object that (in the form of a
hallucination) is experienced as real. The subject can distinguish only
imperfectly between himself and the object representation; the two are
linked symbiotically.

It was possible to derive this process from less drastic disruptions in
object relations during our interviews. Death means separation and

irrevocable loss—the worst possible disruption. The description given above corresponds more or less to the institution of mourning in Western cultures. The difference lies in the fact that we hold fast to the lost love object as an introject until our mourning has done its work and we have gotten over our loss, whereas the Anyi view the lost love object as existing outside themselves but have a very special—a symbiotic—relationship to it. One could also express it by saying that they reproject or externalize the introject. With us grief does its work step by step, more or less completely. Reprojection, in contrast, follows the law of all or nothing, the narcissistic mode of experience represented by the omnipotence/impotence polarity.

This explanation may help us place into a meaningful psychological context the concept of a discontented, vengeful spirit that refuses to go away.

Before we attempt this, however, we must bear in mind that by no means all, or even a majority, of the funeral guests necessarily undergo exactly these psychological processes. Without changing it in any way, the Anyi could continue to adhere to this custom with lukewarm faith and without any inner participation in the ritual, or they could invest the ritual with new psychological significance; for example, assign it the purpose of consolidating the cohesion and the group identity of the mourners.

On the other hand, when a ritual that so decisively affects all areas of life and gives rise to so much strife is retained in spite of the fact that even those who practice it consciously deplore it, we are justified in assuming that unconscious emotional factors must be responsible. And this in turn indicates how much weight such emotional attitudes may have for other sectors of social life as well.

The dead sing, through the voices of the mourners:

> I have visited your compound,
> I have been together with you.
> I had my family about me,
> And I had my house,
> And I had my compound.
> Then I had to depart,
> I had to go away.
> You lied to me.
> You betrayed me,
> You betrayed me.
> I am alone,
> I have no one.
> I went away alone
> And now I am returning.

In other words, it was a cruel illusion to believe that one could rely on one's family and friends. The dead see through this deception. And this is what compels them to come back among the living, who are just as cruelly deceived. The act of separation is undone.

> I went out into the fields
> To pick chili peppers.
> They told me the pods were ripe,
> But they deceived me.
> They told me to go.
> I was deceived,
> The pods are not green,
> The pods are not red.
> The peppers are black.
> I have been betrayed.
> Why should I go away?

The Anyi do everything in their power to ensure that the dead remain where they belong. A dead person must be buried in the cemetery of his native village, beside his ancestors, who will receive him and take care of him. Then perhaps he will stay with them. If he were to be buried elsewhere, far from his home, he would assuredly come back. Every river across which a body is transported has its own spirit, which must be placated by a sacrifice (in the value of one sheep). Boatmen and the priests of the river gods demand exorbitant payments—and get them.

And even so the living are not safe. They provide the body with everything they themselves like, with money to pay the fare across the river that, they hope, will keep the living and the dead apart, with cloth, gold, and slaves. Even today many young people are terrified that they may be called upon to accompany a dead dignitary to his grave, to be sacrificed like the slaves in olden times.

The impossibility of taking revenge on the dead for the pain their death causes accounts for the reaction of turning aggression toward the self. With us this leads to pathological grief and sometimes to suicide; with the Anyi it leads to voluntary self-sacrifice of slaves for their dead masters.

As long as the separation is incomplete, grief remains concentrated within. Outbreaks of quarreling and animosity provide a measure of relief from the violence of the aggression initially directed against the self. Killing a slave with one's own hands must have had an even more salutary effect. Consciously, the mourner regarded the dead person as being elsewhere, outside, and gave him the slave to accompany him. Unconsciously, he was dispatching the painful introject once more.

Once upon a time a dignitary from the Ashanti state was on his way to report the death of his king in Gyaman, accompanied by a large escort of bearers. In his own words, "Every time I was overcome by grief at the thought of my dead master, I cut off one of the bearers' heads, and by the time I had arrived in Gyaman, I had killed all but one of them with my own hands" (33).

The earlier psychological explanation (7, 33) for the exaggeratedly ostentatious cult of the dead was the fear that dominated the relationship of the living to the dead and to all spirits in general. For they are never benevolent or neutral by nature. Even a plea to one's ancestors for some favor or other was in reality a plea not to be so mean for a change.

Modern Europeans would find a different explanation more plausible—namely, guilt feelings toward the dead, to whom one has done or wished evil wittingly or unwittingly, and the resultant qualms of conscience. Ritual offers an opportunity for atonement.

And there is no doubt that the Anyi have good reason to feel guilty. The sick are practically uncared for; an accident victim is left moaning out in the sun, passersby pretending not to see him, until the village chief or the chief of the young men learns of the accident and orders the victim brought to his family. They react with great excitement and shrill laments, but no one thinks of helping the injured man to bed or giving him a sip of water. Whenever we recommend taking a gravely ill patient to the hospital, the family first sits down and coolly calculates how much or how little he has worked and how much money he has contributed in order to decide whether it is worthwhile, in view of the high costs of transporting corpses, in case he should die in the hospital. And the aggressive tensions between married couples and among family members probably—in fact are bound to—result in guilt feelings when the unconscious wish for someone's death is fulfilled.

Thus there is perfect logic in the old custom that marriage partners used to be subjected to severe punishment, that wives used to be forced to confess at their husbands' deathbeds whether and with whom they had committed adultery. It was believed that only then could the dead husband find peace. The uncle of the "clean old man" in Yosso had punished him for the rest of his life by inducing in him an agonizing compulsion to wash continually because he had squandered his inheritance instead of using it to erect a worthy tomb for the uncle.

The guilt anxiety of the Anyi is penetratingly obvious. Every person who dies has his magic-working murderer. If it is not already common knowledge who it was that injured him, devoured his flesh, or put a spell on him, the Anyi ask the corpse. Young people load the bier onto their shoulders while the other villagers crowd around in a circle. Every single person must be present. The bier begins to twist and turn. The person at whom the corpse points is the witch and has to pay a fine. Only rarely is the cause of death so satisfactorily clear as in the case of Assoua. When he drank the hallowed water of the mediator Edjro, he swore that he had already confessed all the spells that he himself had worked. He died because he had neglected to mention three misdeeds. His death was nobody's fault but his own. One of Ahoussi's wives ("the good woman") was the only person we ever heard of whose death was attributed to natural causes.

The flaw in this explanation is not that it assumes a projection of personal aggression to a relatively unimportant, defenseless member of the maternal kin; it lies in our own conception of conscience and superego. The people of Bébou do not feel themselves in the least responsible for the health of those dear to them, and their contact with the Christians has given them only a superficial acquaintance with the concept of a charitable duty toward one's fellowmen. They are perfectly capable of directing sadistic aggressions, along with their love, against members of their families, their mistresses, wives, and children. We cannot do this even while they are alive. We are compelled to be compassionate, to repress our hatred.

The Anyi's relationship with his fellowman is just like his relationship to the material things he owns and to the objects from which he hopes to derive profit; it has an anal as well as an oral parasitic nuance. If this relationship, which in itself does not give rise to feelings of guilt (or bring about "more humane" behavior toward wife and children either), is disrupted by death, the result is a regression. The spirit of the deceased wanders about, restless and thirsting for revenge, and threatens the mourners with the same oral rage that his loss has released in them. The following lament makes this clear:

Why have you come back?
Why have you come back?
You crushed my arm,
You devoured my leg.
Why have you come back?
Why don't you leave us in peace?
We are here,
We are here for you.
Leave us in peace.
You return to devour us.
Why? Why?
We are your children.
Leave us in peace.

We are here for you.
We didn't drive you away,
We've done nothing to harm you.
Why have you come to devour us?
Why do you steal our flesh?
Why do you devour us?
Leave us in peace.

And a pious inscription on a gravestone down at Aby Lagoon reads as follows (30):

Here lies the body of Emil Bacua.
Let those who love him pray,
And those who hate him laugh.
But do not believe that he is dead,
If you do, you will regret it.

Emil Bacua is not dead. In the philosophy of the Anyi, the god Nyame and all the gods and spirits and wandering souls are merely various aspects of the only real world, the spiritual world. All dead matter is made animate, above all the recently deceased. Animism is nourished by the projections of those preobjects that are imperfectly demarcated from the self, reflections of one's own needs, embodiments of oral hatred and consuming love. Let the tree carry me, as a mother carries her baby. The spirit of game killed in the hunt must be placated; otherwise it may take up its abode in my grandmother, and she will steal my flesh and sell it to a woman who is greedy for the flesh of her daughter.

The spirits of the dead, akin to and partaking of the divine spirit, are moved by the same passions as the living, by their joy and their grief; they too yearn for gin, for food, for love. Since they are no longer able to obtain the delights of the world, they hover about as restless spirits. They might take revenge on those who are still able to enjoy all the things they long for, the living who try so hard to appease their dead with ostentatious ceremonies and succeed only in reviving them projectively again and again out of the depths of their regressions.

The gods of the Greeks were endowed with human passions; they were larger than life, idealized human figures. The dead ancestors of many African peoples not only live on with universally human features but even retain the character traits and specific qualities that they possessed in life. Only their power is greater than that of the living, and their idealization is limited to endowing them with a willingness to help their descendants as long as the latter adhere to their commandments and fulfill their demands. The spirits of the Anyi dead have tremendous power over the living. But they have not been idealized and, left to their own devices, they have no ambition to come to the aid of the living. On the contrary, they have been reduced to the status of disappointed and frustrated beings, helpless prey to their passions. They are no longer subject to the control exercised by common sense and social ties, as they were in life. They are like living persons who have been insulted and betrayed and, in consequence, have become solitary and vindictive, the playthings of their own greedy passions. The spirits of the dead display the same ego regression and the same tendency to succumb to instinctual urges as living persons who have suffered a loss. The externally projected introject is endowed with omnipotence, the self with impotence. The representation is altered during this process; it becomes a mirror image of the unconscious perception of self.

The Anyi have a deep fear of death, and they are able to cope with it only with difficulty. The separation it represents evokes rage at the person who dies, that is, the frustrating object, and also a feeling of omnipotence, the feeling that the individual himself has brought about (not merely wished!) the death. Their funeral rites enable the groups that attend them to take part in a collective regression, in which the mourners identify with one another.

As it came time for us to leave Alangouan, the prevailing mood was gloom. We were afraid that the inhabitants of Bébou would be unable to bear the coming separation, that they would want to keep a part of us, that they would rob us, hate us. A few days before our departure, we began to be very formal. We drew up what we felt was a fair and just list of what parting gifts each villager should receive—the most to those we had been closest to, those who had worked with us, and progressively less to those with whom we had had little or no close contact. Since we had shown ourselves to be strong, invulnerable and nurturing, good objects, the rage and greed directed against us were very slight. Instead, there was a withdrawal of desires and wish fulfillment in the form of fantasies. Only a few children showed up at our last medical consultation hour. Many people left Bébou to visit relatives in other villages, so that they would not have to bear passively the pain of being abandoned. A painful parting can be avoided in this way; death cannot.

The older, more sensible inhabitants paid us a great compliment— "This year we've had no deaths in the village. Last year there were more than thirty. As long as you were here, there was no need for anyone to die. We had no funeral ceremonies to ruin us. Next year all the more will die."

And, really, only one man had died during our stay in Bébou. That there were no other deaths was certainly due in part to the medical services we provided, to our treatment of malaria, pneumonia, and above all children's diseases, and to our insistence on prompt transferral to a hospital for the gravely ill—much as the population hated this last measure.

But apart from their being spared the usual number of deaths, the period of our stay was not an entirely happy time for the Anyi. Our medical assistance brought it home to them all the more clearly that they were incapable of protecting themselves, least of all against death, without outside assistance. This realization is all the more bitter once one has seen that things can be different. "We were surrounded by menace before, and we will be again next year. And in all the years to follow—till the end of eternity."

4 Childhood

Suzanne (Goldy Parin-Matthèy)

Suzanne is a blood niece of Thomas Assoua. She has a secondary-school education, which is why Thomas asked her to talk with "Madame." She is an unusually lovely, neatly groomed girl of seventeen or eighteen and the mother of a healthy little boy about ten months old. Unlike my second subject, Elisa, whose expression was surly, often passionate, and so wild as to be almost tragic, Suzanne impresses me as a gentle, well-brought-up young lady, rather like a "girl of good family" in Switzerland. Her awareness of her own beauty finds expression in a kind of queenly detachment in her attitude toward me and toward her environment. I never observed in Suzanne the rather aggressive coquetry and provocativeness that characterize other Anyi beauties.

I had thirty-eight hour-long interviews with Suzanne between 3 February and 24 March 1966.

She tells me she picked the name Suzanne because she liked it so much; her full name is Suzanne Kouassi because the father of her son, whom she has christened Syrien, is called Assima Kouassi. Assima has selected Paul as his Christian name, so Suzanne also calls herself Pauline.

Later on I discovered that her real name was quite different—Eba Akoumbra. She never uses her father's name (her maiden name), and once I had found out something of her family history I could easily understand why.

Her lability in dealing with her own name reflects the insecurity of her feeling of identity. She is uncertain of her place in the family and of what role she is allowed to play and is capable of playing.

Suzanne's maternal grandmother, Nja Messan, is the first wife of the influential dignitary Anoh Assoua (Thomas is the oldest son of Anoh Assoua's second wife). Her oldest daughter is Suzanne's mother (Assoua Amma), who, at the age of twelve, was promised in marriage to a gentleman named Eba from Aniassué and joined his household when she was sixteen. She bore him two daughters before Suzanne, and a son and daughter after Suzanne's birth.

When Suzanne was about three, her father Eba gave her away to his older sister N'Guessan, who lived in Bébou. He did this because his sister was a shaman and had no children of her own. At that time there were four other children living with N'Guessan: the girl Amarane, who had been given to her by King Ahoussi de Bernard, and three children of Eba's older brother—Suzanne's girl cousin Atta and two small boy cousins who were later killed in an explosion. The number of children entrusted to her is an indication of the great esteem enjoyed by this shaman—and perhaps also of the fear the inhabitants of Bébou felt toward her.

From that time on Suzanne lived in the compound of her aunt, the shaman, and helped her run the household.

Later, when she entered school, Suzanne was summoned by her grandmother to the court of the maternal family to take her meals with them; she continued to sleep at her aunt's compound.

A year later the shaman, her aunt, became seriously ill, and her brother Eba, Suzanne's father, came to Bébou. At that time the shaman said to her brother, "You ought not to return to Aniassué; they'll kill you there." Suzanne was delighted at this pronouncement. The father refused to heed his sister's warning, saying that he had cocoa plantations to care for and had to go back. Soon afterward, the shaman died and Suzanne moved in permanently with her grandmother, Nja Messan, in the court of Anoh Assoua.

Suzanne recalls going home for a visit to her parents during the holidays after her second year of school. It was while she was at home that her father died.

During our first interview, Suzanne relates how her father drowned while fishing in the Comoë River—"The devils killed him."

"There in Asinassué, where my father was, we had everything; here we have nothing. Here we have to buy everything. The machine demolished our plantations in Bébou. [When the bulldozers cut roads through the rain forest, they level whole areas.] Now we have our coffee plantations on the other side of the Manzan River. We've started plantains, too, but they're not bearing yet. In Aniassué we had big plantations with trees old enough to bear, and the harvests were good."

Then Suzanne begins to speak of her husband. He is the father of her small son Syrien, but he already has a first wife. "She's so mean. She has three children from my husband, but she's really mean. My husband is going to send her away. He'll give her seven thousand francs and tell her to go to the devil!" (Suzanne's eyes blaze, and she beams at the prospect.) "I lived with him in Zaranou for six months, until he lost his house. The machine destroyed it as it did our plantations." Since then she has been living with her son in the court of her mother's family in Bébou. "As soon as his new house is ready, I'll join him in Zaranou. By that time he will have gotten rid of his first wife."

What I have heard from Suzanne leads me to suspect that even as a child she perceived her mother as a rival, since the mother—as her husband's first wife—was allowed to stay with Suzanne's father while Suzanne was sent away. In the same fashion, she now considers her own husband's first wife a rival. She hopes that he will send her away, just as she had wanted her father to send her mother away and keep his daughter with him. The other woman must go—this is Suzanne's main desire and her plan for the future; it is also the topic of our first conversations together.

In the very first interview she identifies me with her husband. "My husband can drive a car too—like you, Madame."

Suzanne appears for her next interview all dressed up and carrying her handsome little son on her back. She seats herself and, absorbed in what she is doing, gives him her breast. She does not speak, but plays a scene for me. Today, apparently, she plans to introduce me to the most important persons of her environment. Her mother stops by to greet me, takes the baby on her lap, and then leaves with him.

The next visitor who appears to greet me is Suzanne's husband, Paul Assima. He is a very good-looking young man in European dress. Unlike his wife, though, whose behavior is always natural and confident, he seems inhibited and embarrassed. Obviously his attitude toward me contains so little of the phallic component that he has felt it necessary to bring along his little brother for support. The boy is carrying a cage containing four captured rats. It is evident that Paul has arranged the entire scene to cover up his own feeling of insecurity. He was probably a bit intimidated at the thought of meeting Madame and Suzanne all alone. He shows me the rats and explains that he will feed them until they are big and fat and then eat them. Hurriedly and awkwardly, he says goodbye, without a glance at Suzanne, and departs with his brother and the rats.

Suzanne asks whether I also eat rats. I explain that our rats live on garbage, and that therefore we don't eat them; here, however, the rats are fed good plantains, so the situation is quite different.

This makes it clear to Suzanne that I am not just like her husband after all. Also, she has probably realized that he must have impressed me as a rather sorry figure, full of inhibitions, and this tempts her to identify with me, just to see what happens. Suddenly she announces that she would never eat those rats and spontaneously launches into a hymn of praise to European medicine. She tells me that she had watched me at work in the clinic last evening, and that she had had her baby in Aben-gourou and not in Bébou, where there are too many devils. She adds that later on she intends to learn how to type, as she has seen me doing.

The next time, Suzanne appears punctually and beautifully dressed, but without her baby. She talks about her husband, who will soon pass his driver's test and be able to drive around in an automobile, like Madame. Apparently her husband has regained the same status as I have in her eyes. The news of her husband is followed immediately by a story about a woman thief who is told to go to the devil.

The tale of how the bad woman, the thief, is driven away comes right after the identification of her husband with Madame at the wheel of a car. What is it that Suzanne is trying to express? Perhaps the following: It had lain within her father's power to keep his daughter with him and to send his wife to live with his sister instead. Today it lies within the power of her husband to send his first wife away and to put Suzanne in her place. The power to cope with rivals that she attributes to me is now supposed to be magically transmitted to Paul, through the identification of him with me, enabling him to deal with her rival—that is, to get rid of her. If she succeeds in establishing a contact between her indecisive husband and Madame, to whom she attributes so much power, then her husband will be strong enough to fulfill her heart's desire, namely, to have her take the place of the rival/mother, the first wife, this thief. She is making use of an unusual form of participative projection with me; the phallic power with which she has endowed me is supposed to enable her husband, via the identification of my person with him, to give the proper expression to her own feelings of rivalry.

As if the whole thing had been planned and rehearsed in advance, a little girl now appears like a herald at the fence surrounding our tent area, with a group of even smaller children in tow, to announce that one of the older girls is on her way to us with the baby, Syrien. As soon as the girl has brought him, Suzanne places him at her breast and begins to play with him absorbedly. There is no need for her to speak. Her behavior reflects a complete withdrawal from her relationship with me to an autoerotic narcissistic gratification, in which, however, she obviously perceives herself as perfectly equal to me, on exactly the same footing, and in total harmony with me.

But what is the reason for this sudden withdrawal to an inaccessible, unapproachable Mother-of-God posture? The entire scene, the way she arranged for the baby to be brought to her, was surely intended as a dramatic underscoring of her own phallic completeness, to stress for my benefit that she is at least as perfect as she considers me to be. It is possible that the transferred wish that I fight her rivalry battle for her was threatening to make her too dependent on me. In this case I would be invested with such unequal phallic power that I might come dangerously close to resembling in her eyes the early phallic mother. She also might be drawn into an erotic admiration for my power. Whatever the reason, she has gone to a good deal of trouble to stage the dramatic entry of her son. With her baby on her lap she can enter into a phallic identificatory relationship with the alien white woman without risking an oedipal or preoedipal dependency conflict. Not even my interpretations are able to dislodge her from this relationship with me—any more than they could Elisa. The phallic significance of the little boy is so obvious and so genuine that Suzanne, armed with the baby, is usually able to appear punctually for our interviews—unlike Elisa, who feels a constant need to substantiate her phallic identificatory relationship with me by acting out.

Carrying Syrien on her back, Suzanne comes to pick me up. I notice that she bends forward as she walks. I open the tent and we go inside. She sits down without speaking. The baby is becoming restless, and she cuddles him to her breast and then puts him down on the ground. At first he crawls about happily, smiling. Instead of the dirty piece of wood he is about to put into his mouth, she gives him the cord with a cowrie shell that he wears around his belly and that has become unfastened. He plays with it actively, setting it swinging with one hand and trying to catch it with the other. To break the silence, I remark, "The baby is playing catch." Suzanne smiles in agreement. There is a pause. Finally she says:

"My husband didn't come. My sister met his first wife and she said that he had gone to Ebilassekrou."

The baby begins to cry and wants her breast, which she gives him; then he spits out the milk. I tell her that she is probably worried about what he is doing there. "No, Madame," she replies. The baby is howling now, and she tries unsuccessfully to soothe him by placing him at her breast.

> *Madame:* But you can tell by the baby's behavior that you're worried about something; today he's not so cheerful as usual.
> *Suzanne:* I'd better put him on my back [does so]; children are unhappy when their papas are away.

I explain that she is worried about her husband, and also uneasy with me, but that when she is upset and unable to talk about it, the baby expresses her mood.

Out of the blue, Suzanne remarks, "My grandmother asked me why the white woman doesn't wear any earrings," and shows me her own, a gift from her husband some time ago. Now she has an advantage over me. Obviously she cannot admit to me that anything might be wrong. Her husband is good; after all he gave her the earrings.

After I have explained Suzanne's presumable worries and possible jealous apprehensions to her by referring to the behavior of the baby, she appears punctually for the next three interviews, beautifully dressed as usual, but without her son. She chats charmingly and noncommittally, and each time she has arranged to have the group of children bring Syrien to her in the dramatic fashion described above. Sometimes she pays no attention; then the children squat down with Syrien outside the fence, but within sight, and play with him. Suzanne smiles and nods in complete agreement when I interpret this form of equality between us as practical for her but conducive to maintaining resistance. This way, there is no longer any need for her to say anything. On one occasion, Syrien pulls himself up, clinging to the fence for support, and Suzanne describes how he holds on to the bamboo poles at home and tries to stand. Another time a little girl lifts Syrien over the fence and gives him to Suzanne. She cuddles him to her breast, the atmosphere is relaxed and happy. When the hour is over, she departs with the baby, smiling radiantly.

The following three sessions pass in much the same way, with Suzanne appearing punctually and in a happy mood, giving me her "first news" and "second news" in keeping with the ritualized forms of contact among the Anyi—her remarks completely impersonal—and then devoting herself absorbedly to nursing or playing with her little son. The pattern becomes clearer—Suzanne, I, and the baby are an ideal family. She beams at me and we admire the little boy together. Here she enjoys the peace and freedom from conflict that is impossible with Syrien's real father, who is away.

Yesterday evening and early this morning, we witnessed some highly dramatic scenes among the women of Bébou. The cause: one of the husbands from Suzanne's compound has been caught committing adultery with Ernestine, a young unmarried woman with a four-year-old boy.

Act One: The injured wife boxes her husband's ears, and he puts up with it patiently for a while. When he makes a halfhearted attempt to defend himself, the wife throws herself on the ground with a scream, bursts into tears, and complains that her husband—on top of committing adultery—is also beating her. Exit the husband.

Act Two: The young women of Bébou, including Suzanne with Syrien on her back, gang up on Ernestine, shouting at her and threatening her. The wronged wife is determined to throw herself on Ernestine and is egged on by one group but held back by another until Ernestine can flee behind our compound to her friends.

Act Three: While one group howls with rage and the other laughs with glee, Ernestine speaks up in her own defense: "If I had a figure like an ape the way you do, your husband would never have slept with me!" It is like a Greek tragedy, with sweeping gestures and a chorus, and the young girls of twelve or so find it great fun to imitate the fight going on between the grown-ups. The foreign laborers stand around and laugh.

After this spectacular domestic quarrel, which had the whole village up in arms, Suzanne arrives late for our session, carrying her baby on her back. Evidently she has slept badly and is still upset, but she says nothing, assuming that I already know all about what has happened.

Finally she remarks, "Ernestine came and took the husband and slept with him. She has no husband. She was in Abidjan and she should have stayed there. Why did she have to come back? She even sleeps with children!"

At this point her speech becomes blurred, and all I can understand is that her husband once slept with "that woman," too, but that she, Suzanne, had not made such a fuss about it.

This, incidentally, was the only time during all our interviews that Suzanne exhibited a slight deterioration in speech—something that happened often to Elisa. Suzanne apparently has other forms of defense that enable her to cope with overwhelming emotions. By now the baby is very restless, and Suzanne gives him her breast. I remark that he probably had a rather upsetting morning; after all, he had been there during the uproar too. Suzanne agrees and begins to play with him. The baby's behavior is strikingly different today. For the first time he struggles actively to get away from her and come to me. He smiles and reaches out to me, and, for the first time since I have known her, Suzanne pulls him back roughly and thrusts her nipple into his mouth, though he shows no sign of wanting the breast at the moment. Her behavior expresses her jealousy of her son. I watch the two of them, doing nothing to encourage the baby. His glance falls on the pole of the tent and he tries to reach it. Suzanne loosens her hold on him for a moment, then pulls him back from the pole with unusual roughness. Finally the little boy manages to grasp the pole with one hand and is delighted at his achievement. He stretches out his other hand, takes hold of his thumb, pries it away from the pole, and pulls both hands back together. He has just invented a new game—grasping the pole with one hand, catching hold of his thumb with the other hand, and pulling both hands back—and he plays it enthusiastically over and over again. Suzanne keeps trying to entice him back to her breast; he screams angrily and wants to keep on playing his game.

At the end of the hour I interpret his behavior for Suzanne: "The baby can't talk yet, and you refuse to talk, but the little boy shows me exactly what you feel in your heart. You saw the game he was playing. He wants to grasp this alien thing, the pole, the other woman, and hold it fast. And that's what you're afraid of in your husband, and what happened to that woman in your compound yesterday. That's why you try to tear your baby away from his game. But he shows me something else, too. Once he has caught hold of the pole, it's his own thumb that interests him; he pulls back both hands, lets go of the pole, and is content with what he has, his thumb. This is his way of expressing the fear and the desire of his mother—he shows them both clearly. You can see it, and you don't have to put it into words. One can deny what one has seen and close one's eyes to it; then it just didn't happen. But when one puts it into words, the words can't be erased. There might be trouble; it's safer to say nothing."

Suzanne listens eagerly and agrees, "Yes, that's it exactly." She stands the baby upright on her lap and he urinates in an arc that splashes on the wall of the tent. Both mother and son seem proud of this urethral demonstration. Since Syrien is still trying to reach me, I tell Suzanne, "Today it bothers you to see him flirt with a strange woman." She laughs and puts him down on the ground. For the very first time, Syrien succeeds in pulling himself upright without adult assistance by holding onto a stool and crows with pleasure. He bites the wood and hammers on the stool with his hands. The hour is at an end, but today it is difficult to get him to leave. Suzanne puts a fifty-franc piece into his hand. I mention that today he was the one who did the talking. With a radiant smile, Suzanne goes off with her son.

My interpretation was based on the assumption that the baby actually had acted out in play the jealous urges and apprehensions of his mother. Once I call her attention to this, Suzanne experiences a phallic narcissistic heightening of her self-esteem, because I have confirmed that in this way she has managed to cope with overwhelming ego-threatening emotions without losing face. Her son expresses the satisfaction that autonomous functioning brings for self-esteem, first in the form of a phallic urethral feat and then—in newly acquired mastery of his body—by standing upright all by himself for the first time.

Even so, some of Suzanne's jealous distrust of me seems to persist. For the next five sessions, she arrives punctually at my tent, but without the baby. Nor is there any sign of the group of children who regularly play outside the tent when Suzanne and Syrien are inside with me.

Suzanne chats unconcernedly about the dancing at the funeral ceremonies being celebrated at the moment and explains to me which musical instruments and which songs are used at each stage of the ceremony. Then she goes on to speak of the redistribution of the fields that belonged to the deceased and of the appointment of a new family chief and tells me what aunts and uncles have come from other villages for the ceremonies. On one occasion she shows a slightly jealous reaction toward Elisa, whose sessions with me take place right after hers, but soon afterward she reports that she has made up with her. In reply to my comment that she has probably stopped bringing her little son along because it upset her to see that he was expressing her own secret thoughts, she says—with surprising harshness and abruptness—"I don't think anything."

After this she begins to talk about her husband. When his mother lay on her deathbed, he was ten years old, and the dying woman said to his older sister, "From now on, you are his mother; you are the one who has to take care of him." The older sister refused, protesting that "Your child doesn't concern me. I don't want to be his mother." Hereupon the mother threatened her and said, "All right, then I'll kill you as soon as I'm in the other world." After this the sister apologized and took the boy under her care.

Suzanne: That's the way things are with us; when a mother or a grandmother or an aunt has no one to help her, we give her a child—"this girl or this boy now belongs to you." Then that person becomes the child's mother and has to see that it is clothed and fed—the child is then her own.

[I ask whether she would give Syrien away like this.]

Suzanne: My husband wants to give Syrien to his older brother in Abidjan.

Madame: And what do you think about his plan?

Suzanne [once again abrupt and harsh]: I don't think anything.

I ask her whether she has met the older brother in Abidjan. She replies, "No. They say that the son of my husband's first wife lives with him. They say that he was thin, very thin, when he lived in Zaranou but that now he has gained weight. He's quite fat now."

With her story of how her husband acquired a new mother when he was a small boy, Suzanne has told me something about her own fate that I had no way of knowing at that time. Calmly and without any intense emotional involvement, she speaks of the fact that her son will now suffer the same fate; her husband wants to give Syrien to his older brother in Abidjan. It is only when I ask her directly what she herself thinks about the plan that she replies with this brusque "I don't think anything." She reacts in just the same way when I say that I can tell how sad and upset she really is about the whole thing.

"I don't think anything"—with these words Suzanne denies her emotions without actually suppressing them. This phrase enables her to remain within the ritualized framework of the social order and to save face. It is as if she were afraid of being humiliated, afraid of a shameful outbreak of emotions that would make her small if she showed her grief and her concern. "I don't think anything; it's best to say nothing"—this is Suzanne's method of keeping up her own courage. This is why she does not bring Syrien along to the next five sessions; he has betrayed some of the emotions she herself feels.

Evidently Suzanne was seriously upset by the domestic crisis in her compound, even though she dislikes the wife who was wronged and calls her a mean and stingy woman. Because Suzanne fears that the same fate may befall her, she identifies with the wife and carries over the crisis into the established domestic happiness of our sessions together. She is not angry with me, but she is distant and polite, and she is just as careful not to show any weak points in front of me as in front of her husband by revealing her anxiety and sadness, for in her position a stiff-necked pride is the only weapon that a woman who is aware of her own beauty can use against a man upon whom she cannot rely. She has already eliminated the child from our interviews, as if she were preparing for a divorce.

Prompted by a faint signal, Suzanne has become afraid that her husband might leave her and has reacted with narcissistic withdrawal. As long as she can maintain a behavior that demonstrates invulnerability, and as long as she is able to suppress her desire for dependency by convincing herself and the world that she is capable of leaving voluntarily herself, her self-esteem does not suffer.

Then she comes again with Syrien on her back; the baby sleeps the whole hour. She sits down on the hard stool, assuming an uncomfortable posture in order not to wake him. After we exchange our "first news," she reports that the jealous quarrel among the betrayed wife, the husband, and Ernestine has now been settled. The man had to pay his wife five hundred francs for the light blow he gave her and to donate wine in the amount of one thousand francs to the family council. He had to promise never to sleep with Ernestine again and not to marry her. Now that order has been restored in her compound and adultery atoned for according to custom, Suzanne can bring her son with her again. She says, "My husband stopped by to see me yesterday, but he left again this morning." Perhaps this is also one reason why she is able to reestablish the satisfying family situation with me—father-mother-child. Laughing, she turns to look at the baby on her back and says, "He sleeps much better on my back than at home. He doesn't sleep well at home." Our happy little family in the tent is established once more.

Today a radiant Suzanne enters my tent. "My husband came today and asked me to cook for him. I didn't just make rice, but *futu* and sauce, too." She has been to the hairdresser and her hair is beautiful—straightened and tarred jet black. She is happy and obviously in love with her husband. And she tells me right away, "Today my mother said that I ought to learn to type, like Madame." No sooner does Suzanne's husband give her reason to hope that he will choose her as his only wife (after all he asked her to cook for him; otherwise he ordinarily would have gone to some other family he knows well) than she identifies with me in my role as a wife.

Suzanne went to Zaranou with her husband—"but I was already back by midnight. He wanted me to sleep there with him, but I didn't want to." There is a pause, then I remark: "There are a lot of reasons why a girl doesn't sleep with her husband. Maybe you'd rather be here with me in the tent?" Suzanne is silent, playing with the little boy, who is now able to stand up by himself almost every time and who drums away on the stool with great enthusiasm. After a long pause Suzanne says, "The kitchen in the new house isn't finished yet." At this point Syrien begins to cry and wants to suck, but even this fails to soothe him. While she tries to calm the wildly thrashing baby, Suzanne tells me that the first wife of her husband has offered to forgive him, and now the husband's older sister has decreed that he should not divorce her after all.

"And you, Suzanne, what do you say to that?" I ask. With blazing eyes and the harsh, abrupt reply "I don't have anything to say," Suzanne once again saves face. The baby at her breast is quiet again, and Suzanne talks matter-of-factly about her husband's plantation, where his first wife works.

I cannot help but be impressed at the way Suzanne informs me of this very serious turn of events, that her rival has won the day and is to remain her husband's first wife. This means that all Suzanne's hopes of remaining with him are shattered, but she is able to tell me about it calmly and objectively, with no sign of linguistic regression. The affective assault commensurate with the destruction of all her hopes is expressed by her child on her behalf.

During our next sessions Suzanne assures me again and again that she would not discuss even her deepest sorrows with anyone, not with any of her girl friends and not with her mother, and least of all with her husband. "A woman can go away, that's her strength." She relates how her mother, who was her father's first wife, lived in the same compound with his three later wives. Suzanne had never spoken a single word directly to these stepmothers. She tells me that she will never live together with other wives as her mother did.

Can it have been Suzanne's jealous pride and her complete and utter refusal to talk things over with her husband's first wife that brought her husband into this dilemma?

Suzanne informs me that yesterday evening a chauffeur sent her a message to the effect that her husband had already purchased vitriol with which to take his own life. He had had a fight with his sister, who had taken the place of his mother, and was now determined to swallow poison. There is a pause—followed by nothing. Suzanne plays with the baby, who has begun to flirt gleefully with me; then he becomes restless, and she takes him to her breast. I remark to Syrien: "That's good milk and not a nasty medicine. You haven't quarreled with your mother yet, and I hope that later, if you ever do, you will talk with her. There are better ways of working things out than swallowing nasty milk, poison."

Suzanne smiles at me to indicate her wholehearted agreement and says nothing. But now she begins actively to play the game with the tent pole with him, the game that she had tried to keep him from playing when she was jealous. When I point out, "That's the same game as before, when you were jealous, and now you're playing it yourself," she smiles broadly and goes on playing.

She shows me in this way that our relationship is now different and that she trusts me. Evidently she feels much closer now to me as a woman and senses that I understand her.

Her son is beginning to fuss, and she takes him to her breast. He struggles to sit upright and she places him on the stool and tries to play a clapping game with him, but he wants to suck. She is clearly uneasy, fearing that I will notice her own worry in the baby's behavior. I ask whether she thinks that she will be able to comfort her husband. Calmly and confidently, she replies, "Yes, of course. I'll go to see him this evening." And, as if her son had sensed her confidence, he stands up in her lap and urinates triumphantly. Extremely pleased with himself, he hammers with his fists on the stool and waves a leaf in his hand, then invents a new drumming game. Suzanne smiles at him devotedly.

I tell Suzanne that I can understand her: "As long as Syrien is such a sweet little boy and so much an extension of you that he is always able to express your feelings in harmony with you, you feel complete and no real sorrow can affect you. You don't even have to suppress your worries and your unhappiness, your feelings overflow, and Syrien is allowed to express them for you. You're safe, and for the moment you have everything you need. Later on, when he is able to walk, that may change. You will have to share him with the world, and then he will have wishes and desires of his own that are no longer quite the same as yours, and he will grow away from you—but that won't happen till later."

Syrien has now discovered another new game and begins to wave the large leaf he is holding. Smiling, and waving with him, Suzanne departs.

Now we revert to the earlier pattern. Suzanne arrives without the baby, then the children come to announce that someone is bringing him. When he arrives, Suzanne takes him on her lap and sits there demurely and silently. Today, though, the little fellow is restless and unable to concentrate on games. He tries again and again to eat roots, leaves, and twigs, not just chewing or sucking on them, but actually trying to swallow them. Suzanne is constantly busy gently but firmly trying to force bits of root from between his tightly pressed lips. In response to my comment that he is just like his mother—that she too has bad things in her mouth and refuses to spit out the bad words and thoughts, she gives me a bright smile and says, "Yes, that's exactly the way it is." The little boy struggles in her arms; he simply cannot sit still. Suzanne is entirely taken up with trying to amuse him, giving him the breast, helping him to stand up or crawl, and so on. Finally she says:

> *Suzanne:* The day before yesterday the band from Niabley played in Zaranou and I danced with my husband.
> *Madame:* Oh, then he didn't take the poison after all?
> *Suzanne:* No, they took it away from him and hid it. Some woman told me.
> *Madame:* You didn't ask him directly?
> *Suzanne:* No, I didn't ask.

There is a pause. The child struggles to sit up and pushes against her. Suzanne puts him on her back, saying, "I'll go now, then he'll be quiet." But she remains seated, and I interpret for her once more: "It's easy when you refuse to speak; disagreements remain under the surface and in abeyance. But by the same token distrust remains in your heart—distrust of me and of your husband."

> *Suzanne:* I did speak with him. I told him I would go away if he went on doing such things.
> [Pause.]
> Today the band is coming here from Zaranou. There were a lot of people there. They play both Anyi and Cuban music. Today I'm going to go dancing.

Then she begins to rock the baby gently on her back and sits there without speaking until the end of the hour, entirely absorbed in rocking the child.

In the form of a hint, she threatened today to leave me, too, when the baby made such a fuss. Then she stayed after all, just as she stayed with her husband, with whom she is apparently going to celebrate their reconciliation when they go dancing. In telling me about the dance and in rocking the child, she is obviously making up with me as well.

Later Suzanne tells me how she actually did make up with her husband at the dance. She had sent a message through a friend letting him know that he would have to ask her forgiveness. Then he came to pick her up and they spent the whole night dancing together.

Suzanne appears obediently at the appointed time for the next five sessions, bringing Syrien with her, and chats politely and unconcernedly about general matters—about women, clothes, jewelry. Her favorite topics are musical instruments and dancing. Whenever she talks to me about dancing, she feels that we are reconciled, just as she and her husband were on the dance floor. Every day Syrien invents a new game—he is extremely lively. Suzanne withdraws more and more from me to devote herself to him. Sometimes she sits there lost in a dream and seems even to have forgotten that I am there.

Superficially, Suzanne has forgiven her husband. By transference I have taken his place, but she realizes more and more clearly that she cannot rely on me either—that I too am unable to give her the home she so desperately wants. She must avoid at all costs touching upon anything that might provoke overwhelming emotions, a breakdown of the barrier erected by her pride. She is extremely wary with me during the sessions following the "reconciliation" with her husband. She does not dare mention any explosive, emotion-laden topics. In short, she is practicing a stoical attitude on me, an attitude intended to help her deny the hopelessness and despair she feels.

I have learned from other sources that Suzanne's mother, who returned just a few years ago to her parents' court in Bébou, is leading an increasingly immoral life. There have been some dreadful jealous scenes with a Mossi man, her lover. Suzanne mentions not a word of this to me; absolutely nothing that might endanger her precarious harmony with me—her husband—must be allowed to intervene right now.

She talks about her husband's wish that she should join him in Zaranou as soon as possible. He wants her to live with his sister, who had taken the place of his mother, until his own house is ready. Then again, Suzanne says that she intends to go to live with an uncle in Abidjan and train to be a secretary. "My husband has nothing to say about that," she declares proudly. She would leave Syrien with her mother, who would then give him to Suzanne's older sisters. She plans to do this as soon as Syrien can walk.

At this point Syrien, who has been sitting happily in her lap playing all his games one after the other—grasping the tent pole and pulling back his hands, a game with my cigarette lighter, which he bangs on the floor and then plays hide-and-seek with—begins to howl. It's impossible to talk for the next fifteen minutes because the baby is thrashing about and refuses to be quieted. When Suzanne tries to nurse him, he bites her breast hard. She finally ties him firmly on her back and he calms down. Suzanne states: "As a secretary I would be independent." Rocking her child, she begins to daydream. After a fairly long pause, she says: "These coffee trees here belong to the old woman. When the machine [bulldozer] came to make the road here, she cried and cried. She lost a lot of coffee trees and they didn't pay her anything for them."

During our first interview, Suzanne spoke of the bulldozers that had demolished her family's plantations in Bébou. Before that time, as long as she was still allowed to live with her father and in her family, her world had been whole. Later, as a young girl, she had spent one year with her husband in his mud house in Zaranou, happy and in love; at that time his first wife played no role. But then the bulldozers came and knocked down the house, and once again Suzanne had to go away, this time from her husband, as she had had to leave her father as a child, in order to live temporarily in the alien court of her grandmother. I have the impression that she has lost all hope of ever being able to go back to her husband now that his first wife is living with him again—just as her mother had remained with her father when Suzanne was a child.

And now the third separation is imminent—the separation from me. The bulldozers destroyed the old woman's coffee trees right here, on the spot where my tent now stands. When I fold up my tent and depart, Suzanne will be alone once more, and once more her dreams of a safe and secure nest will have been shattered.

That same evening Suzanne and Syrien come to the clinic. Syrien is sick. And the next day she comes back faithfully with him to show me how sick he is and how worried she is about him. She says almost nothing but is completely taken up with Syrien, who is crying and thrashing about, and with her attempts to distract and comfort him. Today she has no other function but this, for Syrien is expressing what she feels when the ravaging bulldozers come back, that is, when we pack up our tent and leave and her idyllic relationship with me, like her harmonious life with her husband and before that with her father and mother, will be destroyed.

I ask whether she would mind if I took a movie of her bathing and grooming the baby at her compound in the morning.

When I arrive the next morning with my movie camera, she seems perfectly all right and bathes and cares for Syrien with her usual calmness and efficiency.

What strikes me, though, is the corner she has selected for herself in the compound of her maternal kin. She has a nice large room with concrete flooring for herself and Syrien, right next to the little house occupied by her grandmother, Nja Messan. She has no cooking area of her own and uses her grandmother's—not her mother's. But Suzanne has squatted down right in the rather narrow passage linking the front and rear courtyards, somewhat apart from the other women in the rear courtyard, who are already going about their morning tasks loudly and cheerfully. This is Suzanne's place—a temporary abode in between the permanent ones, unsuited as a permanent residence. It is clear that she is living here in her maternal court like a respected close relative who has come temporarily on a visit. She has no functions within the group. She does not go out to the fields with her mother. Only rarely is she invited to take part in the joint activities of her extended family. This is why she beams with happiness when she reports that she has been asked to help with the coffee-sorting going on now—during the harvest season—in all the courtyards.

I always find Suzanne happiest when she is doing her best to integrate herself into the group of approximately fifteen-year-old girls who do not yet have children, when she is taking part in their festivities in celebration of one of the girls' first menstrual period, or when she goes fishing or gathering snails with these still carefree comrades.

Here she lives as if ready to depart at any moment, in the court where she had been taken in as a child only for her meals, being sent back to her aunt, the shaman, to sleep. While she was at school in Zaranou, she fell in love with the man who made her pregnant and lived with him in the belief that, as his only wife, she would finally find the stable position she had longed for ever since her parents sent her away.

During the period covered by our interviews, she carried over to our situation this dream of her desire for a place all her own. Thus, during transference, she relived with me the brief period of happy family life with her husband, a happiness patterned after that she had felt while living with her parents. She wanted to maintain this relationship with me as long as she possibly could, and no disturbing element was to be allowed to interfere with our imaginary happiness. The whole time, however, she was fully aware—as playing children are aware of reality—that in the end I would abandon her just as had her parents, and now her husband. Realizing that this game of pretend was bound to end sometime, and perhaps precisely because of this realization, she gradually, step by step, came to achieve a more realistic appraisal of her situation. Our talks, during which she grew more and more clearly aware of her transference love, helped her against her will to grow up a bit. Her main defense against the pain of being abandoned was to deny all emotion and to build up an attitude of pride as a countercathexis in the self, to demonstrate to the world that "no one can hurt me any more."

The aggression provoked by the experience of abandonment finds expression in the rigid pride of a head held high. In addition, she rejects any thought of an appeal for sympathy and voluntarily breaks off communication with the group. In compensation, this defiant attitude of "standing up to misfortune" expressed in her carriage gives her the satisfaction of feeling herself in conformity with an inner attitude fixated in the ideal self, namely a sovereign denial of unhappiness. In this way she isolates herself from the group but remains in harmony with the ideals of society. And this brings her a narcissistic bonus. Moreover, the ideal self, whose content is this awareness that "no one can hurt me any more," contributes to bringing about and stabilizing the denial of emotions. This defiant/melancholy pride, which serves as a defense against anxiety and pain and which Suzanne has firmly established within herself as a permanent character trait, guarantees her ego autonomy. Whenever painful loss emotions threaten to overwhelm her, she reacts with this reinforcement of the narcissistic cathexis of the self.

Like all Anyi children, Suzanne was forced to undergo a good deal of unhappiness during childhood, being laughed at when she burst into tears and tried to communicate her grief to the world. As a consequence, an attitude of proud stoicism is very highly regarded in the Anyi structure of social ideals. Tears and sobs are all right for children, who are laughed at and put to shame. Whether Suzanne unconsciously associates crying with childhood incontinence or soiling is unclear. The tone in which she assures me that "a grown-up girl will never cry" seems to point in this direction. In any case she functions more efficiently with this defense mechanism stabilized in her character than does Elisa, for example, who must suddenly withdraw and abandon object cathexes in order to avoid emotional deluge.

But pride as a character defense is not overly rigid either. Suzanne is capable of expressing her love for me very movingly, by showing me—or having her son show me—how much they enjoy coming to my tent. Armed with this stable defense, she can be punctual and dependable, while other Anyi put off day after day the effort it costs them to come and talk with me.

At the time of our interviews, Suzanne enjoys the privileged position of every Anyi woman with a baby at her breast. Her son Syrien is external evidence and internal proof of the fulfillment of her phallic narcissistic desire for completion and at the same time is a gratifying object for autoerotic acts. The intense, empathic relationship between mother and child enables the child to serve as an organ for the expression and discharge of emotional assaults that might otherwise endanger the mother's ego.

It is striking that neither Suzanne nor any of the Anyi mothers enters into verbal communication with her baby. The whole time we were together, Suzanne never once addressed a word to Syrien. The employment of words would evidently imply the presence of a partner; words are intended to bridge a spatial gap. The relationship between Suzanne and her son is exclusively a preverbal union, in which mood transferral repeatedly reinforces their satisfying unity.

Later on, "when the baby learns to walk," the mother will communicate verbally with him in the form of commands. In this way the child will learn to talk and, at the same time, will become a completely different, alien being for his mother, one whom she can no longer use for autoerotic gratification or as an organ for the expression of emotions. Once the child starts to show more unmistakable signs of independence and to express his own separate emotions and desires instead of merely hers, the mother's self-esteem is bound to receive a deep wound. It can only be the disillusionment caused by this separation that changes so radically, from this moment on, the mother's concept of the significance of having a child and transforms the child so suddenly from a highly cathected object of value, an object capable of guaranteeing happiness, into mere property, an exchangeable commodity. The being that an Anyi woman perceives as "my child" is always that child that she happens to be nursing at the time, the being with whom she is united in a brief, preverbal happiness. This explains Suzanne's remark to me—"As soon as Syrien can walk, I'll have my next baby."

Syrien is often restless now, cries during our interview sessions, and is dissatisfied with everything. Suzanne explains, "Yesterday evening Syrien cried and cried because his papa is gone." I remarked that both the baby and Suzanne herself are sad because I am leaving and will soon be gone, too, like Syrien's papa.

> *Suzanne:* A girl will never cry; she'd be ashamed of herself if she did. Only when she sings can she speak of personal and unhappy events and feelings without being laughed at. Jacqueline and I will sing for you before you leave.

In the third-to-last interview I ask Suzanne whether she would like to take a Rorschach test, and she agrees. To isolate the test from our sessions and to make the conditions more neutral, she is to take it in the Anyi language, using François as an interpreter.

Suzanne brings Syrien along, and he plays happily. The moment I make a blot to show her how it is done, she recalls that she was present when the dignitary from Zaranou, the one who died yesterday, took the test with me. It was only yesterday, she reminds me, that I had attended his funeral rites, at which her mother and grandmother were also present. I realize that Suzanne vaguely associates the idea of the test with "dying," so I explain her fears to her and assure her that she need not take the test if she would rather not. But she replies very calmly that she is not afraid and wants to go through with it. When I present the first card to her, Syrien has a bowel movement, although he has already had his morning enema. Suzanne takes him away to wash him, and I clean up the floor of the tent. She returns without Syrien and begins with the test, attentively and matter-of-factly, like any other woman who had never been interviewed by me. When we get to the second card, her freshly bathed baby is brought in and she places him at her breast while she continues with the test, concentrating calmly and without any expression of emotion.

The fright Suzanne experienced when I confronted her with the death-dealing cards has been demonstrated by her son on the tent floor. As a result, she herself is able to handle the cards unconcernedly, in fact more attentively and matter-of-factly than a great many other subjects. The feelings of anxiety and pain occasioned by our approaching separation, emotions that represent a kind of dying and that manifest themselves in the baby, must be banished into her body by her rigid pride; Suzanne becomes ill. Apparently she recognizes the connection between her sickness and our separation. She does not mention it—refuses to say anything—and that evening comes quasi-anonymously to our medical consultation hour. The following day, however, she is no longer able to conceal her despair.

Heavily made up with kaolin and yellow clay and running a high temperature, she enters the tent and admits that she feels terrible. Later I pay her a visit in her compound and bring her some Nivaquin, for on top of everything else she also has malaria, as Syrien had ten days ago. She is a pitiful sight, lying on the ground alone and ill in one corner of the covered terrace of her compound, her little son cuddled up asleep at her back.

Now she is finally able to give way to her tears, and she is fully aware of the cause of her illness, which is simply a manifestation of her sadness and despair over our separation; for her separation from me is just a repetition of her abandonment by her parents and her husband.

But the very next day, when she comes to my tent—heavily made up and still feeling miserable—she announces: "Grandmother says that she will cry a great deal when you go away." Her need to hold her proud head high is greater than ever if she is to survive the ordeal of our parting; it is her grandmother who weeps, not Suzanne.

Today Syrien is determined to hold fast to Suzanne's breast with his strong little teeth; he pulls at it so hard that she notices it. With a rueful smile she comments, "You can't hold on to people you love; they all leave you in the end"—and then begins to weep.

I still owe her money for our interviews, and she asks me to use it to buy her a pair of gold-colored sandals in Abengourou—the same as her husband once gave her when they were still living happily together. She points to her feet—"They'll soon be ruined now."

Beautifully dressed and prettily made up, she appears with Syrien for our last session in the tent. The malaria attack has passed and she feels fine again. She is now clearly aware of her own situation; she is no longer relying on her husband.

In her court, too, changes are taking place. Louise Ya, her paternal aunt, is returning to her own family in Aboisso, and her grandmother Nja Messan is going to Akasso. Thomas, the newly appointed chief of the Assoua kin, will move into his dead father's house; he is going to make up with his first wife, who had left him, and live there with her. His second wife will stay on with her child in the small compound where she has been living till now.

As for Suzanne herself, she says that she and her mother will join the mother's daughters in Kouassikrou—perhaps for a year or two. Her stepsister has a little boy of Syrien's age. But she plans to keep her room in the Assoua court in Bébou.

Suzanne is sad but not depressive. She has a much clearer perception of her situation. Her pride forbids her remaining in Bébou and waiting until her husband—perhaps—makes up his mind to come and get her. She is not the only one for whom our departure is a signal to follow our example.

In fact, it looks as if our departure were a signal for reorganizations, upheavals, and leave-takings in many of the courts of Bébou. The whole village seems to be experiencing it somewhat as it would experience a return of the bulldozers—those machines of destruction with which the Anyi here have to live, which tear down their houses and wreck their plantations. The bulldozers might almost be regarded as a symbol of this restless people, whose only test of stability seems to be constantly letting everything go to rack and ruin and then beginning afresh.

Was it really only coincidence that on this last evening in the tent with Suzanne a tiny red ant fell into my eye and I was so overcome with uncontrollable and painful tears that I was forced to break off our session early, with red, swollen eyes?

In addition to the sandals, I made Suzanne a present of the little table and three stools with which the tent had been furnished. It was touching to see Suzanne sitting on one of the stools under the mango tree that had shaded the tent, watching the men take it down. All dressed up, with Syrien on her lap, she sat there amid her own furniture, envied and admired by the women of the village. For a little while she sat there, holding court, on the spot where, with me, she had played through and given expression to her really very modest desire for a stable home of her own. The furniture, an external, tangible symbol of all this, gives her great prestige in the eyes of the others as well as a certain satisfaction that she has been able to fulfill at least a small part of her desire.

On our last evening in Bébou, Suzanne and Jacqueline, accompanied by the entire Assoua court, sang for us. This is the translation Suzanne gave me afterward:

> The dance we have danced
> Is ending.
> And with it its children.
> The dance, too, will die one day,
> It, too, will die.
> She says her father is dead,
> Her brother, she says, is dead;
> She is left alone,
> She sees nothing.
> She did not know that her father would die,
> What will she do, to be able to go on living?
> If she stays at home,
> Death will kill her, like her father and her brother.
> There is a tree here—
> It weeps like a man.
> It weeps and can never stop.
> All that is left is weeping.

Childhood: Direct Observation
It is a misfortune to be a child.

Brou Koffi is talking with the white man. Their conversation bores his three-year-old daughter. She jiggles the table with the transistor radio on it. The chief shouts at her, without effect, then calls his wife. She enters the room with a long, thin stick and hits the little girl with it, then returns to the kitchen, leaving the child sitting on the floor and crying disconsolately.

Brou Koffi: A child should be beaten once in a while as long as it is small. That way it learns . . . . Yes, she's still too small and hasn't learned anything yet. That's exactly why we have to beat her . . . . You ask whether my mother beat me, too? Yes, I'm sure she must have. I don't think there is any mother that doesn't beat her child . . . . I don't remember exactly, though. When you're little, you don't remember things. That doesn't come till later . . . . I really don't know for sure.

Morgenthaler: But surely you told me just recently that you remember your mother carrying you on her back?
Brou Koffi: That's different. When your mother carries you on her back, you never forget it. That's something that sticks in your memory. Your mother does something good for you when she carries you. That's why you don't forget it.

The chief of M'Basso has discovered for himself one of the fundamental principles of psychoanalysis: childhood amnesia, that ability to forget that serves to blur a good many of the memories of childhood or even to banish them, seemingly once and for all. And he gives the same explanation for this phenomenon as Sigmund Freud, namely that unpleasant (unbearable) events are forgotten (repressed), while pleasant ones are likely to be remembered.

Childhood amnesia is just as typical of the Anyi as it is of us. The psychoanalyst is forced to guess at the most important events of childhood on the basis of the associations, the "new editions," and the transference of the subject. The reconstruction of the decisive events can succeed only with the subject's help. The most important part of psychotherapy is helping the patient overcome his resistance to this task. The result provides the genetic core of psychoanalytic theory.

Direct observation of the child cannot take the place of the work of reconstructing. External events and behavior patterns are not the same thing as the experiences that are most decisive for psychological development. Nevertheless, the systematic observation of children during the first years of life has contributed a great deal to the verification of psychoanalytic hypotheses and to the development of new insights.

Inasmuch as psychological development is decisively influenced by the behavior and attitudes of the social environment, and since the average expectable environment of the Anyi child is very different from that of European children, we had to rely upon direct observation of children, especially babies and toddlers, to be able to formulate more or less accurate suppositions (reconstructive interpretations). These interpretations were then tested in later interviews and sometimes through additional direct child observation.

Our direct observations followed in general the techniques developed at Harvard University for comparative studies on the process of growing up in different cultures (153).

The most serious disadvantage we had to contend with was that we could only guess at the ages of the children concerned. Bébou has no registry office where birth dates are recorded. And even when a baby could not have been more than a few weeks old, neither the mother nor the father was able to tell us the exact age. Questions intended to elicit more precise information—for example, whether the child had been born before or after the last coffee harvest—brought the most fantastic replies. One little boy who was already able to talk was supposed to be only three months old, a baby of about six months was described as two years old, and so forth. The only exception to this general uncertainty was a baby from the Assoua court who was born while we were in Bébou.

The finer points of emotional interchanges in the dialogue between mother and infant (137) show up more clearly in our movies than in the records of our direct observations.

Infancy up to Weaning (during the Second Year of Life)

Direct observation of a number of infants revealed surprisingly small variations in the behavior of the mothers. Throughout infancy, the child stays close to his mother. At night he sleeps naked next to her naked body on a mat or bed, the two of them covered by the same cotton blanket. During the day the mother carries him on her back, wrapped in a shawl that she fastens across her breast. The baby is almost always dressed in a clean cotton undershirt like the ones babies wear in Europe, except when he has soiled it and there happens to be no fresh one available. The babies and toddlers of extremely poor mothers are often completely naked.

When nursing her baby, the mother sits on a low stool or on a door-sill. She lays the child across her lap, supporting his head with her left hand, or places him so that his head rests on her thigh, as on a pillow. Then she leans forward slightly until her breast—pendulous even after the first child—is within reach of the baby's mouth. In this position the baby is unable to see his mother's face while he is sucking, and the mother usually looks straight ahead, only rarely glancing briefly at the child's face (in one typical case, for example, only five times during an entire hour of sitting undisturbed with the baby on her lap, with three nursing periods).

Older babies sometimes sit on the mother's thighs while nursing and lift her breast to their mouths as if it were a bottle; still older ones occasionally stand between the mother's legs and hold her breast in both hands.

The mother often helps a smaller baby find the breast by holding it close to his mouth, frequently taking hold of the nipple with two or three fingers and massaging the milk into the sucking mouth.

The mother never directs a single word to the baby, nor does she react to any sounds he may make. Not until near the end of his first year of life does she begin to address a few unemotional words to him—and even then only rarely. She does, however, examine his skin frequently, scratching away rough spots with her fingernail, clean the corners of his

eyes, his nose, and his navel with the tip of her finger, smooth away
dirt or dampness with her palm, and comb through his hair with her
fingers. And during the long hours that they spend dreaming in the
shade with their babies, the mothers also busy themselves with their
own bodies. Staring depressively at nothing, they massage their
breasts, scratch themselves, brush the dust from the soles of their feet,
moisten their lips, spit, smooth their hair and their hip-cloths.

Unless it is prevented by some unusual circumstance, mothers nurse
their babies at irregular intervals, one to three times an hour during the
day, for about one to five minutes each time, and apparently several
times during the night, without entirely waking. Usually the mother
starts her preparations for nursing (arranging the baby in the proper
position, freeing her breast) before the observer is aware of any signal
on the part of the child. Occasionally there may be some slight bodily
restlessness; very rarely the baby may make a sound. Only under very
unusual conditions and only once during the normal daily routine did
we ever hear a baby under nine months old cry. Sometimes toward the
end of the first year of life, babies scream and cry in anger and defiance,
like Suzanne's Syrien and older infants, but they are soon distracted
and soothed by their mothers.

The most frequent act in the grooming process is the bath, very thorough in the early forenoon and somewhat more superficial in the afternoon; on hot days babies are bathed in between as well, just to cool and
refresh them. During this very complicated procedure, the mother's
expression remains unchanged—either grave or sad. Her movements
are graceful, skillful, gentle but firm.

The following is an excerpt from our records:

Hangar woman, Yosso, twenty-five years old; 25 January 1966, 8:45–
9:35 A.M.

Children: one six-year-old girl, one three-year-old girl, one two-
month-old, healthy-looking baby; toward the end of the observation
period, four female visitors between the ages of twelve and seventeen, the oldest with a baby on her back.

The mother is bathing the two-month-old baby under the projecting roof of the hangar. She is sitting on a stool and has already laid
out everything she will need; a large basin to the right behind her,
with powder, towels, kaolin, soap, etc. In front of her is a basin filled
with soapy water, and under her knees one with clear water. The
three-year-old girl is playing quietly behind her; the six-year-old
comes and goes.

The mother, dressed in a hip-cloth, holds the baby on her bare
knees, her left hand steadily supporting his head and shoulders.
Very patiently, her movements gentle but firm, she takes one object
after the other from the basin behind her and bathes him, going
through the following steps: (1) removes baby's clothes (undershirt),

places clean towel across her knees and lays baby on it; (2) washes baby with clear water; (3) soaps and rinses baby step by step, always beginning with the front of the body, then the head, particularly the face, using fresh water; washes the baby's genitals, but no more thoroughly than the rest of his body; (4) dries baby; (5) takes kaolin in her right hand—after having had to rummage for it for approximately three minutes among the other objects in the basin—and crumbles it finely; rubs baby's entire body, including face, with kaolin; (6) after patting the kaolin dry with her fingertips, rubs the baby's body with shea butter (vegetable fat); (7) dusts baby's body, excluding face, with baby powder; (8) tells the six-year-old girl standing behind her to bring a clean shirt from the clothesline; (9) turns the baby over, dresses him carefully, pulling the shirt over his arms and fastening it with safety pins that she takes from the basin, then turning the baby over on his stomach and tucking in the shirt behind; (10) carefully combs the baby's very abundant hair with a European comb, up over the ears and back.

During the entire time the mother has glanced over at me perhaps four or five times for about five to ten seconds, giving me a smile and then going on with her task without paying any further attention to me. The baby does not smile or look fixedly at anyone or anything, and he never once looks up into his mother's face.

Just as the bath is over, four young girls appear on the scene. That is, one of them has a baby on her back, probably her own, and so is really a woman.

At this point the three-year-old who had been playing behind her mother begins to fuss and scream. Her mother picks her up with one arm and places her on her back, tying her fast like a baby, then gathers up the things she has brought with her for the bath, moving a bit more energetically than is necessary. The little girl calms down after about twenty seconds. The mother keeps her on her back. The mother's expression remains calm.

In the meantime the girl has put the baby in my arms, and I rock him gently. After about three minutes I give him back. Another girl takes him in her arms, strokes his hair and rocks him. I leave. The girls laugh, and the mother nods to me.

The two-month-old baby did not cry once; he only fussed a little when he was having his nose cleaned. The mother did not smile at her baby a single time, yet she handled him so skillfully that he stretched and squirmed with pleasure throughout the entire procedure. The baby displayed a spontaneous Babinski reflex.

After the sixth step (above), before the mother starts looking for the shea butter, she places the baby at her left breast and lets him suck for two and a half minutes till he turns away and begins to squirm. Then the grooming process continues.

I had not noticed anything to indicate that the baby wanted the breast, except perhaps that his squirming may have become a bit more active.

The three-year-old girl was quiet the whole time until the mother had finished bathing the baby. Then she began to fuss, whereupon the mother picked her up immediately (after ten seconds), without speaking a word to her.

The six-year-old interrupts her play immediately when the mother tells her, in a low voice, to bring the baby's shirt from the clothesline. First she brings the shirt, then, after a few minutes and without waiting to be told, she goes and gets the baby's panties as soon as the mother has finished the complicated business of putting on the shirt.

If a baby soils itself, the mother wipes it clean. Usually she notices in time when the baby is about to defecate and holds it out away from her. All children, from their very earliest days, are given enemas once or twice a day (see section on toddlers).

Though a shirt and panties are considered a luxury, a string of beads worn around the belly of the girls and as an anklet, necklace, or around the chest of the boys is almost mandatory; the beads are not removed when the child is bathed.

As long as she is nursing her baby, the mother works as little as possible; if she lives in a compound where there are many women, she can devote almost her entire day to the baby. If she happens to be the only young woman in the compound, however, she has to perform her usual tasks—including fetching water and kindling and going out to the fields to get food—and has little time for the baby.

Some mothers carry their babies on their backs the whole time they are working. But most give the baby to some other woman when it gets in the way, especially when they are engaged in heavy work, and leave it at home when they go out to the plantations. This means that the baby, who ordinarily can nurse whenever it feels the urge, often has to wait several hours between feedings.

Only once did we see a nursing mother simply place her nine-month-old baby on the ground and go away. A young man had appeared with whom she felt like flirting. She interrupted her work right in the middle of drying the baby after its bath, told a girl to clear a place on the ground, and did not even look back at the happily crawling baby.

It is customary for the mothers to place their babies in the arms of any female visitor. Women who do not happen to be nursing a baby at the moment often borrow one "for show," to stroll proudly through the streets with it, or to take it along when they pay a visit. These substitute mothers behave differently from the nursing mothers; they play with the baby, give it objects to hold, rock it, and even talk to it. When the baby demands the breast and refuses to be distracted, they invariably try to let it suck at their own dry breasts. When the baby starts to howl and insists upon being nursed, the real mother sometimes reacts at once; on other occasions, though, the same mother may let the baby cry for as long as ten minutes before she gives him her breast.

Substitute mothers handle a baby in much the same way as a young European mother does. But they too are extremely chary of verbal communication and tend to play rather roughly (throwing the baby into the air and catching it, holding it by the legs and whirling it around) until the baby starts to scream, whereupon all those present—including its real mother—usually laugh loudly.

The nursing mother herself displays quite a different attitude toward her baby, one that seems very strange to us. Until the child is about nine months old, the mother almost never plays with it, smiles at it, praises or scolds it, or even talks to it. Even when the babies are older such forms of communication are observed only rarely. This is particularly striking when an older baby has just been playing and prattling with a substitute mother and then reverts to nonmimic and nonverbal dialogue with the real mother.

While nursing, the babies do not gaze fixedly at the mother's face until they are old enough to suck sitting up in her lap, that is, after they are about nine months of age. And even then they very seldom smile at her or communicate with her by sounds, except when they cry or howl.

In summary, three points should be emphasized: (1) Within the framework of the details described above, the relationship between mother and infant seems to be undisturbed. (2) Whenever a baby appears on the scene, it automatically becomes an object of intense emotional interest to the adults present, though this interest suddenly subsides after a shorter or longer interval. (3) The preverbal dialogue with the mother develops according to different rules and is made up of different elements than with Western children. Anyi children obviously learn certain forms of communication (gazing fixedly at someone's face, smiling, playing, exchanging sounds) with persons other than the mother. The maturation of these behavior modalities does not seem to take place any later than in European children (insofar as the uncertainty in the estimated ages permits a comparison).

Children of both sexes and all ages enjoy handling a baby and in fact are usually gentler with it than adults are; toddlers are gentlest of all. The men show just as much interest in a baby as the women and handle it in much the same way, but for shorter periods. The fathers have a habit of grabbing a baby suddenly, tossing it about in a well-intentioned but rather rough game, then passing it on to the next adult.

When the baby is a bit older, it is the mother who gives it supplementary nourishment, in a manner as casual as it is skillful—a sip of water before nursing, or a few little balls of cooked rice.

The mother encourages the child to use its body at an early date, helping it to crawl, to stand erect, and so on, as we observed with Suzanne and Syrien. During the baby's very first months, the mother helps it to practice sitting up (with support).

Toddlers (from Weaning, during the Second Year, to the Age of Five or Six)

Weaning marks a drastic turning point in the life of the Anyi child; it takes place "as soon as the baby is able to walk well." Thus it may be postponed until this stage is reached. The three children in whom we observed the process of weaning were approximately one and one-half years old, could walk well erectly, and were more or less accustomed to supplementary foods.

The toddler no longer sleeps at its mother's side at night, but sleeps with other children in the same or an adjoining room. During the day the mother limits her attentions to the child to the "necessary" minimum and—like all other adults—has withdrawn from it emotionally. One can say that children of this age live in the compound, in the same environment as their mothers, but take no part in the life of the group.

One of our observation reports (15 February 1966, in the compound of the Boa, Erneste, in Yosso, from 9:45 to 11:35 A.M.) deals with the busy activity in the courtyard during the forenoon. There is one infant of five months, from time to time another one about eight months old is in evidence, then a three-year-old boy and two girls of about four and a half, a boy of six, one of seven, and—during the entire observation period—three adults. Counting visitors who come and go, there are never fewer than eight, occasionally as many as fifteen persons in the courtyard. All the adults, except for one teenage boy, busy themselves with the infants intensively and with obvious emotional engagement, for periods of varying duration. As regards the toddlers, our notes report the following:

> During the entire period not a single person spoke to any of the children who were between three and four and a half. Now and then, when they felt like it, they tried to help with the preparation of the plantain mash and were pushed out of the way once or twice, but basically no one took any real notice of them. It was only at the end of the period, when I asked which child belonged to whom, that Marguerite seized her four-and-a-half-year-old girl by the hair and drew her to her side to indicate that this child belonged to the compound, while the others did not. None of the children exhibited visible signs of jealousy at the attention and care being lavished on the babies.

...The somewhat older children (six and seven years of age) are sometimes given orders, but no one seems to take the trouble to see that these are carried out. These children are already able to do most things independently; only the stranger François has to explain to them exactly what he wants them to do. One of the children asks his older brother for something to eat...who then tells him where he can find some food....

...Even this peaceful scene makes it clear that children who are already weaned but not yet old enough to join in the play of others, in other words, those between one and a half and five years old are usually neglected and left to their own devices. For the older playmates are constantly running about, and the smaller ones cannot yet keep up with them. They live "at home," but no one pays any attention to them.

The mothers continue to provide for their bodily needs. They bring them food, or the children can scoop it out themselves with their hands from the pot in the kitchen or from the bowls of the adults. Only rarely does a mother help a child drink from a cup, and she never feeds him. More frequently, the older children try to help a little in this respect. Sometimes the children eat at the same time as the adults; otherwise they have no regular schedule for meals. They never refuse food when it is offered them.

The toddlers are still bathed by their mothers, but the mothers are no longer gentle—in fact they are often quite rough. The child stands in a basin, is soaped with scratchy palm fibers, and is rinsed off by having a bucket of water poured over him.

Commands and prohibitions are the most important verbal utterances that toddlers hear from their mothers and from the other adults. Until about the age of four, the commands are very short, often coupled with threats, and repeated in a loud voice. Later come more detailed instructions. Any older person has the right to order a small child about. If it refuses to do as it is told, it is frequently ignored, laughed at, ridiculed with scornful words, or sometimes even spanked by its mother or a substitute mother. If it cries, the only reaction it elicts is derision.

On several occasions we witnessed corporal punishment that can only be described as sadistic:

28 February 1966, compound Be, Bébou
A four-year-old girl is crying monotonously, her attitude obviously a mixture of resignation and defiance, and writhing about on the ground. A young woman (the sister of the child's mother) sits nearby, smiling, with a small stick in her hand, with which she strikes the child every ten to twenty seconds on the stomach, back, or buttocks. The child howls; the young woman smiles and keeps on hitting her. In the meantime, the aunt's baby is splashing in the

basin, trying to sit up, crowing happily. A twelve-year-old girl appears on the scene, drags the four-year-old to her feet, draws her to her side and puts her arm around her, thereby soothing her immediately. The other children present in the courtyard have shown no reaction whatsoever; they might as well have been deaf.

Fifteen minutes later, the young woman comes to pay us a visit, the freshly bathed baby on her hip and the four-year-old she had beaten clinging to her skirts; the little girl seems quite happy and shows no fear of us as strangers.

From their very earliest days, all the children are given enemas once or twice a day with a suspension of ground chili peppers. The instrument used is a rubber balloon with a hard-rubber pipe attachment. Immediately after the enema has been administered, the baby is held between the mother's knees over a chamber pot; the toddlers are placed on chamber pots nearby, while the older children are expected to find their own spots to relieve themselves. The enema is followed immediately by a thorough bath.

Babies, whose first enemas contain only one ground chili pepper, writhe as if with colic, but they never protest or cry. After the child has been weaned, its behavior changes. By now the emetic suspension contains about six chili peppers and possibly a bit of grated ginger and herbs as well. The children await the procedure bent over, heads down, buttocks thrust out, hopping from one foot to the other, sometimes whining quietly. They do not try to run away, or go just a step or two, so that they can easily be caught again. The mother lays them belly-down on her lap. Usually they begin howling and kicking wildly. Another woman holds their legs still. Then, seated on the chamber pots, they no longer squirm about like the babies but press their hands to their bellies, cry, or stare silently straight ahead. During the baths that follow, they struggle and resist; the mothers handle them roughly and shout at them.

In later babyhood, most of the children experience brief fits of active protest and defiance, as did Syrien. During this period, their rages subside quickly; howling, they may throw sticks or stones at other children or at adults, but the only reaction is laughter. Usually this defiance becomes passive or dispairing; very often these children run off and hide.

The following is an excerpt from a report about the same three-year-old girl whose mother picked her up immediately when she started crying after her three-month-old brother had been bathed.

Hangar woman, Yosso, 17 March 1966, 6:55–7:55 A.M.

. . . the baby on her back, holding the three-year-old by the hand. The little girl does not see me; she is trying to pick up a bowl and can't quite manage it. Begins to weep monotonously, first softly, then more loudly. Withdraws into the bamboo shed. Sits down on the ground in a corner, her face turned to the wall and her legs stretched out in front of her.

During the whole hour the little girl remains sitting there, her body bent forward slightly, sometimes rocking rhythmically. In the beginning she weeps quietly to herself, stops after five minutes, but resumes her monotonous crying from time to time. The rocking movements and the weeping sometimes occur simultaneously, sometimes alternately. She makes no attempt to amuse herself by playing.

The mother, separated from her only by the bamboo slats, does not pay the slightest attention to the child the entire time; she does not look at her once or say a single word to her.

A young woman who comes in with her baby to visit with the mother glances through the slats into the shed and speaks a few derisive words to the child. No other attempt is made to rescue the little girl from her loneliness and despair.

This is in extreme contrast to the way the mothers behave toward their babies.

The infant (now four months old, being held by the visitor) starts to cry once for about two seconds but is immediately soothed when the visitor kisses it, pets it, helps it to sit up on her lap, rocks it in her arms, suckles it, or simply turns her face toward it.

Toddlers are afraid of strangers. One often sees them in strangely cramped, apparently catatonic positions, crouching, lying, or rocking back and forth in a corner, rhythmically rubbing or knocking their heads against a wall, either completely mute or crying monotonously.

When one approaches them, they run away. Some will let themselves be seized by the hand and dragged away by the others. When the mother picks up a child in this state—to have her picture taken with it, for instance—the child is immediately reassured and even begins to smile. The mother routinely holds her child like a madonna in a painting, not saying a word, her glance not resting on the child but directed beyond it, straight ahead. A stranger can soothe a child in this state just as easily; ordinarily it is the girls and boys in the latency age and the somewhat older girls who occupy themselves with these children. The adult women are usually scornful; the men show no interest whatsoever. Not infrequently, though, children in the phase of latency like to tease the smaller ones and enjoy making them so furious that they burst into tears. The quickest way to bring these children back to normal is to bathe them.

Some toddlers show signs of initiative and start playing, at first alone and then with other children. We often watched children of this age imitating adult activities, plantain mashing, for example, which seemed to calm them immediately. One small girl doing this was called away by her mother for her bath. She ran away and would not let herself be caught. Two minutes later she was bathing all alone in the basin her mother had prepared for her and had calmed down completely.

Now and then small children were dragged up to have a look at us, and—either just for the fun of it or for pedagogical reasons—the others would try to instill a fear of the white man in them; this always led to terror. On two occasions little girls were told that the white man would give them injections in the buttocks if they persisted in wetting their sleeping mats at night, and once a two-and-a-half-year-old boy was frightened with the threat that the white man would cut off his penis. These threats were repeated with graphic demonstrations until the children broke into paroxysms of terror, tore themselves away, and ran off crying rhythmically. These were the only methods of "toilet training" we ever observed.

When the mother of a toddler is nursing her latest infant, small children often stand around watching. They may caress the baby, act indifferent, or even strike or pinch it covertly. The mother pays no attention to the toddler unless it threatens or disturbs the infant. Then she screams at it, "Leave my baby alone!" and chases it away, sometimes throwing a stick at it.

Many such jealousy-frustrated children take to rocking or masturbating, both of which are routinely ignored by the adults.

Report on compound Assoua, 4 March 1966
The mother is holding her seven-month-old son on her lap. Several women and children present.

While I am speaking with the older schoolgirl who has brought the baby to its mother, the two-and-a-half-year-old sister of the baby crouches down in front of the mother, takes hold of her little brother's penis and plays with it, takes it into her mouth and sucks it.

The mother and her sister laugh and do nothing to stop her. The little girl seems to be sexually very excited. I have the impression that she is jealous and would like to be nursed herself.

Suddenly the little girl starts crying and demands something to eat. . . . They laugh at her a bit, then the mother brings a small bowl of *fufu* and sauce from the kitchen and gives it to her. The child clutches the little bowl greedily, sits down close by, and begins to eat clumsily with her fingers.

When a toddler who has been weaned annoys the adults by pestering them or crying too loudly, the mother often pulls it to her roughly and puts her nipple into its mouth—let it suck! Some children can be soothed by this method, and some start crying on purpose so that the mother will nurse them, but most of them have no desire for the breast and scream all the louder. They seem to be in a state of desperation. Sometimes, when a man picks them up, they feel for his nipples and try to suck.

There was hardly ever a moment, day or night, in our court (situated in the middle of the village) when we could not hear at least one small child crying bitterly. Among the children we observed regularly, there was not a single one whom we did not see at least once in a state of despairing loneliness or helpless defiance. In addition to the specific observations detailed here, of course, it must be borne in mind that the mothers by no means neglect the bodily care or the feeding of children of this age group, that most toddlers play undisturbed for hours every day with others of their own age or older, and that very often they eat their meals quietly and relatively independently, sometimes being helped by older siblings.

Conflicts that flare up in the absence of adults are much shorter in duration and rarely lead to serious withdrawal. Fighting and wrestling among boys and girls of the same age is common; as soon as adults—especially younger women—appear on the scene, they urge the fighters on, as at a cockfight. They are obviously very excited, and the fighting among the children becomes savage and stubborn.

The toddlers are happiest in a large, mixed group made up of many children; they become uneasy when their mothers are nearby; left alone, they often become despondent.

Latency (from the Fifth or Sixth Year to Puberty at Twelve to Fifteen Years)

There is a clear demarcation between the latency period and the age of the toddler. Though there are no social institutions specifically for them, since school attendance usually begins only at the age of eight or nine, and though there is no significant alteration in the adults' attitude toward them, the five- and six-year-olds embark on a new phase of life. At this period boys and girls form social groups according to sex, even though they still play, eat, sleep, and attend school together. After repeated attempts, rebuffs, withdrawals, and renewed attempts, the small boys gradually succeed in being accepted in the games of the older ones, the process being initiated and helped along by their increasing mastery in imitative activity. Sometime between their fifth and twelfth years, the boys of a village band together in cliques and groups, irrespective of the families and courts to which they belong. During the day they play together, but they still sleep with their parents or foster parents, very frequently in the parents' room until after puberty; otherwise the "brothers" may sleep in a separate room and the sisters with the women.

During this period the children impress the observer as being interested, alert, and receptive. Boys play a variety of quiet, active, and sometimes even wild group games (shooting marbles, soccer) and make toys for themselves with a fairly high degree of manual dexterity. Sometimes they go fishing or rat-hunting together, or collect sap for palm wine, and share their booty. In general they enjoy school, and their academic performance is good. They usually do their assignments in the evening under the supervision of one of the better pupils.

They take their meals irregularly, snatching a moment between games and eating in the courtyard. Some of them share the common meals of the women, who see that they mind their table manners, and here they often help feed the smaller children with surprising patience and gentleness. On the other hand, while one often sees them carrying babies around and petting them, just like the grown-ups, they also enjoy teasing the toddlers or laughing at them. At this stage they are able to take their daily baths without assistance, the mothers merely putting out soap and fresh clothing for them. By this time they have already developed an addiction to the daily enema. They cannot live without it, and if they do happen to skip one it is only because of childish carelessness. The following day, however, the need makes itself felt.

They perform the chores that can be expected of small boys in the household and on the plantations like adults, independently and without supervision. They carry out without protest the orders given them.

Thomas's eleven-year-old nephew leaves his playmates without a murmur to scratch his very inebriated great-uncle's back, though he obviously finds the task repugnant. It can also happen, though, that boys of this age do nothing they are told to but simply continue playing and refuse to let themselves be bothered by curses or threats. They are rarely punished for disobedience because they simply answer back and run away. This leads to dissension, which sometimes results in the child's going to live at another compound—leaving his parents, for example, and moving in with a grandmother or uncle.

The eleven-year-old son of the leading female shaman of Yosso has been living with a foster family in Bébou for two years in order to attend school here. One day he turns up at our car with his bundle in his hand.

He has decided to give up school and return to Yosso. His mother just happens (?) to be sitting in the car waiting for us to leave. A couple of playmates, two teenage boys and two men are trying to persuade the boy to give up his unreasonable plan. No one knows and no one cares what his reasons are for wanting to leave school and Bébou. He sits in the car, silent and defiant; when they try to pull him out by the arm, he holds fast. Finally his mother intervenes. Without turning around to the rear seat, where her son is sitting, and without raising her voice, she delivers a brief speech to the effect that her son will get nothing to eat from her and will not be permitted to sleep under her roof if he insists on having his way. He replies, "I don't care," then relapses into silence and rides to Yosso with us without his mother's addressing another word to him.

During quarrels of this kind, the Anyi sometimes treat their children like material possessions with no wills of their own, and sometimes treat them like adults. As a result, a dispute with a child is often handled like a dispute with any other responsible individual and is brought before a court of arbitration.

No matter how cheerful, lively, and healthy these groups of boys may seem at work or play, or how similar their activities and pranks are to those of somewhat neglected children in small towns in Europe, the picture is not yet complete. A trivial quarrel frequently leads to disproportionately intense rage, mortification, and withdrawal. The weaker boy withdraws from the group, sobbing monotonously to himself between recurring helpless fits of rage, very like a toddler. Sometimes he recovers his equilibrium quickly, sometimes he is able to return to the group games after a few days, and sometimes he remains permanently isolated. We never observed that a group of boys deliberately ostracized or expelled one of its members; it was always the offended boy who withdrew voluntarily.

One often encounters boys of this age group playing alone. One boy made himself a very neat little cooking area, like the ones the women use. When Madame comes to admire his work, he destroys it and sits there in deep depression. An undernourished seven-year-old boy who has been living next door to us for some time with his mother and an older sister comes staggering into our courtyard and throws himself down on a bench in the unbearably hot sun, assuming the strangely contorted position often observed in catatonics. His eyes are closed, and he does not reply to our questions. After about ten minutes his mother appears and seizes him by the arm. Resisting, he is dragged away.

The girls, like the boys, imitate the work of the women in the household. But with the girls this play gradually develops into useful work, while the boys soon begin to act as if they were above all this sort of activity. At an age when our children are still playing with dolls, Anyi girls are already taking care of their smaller siblings. We observed repeatedly that these spontaneous activities lead to an improvement in bodily skills and to a more active interest in the life of the community. Instructions given to the girls very often develop into personal conversations in which they ask questions freely, and the women—the older ones in particular—take time to talk with them instead of simply laughing at them. The life of a twelve-year-old girl is pretty much the same as that of an adult woman, and her position in the compound is much more firmly established than that of the boys. So far, though, her duties are not fixed. She is allowed to be lazy and play when she feels like it, then she helps for a while with household chores, without, however, ever receiving a word of praise for her work. In addition, the younger girls are still allowed to take part in the games of the boys; older girls have their own common play groups with which they do things outside the home (gathering snails, fishing). They obviously enjoy these activities and are extremely good at them.

In general it seems that children are reared in keeping with the needs of society. The girls develop a greater feeling of closeness to their mothers and sisters and perform their daily chores dependably, in accordance with their later role as custodians of the cohesion of the maternal lineage. Boys have to free themselves of their attachment to the maternal world, to change their identity, and to assert themselves in the outside world, that is, in the groups they form, with virtually no paternal example to follow. Later on, as adult men, they will have to be capable of acting independently. For the time being, however, they live in the paternal family (where they will not be permitted to remain) and not yet in the court of a maternal uncle. Their lack of ties within the family system can be attributed to the fact that, in reality, they belong nowhere.

The subsequent phase of development, however, does not lead directly to social integration. During school age, Anyi children go through a genuine period of latency, just like Western children. In other words, their infantile sexual exploration and certain sexual and aggressive activities do not entirely cease, but during this developmental phase they are no longer dictated—or at least only rarely, in exceptional cases and special circumstances—by the conflicts that characterize early childhood development. These conflicts, with the Anyi as with us, reemerge with even greater intensity at puberty.

Our direct observations show that the external behavior of children who were given away to a foster family does not differ from that of children of the same age who have remained with the real mother.

It should be emphasized once again that while direct observation does help us reconstruct the inner events of childhood, it does not permit direct conclusions about the development of psychological structures. Here, of course, we are at variance with the theories concerning the learning of culture-dependent behavior. We do not deny that social behavior is acquired during childhood. We maintain, however, that the outcome of the learning process, the molding of the individual, is determined by the outcome of conflicts that are for the most part unconscious; the content of what has been learned and the recurrence of exposure to specific experiences play only secondary roles.

Children in Our Medical Consultation Hours

Babies were frequently brought to us by their mothers, but sometimes by a grandmother, some other woman, or the father. Toddlers, on the other hand, were seldom accompanied by the mother; they were brought to us most often by an older sibling or some other person. Children of school age came alone. These were our first patients, and they came with festering sores on their arms or legs; first the little boys, usually in groups of two or three at a time—to help keep each other's courage up. As soon as they discovered that the sores stopped suppurating and healed over with our ointments and bandages, they brought us their younger sisters and other little girls. The girls were usually timid, some of them almost in tears, so that their brothers frequently had to drag them to Madame's dressing table and hold them still when they had to have an injection; the boys were just as delighted as their sisters when the ulcerated, swollen spots healed over.

The mothers were the exact opposite in communicativeness. When they brought in their babies, they would tell me, "It's runny" (i.e., it has diarrhea), "It's hot," or "It has a headache." This was supposed to mean that the baby was running a fever, because adults have headaches when they have malaria. It was practically impossible to elicit any further information. During examinations they handled their babies so stiffly and clumsily that they began to cry, though they could soon be soothed in the doctor's arms. Several times mothers brought us completely dehydrated, seriously ill babies with the laconic complaint that they had a sickness "here"—somewhere on the skin. This usually turned out to be an almost invisible pimple or an insect bite, so that we had the feeling the mothers had completely overlooked their babies' general condition. Nursing mothers could not even tell us whether the baby had had a feeding the same day. They felt their own breasts to see how full of milk they were.

Almost without exception the toddlers were terrified, kicking and screaming in desperation. They were treated roughly, shaken, shouted at, and pushed onto the table in positions that made examination impossible. The adults who happened to be present found it unnecessary and ridiculous when we tried to quiet a screaming child by talking to it and petting it, though it was surprisingly easy to do if the adults could be gotten out of the way. The persons entrusted with caring for the toddlers were usually not there. When we had them called to obtain more information on the course of the child's illness, they came only after long delays and acted as if they knew nothing at all about the child. They expected miraculous cures from injections, or at least from medicines; they seemed to be quite incapable of preparing for a sick child the diets we recommended, such as the rice that the villagers ate in any case.

Quite often we succeeded in bringing about informal group conversations, during which it became apparent that at least some of the persons caring for the children had observed their charges quite accurately. This impression was substantiated by the fact that the children brought to us for examination were usually really ill, except for a very few otherwise healthy children with minor skin ailments.

At the beginning of our stay we had gotten the impression that the mothers and other adults were extremely cold and indifferent toward the toddlers; toward the end, though, we concluded that they were denying their fears for the child and thus refusing to take a rational attitude toward the illness. Sometimes it was evident from the mother's behavior that she was furious at the thought that her child could reduce her to a state of helpless worry and fear; as a result, her aggression was directed toward the child and her skeptical expectations of a miraculous cure toward us.

The schoolchildren were almost the only patients who seemed sincerely overjoyed when we treated them successfully; they would come back to show us their healed injuries (or for treatment of new ones, which they regularly managed to acquire between visits) and were the only ones who ever expressed their thanks. Adults, including mothers whose children would have died without treatment, never showed us by a word or gesture that they were grateful for what we had done.

Childhood: Adult-Child Relationships
When your child pretends he is dying,
then act as if you were digging a grave.

Even today child mortality is high in Alangouan. This statement is based on estimates by the doctors in Abengourou; no statistics are available. Elisa says, "Last year thirty-five children in Bébou died of measles." In earlier decades the mortality must have been enormously high, as is evidenced by the present underpopulation and by the immigration of foreign laborers—and also by the countless women who have borne ten, twelve, or fifteen children and have managed to "keep" only one or two. There is also that mother in Yosso who has had twelve children and is considered unusually fortunate because six of them "have remained with her"; evidently she must possess a highly potent amulet.

The strange—and to us extremely unsettling—way Anyi mothers treat their children might perhaps be traced back to an unconsciously operating need, a need to do everything in their power to reduce the pain they know they will not be able to bear when—as is only to be expected—one child after another has to die.

There are known cases of contraception and abortion. Anyi men consider both to be criminal. Men and women are unanimous in their conviction that only a woman who has borne many children and lost them (through death) soon afterward could be capable of anything so perverse. For she probably thinks "Why should I always hope and hope in vain, when none of my children wants to stay with me?" According to an ancient belief of the Akan, children are not of this world. A newborn baby still belongs entirely to the world of the spirits. The mother does not start nursing the baby until a few days after its birth, when the baby itself demands the breast, thus signaling its desire to remain in this world. The naming of the baby by the father and his clan can be viewed as an attempt to detach it from the spirit world of the uterine lineage, to which it still belongs and to which it can return at any time. Another important step has been taken when the baby is able to sit up, which is why it is encouraged to do so as early as possible. Once its buttocks touch the earth, it has acquired a modicum of earthly posture. Adults are sedentary beings, and the symbol of the Akan kings is their stool.

When a child dies, the funeral rites are very simple; after all, it hadn't yet made up its mind whether it wanted to remain among the living.[1] Thus, when a small baby dies, it is buried just anywhere and its body is whipped to show that the adults have seen through its game and refuse to be led around by the nose; the spirit had only pretended that it wanted to stay in the world in the form of a child—in reality, from the very beginning all it wanted was to fool the living. Not until the pubic hair appears, indicating the onset of puberty, is a child regarded as being truly of this world. Physical maturity signifies its ability to contribute its share toward multiplying the kin. At this point the mother loses her child to the community, a child that she has never really perceived as a completely independent being.

During the nursing period the mother has developed a kind of physical union with the baby. If it should die, she would lose a part of herself—which can always be replaced by another child—and not a being whom she loves. Once the baby is weaned, she continues to feed and care for it, of course, but she treats it coldly, saying, "It's still too small, it can't run away." Apparently she has been able to avoid developing a close personal bond. In caring for the child, she is merely conforming with custom; she is responsible to her kin for preserving their property in the form of her child. The ritualized steps in caring for it give her a self-esteem that is not menaced by loss or separation anxiety. Suzanne, for example, can face with perfect equanimity the prospect of soon losing her adored Syrien to the manipulations of her kin.

There are two principles that govern dealings with children: one must see that the children remain alive, thereby ensuring the continued existence of the kin; and one must avoid the pain and grief of mourning.

These principles are abstractions, not the motivations of human behavior. The motivations themselves are more varied and more tangible than the half-forgotten Akan theology of the soul or the nonexistent statistics on infant mortality. Some important ones—to name just a few—are the recurring reality of the grief a mother feels at the death of her child, the danger of diseases that constantly threaten to snatch children from life, the struggles of the kin to obtain a better place in society, and their never-ending need for a larger labor force. Nevertheless, these principles ought to be kept in mind because they can help us to view psychological processes and given realities as a single complex.

Reference to the ancient wisdom preserved in proverbs and sayings is not sufficient for an understanding of the attitude of the Anyi toward their children. Prevailing opinions and value systems as well as personal experience often contradict social norms; direct observation and psychoanalytic interpretation provide additional aspects of "reality."

When the inhabitants of Bébou are asked what is meant by the saying "It's a misfortune to be a child," their usual reply is this: "That refers to the boys between seven and ten who don't yet go to school and whose parents don't look after them." Subjectively, toddlers are probably far more miserable than these freely roaming boys of school age. But the Anyi say that the toddlers are not yet intelligent enough to perceive their unhappiness. As the conversation continues, opinions become divided; the men maintain that the women neglect the children and spend their time on love affairs, while the women declare that the fathers do not provide adequately for their families and that the children are unhappy for this reason.

Even pregnancy is marked by a certain ambiguity of attitude on the part of the mother-to-be. Young girls are taken by surprise when they skip their period and assume that they are sick; they are not told the facts of life until they dare to ask their mothers or some other woman. Usually they wait so long that their pregnancy becomes visible. Many girls, and naturally all women who have borne a child, know very well that a baby is conceived during intercourse, that menstruation then ceases, and that a pregnancy lasts nine months. None of them, though, ever bothers to figure out her delivery date on the basis of this knowledge. Hypochondriac bodily sensations, the feeling that the belly is "heavy," and the decreasing desire for sexual intercourse tell her that the child will soon be born. She then begins to make preparations for the trip to the hospital in Abengourou.

From this point on, a kind of dual-track motivation becomes apparent. It is regarded as better to give birth in a hospital, even though this goes against custom and entails financial burdens. For at home in the village many women die of childbed fever and many newborn babies die of tetanus. The rationalization for preferring the hospital is rooted in the realm of magic; in the village there are too many witches, and they might kill the baby. It is considered wise for a girl who has just had her first child to go home to her mother to learn how to care for it. The conscious motivation is a phobic, hypochondriac fear that the young mother might be overcome by a feeling of weakness in her arms and might drop the baby and kill it if the mother were not there. One young mother, whom I had watched bathing a neighbor's baby carefully and efficiently just two weeks before she herself gave birth, was convinced that she would never be able to care for her own baby without instructions from her mother.

Nursing mothers regard themselves as instruments designed to satisfy all a baby's needs immediately and completely. They describe their own role as a passive one; it is the baby who wants, desires, needs—they themselves are merely appendages or executive organs to carry out its wishes. The act of nursing is invariably performed efficiently. Our psychoanalytic interpretation, however, is that the infant, regardless of sex, has the significance of a phallus for the mother; that is, it gives her a symbiotic feeling of completeness and, as a part of her own person, provides narcissistic sexual gratification. Although she was not aware of our assumptions, Dr. Kulka, a child psychiatrist in Santa Monica, wrote the following after having seen our movies of nursing scenes:

> I believe that these mothers . . . in spite of their intense and concentrated absorption in their babies, do not feel any motherly warmth or affection, but are using the nursing act for their own

sexual gratification. I saw very little of playing, laughing, or even just being happy with the baby in their faces, but chiefly their own satisfaction—in the baby's sucking at their phallus; and they themselves do the rest—as if they were only using the baby to carry out masculine masturbation. Even the bathing of the baby and the oiling of its skin seemed to me to be self-gratification; therefore, when the baby can no longer be used in this way, aggressive "treatment" takes over and the enema tube replaces the phallus.

During the first few months of life, the mother's dialogue—or rather monologue—with the child is characterized by a variety of communication modalities that do not require the presence of a partner or a demarcation of the object, but instead encourage the development of a vague symbiotic bond and primary identification. The mother sometimes continues dreamily to massage her nipple long after the baby has stopped sucking. In every activity—from smoothing and caring for the baby's skin to bathing it, administering enemas, dressing it in modern clothing, from skin eroticism to vanity—the mother can perceive the baby as a part of herself. The baby lends expression to her emotions, as we saw with Suzanne's son Syrien. The mother has temporarily lost her adult sexual needs.

Other forms of contact that create a distance and demand a partner (and thus gradually awaken in the baby an awareness of the mother as an object separate from itself), such as smiling or looking at it, or talking to it, are alien to the mother. Is she trying to avoid as long as possible cathecting this small being with object-oriented libido? Is she afraid of losing this satisfying, pleasure-giving part of herself and her body that she has finally discovered? Or has she already achieved separation, behind the immobile facade of her face, her eyes staring straight ahead into emptiness—is the child already a part of her fantasies, as a permanent possession that provides her with security against the anxieties of her loneliness?

It is the visitors—other women, girls, and men—who provide the baby with those communication modalities that the mother does not yet employ. Their interest in the baby is secondary narcissistic, in much the same way as we, too, are able to enjoy a bit of the childish and instinctual by identification when we play with a baby. For them the child is a part of their own past, of their prestige, a further multiplier of the kin, but not a part of the self or of the body image. They need have no fear of being maimed or castrated; the loss of the child would not affect them emotionally; they would be able to withdraw their cathexis without suffering too greatly.

The baby is weaned as soon as it is able to walk without assistance. The reason for weaning is often given as the potential danger of continued nursing to the health of the child. If it develops digestive troubles at this time or the mother is afraid it might become ill, this is taken as a sign that her milk is poisoned. Or the mother may feel that the time for weaning has come for other reasons; she may be pregnant again, and in that case her milk is certainly poisoned. Or she may feel a need for sexual intercourse, or have a feeling of weakness or emptiness after the menstrual period. In short, there is no place for the baby any more.

Loss anxieties, oral aggression, and reactive evasions prepare the way for the mother's decision, which—once taken—is put into practice with desperate suddenness. She may rub her nipples with sharp or bitter herbs, or cover them with adhesive tape. Since she is unable to deny her baby the breast if it insists on sucking in spite of these obstacles, she has no choice but to flee, to abandon the child and not to return until it has "forgotten" both her and the breast.

The sudden decision to wean a baby is not shaken by its obvious desire to keep on being nursed. After all, it can run around now; its place has become free for another.

What has happened is exactly the same thing as Margaret Mahler (124) describes in certain mothers of disturbed children in the United States:

> Many mothers, however, take the very first unaided steps of their toddler, who is, intrapsychically, by no means yet hatched, as heralding: "he is grown up now!" These mothers may be the ones who interpret the infant's signals according to whether they feel the child to be a continuation of themselves or a separate individual. Some tend to fail their fledgling, by "abandoning" him at this point, more or less precipitately and prematurely, to his own devices. They react with a kind of relative ridding mechanism to the traumatization of their own symbiotic needs. These needs have been highlighted by the fact that maturational pressure has both enabled and prompted the child, at the very beginning of the second year, to practice the new "state of self": physical separateness.

> When . . . a woman who feels herself castrated seeks to compensate for her lack with a "penis baby," the main cathectic energy will be directed to her representation of self, while object representations become less important. This will be substantiated in the behavior of such a mother; she will try her best to suppress all the child's attempts toward self-realization. [97]

The Anyi mother does not suppress her child; she is already expecting the next. Her narcissistic instinctual cathexes are not withdrawn entirely; instead, they change in a very specific fashion.

After weaning, that is, after the interruption of parasitic symbiosis (Mahler), oral urges acquire paranoiac overtones—the anxiety that a mother-witch may devour, poison, or sell the child. An effective defense against this anxiety is oral abandonment, which—in its external manifestation—feigns complete libido withdrawal. An Anyi mother nursing a baby may say to a slightly older sibling who is leaning over it, "Leave my child alone!" In other words—"The child who has been weaned is no longer 'my child'; I deny that it ever belonged to me, because then I've never lost it."

The mother expects to regain the penis she has lost when she has another child, either by her husband or, better yet, by a new lover (whose penis she has not yet taken). Finally, she replaces it as an anal penis in the form of the enema tube and of the now anal cathexis of the toddler. She declares: "I made it; it belongs to me" and, above all, "It's still too small to run away; why should I look after it?" Yet she does continue to take care of it, in anal fashion, and this finds dramatic expression in sadistic beatings.

The cathexis with phallic narcissistic libido is less apparent; it becomes evident when a mother wants to use her child for self-ornamentation and adopts a madonnalike pose before the camera, and when she continues skin care and skin eroticism while otherwise almost completely neglecting the child's mental and physical well-being. When a mother points reproachfully and full of concern to a blemish on the child's skin, which is supposed to be "beautiful" above all else, she reminds one of European youths at the age of puberty when they complain that their penises are too small. The mothers' evident pleasure in seeing their children masturbate (even though it may be only out of desperation) and their occasional shame at their own reaction no doubt go back to the same phallic identification.

Anal sadistic activities are probably the most important as a continuation of the dialogue with the child; in any case they are the most conspicuous.

Just when the West Africans learned to give themselves and their children enemas is unknown. The psychologist can provide a facile answer: as soon as they had found a way to calm hypochondriac anxieties by means of an active measure with passive goals. The medical historian will confirm that nowadays no European nation indulges so intensively in the enema cult as the Portuguese, that the Portuguese were the first to establish trading settlements along the Gulf of Guinea, and that they were just as ready to incorporate Negro customs into their repertoire of habits as the Negroes were to adopt theirs. It can also be pointed out that many West African peoples, particularly the Akan peoples in the rain-forest belt, make a habit of taking enemas—though few go to such extremes as the Anyi—and that all these peoples not only are threatened by the same tropical intestinal complaints, but also, as far as we know, show the same syndrome, namely hypochondria about the contents of their bowels, a belief in witches, and certain customs in connection with enemas. In earlier times, and even today in very remote villages, mothers administer enemas by taking the suspension of ground red chili peppers into their mouths and blowing it through a bamboo pipe inserted into the rectum. Adults were given their daily enemas by persons of the same sex; nowadays they do it themselves with a rubber syringe.

The conscious rationalization, namely that chili peppers protect against or cure intestinal ailments, is generally advanced, but without much conviction. There are many babies who suffer seriously from the enemas; in the Abengourou hospital alone, forty to fifty die each year of ileus as a result of overviolent cramps following enemas. In spite of this, the doctors have not succeeded in banishing this custom, which they regard as a dangerous superstition, from the wards of their hospitals. All Anyi are deeply concerned about the contents of their bowels and are constantly worrying about the composition of their feces. During our medical consultation hours, there was not a single male patient who failed to complain of the frequency—or lack of frequency—of his bowel movements and the consistency of his feces, and not a single woman who did not, in addition, mention her too rare or too frequent menstrual periods or complain of losing too much or too little blood.

The bond of hypochrondriac anxiety between mother and child seems to persist. The mother's inability to hold back with nursing until the baby shows signs of being hungry seems to have a sequel in her impatience to have it empty its bowels as soon as possible. Once or twice each day, after pedantic preliminaries, a latent tension is discharged in the orgiastic act of anal penetration. There are depressive women who have given up all other activity and who are no longer interested in sexual relations who spend the entire day lying in wait for children they can give an "injection" to. The mingled fear and pleasure with which toddlers wait for their enemas makes one think of the children of psychopathic parents in the Western world who have learned to expect a spanking as the only physical sign of parental attention. The adult Anyi who beg a white man to give them an injection even though they are convinced that he means to do them harm reflect a peculiar mixture of castration anxiety and passive instinctual desires.

During the child's "second eighteen months of life," during which it must develop its independence, withdraw from the symbiotic union with the mother, and ultimately become an entity in itself by imitating and identifying, the Anyi mother is neither an empathic tower of strength nor a partner for the child. In addition to passive anal violation, the child experiences stimulation of the anal erogenous zone; thus one can say that during this period anal penetration is the modality used by the mother to express her affection toward the child. For the rest, she leaves it up to the child to develop independence, to do whatever it feels like until it is "intelligent enough" to obey orders.

It struck us that Anyi children do not begin to talk any later than Western children. Our questions elicited the unanimous opinion that the children start talking of their own accord and then acquire a vocabulary through listening to instructions and commands. They learn to say "papa" and "mama" by hearing such commands as "bring these bowls to mama" or "go get papa's basket." Children who speak spontaneously to adults are extremely rare. It is probable that, in learning to talk, imitation and the primary identification with a function promote the acquisition of the faculty just as rapidly as interchanges and encouragement do in other cultures. The enormous vulnerability of the adults to speech disturbances, and the high esteem attached to the ability to speak well as an attribute characteristic of the great of this world may be simultaneously cause and effect of the fact that Anyi children, once "abandoned" by their mothers, obey as the recipients of orders and learn to speak without partners.

The restriction of the object relation with the mother to so few modalities during the toddler phase can be correlated, in our opinion, with two phenomena: with the relatively low incidence of envy of younger siblings, and with the conspicuous tendency of the children to drop even violent defiance reactions the moment the mother pays attention to them. The toddler does not envy the baby his mother's affection, but solely her nurturing functions; identification with the baby and autoerotic gratification can provide a substitute. Even passive defiance is weak in these children. To sustain stubborn defiance, a child needs a certain retentiveness, a certain ability to bide his time before taking action, and above all a constant object—not a person who immediately turns away with a scornful laugh the moment he is "naughty."

Scorn and mockery, poured on the heads of naughty, disobedient, despairing children repeatedly and without rhyme or reason, at the whim of some adult, are hardly suitable methods for rearing a child, although such experiences naturally leave their marks on a child's character. This attitude of scorn on the part of the adults seems to go back to a specific feeling of helplessness that overcomes them when commands and punishments prove ineffective.

The mother's practice of keeping a toddler quiet by thrusting her nipple into his mouth, even after she has managed to accomplish his weaning only by flight and the resultant traumatic separation, is a further expression of this feeling of helplessness. It never occurs to an Anyi mother to react actively instead—to give the child a tidbit or a kind word. François told us that he could remember taking his mother's breast in his mouth and biting it viciously when he was already old enough to go fishing alone on the Comoë River. His mother had struck him with a stick, but had not been able to make him let go of her breast. Some children reject this all too tardy attempt at oral seduction; others violate the mother who beats them and scolds them so scornfully and take revenge for her anal violation by sucking and biting.

A peculiar lack of closeness characterizes the parents' dealings with their children. A mother cannot expect her child to do something "because he loves her." She herself has renounced and evaded the libidinal cathexis that was so unbearably threatened. Nor can she appeal to a superego in her child, for in its structure she would find her own moral person in the guise of a commanding, punishing, and rewarding introject. When dependency and the fear of punishment prove ineffectual (as with the son of the female shaman), the mother turns away in scorn. The child reacts with narcissistic withdrawal accompanied by various regressive phenomena. For the moment parental authority has reached its limits. Not until the latency period, when identificatory ties have become stronger, when a clan conscience and a ritualized etiquette have become firmly established, and when mature understanding argues in favor of accommodation in accordance with the pleasure principle, can parents once again play an active role in rearing their children.

In these circumstances it is no wonder that chiefs often remove their favorite sons from the care of incompetent women even in infancy and bring them up themselves—as father and mother in one person—caring for them with affection and rearing them with strictness.

Social norms dictate, and a wealth of sayings and proverbs explain, how children ought to be dealt with, or rather how the deficiencies of a natural upbringing can be overcome; some of the parents in Bébou and Yosso try their hand at applying these guidelines with older children. Parents are supposed to be strict—"If a child is to succeed, he must not lie in a soft bed." A child must not feel that he is better than his parents—"When the calf of the leg grows longer than the thigh, that's a sickness," or "If a child behaves like an adult, it must suffer [the same punishment] as an adult."

The Anyi place their hopes on learning by imitation—"If you walk behind your father, you will learn to walk like him"—and by experience—"If a child wants to grasp a glowing ember, let him."

Anyone seeing the merry, independent little boys of Bébou at play or the busy little girls at their household chores or taking care of smaller children will probably agree with Ahoussi when he says: "The children here are not unhappy. On the contrary. Children are so foolish that they don't even know that they are unhappy."

5 The Life Cycle

Anoh Michel (Fritz Morgenthaler)

We had hardly established our headquarters in Bébou before the sick began coming to our compound and asking for medical help. We decided to hold fixed consultation hours. On the third day of our activity as doctors, we had to transfer a seriously ill middle-aged man to the hospital in Abengourou to be operated on for a strangulated hernia. The surgeon happened to be away, so the patient was taken to the capital, where he died during the night. This man belonged to the family of Anoh Michel.

A few days later Anoh Michel, a slender young man twenty years of age, came to our consulting hour. He complained of sleeping poorly and declared that he had been having bad dreams ever since his uncle's death. My impression was that he was a haunted, unhappy young man. He agreed to my proposal that he come to my tent for an hour every day and talk over his problems with me. During our stay in Bébou, I had fifty interviews with him.

When I tried to fix a time for our first talk, he told me that he could not come that day because he had arranged to meet Thomas Assoua. He explained that Thomas and he were friends and that they also worked together. Later I found out that Anoh Michel had not had an appointment with Thomas at all, and I assumed that he had invented it as an excuse out of fear of becoming involved with me.

Our first interview took place two days later. Anoh Michel reported that he had had no further nightmares and was feeling better. It turned out that in the meantime Thomas had been called upon to explain to Anoh Michel's mother just what the white man wanted with her son. Only after his mother had given her consent could Anoh Michel come to talk with me.

Thomas acted as our go-between. He had been the first villager to declare himself willing to talk with me an hour every day in my tent. Anoh Michel was a member of Thomas's work party. There were four of them in all, all of them quick and reliable workers. Even before I met Anoh Michel, I had made the acquaintance of the other two, Etienne Lazare and Bléou Boni. I had begun interviews with both of them before I found out that they planned to leave the village and would be away for some time. The four friends were accustomed to working as a team, one or two days on one's plantation, then a day or two on the plantation of the next. Almost three months before our arrival in Bébou, Thomas, Etienne, and Bléou had begun going out to work alone more and more frequently, while Anoh Michel stayed at home. Something had gone wrong in his relations with his friends. He seemed depressed over this and could not understand—or so he told me—why Thomas wanted no more to do with him. When Etienne Lazare and Bléou Boni then started moving from village to village with their pest-control equipment to earn extra money, it became more and more obvious that Thomas was deliberately avoiding Anoh Michel. He now preferred to go out to work alone on his plantation.

Since Thomas came to my tent regularly and had also done a great deal to dispel the villagers' distrust of us, Anoh Michel was now trying to establish contact with me in order to get closer to Thomas. A new group emerged in which I, too, began to play a role.

During the first six sessions it became clear to me that Anoh Michel had difficulty in feeling that he was an Anyi. From this standpoint he welcomed the contact with me, for he found himself better able to display the traits of the Anyi personality in the presence of a stranger. He played them all through, one after the other, and enjoyed himself tremendously in the process. This is the way things began:

Anoh Michel: I'm thinking of my uncle, the one that died.
Morgenthaler: Were you fond of your uncle?

Anoh Michel: My uncle belonged to our family. He always said that he was going out into the forest to work, then he would take a sleeping mat under his arm and disappear. My uncle never worked. Out in the forest he would lie on his mat next to a palm that had been chopped down and drink palm wine. Evenings he would come home drunk . . . . I don't drink. I go to work on the plantation with my mother. I don't earn anything, so I don't have anything. I'm always the one that gives, I never get anything.

My question about what it was that he was always giving led to a conversation in which it transpired that Anoh Michel had worked last year for a wealthy Anyi in the village. After the crop had been harvested and sold, Bra—the rich man—was supposed to pay him. Bra refused to pay him and demanded additional work, telling him to clear the fields of weeds. Anoh Michel was indignant and complained bitterly about Bra, who—Anoh Michel says—sits around in the village doing nothing the whole day. All the immigrant workers employed by Bra had received their wages, and Anoh Michel was the only one who was paid nothing—as usual.

Anoh Michel: I had a special agreement with Bra, but there was nothing in it about having to clear the fields before I could get my wages. My mother negotiated with Bra for me; she's always present when we discuss wages.
Morgenthaler: What kind of arrangement did you have with Bra?
Anoh Michel: I stood there and listened, then I left. That was all.
Morgenthaler: And what are you going to do now?
Anoh Michel: Nothing. Wait and see whether Bra pays me. If he doesn't want to pay me, he doesn't have to. Maybe I'll be sick tomorrow. Then I can't go to work anyway. And if I do go out to the plantation, I can always cut my leg with the bushwhacker so that it bleeds and I can't go on working. I don't care one way or the other. If I get sick or hurt myself, then Bra can keep his money. I never have any money, and I never get any either. I'm always the one that gives.

With these words, Anoh Michel is trying to prove that he is a true and worthy Anyi. In the proud feeling that he is not dependent on the benevolent gesture of another Anyi, he intended to wait and do nothing. This posture was more important to him than the trifling remuneration that any laborer, even a foreign one, is—quite rightly—entitled to. But Anoh Michel's indignation at the wealthy plantation owner was directed less at the envied person of Monsieur Bra than at me. For with me Anoh Michel was a foreign laborer of a very special kind. He had already attached himself to me. The greedy desire to get as much as possible had made itself felt, and the inclination to react with disappointment was great. Anoh Michel was not consciously aware of the conflict with me; he was acting it out in his relationship to Bra. The memory of his mother's having helped him last year in the negotiations with Bra calmed him. He himself was well out of it. The only thing that seemed to bother him was that now something was being demanded of him once again. He tried to appear indifferent and managed to get out of the unpleasant situation with the help of fantasies in which he inflicted injuries on himself. Afterward he lay on the cot, relaxed and cheerful, and said at the end of the session:

Anoh Michel: This evening I'm going to see Bra with my mother. She'll talk to him. She'll explain everything, and then he'll pay me my wages.

[He laughed. And at the beginning of our next interview the following day he was still in a cheerful mood. Dreamily and aimlessly he relaxed on the cot, in the same way perhaps as his deceased uncle, who used to spend his days lying under the trees in the forest.]
Morgenthaler: Did you speak with Bra? Is everything settled now?
Anoh Michel: We were there. My mother talked with him for a long time, but she couldn't change his mind. He still insists on what he demanded.

[Pause.]

It would be best if I went away. I could earn money more easily somewhere else. Then if I came back and had a lot of money, all the people in the village would respect me. And my wife would be satisfied. I could buy her anything she wanted.

[Pause.]

Here in Bébou you can't earn anything. You work all the time and still you don't have anything.

Anoh Michel was now downcast. He recovered quickly, though, and told me that he had been having a foreign laborer build a house for him. Now the house was finished, and the man was demanding his wages. But since he had nothing himself, Anoh Michel couldn't pay the laborer. This provided a new reason to complain about Bra. It was pointless to start with the work, said Anoh Michel; it would take him two weeks to finish. This was greatly exaggerated. But he insisted that there was no point to anything, no matter what you did, no one took you seriously.

Anoh Michel: Give me some pills. I feel sick.
[The following day, his sickness completely forgotten, Anoh Michel appeared in a happy mood.]
Anoh Michel: Yesterday evening I received some money I hadn't expected—2,500 francs. Last year I worked for somebody who hadn't yet paid me. Yesterday this man sold his coffee crop. Then he came to me and brought me the money. I gave it to my mother right away. Now I can pay the man who built my house at least part of his wages. I'll owe him the rest.

Anoh Michel turned the money over to his mother immediately. This act was in keeping with the traditional custom. This is what an Anyi does. For the moment this aspect is more important than that reflecting the infantile need to remain dependent on the mother. The act becomes ego-syntonic through institutionalization of the infantile need.

Anoh Michel: It would be dangerous to keep the money in my pocket. I might lose it. Somebody might steal it out of my pocket. When you have money, you're all too easily tempted to go into a store and buy something good to eat. Or I might run into somebody who asks me to lend him some money. And if I had it in my pocket, I would have to give it to him. So it's better for my mother to keep the money at home.

At this point we were interrupted. A man standing at the fence in front of the tent spoke to Anoh Michel. It was the immigrant worker who had built Anoh Michel's house and now insisted upon being paid his wages.

Anoh Michel: I have to go with this man to see my mother. He wants his wages.
Morgenthaler: Tell the man to wait until our hour is up.
Anoh Michel: He doesn't want to wait.
Morgenthaler: He can go alone to your mother. She has your money and she can pay him.
Anoh Michel: But you can't just pay out money like that. There always has to be a witness; otherwise the man could come back later and claim that I hadn't paid him.
Morgenthaler: Oh, then your mother will be a witness that you have paid him?
Anoh Michel: No. My mother will pay him the money, and I will be the witness.

Anoh Michel had the luck of the Anyi. Just at the right moment a man who had owed him money for a year turned up unexpectedly and paid him. And then, to make things perfect, the foreign laborer appeared with his demands at the fence surrounding the tent in which we were sitting. Anoh Michel was now in the same position as Monsieur Bra, and he was obviously enjoying the role.

Morgenthaler: Your mother takes care of everything for you. She deals with Bra, she keeps your money for you, and she pays your laborer. You're only the witness and don't have to get involved personally.
Anoh Michel: I have no father. He died when I was still very small. So my mother took care of everything and I have become what she wanted me to be. When you have a father, then you become a little like him. You watch what he does and then you do it too. But if you

don't have a father, you do everything your mother tells you and you become like her.

Morgenthaler: You say your father died when you were very small?

Anoh Michel: Yes, he died . . . . When my uncle died, the one you took to the hospital, I felt sick. There were too many thoughts in my head. At night I couldn't sleep.

Morgenthaler: What were those thoughts that were bothering you?

Anoh Michel: Every night I dreamed. Now, since I've been coming to you, I don't dream any more.

Morgenthaler: And what did you dream?

Anoh Michel: Terrible things.

Morgenthaler: What things?

Anoh Michel: That I was out in the forest. Three black cows were grazing there. When I caught sight of them, all three looked at me at the same time and started chasing me. I was scared and ran away. I got to the river and jumped into the water, but the cows were coming after me. Then my wife woke me up and asked what was the matter with me. She said I had cried out in my sleep. I didn't remember crying out.

[Pause.]

Or something else—I was somewhere and I saw a lot of people. They all rushed at me to hit me. I couldn't do anything. I tried to run, but I couldn't. Finally I flew away—yes, I did, Monsieur—I flew away like a bird. That's possible in a dream.

When he came to the end of his dream, Anoh Michel was excited and almost reproachful. He had tried to find his lost father in me, to bring back his dead uncle. After he had finished relating his dream, he mentioned that Thomas had suggested for the first time in months that they should work together again.

Anoh Michel: When Thomas asked me whether we could work together again, I thought for a moment that I would refuse. But then I said I would.

The next day Anoh Michel came to me after he and Thomas had been out working. He was exhausted and felt ill. At the same time he announced that he intended to go away for a few days on a trip.

The funeral rites for old Assoua were soon to take place, and on this occasion Thomas was to be appointed head of the family. The entire village could talk of nothing else. The festivities had been scheduled for after the coffee and cocoa harvests, because at this season the villagers always have a little money on hand. Anoh Michel is Thomas's brother-in-law, since his wife belongs to the Assoua family. In these circumstances he well knew that certain demands he was unable to meet would be made upon him at the ceremonies. There had already been two Assoua funerals at which Anoh Michel had had to plead insolvency. On the last occasion old Assoua had said to his son Thomas, "Anoh Michel will have to pay at my funeral ceremonies; otherwise misfortune will befall the family." Anoh Michel knew that Thomas would take his father's words seriously. He wanted to borrow money somewhere outside the village and then hire out as a plantation worker for the following year. This was the external motivation for his trip.

Three days later Anoh Michel returned to Bébou. He was bright and cheerful. He had run into acquaintances everywhere he had been.

Anoh Michel: I met a friend in Bokakoré. He comes from Bébou. Last year he was so deeply in debt that he borrowed ten thousand francs from a woman in Bokakoré. Then he moved there and worked on the woman's plantation. He has just earned thirty thousand francs harvesting coffee. You can earn a lot of money outside Bébou.

Morgenthaler: Does your friend intend to stay in Bokakoré?

Anoh Michel: No, he'd rather come back to Bébou. I've come back without any money. Yes, I went away because I didn't know what to do.

Morgenthaler: Why did you go away?

Anoh Michel: I don't know.

Morgenthaler: I think you simply had to go away, to get rid of Thomas and of me, too.

Anoh Michel: Thomas is mad at me now. He won't speak to me. I've heard that he complained because I didn't say good-bye to him when I left on my trip.

[Pause.]

That's always the way it is. All my friends desert me.

Morgenthaler: But you were the one who went away and left Thomas.

Anoh Michel: I have to go now. The nets are still in the river and I have to pick them up before it gets dark. I'm afraid to be out in the forest alone after dark.

[Pause.]

There are still pygmies out there—those little jungle men with long hair down over their shoulders. They're very dangerous. If you meet them, you're unable to speak. They have herds of antelopes, and they split their ears—that's the way they mark the animals that belong to them, so that they can always recognize them. The pygmies sleep in holes in the ground with the snakes. If one of them catches you, he gives you a thrashing or marks you in some way. Then you're like a tame animal and you can't think any more. You have no brain, just a tiny one. You have to follow the pygmy's signal. He lures you into a hole, and when you're sitting in the hole, then a lot of pygmies come and beat you. They beat you to death.

Morgenthaler: That's what you were dreaming of recently, when you flew away like a bird.

[Anoh Michel's tenseness relaxed immediately. He laughed and was delighted to see that I had remembered his dream.]

Anoh Michel: You never know where they are, these pygmies. Nobody goes out into the forest at night, everybody is in the village. When I'm alone in the forest and hear footsteps . . . who can it be? It must be a pygmy.

Morgenthaler: It could be someone taking a walk in the forest in the evening—a white man, for instance. It could be me.

[A few days before, my wife and I had gone for a walk in the forest one evening. The whole village knew about it.]

Morgenthaler: You're afraid of me and you're scared of being pursued by me the way the pygmies pursue you. You expect me to reproach you for having run away.

Anoh Michel: I'm not afraid of you, but there's nothing I can do about Thomas. He won't say hello to me, and he won't talk to me any more. I'll ask someone to give him my apologies.

In cases like this the Anyi custom is to ask a mediator to take the preliminary steps toward a reconciliation. Thomas's annoyance with Anoh Michel had brought about a relaxation in transference. Now Anoh Michel was more afraid of Thomas than of me. Thomas had become a powerful, threatening figure, because Anoh Michel dreaded the coming funeral festivities.

Anoh Michel: I've had a quarrel with my wife, too. She reproached me with all sorts of things. She wants to leave me.

[It turned out that Anoh Michel had hidden from his wife and gone to bed early when he returned from his trip.]

Anoh Michel: When my wife came home, I pretended to be asleep. She waited a little while, then she began to heap reproaches on me, in the middle of the night.

Morgenthaler: In reality, it is you who would like your wife to go away.

Anoh Michel [laughing]: Yes, that's right.

Morgenthaler: You pretended to be asleep so that you wouldn't have to have intercourse with your wife.

Anoh Michel: I had the feeling that I wouldn't be able to. And then I thought it was better not even to try.

Morgenthaler: Your wife sensed that you didn't want to sleep with her. That was the reason for her reproaches and for her wanting to leave you.

Anoh Michel: You've just expressed it exactly.

[Our hour was up. We stood up and went out of the tent to say good-bye.]

Anoh Michel: Right now I feel something in my buttocks. It's as if you had given me an injection.

Anoh Michel had been afraid of Thomas and the dignitaries. He left the village and, when he came back, talked about the pygmies that pursue people. Then he hid from his wife and was afraid of her. After we had talked about his fears, he adopted a passive, homosexual attitude toward me. Now he was trustful and confiding and found pleasure in the thought of my giving him an injection.

The following day his apprehensions concerning the approaching funeral ceremonies had increased. Thomas was no longer speaking to him. The relationship between the two friends had been broken off almost entirely.

Anoh Michel: I won't be able to pay anything when they collect the contributions. I have nothing, but it's not my fault that I don't have anything. How could I be expected to change things. My grandfather and I . . . that's impossible.

Morgenthaler: Do you mean Tanoh Ane, the old man who owns the court where you live with your sister and your mother?

Anoh Michel: Yes, Tanoh Ane. He was good to me when I was little. Later he even sent me to school in Abengourou. I was always near the top of the class, and my grandfather sent money regularly. Then came the year 1962, and Tanoh Ane stopped sending money. First I tried to find work, but I had no luck. Then I came back to Bébou. Grandfather wanted nothing more to do with me, and that's the way things have remained up to today. When he has a job to be done, he'd rather hire a stranger than me.

[Pause.]

At night, when I'm alone and can't sleep, I start to cry and feel absolutely miserable. They've ruined my life. Why did they send me to school? Why did they let me think that I would be able to go on to college and get on in life as an educated man? It would have been better if they hadn't sent me to school at all. I would have become a planter, and today I would have a big plantation of my own here in Bébou. I'd earn a lot of money with my crops. But no . . . they sent me to school until . . . yes, until I'm now so old that everything is ruined. I have nothing. It takes years for a plantation to start paying. A while ago, when I went out there, I saw that all the cocoa slips I planted two years ago are dead. This year was too dry. They all died.

[Pause.]

And what kind of figure will I cut now at the funeral ceremonies, without any money? They'll all point their fingers at me.

But no one pointed his finger at Anoh Michel two days later, when the ceremonies took place.

For on this day he appeared in European dress—a white shirt and long gray flannel trousers. He was in a cheerful mood. His mother had given him four hundred francs. He still had three hundred himself, and his mother thought that seven hundred would be enough. As was only to be expected, the dignitaries refused to accept Anoh Michel's small contribution. So he went back to his mother, and she gave him another three hundred francs; this gave him a total of one thousand francs. Though a brother-in-law's contribution is usually set at two thousand, Anoh Michel's sum was accepted. Afterward he stood there together with his kin, watching eagerly as the others' turns came. His delight when someone was rebuked for trying to get off cheaply was not untinged by malice.

The day after the funeral festivities, Anoh Michel continued the story of his life.

Anoh Michel: When I first met my wife, everybody was against us, the Assoua family and my family too. Every day they beat my wife when they caught her with me, but my wife was full of courage, and she cried, "I love only Anoh Michel and I want to marry him." Then her family sent her away to forget me. But she was already pregnant by this time. When her belly got bigger and bigger, her family let her return to Bébou and told her, "Since you're expecting a baby, it's better for you to have a husband to take care of you. Luckily, you have Anoh Michel—he'll pay for everything." So the Assoua kin gave their consent to our marriage. I brought them a bottle of gin, as custom demands, and we were married. My grandfather was the only one who didn't come to the wedding.

[Pause.]

My grandfather doesn't want to have anything to do with me, now that I have married this woman. There's an old feud between the two families.

[Pause.]

It began this way: My younger sister died when her first baby was born, because her husband [who was an Assoua] had deserted her and had not made any arrangements for the baby's birth. My grandfather was very angry about it and declared that the Assoua family was to blame for his granddaughter's death. She died on the fifth of September 1963.

The grandfather had stopped paying for Anoh Michel's schooling because it was the fault of the Assoua family that his granddaughter had died in childbirth. Later, Anoh Michel's wish to marry an Assoua woman added further fuel to the feud between the grandfather and the Assoua kin. There was some justice in Anoh Michel's accusation that his grandfather was responsible for his unfortunate fate. He was resentful. And he had transferred this long-standing resentment to his wife, with whom he had now had a fight.

Among the many guests who had come to Bébou for the funeral festivities was a young man who used to be the boyfriend of Anoh

Michel's wife. The two had met on this occasion and renewed their friendship over a considerable quantity of palm wine.

Anoh Michel: I'm almost sure that she slept with this fellow. If she gets pregnant now, I'll send her away. She can go to the man that gave her a baby.

Anoh and his wife got into a loud and abusive quarrel in the village street. She told him she wanted a divorce so that she could go away with her friend.

The scenes between Anoh Michel and his wife attracted little attention in the midst of the countless disputes that had flared up in the village on the occasion of the funeral festivities. Strife prevailed throughout the village, even in Thomas's family. But everybody seemed very cheerful in spite of this. Anoh Michel, too, was unusually cheerful and optimistic during these days. The tensions in his marriage and in his relations with Thomas, which seemed to be growing more acute, remained in the background during our interview sessions. During the turbulent days before and after the funeral festivities, Anoh Michel concentrated on his childhood memories and fantasies in our talks.

Anoh Michel: I was not born in Bébou. While my mother was still carrying me on her back, we lived with my father in Elasso. That's in Sanwi, a long way from here. One day Ahoussi, the village chief of Bébou, and my grandfather Tanoh Ane appeared in Elasso and demanded that our family come back to their village, to Bébou. My father didn't want to leave Elasso because he had his plantations there. So my mother moved to Bébou with my younger sister and me. My older brother stayed with my father. What I want most of all is to go back to Elasso. Everything would be better there, and my father would give me work and money. But since I don't know the way, I can't go back. [Anoh Michel's father had died when he "was still very small"!]

He goes on to relate how his stepfather, the man his mother had married in Bébou, was killed by a young man while they were out hunting monkeys. It was an accident, he says, and he grows more and more excited as he relates his story, which he embroiders with ornamental detail—a confused mixture of betrayal, flight, pursuit, and deceit. It was impossible to tell what he had invented and what had really happened. He spoke in a rush, hardly stopping to catch his breath. The end of our hour had long since passed. Finally, I stood up to indicate that we would have to finish our conversation the following day.

Anoh Michel [excited]: If my wife runs away, that's fine with me. I'll give my sister what I've given my wife so far. I feel closer to my sister. Before I came into the world, my sister was my wife. I was born first, then my sister. So you understand why we belong together. If my wife leaves me, I can stay with my sister.

When I declared that day's session at an end, emotions were revived in Anoh Michel that reminded him of the loss of his father. He had been talking of good father figures, all of whom he had lost. I had taken their place now and was expected to replace them for him.

The next day Anoh Michel was full of bitter accusations against Thomas. In pouring out the drinks during the singing of the songs for the dead, Thomas had not even offered him a glass. This is very serious for an Anyi.

Noteworthy was the fact that Anoh Michel now felt that he could voice his complaints to me. He had taken me into his confidence. Then he started telling me about his sexual relations with his wife. He always had to be careful, he said, to make sure she did not become pregnant again. Their first child was still too young. That was why he regularly interrupted intercourse. Then he mentioned a book on sex relations, which recommended the use of condoms.

Anoh Michel: When there is an older brother, he has to tell the younger one what to do in life. So you could bring me some condoms from Abengourou, if you know where the pharmacy is.
Morgenthaler: So I'm supposed to be the older brother?
Anoh Michel [with a laugh]: That's right. You're sort of like a father.

During the following session, Anoh Michel began to talk about the life of the whites. Soon he drifted off into a "fantasy of fame and fortune in far-off lands" and described how wonderful everything would be if only he could live where we come from. Only the languages—he admitted—might be hard to learn. He explained that there are a million languages in the world, in fact that there are nations so huge that it is impossible to count how many people live there—like China.

Anoh Michel: If the Chinese ever come to the Ivory Coast, there won't be anything left to eat. The Chinese eat up everything. But our president has refused to let them in. They have to stay in Ghana.

It was absolutely impossible to shake Anoh Michel's conviction that when foreigners (whites) come to a country, they automatically take everything they lay eyes on. Then he recalled the controversy between Guinea and the Ivory Coast. He described how the uncle of Sékou Touré had been abused, beaten, and finally killed by the whites. Next he spoke of religion. He himself was a Christian, he told me, but right now there was a fasting period of forty-four days, just like the Moslems. He hadn't eaten anything since that morning.

Anoh Michel: Jesus Christ suffered for the sins of the world. Now people ought to suffer a little bit, too. When you do something wrong in life without noticing it, God does something good. He takes away some of the wrong, and you don't feel so unhappy. [He points to his arms and legs.] They'll get thin and I'll be a different person.

After this he told me about a boa constrictor that almost caught him. His words become more and more implausible as he relates how terrifying it was and how he had to take huge zigzagging leaps to escape the snake. He worked himself up into a state of growing excitement before my eyes. Suddenly, for no apparent reason, the snake was forgotten and he began to talk about his wife, about her clothes and how much they cost; he gradually became confused. His French became so bad that I could hardly understand what he was saying.

Anoh Michel: Never me money . . . none . . . everything . . . never—yes, until—until . . . young . . . but money . . . only . . . yes, the old men, these old men. [At this point he recovers quickly. Something else occurs to him. He sits up straight and speaks normally again.] Yes, when you're old, you have money. But then you can't sleep with women any more. You have a wife and you pay for everything. That doesn't matter because you have a lot of money. There are some old men who keep their money in boxes and trunks and don't even know how much they have. The termites come and eat up the bills, eat them all up till there's nothing left. That's the way things are when you get old. Your wife cooks your food, a big plateful [he makes a gesture with his arm to indicate the size of the plate—as big as a cartwheel], and she brings you water, and that's all. But because you're old and have lost your key in the Manzan [River], she goes off and amuses herself elsewhere.
    [Pause.]
    We say "key" for penis, you know. And when we say we've lost our key in the Manzan, that means we're completely impotent, completely. Everything's over. There are some old men that say to their wives, "Don't leave me, stay with me and bring me my food and water. At night you can go out and make love with other men if you want." Really, there *are* old men that say that. There's no doubt about it. And there are wives that do what their husbands tell them, and then when they have a baby, the old men say, "That's for me, it's all for me." The old men accept the children, even though they were begotten by another man. That's the way old men are.
    [Pause.]
    But I don't want to wait until . . . until . . . [and Anoh Michel draws out the final consonant until he has to pause for breath, then lets it die away softly]. I want money now, a lot of money. If I had it, I'd buy myself a car like the one you have. Then I'd go for long drives, far away; I'd do absolutely nothing—yes, then I'd be happy.

Anoh Michel was beaming with pleasure. He was absorbed in his new fantasy of bliss, in the idea of owning a car, like me. He wanted to drive away with me. He needed the help of a father, and since he had lost all his other fathers, he felt dependent on me. His desire to go with me to the land of the whites overcharged him and made him feel small and weak. Persons one depends on may also be dangerous, because they may demand too much. Thus he projected his dependency emotions to people who devour, in order to protect himself against demands he was incapable of fulfilling. He himself does not eat; he is fasting. The others were the bad ones. He was absolved of guilt, but he becomes a different person. Behind these fantasies was the oral devouring, cannibalistic mother, the mother who eats up everything. The same dependency feelings then emerged in connection with a phallic castrating object. The snake represented the phallic wife and mother, experienced as a menace.

His reaction was to withdraw, to regress to linguistic deterioration, and ultimately to take refuge in fantasies about the wealth of the old men. But this anal escape into old age did not help him, either. The anal phallus, that is, money, was threatened once again, this time by the termites that devour it and by the sexual impotence of the old men. In this way, however, his phallic desires were projected externally. He retained the oral ones, and that was good, because they permitted him to identify with me as soon as he had gotten rid of his castration anxiety. Once all the dangers had been conjured away, he could have what he needed to be happy. He told me two highly improbable stories about people from the village, already dead and buried, who were "away on trips" and sent their relatives greetings and instructions through mediators. There was no one in the village more clearly "on a trip" than we whites, who had come from far away and would soon be leaving again. In his fantasies, Anoh Michel was turning me into an ancestor.

After this hour, I had an interview session with Thomas. Anoh Michel wanted to belong to me completely and to be just like me. I was to act as a mediator to help settle his quarrel with Thomas. He came to the tent while Thomas and I were talking and wanted me to settle things right then and there.

Each reproached the other with the fact that the old men of their respective families had long dealt unjustly with their own kin. Hereupon I interpreted for them the rage they both felt toward the old men.

Morgenthaler: During the period before and after the funeral festivities, you were both in a difficult position. You were both afraid that the old men would steal all the money you possess. So you were both furious at the old men. But we can't show feelings like those; we always have to be polite and to smile. As a result we suppress our anger, we swallow it. But this anger has suddenly broken through again, and since it can't be directed toward the old men, each of you has directed it toward the other, because it's much easier to be mad at a friend. You're not so much afraid, and also you know that you can easily make up again.

Up to that time I, as a stranger, had not been in a position to be of effective help. Now, however, in my capacity as an ancestor I was—for, in contrast to the whites, the ancestors really are endowed with omnipotence.

After this Anoh Michel developed a childlike attachment to me. He put on his most gorgeous toga for our appointments, one embellished with two huge batik portraits of Kennedy against a background of blue stars.

> *Anoh Michel:* I picked out this material because I find the name Kennedy so beautiful.
> *Morgenthaler:* Who is Kennedy?
> *Anoh Michel:* The president of the United States. He was assassinated.
> *Morgenthaler:* Do you know why you find the name so beautiful?
> *Anoh Michel:* If I ever have a son, his name will be John Kennedy. He will be Anoh John Kennedy.
> *Morgenthaler:* You would like to be the kind of person Kennedy was.
> *Anoh Michel:* Yes, I'd like to know as much as the whites. I could have gone to school, too, if my grandfather had not refused to help me. But maybe things will be different later on.
> *Morgenthaler:* What do you mean by later?
> *Anoh Michel:* Yes, later, in another life. Perhaps I'll be born in Europe as a white man in the next life. Then I'll be like you. In this life I'm stuck as a planter here in Bébou, and that's awful. Whoever invented the profession of the planter ought to be caught and punished!
> *Morgenthaler:* What would you do to him?
> *Anoh Michel:* Whip him, beat him—he ought to be whipped within an inch of his life!

Then he tells me about Ferdinand, one of his wife's former lovers. Childishly, he boasts of his own qualities. Ferdinand, in contrast, was an ugly fellow. His nose was so broad and flat that all you could see were his nostrils. "He breathes right into your face. When he's sick, he infects you right away." Anoh Michel was unable to understand how a woman could choose a man like that, but his wife had met Ferdinand again secretly. On this occasion Anoh Michel had made it clear to her that he always knew what she was up to, and since then she believes it.

Our next session began with Anoh Michel's telling me that he had not dared to enter the tent because I was not yet there. So he arrived half an hour late. He spoke about the evil spirits that pursue anyone who catches fish in the river on a Wednesday and told me that he had neglected to take in his nets on Tuesday evening. "The net is concealed in the Manzan. Nobody will find it. In any case it's a long way from here; nobody goes there."

Today Anoh Michel is rather tired. He turns over restlessly on the cot. Now he has his hands between his knees and is scratching his genitals. He is wearing his Kennedy toga again; he pulls it up over his shoulders, baring his legs so that his undershorts are visible. The toga is around his neck like a shawl. He looks at me and laughs, then looks away again. Suddenly, out of a clear blue sky, he declares: "It's really true that the dead are not dead. Today again something happened that proves it."

And he relates the story of a married couple. The man killed his wife and then committed suicide. A woman from a neighboring village had appeared in Bébou and brought greetings from the suicide victim, whom she claimed to have met on her way there.

Anoh Michel: When I've been in Bébou for a long time and am still in Bébou—for a longer time than you can imagine—then I'm fed up with it and tell myself, "Now I intend to leave." But how can I? I always have to come back because my wife lives in Bébou. When I've had enough, I'll simply leave my body here in Bébou. They'll bury my body, and my soul will go traveling. At night it will return to the cemetery and pick up my body. Then I'll go away forever and never come back. It's good that way, and that way you can go traveling.

Ever since Anoh Michel has endowed me with the omnipotence of his ancestors during our talks, he has had difficulty in separating his feelings of affection from his aggressive urges and from his fears of punishment. Hardly has he revealed his enthusiastic admiration for Kennedy before he begins to have fantasies in which he inflicts humiliation upon himself and in which he is beaten. When he dared to compete with another man, his fears that the man might be sick and infect him were immediately apparent. When he tries to identify with the omnipotence of knowledge with which he has invested me, he expresses his fears of being punished for secretly violating a prohibition dictated by the spirits. Finally he adopts an exhibitionistic pose in my presence and vies for my affection by homosexual means. This makes the process of identification easier for him. He quickly transforms the aggressive impulses that emerge into an anecdote about the suicide who killed his wife. Afterward he is able to perceive himself as the dead man who is continually traveling, like me.

The next day a man was injured when he fell off a roof; I drove him to the hospital for emergency treatment and did not get back in time for my appointment with Anoh Michel. I found him in his grandfather's compound, fast asleep in the hut where he had lived as a boy, before the estrangement from his grandfather. He accompanied me back to the tent, where he began to berate his grandfather and complain angrily about the injustice he had suffered as a result of the grandfather's neglect. I interpreted for him, explaining that his rage at his grandfather had existed since his childhood, but that he had not felt it consciously until the grandfather had begun to ignore him.

Anoh Michel: Yes, you're right. I remember now. When I was very small, at the time my mother had just moved to Bébou with us, Ahoussi said to me, "You belong to your grandfather. Go to him and do everything he tells you to." I said I wouldn't, and I got a whipping. Then I did go to him, but I was furious. They forced me to go out to the fields with the old man, and I went.

Morgenthaler: Little Anoh Michel had no choice but to obey and couldn't show his anger. That anger has existed all the years since that time.

Anoh Michel: It broke through when he turned away from me and refused to pay for my schooling. He has been mad at me ever since.

Morgenthaler: You have been mad at him ever since.

Anoh Michel: I can't talk to him. I can't do anything.

Morgenthaler: How could you be expected to be able to clear things up when you're so angry with your grandfather? No matter what your grandfather does, you'll always be dissatisfied.

Anoh Michel: Then you're saying that I am to blame.

Morgenthaler: I'm not saying that you're to blame, but that it depends on you whether this business with your grandfather can be settled or not.

Anoh Michel: It was in December 1965. The old man's wife was expecting a baby. Then she got sick. She jerked all the time, her muscles got stiff, and her eyes stared straight ahead—it was frightening. Everybody thought she was going to die. My grandfather was very upset and ordered a car to take her to the hospital. That cost him five thousand francs. There was nobody there to help carry her. So I helped, and my grandfather made no objections. In the end I went with them. During the ride, his wife vomited some black stuff, and they said that she was dying. "Turn around!" shouted my grandfather, "Go back to Bébou. There's no need to pay for transporting a dead body, too." But I could tell that the woman was not going to die, and I said, "She's still alive. We have to get her to the hospital." My grandfather shouted at me, "You just want me to get into debt for nothing." I said no, and motioned to the chauffeur to drive on. My grandfather didn't say anything more. He accepted it. At the hospital they gave her a big injection, a serum. She slept for a long time, and when she woke up she was able to move again. She recovered and had her baby. Both are healthy and live in the compound we just came from. Afterward my grandfather admitted, "Anoh Michel was responsible for that, indeed he was." He gave me a hundred francs. Really—only a hundred francs—the miser! Since that time my grandfather hasn't spoken a single word to me. He acts as if I simply didn't exist.

Morgenthaler: Why did your grandfather accept your advice? How was that possible?

Anoh Michel: I don't know.

Morgenthaler: At that time it was clear that your grandfather was still capable of fathering a child. This was proved by the birth of the baby. It was there for all to see. As long as his penis still functions properly, your grandfather is able to accept the fact that the young man Anoh Michel may say and do things that are right. This is why he was able to follow your advice and did not feel that he had to reject you.

Anoh Michel [delightedly]: Yes, that's the truth.

Morgenthaler: How can you say that's the truth? Did you know it all along?

Anoh Michel: Yes. He doesn't want to accept the fact that I'm a man.

Morgenthaler: Your grandfather couldn't face the thought that you were becoming a man and could have children yourself—in other words, that you have a penis that can accomplish what it was intended for.

Anoh Michel: A penis just as good as his—that's true, he was always against that.

Morgenthaler: How do you mean?

Anoh Michel: He always used to beat us.

Morgenthaler: Can you explain to me what you mean by that?

Anoh Michel: Once when I was small—but not a baby, older than that—anyway, when my penis was beginning to look like something, I was playing with Maurice in grandfather's big house. It was sort of dark in there, and we often played with our penises, Maurice with mine, and I with his. We thought it was fun, and besides we wanted to find out how they work. When the women went by, they saw what we were doing. They didn't say anything to us, but they went to the old man and told him. He called us to him and shouted, "What have you been up to this time?" He grabbed a stick and thrashed us. He didn't want us to play that game. He used to get up very early in the morning to wake us up and take us out to the plantation. There he didn't leave us alone for an instant. We had to work the whole time. He was afraid we might hide from him and play with our penises. It was that way every day except Wednesday. The women said that children ought to rest on Wednesday. We said we were going swimming in the river, and off we went. The women aren't allowed to go to the river on Wednesdays, so we were alone.

Then a lot of other boys came. We all went swimming, and then we
all played the penis game together. We looked to see who had the
biggest one. Maurice [at this point Anoh Michel gives a scornful
laugh] had the littlest. His is only so big [he places his thumb against
the middle of his little finger]. I had the longest one. We measured.
Mine was eleven centimeters long when it was erect. We measured
diameters, too, and the boy with the thickest penis was the winner.
That was me. Bléou Boni and I, we had the thickest. Maurice had the
smallest penis, so he had to measure the others and see that there
was no cheating. All the boys stood around together and worked to
erect their penises. One boy would come up to another and rub his
penis for him. Others lay down on the ground with their buttocks in
the air and moved up and down very fast. But one boy always helped
another. For example, I did it for Bléou Boni and then Kouako for me,
and so on. Kouako's penis was bigger than mine, but when we were
not excited we were all the same, Bléou, Kouako, and I. When
Kouako was excited, though, he was the champion—eleven and a
half centimeters or more and even thicker. When we got home the
women asked us why we had been away so long—"You've been
doing things you're not supposed to do." But we said, "No, we
haven't. We have witnesses." We called the other boys over, and
since they had all played the game with us, nobody said anything. So
we didn't get a thrashing. Sometimes, too, we'd go into the forest to
collect dead spiders. We fished them out of their webs and crushed
them to dust. Then the boys would rub each others' genitals with the
dust. That was to make the hair grow better.

After our hour was over, Anoh Michel accompanied me—as he often
did—as far as the crossroads in the center of the village. There he turned
left to go home, while I continued on straight ahead to reach our compound. This time we met his grandfather at the intersection. That had
never happened before and seemed to be an evil omen.

Anoh Michel's stories about the boys' sex play symbolized the forbidden games themselves, and the penalty for such misdeeds lay in the
air. The power of magical thought and experience processes made itself
clearly felt during the days that followed. Our next session, for example,
began thus:

Anoh Michel: Now you've met the old man. Did you notice that he
didn't say a word to me?
Morgenthaler: I noticed. He talked about Maurice.
Anoh Michel: Yes, he gets along all right with Maurice. He hates me.

At this moment we were interrupted by a man who had come to tell
us that Tanoh Ane, Anoh Michel's grandfather, had cut his finger badly
with a bushwhacker. I was to go back to our compound immediately. So I
had to cancel the rest of the hour with Anoh Michel and operate on his
grandfather's finger. The old man's injury required stitching.

The next day Anoh Michel told me that he had felt an intense itching in his face when I left to treat his injured grandfather. The itching had plagued him the whole night, and he had had to scratch his face constantly.

It was evident during our conversation that he was reluctant to talk any more about his own problems. He had gotten a scare when the old man injured himself right after he, Anoh Michel, had told me so confidingly and in such detail about the boys' masturbating.

Instead, he asked me questions about the sun, the moon, and the stars and finally came back to his previous remark that the dead are not dead, but travel around at will. Toward the end of the hour, he suddenly turned to me and moved closer.

Anoh Michel: Look [approaching very closely]: my face is full of pimples.

[I examined the smooth skin of his face. There was not a pimple to be seen, only a few beads of sweat; it had been an unusually hot day.]

Morgenthaler: Yesterday you felt a sudden itching when you heard that your grandfather had hurt himself.

Anoh Michel [evasively]: I felt the itching the day before yesterday.

He felt a strong need to place himself in the same position with me as his grandfather, whose injured finger I had examined carefully and closely. Anoh Michel was identifying with the aggressor in order to repress the anxiety called forth by the strange experience.

My operating on Anoh Michel's grandfather had brought me great prestige among the old man's kin. Tanoh Ane himself was extremely friendly to me—almost a bit servile, and this development was not without consequences for the transference built up by Anoh Michel. Some time later, when I paid a visit to Tanoh Ane in his compound, Anoh Michel was there and—together with many other people— watched what I was doing from a distance.

In Anoh Michel's magical mode of experience, the old man's self-inflicted injury was the punishment he had long wished upon his hated grandfather. But it was more than this. Uncanny guilt feelings had manifested themselves. The injury was the tangible expression of the destructive aggressive urges building up in Anoh Michel as he continued to become more and more deeply involved with me. By rights, so to speak, it was our penalty, manifested in an outsider. In this way, with the aid of projection, the conflict threatening to emerge between us was shifted to the outside world and thus conjured away. But, as a result of this process, the omnipotence attributed to me was now greater than before. Now even the previously dreaded grandfather was in a position of helplessly servile dependency on me. This in turn engendered an intense oral envy in Anoh Michel. He wanted to be just as close to me as the old man, who—injured, timorous, and at the same time greedy—was surrendering a part of his body to be manipulated, in much the same way as a mother manipulates the body of her baby in order to give herself up to the enjoyment of her omnipotence over it. The exercise of my function as a doctor brought me even greater prestige. My manipulation of the grandfather was assumed to give me that self-gratifying absorption in what I was doing that filled Anoh Michel with such envy and such longing to experience these sensations with me, as a kind of passive participant in a duality or fusion with me.

At our next meeting, without any preliminaries, he declared:

Anoh Michel: I think I've discovered a cyst on my body.
Morgenthaler: Where did you find it?
Anoh Michel: In a very hidden spot.
Morgenthaler: Then come to the clinic this evening, so you can be examined.

[My matter-of-fact reply gave Anoh Michel a feeling of having been rebuffed, rejected. At the same time it forced him to face reality. He looked first at me and then at the cot I was sitting on.]

Anoh Michel: You know, you're quite heavy. Where you're sitting, the canvas is almost touching the floor. One can see how heavy you are. But then you're already pretty old.

[Pause.]

I'm too thin. That's not good.
Morgenthaler: Would you like to be fat?
Anoh Michel: Fat is not the same thing as strong. Kouassi Kouadio is strongly built, with very broad shoulders.
Morgenthaler: Who is Kouassi Kouadio?
Anoh Michel: Kouassi, Maurice, and I—we're grandfather's three sons. Kouassi Kouadio still lives in grandfather's court. Today Kouassi went out to the forest to drink palm wine. He drinks an awful lot—all day long. He's not married.

[Pause.]

He only talks with the girls; he's so shy that he can't tell them he'd like to sleep with them.
Morgenthaler: Did he tell you that?
Anoh Michel: Everybody in Bébou knows that. The girls laugh at him. They say that he never sleeps with a girl because he couldn't if he wanted to. [He laughs maliciously.] I'm different there. I just go up to the girls and ask them to sleep with me. Naturally they like that.
Morgenthaler: Kouassi Kouadio is afraid of women.
Anoh Michel: He has often asked me to find a girl for him. I did once, and brought her to him. When the girl came to his house, he did nothing but talk her to death. Then finally he sent her home and still hadn't slept with her.

[Pause.]

Kouassi is a very handsome fellow. He's better-looking than I am.
Morgenthaler: But you have more success with the girls.
Anoh Michel: He wasn't in our group when we were small. He lived somewhere else and didn't come to Bébou till he was older.

Then, abruptly changing the subject, he began to talk about Elisa, the pregnant girl whom Madame Parin was seeing every day in her tent. He told me that Elisa's husband was a schoolteacher in Man, who had once come to Bébou on a visit. Elisa and the teacher had slept together the very first evening. He was a good-looking fellow—big and strong. At these words, Anoh Michel looked down ruefully at his own body and said, "I'm thin. The life of a planter is too hard. No matter how much you eat, you stay thin." After a moment he continued, "I wish I were fat."

When Anoh Michel wanted to show me the cyst in a hidden spot on his body, he was a bit like a child eager to show something to his mother and a bit like a homosexual bent on seduction. My curt remark about coming to the clinic left him feeling abandoned and rejected. I acquired the features of the cruel, rejecting mother of his childhood. It turned out later that he had perceived his mother as stout and heavy. That was the image of the pregnant woman. Anoh Michel experienced an emotional conflict as regarded his relationship with me. Should he identify with the phallic mother, whose gigantic phallus was her belly, big with child, or should he hold fast to the image of the handsome young man who seduced the girls with his masculinity? He made several attempts to assert his youthful maleness. "Fat is not the same thing as strong," he stated, and mentioned the good-looking Kouassi Kouadio. Then it turned out that this young man was constantly drunk and impotent to boot. In comparison with Kouassi, Anoh Michel was now the great seducer, and in his transference he made me into the woman-mother without a penis, who talks with him interminably without ever permitting any physical contact. This was a clear reflection of his wish to be raped homosexually by me. He expressed his disappointment at my failure to fulfill his wish my making me impotent. But this made it impossible for him to maintain his self-esteem as a male, and therefore he told me that his friend was better-looking than he was. Finally, he identified with the pregnant Elisa and wanted to be fat like her.

This homosexual wooing of me and his longing for close physical contact with me awakened unpleasant sensations in Anoh Michel, and for this reason he preferred to emphasize the image of the benevolent, omnipotent father once again. He described his views on four professions, two that appealed to him and two that he found unattractive.

What he found attractive and what he rejected corresponded to the components of his ambivalent emotions in the transference he had built up toward me.

Anoh Michel: When I was little—oh, that was a long time ago—when I was still going to school in Abengourou, I thought it would be nice to be a policeman, or maybe a doctor. It's good to be a policeman, then you have a good reputation.

Then he told me the story of a murder in Amélékia, which had caused a sensation throughout the village just a few days before. Two coffee buyers had been killed on the road to Taakro, the bodies robbed and then buried under the refuse from a coffee-husking machine.

Anoh Michel: It was dogs that discovered the bodies. Then the police came. If I were a policeman, they would have sent me out to look for the thieves. Then I would have come and caught the murderers. People everywhere would have praised me and said, "That was Anoh Michel." [He laughs to himself with pleasure and continues.] It's also good to be a doctor. When somebody is sick and the relatives come and say, "Please, doctor, come and help us"—then I would come and do whatever was necessary, and the sick person would be cured. Everyone would say, "That woman there was so sick that she was going to die, but Anoh Michel cured her." That also gives you a good name.
[Pause.]
Schoolteacher, though—that's bad. I'd never want to be that.
Morgenthaler: Why not?
Anoh Michel: Aw, what's a schoolteacher? All he does is talk. He stands there and talks and talks. He has to talk to the children all the time so that they'll learn something. After school he just can't stop, so he keeps right on talking. Finally all that talking makes him dizzy. Last year the teacher here in Bébou went crazy. Really—he kept talking and talking and nobody could understand what he was saying. Then he started to undress—first his shirt, then his trousers, and then even his shorts. Just as he was about to pull down his shorts, they came to take him away—far away from here. That's what happens to you when you're a schoolteacher.
[Pause.]
And attending a seminary—I wouldn't like that either.
Morgenthaler: What kind of seminary?
Anoh Michel: A religious seminary—no, I'd never do that. You can't make love there. I wouldn't want a profession where I couldn't sleep with women.
[Pause.]
Yes, sexual intercourse. That's very important in life. At night, when you're asleep, you suddenly feel sexually excited. You wake up. When the ejaculation comes, you're calm again and can go back

to sleep. Recently my wife was in Zaranou. She was gone for two weeks. When you can't have intercourse, you get excited every night, and it begins to get on your nerves. You can't go back to sleep. In a case like that, I think it's better to help a little with my hand. You come quicker, and it's over. But if I do that when my wife is at home, she makes fun of me . . . yes, or she gets mad.

For Anoh Michel, policemen and doctors embody phallic ideals, while schoolteachers and priests evoke alarming notions. He attributes a complete lack of drive inhibition leading to madness to the teachers, and asceticism and self-denial to the priests. These frightening fantasies revive experiences from early infancy. That these experiences were erotic in nature is illustrated by the fact that they prompted Anoh Michel to start talking about his sex life once again.

The following day Anoh Michel came an hour late. He had been out at his plantation, burning off the dried brush to clear the land. There had been a danger that his fires might spread to neighboring plantations, one of which belonged to Monsieur Bra.

Anoh Michel: He's making a perfect fool of me . . . . For days now I've been going to Bra and demanding my money. But first he wants to see for himself that the work has been done properly. All he has to do is go and look. But he refuses to go.
[Pause.]
Bra is a Moslem. He prays in his own way. There are not many Moslems in the village. A lot of people are Catholics, but most of them don't believe in anything.
[Pause.]
Today we don't eat meat; it's Friday. When you eat meat on Friday, it's as if you were eating human flesh.
Morgenthaler: Who told you that?
Anoh Michel: The priest. He says so.

Anoh Michel described how he had always been at the top of the class in religion and how the priest had given him a stick as a reward. He was supposed to use it to hit the pupils who were unable to recite the catechism by heart. When the time came to take the test, and a white priest from the city asked the questions, Anoh Michel was unable to answer. He sat there, incapable of uttering a single word, though his comrades tried to whisper the answers to him. Many of them passed the test and were baptized. Anoh Michel was rejected. He cried over his failure for a long time, but later refused to sign up to take the test a second time.

Anoh Michel: When people have been baptized, their souls are always clean and pure. When they make mistakes, they go to the priest, kneel down, and tell him everything. Then it's all right again.

Other people can't do that. Their souls remain all black, all full of error. They stay that way, and that's very bad.

Then he related how the priest collects money every year from the people who are baptized. In return they receive communion; the priest sticks something into their mouths. Anoh Michel would have liked that, too. But he always had to stand at the back of the church and was only allowed to watch.

Anoh Michel: When you've slept with a woman, you just go to the priest and tell him. Then everything is all right. The priest tells you what mistakes you've made. Often you don't know yourself. Sexual intercourse is one of these mistakes.
Morgenthaler: At least you don't have to pay anything, since you're not baptized.
Anoh Michel: That wouldn't matter. The priest brings the money to the priest in Abengourou, and he gives him part of it to live on. He uses the rest for a trip to Mecca. There he also keeps part of it for himself.
  [Pause.]
  My wife is baptized. Maybe she'd be more willing to stay with me if I were, too.
  [Our hour was up. Thomas appeared outside the tent. He had killed a monkey the day before, and the two friends were talking about it.]
Anoh Michel: If you cook it long enough, monkey meat is good to eat. The eyes are like eggs. You have to bite into them firmly. Then you get a white liquid in your mouth. Usually it's the women who eat the head. The men eat the buttocks and the tail—that gives them strength.

The part of the monkey the women eat is carefully separated from the part the men eat. Buttocks and tail are phallic symbols. The head and the eyes with their white, jellylike liquid—half milk, half sperm—are the expression of what women devour, symbols of the souls of their own children. Anoh Michel is unable to keep objects separate. He eats the cooked eyes of the monkey with the same enjoyment as the women, and at the same time, as a man, he also eats the tail, which gives strength.

The following day, Anoh Michel was in a bad mood. He said that his wife was getting on his nerves. She kept on doing things he didn't like. Besides that, she lied and told people that he beat her. Whenever she met another young man, she wanted to go away with him immediately. Anoh Michel announced that he intended to take a second wife later on.

Anoh Michel: I've already picked her out, but I have to wait until she is a little older. Then I'll sleep with her. I was Jacqueline's first man, too. That's good. Then the woman won't ever forget you as long as she lives.

[Then he tells me the story of how they met. Both were children.]

Anoh Michel: Jacqueline didn't have any breasts yet, and she didn't want to sleep with me. When her breasts developed, I thought the time had come. I enticed her inside with some excuse and then locked the door of the hut. We tried it, but she began to scream as soon as I got near her. Later it was fine, and she used to come to me every day. She would lie on the bed and I'd stand at the edge. That was how we first made love. Later on we sometimes made love in different positions. We would lie one on top of the other, in the form of a cross. It's good that way.

Morgenthaler: You enjoy it most when only your genitals are touching.

Anoh Michel: Yes, I do. But we're often tender with each other, too. I often stroke Jacqueline's skin—I do it so that she'll stroke mine. The best is when she sucks my penis.

[Pause.]

But that can be dangerous. The Baoulé women do that, but you shouldn't do it with African women. If you're not sure that a woman loves you, and if she has somebody else she doesn't tell you about, then she wants to suck your penis. Then all of a sudden she bites hard, and you've had it. Everything is destroyed, and no other woman will have anything to do with you. Then she leaves you and sleeps with somebody else. African women are dangerous. You have to watch out for them. When a woman takes your penis into her mouth, she can bite off half and eat it as easily as not. I've noticed that there's a little bone in the tip of the penis, and that bone might break.

[Pause.]

Morgenthaler: A little bone?

Anoh Michel: We killed a monkey and cooked its testicles. They're very good to eat. Then we cut open the penis and found the bone.

He laughed with delight and related the story of a man who had had his penis bitten off. He wasn't able to urinate properly any more, Anoh Michel declared, and added, "When he drank water, it flowed right out the other end."

Anoh Michel was very excited. He told me increasingly improbable tales about the penis-devouring African women and repeated with passion his warning about how careful one has to be with them.

Since the funeral festivities, when Anoh Michel seemed to be losing his friends and I succeeded in gaining his confidence, the transference had become increasingly firmer and deeper. I became a benevolent, fond father figure, endowed with phallic omnipotence. By leaning on phallic fathers of this type, Anoh Michel is constantly endeavoring to

bolster his self-esteem as a male and to acquire a bit of phallicity himself, which he can then direct outward to gain prestige in the society in
which he lives. Thus armed, he can confront his fellows and enter into
relationships with them. As soon as aim-inhibited affectionate emotions or even sexual urges begin to play a part in these relationships, the
old longing for the mother of his infancy is revived, and the objects
concerned take on the cruel features of the mother who withdraws and
abandons her child. The anxiety thus engendered destroys the unstable
phallic cathexis of the self, whereupon the former condition of apathy
and hypochrondriac-tinged difficulty in establishing and maintaining
contact reappears. In this state Anoh Michel resumes his search for a
paternal figure capable of being idealized as the omnipotent embodiment of the phallicity he so desperately yearns for.

As transference developed, his image of me—as a benevolent, affectionate father—was gradually and imperceptibly transformed into the
image of an omnipotent, terrifying mother, lurking threateningly in the
background and apparently waiting for the moment to pounce upon
him cruelly to perform the final, annihilating act of castration.

The treacherous female stranger who bites off and devours the penis
reflected the stage so far achieved in the development of transference. I
had become the terrifying female figure because Anoh Michel, in his
apprehension of the coming separation, was in danger of being reduced
to impotence and helplessness by his greedy desire to cling to me. He
perceived our separation as if I were devouring a part of him and thus
taking it away with me.

Anoh Michel came to his next interview with a knife and a stick,
which he spent the entire hour carving. He was engaged in making a
musical instrument for me. He reported that yesterday Bra had finally
paid him his outstanding wages. A lengthy discussion about money
followed, during which he managed to jumble all the figures he
mentioned. The various demands made by his wife played an important role.

Anoh Michel: Our women always get very angry when they see that
their husbands have nothing.

All that had been uncanny in our relationship seemed to have been
conjured away. Anoh Michel whittled away at his stick. This meant that
he was engaged in making a kind of fetish for me. I was to accept his
gift in exchange for not taking a part of himself. In this way he would
stand aloof from events and remain untouched.

It was the fifteenth of March; Anoh Michel was talking steadily. I
interrupted him only rarely, when I needed to ask a question. He stared

straight ahead while he was speaking. From time to time he turned his head to look at me, as if he wanted to be certain I understood what he was saying.

Anoh Michel: It's all over now with my wife. Yesterday evening she told me that she didn't love me any more and was going away for good. "What are your reasons"? I asked her. She answered, "I have no love for Anoh Michel. Next Saturday I'm going to Abengourou with the white people and I'm never coming back." That's what Jacqueline said.

[Pause.]

I wanted to ask you not to take her when she asks whether she can ride with you.

[Pause.]

I told her she couldn't leave as long as our little girl is still so small. If she goes anyway, I'll sue her in the court in Abengourou. She wouldn't listen to me. We had a big fight.

[Pause.]

It's our little girl that makes me so sad. She'll be unhappy. Jacqueline will sleep around with other men and take the baby with her everywhere. She'll cry and get sick. Maybe she won't want her mother to go with other men. Little children are like that.

[Pause.]

It's only because of the child. Jacqueline ought to stay here until the baby learns to walk. Then it can stay with me, and Jacqueline can do whatever she wants.

Morgenthaler: When you were as small as your daughter, and your mother left your father, you were as unhappy as you think your daughter will be now if your wife goes away. You were always waiting for your father to come and get you. And now, if you go to court and fight for your child, you will be doing what you wish your father had done.

Anoh Michel [looking at me in surprise]: Yes, of course. If my father had come to get me, I would have been very, very happy.

After this, and on the following day as well, he tells me that he has now accepted jobs from some older women to clear their fields of weeds. He haggled with them over the price, and finally they came to an agreement. One of the women said, "All right, I'll give you what you're asking. But what if I meet you on the street and happen to need oil or sugar? Will you give me oil or sugar just to do me a favor?" "Yes," Anoh Michel replied, "I'll buy you twenty-five francs worth of oil or sugar." And the woman said, "That's fine, but make it fifty francs so that I'll have something to rejoice about." Anoh Michel agreed. He managed to get the old women on his side, and they persuaded Jacqueline to make up with him. She changed her mind and decided to stay in Bébou. Now she wanted to bake pancakes with her friends and sell them in the village. So Anoh Michel asked me to bring him flour, oil, and sugar from the city.

I brought him what he wanted. He and his wife seemed to be reconciled, and everything was apparently all right again.

On one of the following days, the petroleum seller who goes from village to village happened to be in Bébou while Anoh Michel and I were having our interview. For the first time, Anoh Michel's wife appeared at my tent and interrupted us, asking him for money to buy petroleum. This put Anoh Michel in a bad mood and led him to complain that his wife was keeping him poor with her constant requests for money. At the end of the hour he was unable to force himself to go home as usual. Instead he accompanied me to our compound and wanted to go along with me to M'Basso. He seemed unable to part with me. Since I drove to M'Basso every day at the same time, there were usually a few people waiting at my car, wanting to be taken along. Anoh Michel elbowed them aside and got into the front seat. One of his friends was also in the car. He wanted to go swimming in the Comoë River and to drive back with me afterward. Thus it happened that we talked about swimming in the river during the drive.

The next day Anoh Michel arrived so early that he had already opened the tent by the time I appeared. He laughed and greeted me cheerfully. He thanked me for having taken him along to M'Basso the previous evening. He then began to talk about his wife, who now had every reason to be satisfied with him.

Anoh Michel: I gave her everything she needs to bake her pancakes, and she can keep the money she earns for herself. So she won't need to ask me for anything more.
[Pause.]
From now on I'm going to be the one to say whether she stays or goes.
Morgenthaler: You've put your relations with your wife on a different footing than before.
Anoh Michel: That's because things are different now. If she nags me any more, I'll throw her out. I've no use for a wife that's good for nothing.
Morgenthaler: Today for the first time you're talking about your wife without being afraid. You have a mind of your own and you're behaving like a man. Up to now you were always like a woman yourself. With me, too. You used to lie on the cot and look at me dreamily, as if you were in love and were waiting to be raped, like

makes you unhappy and afraid. You're different today, for the first time.

Anoh Michel: What you just said about a woman being in Anoh Michel is true. A soothsayer once said the same thing about me. He said I wasn't a real man. Part of me was a woman and that would cause me trouble in life. It's true. It's the third time I've been told that.

Morgenthaler: The third time?

Anoh Michel: I've known for a long time that there's a woman in me. When I was little, I wanted to be a girl.

He related how, at the age of seven, he had refused to go to school. He had insisted that he wanted to stay at home with his mother, like his sister. His sister didn't go to school either. Then his grandfather had declared that his sister was a girl and was supposed to stay at home, but that he was a boy and had to learn things.

Anoh Michel: I said, "Give my sister what it is that makes me a boy, and I'll take what she has. I want to be a girl." Yes, that's exactly what I said, and then my grandfather hit me. After that I went to school.
   [Pause.]
   Today you said that the man in Anoh Michel has come to your tent. The woman has left. On the day you leave Bébou, the woman will come back. I know that even now. I'll be very sad and I won't eat a thing all day. But two days later I'll drive away the woman in me forever.

Morgenthaler: You said today that you would send Jacqueline away if she nags you any more. Maybe you didn't mean your wife, but...

Anoh Michel: ...but the woman that lives in Anoh Michel.

Morgenthaler: When you drove with me to M'Basso yesterday, you were so affectionate and so sad at the same time. You could hardly bring yourself to part from me. Have you ever felt that way about a man before?

Anoh Michel: When I was going to school in Abengourou, I had a friend—his name was Marius. We were always together. He followed me everywhere. Marius and I—we were in love with each other. We would go for walks together and hold hands, and when we met again after a separation we hugged and kissed each other.
   [Pause.]
   One day Marius said to me, "Come on, let's go swimming in the river." I knew right away what he was thinking of. We went down to the river and got undressed. But instead of going swimming, we stood there together and looked at each other and measured to see who had the bigger penis, just as we had done before as boys down at the Manzan River.

The following day Anoh Michel again seemed downcast and unsure of himself. During the entire hour he played with a pair of scissors he had borrowed from Thomas to cut his daughter's hair. He would put the blades into his mouth, pinch his lips between them, stick the points in his ears, or prick his nose playfully. Then he started stabbing the supporting straps of the cot with them. He looked at me longingly and complained that he had nothing. Finally it came out; there was going to be a dance that evening. Anoh Michel had made up his mind to ask me for some money so that he could go to it. It took him a long time to get up enough courage to make his request.

At this point I interpreted for him once again, explaining that he was behaving toward me like a woman, except that a woman comes right out and says what she wants, while he is ashamed. Anoh Michel reacted with narcissistic regression, saying:

Anoh Michel: Since nobody loves me [he indicates his body, laying his hands on his thighs, then crossing them over his chest], I love myself a little. I love my body.
   [Pause.]
   But my body is rotting. I love it, but it's sick. I've been running a fever since yesterday.

Anoh Michel had malaria. I gave him some quinine pills. It was the twentieth of March, just a few days before our departure. An attack of malaria is nothing unusual in Bébou, and the next day Anoh Michel came to my tent at the appointed time in spite of it. When I stepped inside, I found him asleep on the cot.

He awakened, sat up, and looked intently at me. All the softness was gone from his expression. He was obviously thinking hard, trying to decide what to say and what not to say.

Anoh Michel: I thought you were going to stay here for a while. And now you're already leaving on Monday.
   [His expression had changed completely. He was staring unhappily in front of him.]
   When you leave, I'll be losing something. It's the same as with the little monkey. He has to clasp his hands firmly around his mother's belly when she springs from tree to tree. If the little monkey falls off her back, he can't climb. He'll have to run around on the ground like the other animals. He's lost his mother.
Morgenthaler: You've become very attached to me, and now you're reexperiencing something you've gone through before. When you were very little and your mother carried you on her back, you were happy, just as you were happy here in the tent with me. When you were able to walk, your mother put you down on the floor and left you alone. Your sister was born and your mother carried her on her back. You were desperately unhappy and felt abandoned, just as you do now that I am leaving.

Anoh Michel: Here in Bébou you can see lots of little children that cry all the time. Their mothers have abandoned them.
Morgenthaler: What you have experienced with me has only very little to do with my person. Most of it is a repetition of experiences you had as a child, and all of them ended in disappointment.
Anoh Michel: It's easy for you to talk that way—you'll be leaving soon and you're happy to be going home. But we're the ones who will be left behind to bear the unhappiness. Everybody in the village says so. When the white people leave, many villagers will die.
[Pause.]
Last year seventeen persons died. If you hadn't come this year, Anoh Michel would already be in his grave.

Then he inquired with interest about our approaching journey and wanted to know our plans in detail. He soon became cheerful again and even admitted that life in Bébou was actually pretty good when I told him about the lives white people lead in Europe. But Anoh Michel became ill again, this time with dysentery. He felt very weak and looked quite ill. He spoke about the cruel treatment meted out by the medical orderlies from the city who went out to the villages to inoculate the population. Anyone given such an injection in the buttocks could die on the spot.

This was Anoh Michel's way of saying that the sickness he now felt in his body had been implanted there from without, by some person. He projected this power to cause sickness to me and thus perceived once again how devastating our separation was for him. Then he changed his mind and, on our last day in Bébou, he presented me with the musical instrument he had made himself: "The women use this instrument to make music. When they sing, the tom-tom accompanies them. I don't know how to do it. When I play it, the voices and the tom-tom are never in time with each other."

The instrument has the significance of a phallic symbol. Anoh Michel's words made it clear that only the women can play it properly. He himself cannot. But he gives it to me as a present, thus indicating that his self-esteem as a man doesn't really belong to him, but was borrowed, so to say, from the phallic mother. If this mother pounces on him, greedy to devour him, he actually has nothing to lose. The rapacious women simply seize what is their due in any case and what they have to devour again and again in ever recurring greed.

On the day of our departure, Anoh Michel was cheerful. Happily he dragged the furniture we had given to him to his new house, now ready to move into.

Anoh Michel was now far away, one individual among all the Anyi of the village we were leaving behind.

After I had left, Anoh Michel slept with his wife and made her pregnant. Nine months later I had a letter saying that Jacqueline had given birth to a daughter. Anoh Michel wrote that he had wanted a son and that in his daydreams he had already named it after me instead of after his earlier choice, the assassinated American president.

In his fantasies Anoh Michel remained true to the Anyi mother. Presumably he experienced my departure less as the feeling of having been abandoned by me than as the feeling that he had been the one to drop and abandon me. And in the end he was quite right, for I had always been a stranger for him and had never been really close to him.

Puberty, Adolescence, and Sexuality

Was Anoh Michel really an adult? Or had he remained immature, deprived of an ideal by the early separation from his father and uprooted by the forced interruption of his schooling? Was his personality unfinished, was he a belated adolescent, a neurotic?

These questions are based on two inaccurate premises. First, the dividing line between neurotic and normal, between psychically mature and immature is by no means a clear one. It can shift depending upon the social value criteria applied. Second, the phases in the life cycle are differently demarcated in every society and, above all, are characterized by different social labels. Only certain physiological phenomena are the same everywhere—birth, puberty, menopause. Important milestones, such as entry into the production process, the beginning of "adult" sexual relationships, and the onset of old age are influenced by material factors, but even more by social ones. In our description of Anyi childhood it seemed logical to contrast the developmental phases, whose course is determined more or less physiologically despite its high degree of variability, with cultural patterns. This method is useless, however, with regard to the phases of later life.

Either one might describe only the applicable value concepts, without making any attempt to comprehend any deviations, or one might proceed statistically and demonstrate the fairly convincing correlation with the hypotheses and criteria employed. Or, as a third possibility, one might try to establish a connection between social processes and customs on the one hand and ego attitudes on the other, in order to illuminate the interplay of tradition and present-day behavior.

The relationship of the individual to society is determined by traditional customs and habits in every phase of life. Sharing a belief, participating in a ritual improve the performance of the ego and enhance self-esteem. Identification with the leading figures of the group (parents and other ideal figures) and with their values is of the utmost importance in this respect. Harmony with these values leads to a "good" clan conscience (75). The ego must resolve certain inner conflicts as well as conflicts with objects of the external world in such a way that the process and the final resolution are predetermined, a foregone conclusion from the beginning. Whatever lends itself to uniform repetition, quite apart from the saving of energy implied, seems not only to serve the purposes of defense, but also to establish a bundle of secondary autonomous functions in the ego. Ritualization binds instinctual energies and ultimately permits the individual to be "himself" and at the same time the representative of the group ethic (101).

Suzanne can refuse to sleep with her beloved until he has built their cooking area, because when she does she expresses her solidarity with "all the women of her world," who presumably would react in the same way; she is justified in feeling happy when her unreliable fiancé asks her to cook for him, for according to tradition this is a step on the way to the altar. She knows, of course, that pressure will not work, and that her right to claim him as a husband is by no means guaranteed. Still, it enhances her feeling of well-being. The fact that her pride has been gratified gives her the strength she needs to cope with her disappointment.

Not all Anyi by any means are so closely bound to tradition as Suzanne, a "girl of good family" who is in the process of stabilizing her identity as a "distinguished lady." Very frequently traditional value concepts are mutually contradictory in their content. Suzanne rejects the idea of being Paul's "second wife." Thomas, on the other hand, takes it for granted that every girl will accept the institution of polygyny provided the formality of "apologies" has been observed.

Despite all the individual differences in the observance of custom and despite the contradictions inherent in cultural institutions and values, it seems to be the combined weight of many similar attitudes that ensures the constancy of a culture. It is not decisive whether cultural institutions function well or poorly, or whether a smaller or larger percentage of the population, the more important people or the unimportant ones, "conform to custom." A tradition is not abandoned but continues to exist as long as adherence to it provides a needed enhancement of the feeling of identity. The sense of "belonging" may be conscious or unconscious. It is merely one sign of an enhancement of self-esteem and an improvement in ego functioning, neither of which could be achieved in any other way.

With the maturation of the sexual function and the development of secondary sex characteristics, puberty brings a change in the array of libidinal urges. Although in many Western social strata the beginning of adult sexuality does not coincide with physiological maturity but is delayed, as a result of social pressures and psychic inhibitions, until after the years of the so-called second latency period, nevertheless puberty entails deep-seated psychic changes. Above all, the individual must now give up the most important love objects of childhood and invest new ones with libido in their place (103). This process is usually accompanied by critical fluctuations. Infantile love objects are temporarily more intensely cathected and the old conflicts with them revived. Then they are abandoned once again, the libido is concentrated on the self, and other, often fantastic, unattainable objects are chosen, or objects that seem to be alien and directly opposed to the original ones, until finally the shift is accomplished and a real object found.

These processes also operate among the Anyi. In their case, however, the conflicts of early childhood had taken a different course. Some objects were introjected as part objects in the preoedipal phase of development and cannot be discarded; others have been deprived of libido (defensive withdrawal of cathexis), so that regressive revival during puberty is impossible. Thus, instead of a shift in objects, there is a search for new ones. And here the influence exercised by society plays a different role than it plays in our culture, in that the individual's dependence on society, as a continuation of preoedipal ties, is greater. The pubescent ego is less capable of independently achieving satisfactory cathexes and thus must rely to a greater extent on the environment in choosing a love object.

Tradition decrees different treatment for boys and girls. Girls are not permitted to indulge in intercourse until after their first menstrual period, a taboo that is reinforced by magical threats and is generally observed. When a girl has her first period, she parades gaily through the village accompanied by some of her playmates, all of them festively dressed and annointed with shea butter. As they go from courtyard to courtyard, they sing songs containing appropriate allusions and are given gifts, while everybody discusses the happy event. According to the dictates of custom, there is nothing to indicate which of the girls is the fortunate one, so that outsiders will not know. Only a few days later, when the girl concerned pays her thank-you visits, is the public event linked with the person. After this the girl's sex life may, can, and should begin.

Society has devised nothing comparable for boys. This seems to be another manifestation of the organizational principle that a matrilineal society is primarily concerned with its female members, while the males have to manage by themselves—as happened during the latency period as well. In other words, women seek to integrate their daughters, with whom they have closer ties, into the group, whereas the fathers and brothers take little interest at any stage of development in the younger members of their own sex. It is left up to the boys to discover for themselves when they are sexually mature—namely, when the pubic hair begins to appear. For psychic reasons, and because there is no initiation ceremony to mark the role change, the result is frequently an overanxious self-observation with hypochondriac overtones. In homosexual experimenting and play, the boys examine and test their own sex organs and their functions in comparison with those of their comrades.

There are some sayings indicating that sexuality (masturbation and intercourse) is not permitted for boys and single young men. Occasionally a father will try to prevent sex play in the boys' cliques by threats and whippings. Actually, one would expect this ban on sex to fall on fertile soil, since early childhood development gives rise to intense castration anxiety. In reality, however, there is no generally effective sexual taboo like the one dictated in part by the "second latency period" experienced by adolescents in certain social classes in Western society. Instead there is a tendency toward hypersexuality and promiscuity, going hand in hand with persistent sexual anxieties. The main differences, compared with our sexual taboos, are the following: The aggressive prohibitions against sexual activity are not based on a consensus of society. The mothers and the other women approve of the boys' sex play. Nor are these prohibitions traceable to objects with high libidinal cathexis, as with us. Sons do not love, respect, or even greatly fear their fathers. The fathers' role in the home is inconsistent and insignificant as far as the children are concerned; their authority is based neither on achievement nor on power, and (within the Anyi value system) they are not by any means regarded as morally ideal figures. When they do intervene in their sons' sexual experimentation during puberty, the sons experience them as envious—and temporarily more powerful—personal adversaries, not as the embodiment of authority. When the older boys attempt to take over their sexual role, they encounter no taboos of any kind, but merely additional difficulty or danger.

Our reconstruction of the life stories of most of the younger men reveals with striking clarity the traumatic treatment to which they were subjected during puberty, an experience that upset their equilibrium and paralyzed them for years to come. The grandfather (in Anoh Michel's case), the uncle (in Jean-Pierre's case), or the father simply dropped them or stopped paying for their schooling, or they were exiled from the family or given away to strange and unfeeling persons (as in the case of Adou Agnimou); it is no wonder that they came to grief, that they were unable to adjust to a situation for which they had not been prepared. A more detailed knowledge of exactly what took place in a given case serves to substantiate the inconsiderate or indifferent way families may treat adolescent boys, but it also shows that developmental disturbances during puberty usually manifest themselves before external blows of fate and independently of them. Agnimou, for instance, had lived contentedly with a foster family for several years and had been doing well in school until—as he said—the first sexual fantasies of early puberty brought him bad luck, that is, led to a decline in his academic performance.

For one of their problems, however—the choice of an "adult" love object—Anyi society does provide some help for pubescent youths in the form of a strictly defined gender role; an adult male is above all a male who has sexual relations with adult girls and women. Accordingly, boys at the puberty stage are expected to begin having intimate relations with girls. Other socially valid signs of masculinity are of only secondary importance. Psychoanalytic reconstruction confirms that the role definition provided by society guides the boy's sexual identity, still insecure during puberty and fluctuating between homosexual and heterosexual love objects, once and for all in the direction of heterosexuality, without any social disapproval or condemnation of homosexuality. The choice of a specific partner, however, is left entirely up to the young men in present-day Bébou. In earlier times it was customary for the representatives of the two families concerned to select the first marriage partners for their children. Especially with girls, a suitable partner was often chosen while the girl was still very young. The wedding ceremony was performed immediately, but the marriage was not consummated until the bride began to menstruate. Since the young men often found it difficult to make up their own minds, and since the families were always able to revoke their earlier decisions with relative impunity, the abolishment of the old custom is deplored more often than the new practice of allowing greater freedom of choice is praised as a progressive development. It sometimes happened that a dignitary might adopt a young man who found favor with him, in order to make him his son-in-law later on. This practice is supposed to have offered the best guarantee for a happy, lasting marriage, since the prospective bridegroom was very carefully chosen and—now that his own kin no longer felt responsible for him—could count on enjoying fatherly affection and guidance until his marriage.

The period of adolescence, from puberty to marriage, is very brief for Anyi girls, since they usually lose no time in getting pregnant and are then anxious to acquire the status of married women if they possibly can (as in the cases of Suzanne and Elisa). This may be one of the reasons adolescent girls have less problematic personalities than boys. The girls remain in the households where they have grown up, work just like the older women, take care of their sisters' children, and enjoy greater closeness to the mothers than during childhood. They take advantage of every opportunity to flirt and play. No one scolds them if they leave their work to chat with a young man. Moreover, they retain their ties to the group of their playmates. Though this group provides them with agreeable companionship, as a "horizontal" organization it is too unstable to offer material or psychological security if there are conflicts with the hierarchy of the mothers.

Several times we met adolescent girls who had been beaten by their mothers or turned out of their homes after a quarrel. Crying to themselves in the despairing cadence of bitterly unhappy toddlers, they wander around the village in dirty working clothes or run away to relatives in another village. Suzanne and Elisa both showed signs— though considerably less noisy ones—of similar despair. Their peer groups were unable to provide any real protection, and in the end there were only two courses of action open to them—either to make their apologies to their mothers and their kin and submit to the established order, or to go their own way.

We never observed such noisy, toddlerlike outbreaks of despair among the boys. They seem to be protected against them less by the rules of etiquette than by their habit of drowning their worst sorrows in alcohol. It is also possible that they no longer have such close ties to any person that they can be so desperately hurt by frustration.

Both in the opinion of the Anyi themselves and from the standpoint of the psychopathologist, the boys show signs of being far more severely disturbed than the girls. We did not encounter a single one who could not be classified as a problem personality or a deeply unhappy person over a relatively long period between the age of about fifteen and marriage (rarely before twenty or after twenty-five years of age).

Before their teachers' very eyes, boys of school age lose their ambition, interest, intelligence, and even their memory; they grow lazy, lethargic, and undependable.[1] The only way to get them to work would be to use force, and this is no longer feasible.

By the time the boys reach adolescence, the fathers have lost any authority they may have had over them. As long as they were small, the fathers occasionally gave them orders, but never an example to emulate or guidance of any kind. According to the present laws of inheritance, they are not in a position to offer their sons a future or even to oblige them to do any work for the benefit of the family in which they still live, more or less as parasites, but which merely provides a roof over their heads until they inherit from their maternal uncles. An uncle has no authority over his nephew and heir; in fact he is usually suspicious of him and is careful to keep him away from his own family. Mothers and older sisters are the only persons who still have some influence over adolescent boys. Yet, since they cannot refuse them food and shelter, their power over them is not great enough to make them lead more sensible lives. In former times the elected chief of the young men is supposed to have had a certain amount of authority. What the Anyi expect of their young men is not greatly different from what we expect of ours. They want them to complete their schooling, find suitable work, and make themselves independent as soon as they can; otherwise they are free to spend their time with their friends and with the girls and to enjoy life generally.

Within a brief time, the group of active, socially well-adjusted little boys has become a gang of unreliable, psychopathic youths, incapable of useful work and no longer even able to get along with each other. If we could explain this phenomenon, we would be a good deal closer to solving one of the most puzzling sociopsychological riddles posed by the Anyi, for many Anyi men turn out to be social misfits later in life as well.

Older and wiser Anyi and—in their moments of reason—the youths themselves complain of this problem. Ordinarily they place the blame on circumstances that they themselves have no power to change. And certainly they often adduce factors that are relevant when they speak of the inappropriate way mothers rear their children, the irresponsible indifference the fathers display and the bad example they set, the obsolete social order, the overweening role of tradition, the disintegration of tradition, the poor economic conditions, the excessively good economic conditions, unemployment, the present disastrous trends in politics, religion, and morals, and so forth. In short, they are just as helpless as we are when we discuss the problems of our protesting youth.

The problems of male adolescence among the Anyi can be attributed to the coincidence of two psychosocial phenomena: (1) An identity crisis is precipitated at an early age (not at the end of adolescence, as with us, but at the beginning) by the boy's losing his status as a child before his culture can offer him either a job, a livelihood, or a place in society. (2) This crisis takes place in an individual who is exposed to special stress during puberty and whose ego is not stabilized by an effective system of defenses or by lasting identifications.

The early confrontation with the realities of the world of adult work contrasts starkly with the traditional expectations of a distinguished, wealthy race of warriors who can find fame and gold any time they choose. The prospect of a hard, dreary life as a planter, who is forced to wait years before he can fulfill his desires, leads to a kind of despondency that seeks gratification through fantasies. In daydreams, in boastful speeches, and in intoxication induced by palm wine, the ego is invaded by orally gratifying fantasies of wealth and greatness whose content is often anal or phallic exhibitionistic in character. All fourteen of the adolescent youths we were able to study in some detail displayed a depressive-dysphoric despondency, and all of them told us fantastic tales of finding a benevolent mentor who heaped riches upon them and asked in return only that they increase his and their own prestige, or of suddenly having the great good fortune themselves to become great patrons, with a lot of money, numerous adherents, and a great deal of power. These daydreams often are set in the past; something good almost happened, but now it's too late and one's lot seems even sadder. European prostitutes frequently tell such stories to touch their customers' hearts with their misfortunes so they will be more generous. Even when these strong, handsome young men with their skeptical, intelligent expressions talk about the future, their stories usually end unhappily—there is always an envious father or uncle, a malevolent, omnipotent rival in the way.

Renunciation of these depressive fantasies with their hallucinatory gratifications is all the more difficult because palm wine really does make it possible for these egocentric, passive young men to be pleasantly intoxicated every day for almost nothing; thanks to their families and to the bounty of nature, basic subsistence is no problem, and the girls are perfectly willing to sleep with them even though it may not bring them love, because it entails no emotional involvement. During this period of inactivity, the adolescents enjoy a sort of moratorium and are able to escape the responsibilities of adult life for a few more years. Some of them achieve a satisfactory reorganization of their personalities afterward; for others these years represent a reeducation in the direction of psychopathy.

The lack of traditional institutions alone cannot explain why most young people lead lives of idleness. In Bébou it would be possible for every one of them to acquire a share in an existing plantation or to lay out a new one with a group of friends and, within a few years, to achieve a steady livelihood. But the identification with the active household work of the women, as an "identification with gesture," was interrupted during boyhood, and this interruption has made it extraordinarily difficult for them to take up the work of adult men. We were often able to observe young men standing by idly and despondently, watching another group working at a common task in the best of spirits. Only after watching for a long time were they able, all of a sudden, to join the others spontaneously, whereupon their mood would change and they would become eager and cheerful. Sometimes an older woman would try to urge on the melancholy spectator prematurely by suggesting that he join the others in their work—but invariably without result. The young man would refuse scornfully, saying he saw no point in it, and walk away unhappily. The woman's urging was experienced as a command that could be evaded by passive defiance.

An incentive to repeated identification would be necessary, the same sort of motivation that prompts a group of boys to engage in joint activities. The tensions that prevail in the adolescent group, however, are far too acute. Reciprocal active identifications do take place, but they break down again almost immediately.

One very popular method of being modern and European, impressing the girls, prevailing as a group over others, and achieving individual renown is playing soccer. In the land of the Anyi, every village possesses a cleared, leveled area used as a soccer field. During the four months we spent in Bébou, the local team played every Sunday against a team from some other village, either on their home field or "away"—just like soccer teams everywhere—with a neutral umpire and according to the rules. But not a single match could be played out—dissension and quarrels usually put an end to them before the second half.

The reports on our conversations with Thomas and Anoh Michel have demonstrated how a work team falls apart when envy and distrust, personal conflicts, and conflicts rooted in family loyalties prevent an identification with the activity of the group. Cathexis of the goal for which both Thomas and Anoh Michel are striving is not in itself sufficient to maintain the cohesion of the group.

Just about the only factor that genuinely unites the young men is their shared predilection for alcoholic orgies. Thoroughly inebriated with palm wine, they lie out in the forest under the oil palms in a spot they call the bar, "le cabaret." They identify with the group in some of their habits, for example, in their penchant for dressing neatly and fashionably and for daydreaming about money. Even Agnimou's refusal to wear good-looking clothes and his ascetic rejection of money can be interpreted as "negative identification" with the group—I'm not what I myself am, but the exact opposite of what you are.

Very unlike the youth of other West African peoples, Anyi young men are suspicious and wary of one another. They are constantly trying to get one of their number down and to insult him with their scornful remarks. This is not the kind of mockery that is based on friendship, though it does make use of nicknames; but the nicknames stick as "distorted names" and create a latent animosity. It would never occur to Jean-Pierre, for example, to confide in any of his colleagues, to discuss his anxieties with them, or to tell them how much money he has. And yet he feels the need for friendship, identifies immediately with our interpreter François as soon as he starts working for the same "patron," and is forced to give up this friendship, too, from one moment to the next.

The ability to maintain lasting identificatory relations with "brothers" of the same sex has never been able to develop, owing to the experiences of childhood. This disturbance, important in terms of society, goes back to the conflicts of puberty, which coincides chronologically with the identity crisis. Society has no place for its young men. Psychologically, there are two major areas of conflict.

Physiologically intensified instinctual demands give rise to a revival of the oedipal conflict, which in most cases has not been satisfactorily resolved. An exceedingly intense castration anxiety develops out of the traumatic witnessing of the primordial scene, out of the notion that the act of intercourse between the parents is in reality sadistic rape. The child's own experiences with his mother during the toddler stage are just as responsible for this notion as the behavior of the father, an alien interloper who has not permitted himself to establish aim-inhibited ties to his wife and children. When oedipal desires then make themselves felt more strongly in the boy during puberty, a rivalry situation must be avoided at all costs. This results, on the one hand, in passive submission and a renunciation of actively phallic, male desires. The resulting homosexual tendencies lead, in turn, to sadomasochistically disturbed love relations between the boy and his comrades. On the other hand, there is a regression of instinctual urges to the point of oral fixation. And this explains not only the greed for alcohol and other oral pleasures, but also the distrust and jealousy that prevail within the group.

While instinctual and ego regressions account for the tensions within the group and the inclination to passiveness, the lack of personal guidelines—the psychopathic attitude—can be explained by a peculiarity in superego formation. In the decline of the oedipal conflict outlined above, the authority of the father is not introjected as an entity to become a permanent component of the ego, as it is in Western cultures. Instead there is an internalization of part introjects with highly aggressive cathexis from an earlier period, while the most important commanding instances, that is, the powerful figures of the family, remain outside for the time being. As long as the boys continue to take orders, they remain hedonistically free of conflict; in other words, they obey when they have no other alternative and do whatever brings them personal gratification when their obedience is not compelled. Since they are removed from parental authority at the time of puberty, at this stage they ought to acquire an inner compass—to introject guiding figures. But, because of the excessively aggressive cathexis attached to authority figures, this development fails to take place. Since the dangers stirred up by instinctual urges give rise to intense guilt feelings and to anxieties of preoedipal origin, the resulting process of introjection is a peculiar one. The ideals decreed by society are isolated from the punishing components. The former nourish the pleasurable fantasies while the latter, by reinforcing primitive guilt feelings from the oral and anal aggressive phases, promote a tendency toward depressive self-destruction. Such a superego can be denied, perceived as nonexistent, and manipulated magically; it cannot prevent asocial attitudes, and it permits the individual to hold fast in his fantasies to the ideals offered by society.

This course of superego formation during puberty contributes to the identity crisis. An inner need to change things in the external world in order to relieve pressure exerted by conscience never arises. The superego is not autonomous. Instead the youth, and later the adult male, must rely on external guidance by some authority if he is to be able to perform many socially important tasks, particularly those that require active effort. His work ethic, to mention one example, is completely subjected to the injunctions of the clan conscience.

Sexual jealousy plays a surprisingly unimportant role in the young people's conflicts among themselves. It must be borne in mind that love objects are found only with difficulty and are not easily cathected with libido, and that it is sexual activity per se that society demands; the love object concerned is of secondary importance.

Judging from the existing social institutions, one would expect the sex life of adults to be extremely gratifying. Sexuality is highly respected as an instrument of procreation and regarded as the highest enjoyment life can offer. The modesty barrier extends only to exhibition of the upper thighs and the genital area; it has nothing to do with less direct sexual acts, and certainly not with flirting or with talking about sexual matters. The few existing taboos and restrictions are applied with leniency. Though it is not difficult for an individual to acquire an unsavory sexual reputation—since erotic curiosity is great—such a reputation is hardly damaging and is no obstacle to either a man or a woman in finding partners.

The poor development of the ego's ability to postpone gratification also reduces inhibitions. Thus it is no wonder that love affairs have an important place in the lives of the Anyi. Since the ties between partners follow preoedipal patterns, and genital strivings are unable to assert their primacy completely but remain linked with pregenital ones, Anyi sex life is characterized by forms that seem alien to us and is certainly subject to frequent disturbances. Of the four normal young men we interviewed, three (Anoh Michel, Jean-Pierre, and Agnimou) suffered impotence from time to time; the forty-year-old chief Brou Koffi asked us for pills to increase his potency because he felt unequal to the sexual demands of his wives—with the casual remark that he himself was no longer interested in sex anyway; and a number of husbands and fathers came to us for help because they had been impotent with their wives for years.

Insofar as we were able to analyze this problem, it seemed that the unconscious fear of women, coupled with the social insecurity of domestic life, was responsible for most of the difficulties. We were unable to discover whether there are Anyi women who are frigid. In their case it is even more obvious than with the men how frequently sexuality is used as a weapon in the aggressive struggle for power and self-assertion. The intense sexual life of the young men is reminiscent of that of European neurotics with primarily pregenital libido fixations. The function itself is not disturbed, but the pleasure gained is predominately narcissistic; the partner is less a love object than an instrument of gratification; emotional relations with him or her are laden with conflict, but this has little or no detrimental effect on sexuality.

We found it very strange to watch young people flirting with each other. We observed this the first time in Yosso, on an empty street. A pretty young girl was stopped by two young men. One of them grabbed hold of her, held her head against his body with his left hand in a wrestler's grip, and slapped her face with his right hand when she screamed and struggled to get away from him. In the meantime the other boy was fumbling at her hip cloth, trying to pull it up over her legs. Although the boys saw that I was watching them, and the girl's screams were growing louder and louder as she struggled, from her awkward position, to kick away the boy behind her, he finally managed to pull up her hip cloth and seize her genitals. Suddenly both boys let go. And only then could I tell, as a European, that the whole business was not attempted rape but merely a form of flirting. The girl ran a few steps and railed loudly at the boys, who grinned back at her, not very affectionately; then she stopped scolding and came back to one of them, stroking his neck and his loins. After this she calmly continued on her way.

Sometimes love play takes place in much this same fashion, sometimes less aggressively. Usually it is only the two partners who participate. But the general atmosphere is often rather like that of the scene described above.

The concept of perversion is not a part of every culture. The Anyi find rape undesirable, but not incomprehensible. They all believe that formerly many women who went out into the forest alone were raped by strange men. We were told that only now that each village has its own prostitutes, most of whom are not Anyi, has this danger become a thing of the past. Tales about the raping of women recall the Anyi fantasies that there are thieves lurking everywhere; the conviction that this is so has its roots in an unconscious fantasy. We cannot say whether the corresponding sexual version is based on equally imaginary experiences.

The psychic development of the Anyi encourages homosexual attitudes. During puberty, their clearly defined social role and their need for a guiding authority "from outside" seem to restrict most men to their heterosexual opportunities, but homosexual cathexis remains possible in their emotional and fantasy lives. We had the impression that these homosexual tendencies are sometimes partially repressed, as in Jean-Pierre's case or in the case of the latent homosexuality of European neurotics, and sometimes merely suppressed in overt behavior. Bisexual development may be even more common in women. In every village there are some men who, for neurotic reasons, do not have sexual relations with women. A number of them are known to practice occasional reciprocal masturbation with boys. One example is the "clean old man" of Yosso, who suffers from a compulsion to wash himself constantly. Such men are regarded as infantile and undeveloped and as deserving of pity, especially since they cannot find women to keep house for them.

The high degree of tolerance toward deviant sexual behavior going hand in hand with a disturbed sex life should serve as a warning to Western reformers that sexual intolerance is by no means the only reason—and in fact not even the most important reason—for the occurrence of sexual disturbances.

Marriage, Divorce, Polygyny, and Old Age
Don't die, even when it seems impossible to go on.

Inexorably, the achievement of adulthood leads to marriage. Economic necessity, social pressures, the often unattainable wish for a stable interpersonal relationship and, most of all, for the continuation of one's own existence in the form of children all work toward this end. In the matrifocal society of the Anyi (140) it is the wife who exercises the greatest influence within the framework of the nuclear family, while the husband has relatively few functions in connection with more intimate matters, so that he is really more or less interchangeable. These circumstances are reflected in the sayings "One is not always in love with the same man" and—from the standpoint of the man—"A wife is like a bed sheet; if you pull it up to cover yourself it scratches you, but without it you're cold." A third saying, "Fear the person who is close to you," applies to both sexes.

The comparative simplicity of the marriage ceremony among the Akan peoples has been attributed to the fact that the bride is not lost to her family (neither the daughter nor her children) and that the bridegroom's kin play hardly any role, since their only function is to provide a procreator. In earlier times the exact observance of the rules of exogamy was a matter for discussion during the negotiations between the family elders; nowadays it is left up to the bride and bridegroom. Elisa's story shows that incestuous infringements may well serve as a pretext for strife, but also that they are generally accepted with equanimity. The main goal seems to be to reconcile the conflicting interests of the families concerned by keeping open the possibility of a later separation. This also explains why cross-cousin marriages, formerly regarded as the happiest of all possible unions because they lent stability to the closely allied families concerned, have fallen into disrepute. Nowadays it is customary to negotiate the terms of divorce even before marriage.

Before a couple is considered stably married, their relationship may progress through three separate stages, any one of which can continue indefinitely or be dissolved at will:

The short-term love affair (without ceremonial obligations of any kind), which is nevertheless regarded as a basis for a longer alliance.

The long-lasting love relationship, which gives the man the right to compensation from an interloper who disrupts it (as in the case of adultery after marriage).

The marriage itself, made official when the bridegroom presents the "head wine"—two bottles of gin—to the chief of the bride's family.

The custom of compensating the woman's kin with a bride-price has never played an important role among the Anyi. Nowadays the man simply makes the mother of the bride a small present of money, which need not be returned in case of divorce.

From the point of view of reducing the overweening importance of the bride's kin, whose rivalry was apt to place a strain on the marriage, it can only be regarded as a sign of progress that the financial obligations involved have been reduced almost entirely to an exchange of gifts between the bride and bridegroom. But since the husband-wife relationship is overshadowed from the very beginning by intense anxieties, and since the husband is far more afraid of his wife than she is of him, the man feels that he has been exploited, that he has been a helpless victim of blackmail, and that he has been sucked dry.

The wives are not afraid of being betrayed and abandoned by their husbands, though this happens frequently enough. Apparently they accept the inevitability of disappointment and are prepared to drop their husbands as love objects or not to hold them in too high esteem. Officially, and sometimes in practice as well, they have their kin to return to as a last resort. Yet the husband's fear of his wife is not primarily a fear of being abandoned, either. Presumably, the form taken by the weaning trauma and the period of life at which it occurs encourage fixation on greedy oral drive modalities. According to the men, "Women are like chickens; when you scatter corn for them, they come running." The younger women, they say, are insatiable when it comes to clothes, money, and love. A woman is like a used car at a bargain price; no sooner have you bought it than its defects begin to show up, defects you have to pay for until, in the end, you have lost everything. If she wants to leave you and you persuade her to stay, she will probably poison you. Some men prefer older wives because they are beyond the age at which they think of nothing but clothes and other lovers; others try their luck with women who have been disappointed in love or women who have quarreled with their own kin—merely to establish a kind of balance.

Separation is the first remedy for all the anxieties that can arise out of living together. In the symbiotic phase, to which we assign the fixation on the trauma, separation from the object represents a progressive act of defense, which naturally cannot undo the frustration, but which does make it possible to project frustration aggressions externally, to the separated component of the symbiotic self. Separate households are only one of the many precautionary measures. When Adou Agnimou's parents had a domestic quarrel, they established separate plantations. The rules of etiquette forbid men and women to eat together. A wife is not allowed to address her husband in public. Even Thomas, energetic as he is, would never dare to criticize either his wife or his sister, not for reasons of etiquette, but because it would be undiplomatic. He can, of course, turn to their sisters or mothers, but he is likely to discover that all the women tend to form a common front against him, even though they may have been quarreling among themselves just before.

A divorce entails no moral disadvantage for either the husband or the wife. If the wife has been at fault, her kin must return the price of the head wine; if the husband is the guilty party, he may have to compensate his wife's kin for any earnings that have accrued to him as a result of her labor. Male children "belong" to the husband, female children to the wife; in case of divorce, the wife temporarily retains custody of children of toddler age; she is expected to give the male children back to the husband later. The children from the first marriage of Thomas's second wife remain with their mother and accrue to the estate of their stepfather, since their father is unwilling or unable to repay the money spent for their maintenance during the years when he contributed nothing toward their welfare and left them with his divorced wife.

There are a number of grounds for divorce—especially sexual inadequacy on the part of the husband, brutality, chronic quarrelsomeness, and miserliness. When a wife fails to become pregnant or a child dies, it is often reason enough for the husband or the wife to terminate the marriage. Today, all these time-honored reasons are no more than arguments brought forward during reconcilement negotiations carried out by the kin of an estranged couple. Actually, one can always assume willful desertion (not of the common household, because often there is none!) as the reason for a divorce. The process is such that any deeper conflict is likely to lead to the wife's leaving or the husband's disappearing. The divorce negotiations are concerned less with the underlying conflict than with what is to happen as a result of it—whether the partners will remain separated or go back to each other.

In the cases we know of, the husband put the blame on the family—that is, the mother—of his wife, even when it was obvious that the wife herself was unwilling to remain with her husband and had thus gone back to her kin. A wife, on the other hand, is most likely to blame the mother or the older sister of her husband (as Suzanne did). In this way both parties are able to spare their own feelings, naturally upset by the conflict between them; the narcissistic injury is less painful when the breakup of the marriage is due to external forces. Both husband and wife have hit upon a psychological truth—that the preoedipal ties to the mother, or rather their introject, which impairs the phallicity of the man and consolidates the daughter's masochistic bond with her mother, is invariably involved in one way or another in all marriage conflicts.

Adultery is not official grounds for divorce, and sexual infidelity seldom seems to be the most important reason for the breakup of a marriage. Suzanne, for example, is unwilling to accept the subordinate role of second wife; she expects tangible proofs of her husband's love for her, including sexual pleasure. It is important to her that he do what she wants instead of following his sister's advice; his sexual infidelity is simply a consequence of his general unreliability. Tradition demands no conciliatory steps when the husband commits adultery. When it is the wife, however, her "partner in crime" is expected to compensate the injured husband with a sum of money, and the erring wife must tender her apologies to her husband. Anyi husbands were often referred to—enviously and contemptuously—as pimps by the French, who were unable to understand that the husband's right of possession over his wife is viewed more frankly (or more cynically, as the French thought) among the Anyi than in Western cultures as akin to the right of possession over material objects.

Infidelity on the wife's part creates a very genuine problem in that the injured husband is afraid of being poisoned by the adulterer if the latter should wish to continue living with the wife. This, however, can be prevented by social processing.

The adulterer is invested with the qualities of a witch, qualities otherwise attributed only to the women of one's own family. This peculiar exception to the usual belief in witches can probably be traced back to the fact that the husband is simply incapable of tolerating a lasting rivalry aggression that he cannot ward off. He relapses into oral regression. The rival who has succeeded in persuading the wife to stay with him is perceived as a wet nurse who has turned her attention to the next child—that is, to the faithless wife. Experiencing a turn to the passive homosexual, the injured husband feels himself helplessly in the power of this male mother. The milk he gives the husband to drink is poisoned by the latter's own hatred, while his good milk is now reserved for the faithless wife, who has become the object of her husband's sibling envy.

Even a man like Chief Ahoussi is not immune to these fears. When his young wife, Elisa's sister, began her love affair with the schoolmaster, it never occurred to him to take revenge on his rival. On the contrary—he promised the teacher new plantations and other advantages provided he never slept with the errant wife again. This agreement was still in effect long after the chief had been deserted by his young wife. Owing to the general inhibition of rivalry aggressions, it is practically impossible for an Anyi to fight with a rival for his wife. Instead, one either buys off the rival as a mother-witch, as Ahoussi did, or conjures him with the help of magic. In olden times, to be sure, the Akan kings enjoyed the prerogative of ordering the death of any man who seduced a woman from the royal harem. The clans had established this law to give at least their leader and ideal figure some semblance of phallic aggressiveness.

Polygyny is viewed as a necessary supplement to monogamous marriage. For prestige, and also because his household requires a good deal of work, a chief must have at least two wives. For an ordinary man it is a matter of status. His family recommends polygyny; though it may be expensive, it is worth it in the end. When Thomas takes over his court, the necessary steps will be taken to see that his first wife, who returned to her family over a year ago and whose child died while she was with them, comes back to her husband—although in these circumstances she was regarded as practically divorced. If she refuses to stay with him, Thomas intends to divorce her and take another woman as his second wife. He shares the widespread opinion that this is the best guarantee of stability in a marriage. Neither wife could run away, for that would mean yielding her husband to her rival. A husband's two wives usually refer to each other as "my rival." Since a man does not marry both wives at the same time, one is always the second wife. Tradition decrees that a man obtain his first wife's agreement when he wants to take a second one, that the new bride convey her apologies to the first wife—for, after all, she will be diminishing at least the latter's sexual rights—and that the first wife accept these apologies. The man must grant the same rights to both wives, not giving sexual preference to one, and is expected to provide two comparable houses; in return, both wives cook for him and care for his needs. It looks very much as though polygyny is a social institution that lends some measure of permanence to an otherwise unstable married life. On the other hand, Brou Koffi complains that two wives in one household are constantly bickering, that the interference of two mothers-in-law is intolerable, and that—adding insult to injury—sometimes even his two wives and his own sister unite against him.

We have no information on just how many men in Alangouan are really married to two or more wives. Statistics of this kind would be extremely difficult to obtain, since it is impossible either to go by joint households or to rely on the statements of individual marriage partners. The legal position of a couple often remains unclear for years; there may be a concubine, for example, who has no desire to marry, or a divorced woman may still be referred to as a wife. Since girls marry younger than men, and since there are a good many neurotic men or men whose sexuality has been impaired by alcoholism who are not married at all, a statistically significant incidence of polygyny cannot be excluded.

As with so many social institutions, however, the facts may be less important than the psychosocial possibility that a custom sanctions, which thereby becomes a psychological reality. One has the impression that the Anyi men, who do not really feel at home in any of the family systems to which they belong, resort to polygyny to ensure themselves a way out of a monogamous relationship they find intolerable (or at least to keep the possibility of escape open in their fantasies), and that the women accept it because they feel that conflicts with a husband can be handled better when they can be shifted to a rival (or to the sister of the husband). In the last analysis, the highest good offered by the form of marriage practiced by the Anyi is the possibility of simply going away without losing face and without feeling guilt—one is simply the victim of circumstances and meddlesome in-laws. In this way they safeguard their vulnerable self-esteem against narcissistic mortification; they retain at least the semblance of independence and pride.

As the Anyi approach old age, their lives become more serene. Grandparents, particularly grandmothers, have a special status. They have great influence on the rearing of their grandchildren and are regarded as the custodians of morality in their courts. Prestige comes automatically with advanced age—"There was already an old man on earth before the king was born." All this applies to the ideal situation, in which the maternal lineage has grown in number and the old people still live in the courts of their kin.

Soon after we open our medical consulting hours in Yosso, a group of eight to ten old women come to be examined. As the first one sits down opposite me, she smiles contemptuously. She refuses to answer my questions. I explain to her that a doctor must hear his patient's complaints; only a veterinarian can manage without that. The old woman takes off her shirt and points to various parts of her body that hurt her. Her expression is now pained and scornful. She—and the others as well—constantly spit on the floor. I tell her I know exactly why she doesn't want to talk with me—she has so many worries on her mind that she simply can't get around to telling a doctor what is wrong with her. There is a sudden change in the atmosphere. She is now all smiles, friendly and depressive. One of the other women waiting her turn begins to weep. After that first visit, all the old women of Yosso were among our most cooperative patients. The one who started weeping is now about sixty-five, perhaps even older. Her whole body is full of aches and pains. She has spondylitis of the spine and arthritis in her shoulders and elbows. She is lean, old, used up. She has a friendly, mobile face and a melancholy smile. She is divorced, and all her children are dead. Her husband kept all their plantations for himself, and she is too weak to start new ones. She is no longer able to mash cassava or to cook because of the pain in her arms. She has neither brothers nor sisters—only distant relatives who do nothing for her. She gathers kindling to earn a little bit of money, so that she can buy rice from the Djoula.

The rest of the old women are not so bad off. They all have bodily ailments, all ultimately attributed to the fact that their monthly periods have ceased and they can no longer bear children. Thus their lives can never again be what they would like them to be.

The old women are provocative and ironic; they are intelligent and quick at repartee in their refusal to accept sympathy from others. Without exception, they are ready to enter into new relationships, in which they are capable of developing friendly feelings.

The old men, too, are depressive, inclined to despondency. They ward off all attempts at contact by aggressive remarks unless—as frequently happens—they have found a happier escape into intoxication.

But the traditional respect accorded to old age, with the entire body of etiquette designed to ensure it, cannot suffice to compensate for the loss of love objects or for inner loneliness. Since prestige and power are better regulated in the maternal lineage system than is material security, the system as such cannot guarantee that a revered grandparent may not die of starvation.

6 Witches, Female Shamans, and Healers

Elisa (Goldy Parin-Matthèy)

During the period from 7 February to 22 March 1966, I interviewed Elisa Ajé Messou in a tent in Bébou on twenty-three occasions, each interview lasting one hour.

She is about seventeen years of age and is seven months pregnant. She has just returned from the district capital, Abengourou, where she had been for a prenatal checkup. Thomas Assoua, a young dignitary of Bébou, is aware of what we are trying to do here and is doing his best to find women and girls who know enough French to be able to talk with Madame. He now appears at my tent with Elisa in tow.

We sit down together in the tent. Elisa rigid with fear, is dressed in a lovely blue and green toga. With her slender face—showing signs of strain—slightly averted and her dark, expressive eyes fixed on some remote object, she says nothing more than "oui–non, Madame."

Elisa has no incentive to talk with me; she was ordered to: "Since we have sent you to school, you now must speak with Madame." Elisa attended the high school in Zaranou only two years; after that, no more money was forthcoming for her education. And since she was not permitted to finish school, the privilege of speaking French with Madame is understandably clouded with bitter thoughts, with a feeling of having been betrayed.

Since the village has offered us its cooperation, and her family is forcing her to comply, it is clear that Elisa has no choice but to come. This "must" seems more important than my reassurances that the interviews are voluntary and will take place only if she herself is willing. In any case, we arrange for her to talk with me for an hour a day in the tent, for which she will be given daily pin money amounting to fifty francs. If she comes twenty hours in all, she will receive an additional gift of the same amount (a *pagne*, the amount of material needed for a dress, costs approximately four thousand francs). Her only reply, uttered with the same strained expression, is "oui, Madame."

For the first two hours Elisa maintains this passively resigned "oui–non, Madame," and gradually I begin to understand. In any case, I dare not try to force things or to make any demands upon her. Instead, during our third session, I begin to talk about my impressions of the Anyi and to explain why we decided that it was this particular people we wanted to know better. I told her how interesting it was to us that the Anyi, who had so clearly retained their traditional cultural identity, should at the same time play a role on the world market with their cocoa and coffee industries.

And this elicited Elisa's first spontaneous comment: "The women get nothing out of it. The men don't give them any money to feed their children. They don't bother about anything. The mothers grieve when a child dies. The fathers don't even think about it; they leave the mothers alone. And that doesn't make the children any better either. The men even beat their wives. When this happens, the wives divorce their husbands and go back to their families. Yes, divorce is the only defense a woman has."

Elisa's statement reflects intense resentment at the social order. Rebelling, she takes a firm stand on the side of the women; her words, "the women get nothing out of it," represent obvious verbal aggression toward the male. The woman's means of defense is divorce, separation, the abandonment of a relationship.

The next day Elisa fails to appear. Is she using her weapon of defense against me, too?

It is probably simpler for me to try to describe, at this point, Elisa's social situation, her status in society and family, even though this necessarily anticipates facts that emerged only gradually during the course of our sessions together.

Elisa's mother, Aboué, lives in one of the chief's courts with her two daughters Tanoh and Elisa. When this chief, Ahoussi de Bernard, king of Alangouan, began to reorganize his kingdom and to build the village of Bébou in the twenties, he talked with all the families of dignitaries he could reach, trying to persuade them to settle in Bébou. Some of these families came; a good many others, however, who themselves had no desire to move from their homes, gave him one or more of their children for his court—also as a gesture of respect toward him. These children now belong to him; they are his property and he can treat them as he chooses—as his own children or as feudal serfs. They increase the prestige as well as the size of his court.

Elisa's grandfather gave his little daughter Aboué, Elisa's mother, to Ahoussi de Bernard. When Aboué came of age, the chief selected a husband for her—a man she did not like at all but was forced to accept. With this man she had one daughter, Tanoh, Elisa's older sister. Aboué, however, refused to remain with the husband for whom she felt no love and slept with Koffi, a Baoulé. The chief, who after all has supreme power over the persons given to him, was furious and apparently had her bound and beaten.

Hereupon Aboué left her daughter Tanoh with an older sister in Bébou and went away to a small village on the Comoë River to live with her third husband, Messou. It was he who was the father of Elisa, my subject.

But the chief still wanted Elisa's mother to return to Bébou. Her husband Messou refused to come with her. So she decided to come back alone, carrying Elisa on her back; one reason presumably was the memory of her older daughter, Tanoh, whom she had left in the care of her sister in Bébou. Shortly after Aboué's return, this sister died, and Aboué continued to reside with her two daughters in the sister's compound, in one of the courts belonging to the chief.

Elisa never saw her real father Messou again. After his wife left him, he was to have taken over the plantations of his uncle in keeping with matrilineal succession, but he was afraid that his relatives there might kill him. He left his family and disappeared from the village. No one knew where he had gone. In 1961 he was reported dead.

Mother Aboué then married a fourth husband in Bébou, but she had no further children. She is a member of the chief's court.

When the older daughter Tanoh grew up, her fate turned out to be a repetition of her mother's. The chief married her himself, for after all she was his property—and, besides, a very beautiful girl. She found that he was too old for her, though, and she was not fond of him in any case; moreover, he failed to give her a child. So she took other lovers. She too was beaten by the chief.

Chief Ahoussi de Bernard gave some of his plantations to the primary-school teacher in Bébou and ordered Tanoh, Elisa's sister, to go to work there. And there she fell in love with the schoolmaster, who wanted to marry her. But, since she was still legally the wife of the chief, this was patently impossible. Ahoussi threatened to kill them both if they continued living together.

Mother Aboué is also worried that her older daughter will follow her own inclinations, as she herself had done, and would much prefer that Tanoh submit to the harsh laws of the Anyi, laws based on the principle of the ownership of persons. For where could Aboué turn in case the king in his fury should cast her out of his court? She is no longer young and has no family with whom she might seek refuge. To enhance the prestige of this very king and to remain on good terms with him—also, incidentally, to purchase its own freedom of action—her own family had sold her, her children, and her children's children to him, together with all the rights of ownership a family has over its own progeny. This shows the extent to which submission to the king goes among the Anyi.

Elisa gave promise of becoming an intelligent child, and Ahoussi sent her to school. When she proved to be a bright pupil, he even paid for her attendance at the high school in Zaranou. But when her older sister Tanoh deceived him with the schoolmaster, Ahoussi refused to pay any longer for Elisa's schooling because he was angry with her sister.

The child Elisa is carrying was also fathered by a schoolteacher, currently employed in the land of the Bété.

Children are considered the absolute property of their families. They can be pledged as security when the family is in debt; they can be given away if the family wishes to place someone under obligation to it. Elisa shares this fate with many other Anyi. With the fate of her mother and sister before her eyes, it is only natural that she is filled with a rebellious longing for greater equality.

Returning to our interview sessions, we have seen that for the first two hours Elisa submitted passively to the command that she talk with me, only to break out in the third session in a rebellious expression of her own feelings, when she adopted a firm stand—we females against the males, from whom no good can be expected. The next time she fails to come. She feels the need to prevent herself from falling under any compulsion I might exercise over her.

When she appears for our fourth session, she establishes a new situation by bringing the traditional return gift. She presents me with a pineapple. In other words, she is retreating from an unprecedented and dangerous relationship with Madame to a form of contact that is sanctioned by custom and at the same time commits her to nothing. She tells me that the day before her mother had sent her out to fish. I imply that the Anyi custom of exchanging gifts instead of thoughts is a practical one and that it is wise simply to do as one is told; then one has no further trouble. I make it clear to her that I understand that now she has no reason to feel dependent upon me.

We come to speak of the town of Zaranou and of the strange fact that the Anyi there are so punctilious about complying with the government edict that the old mud houses be destroyed and replaced by new ones that they themselves are paying for the bulldozers to raze the houses, which will leave them without any money to build new ones.

This is Elisa's spontaneous reaction, brought forth defiantly: "It's a good thing they have to build themselves new houses there. The ones they have are too old, no good."

She continues speaking, but it becomes more and more difficult to understand what she is saying; she mentions something about the school, but it is as if she had lost the power of speech. I can understand the name "Binger" (one of the early French colonizers and researchers), then her words become completely incomprehensible and she falls silent.

What has happened? My mention of the traditional contacts among the Anyi has apparently been interpreted as approval of her protests against the "old society" and its customs. As early as her third talk with me, Elisa identified herself with me, with Madame, who—as a foreigner—stands apart from this society, who is different and powerful. We women stand together against the men, we substitute new values for the old, inadequate ones. Now, as I fail to agree with her radical standpoint regarding the tearing down of the houses, she senses that this identification is threatened and shaken, and her speech becomes unclear and incoherent. It may well be that the linguistic deterioration reflects the ambiguity of what she now feels toward me. On the one hand, we seem to be partners; on the other hand, there are obviously areas in which we do not agree, and in these she is compelled to stand alone with her aggressive, rebellious wish to destroy.

An overvaluation of my person had reinforced Elisa's self-confidence as long as she identified herself with me. The collapse of this identification led to an undermining of her self-esteem and to a deterioration of verbal expression, a function of the ego.

As if summoned by Elisa, at this very moment her older sister comes running to the tent, carrying a little boy in her arms and crying, "He's going to die!" The little boy's toe has been badly cut. Together with Elisa and her sister, I go to get the materials to bandage it. As soon as the boy's injury has been treated, the two sisters depart together.

Was the sister expressing the fears Elisa herself had just been experiencing? Will she have to die if she identifies herself with me, if she gives expression to her mutinous, aggressive wishes, and then her identification with the idealized foreigner turns out to be untenable after all?

Elisa does not come to the next scheduled session. Then she appears with an excuse; she had been there twice but had not seen me.

After this she tells me laughing that the little boy's injured toe no longer hurts. "He's a regular little rascal; he's always running away" (she laughs). Indirectly, Elisa has informed me that *she* is the little rascal who makes a habit of running away.

But then—as if to justify her running away—she embarks on a tale of a white man who owned gold mines and forced people to work in them. This man, she says, beat her. The story becomes more and more horrifying, her speech deteriorates again, becomes incomprehensible— something about dead bodies buried by a landslide and an old man who laid people on a board and chopped off their heads.

After a fairly long pause, she tells me—her speech perfectly normal and understandable—the story of how people discovered that bananas are edible. A good, courageous woman was the first to bite into the fruit everyone thought was poisonous and thus found a new source of food for her people.

What was the reason for the linguistic deterioration this time? I started from the assumption that Elisa's inability to speak the previous time was the result of her feeling of insecurity regarding her identification with me. If she now demonstrates her admiration for me by behaving like the small child who runs away but cannot be blamed for its naughtiness—in other words, by visualizing herself as small compared with me—then she will soon begin to fear that from behind the foreign white Madame may emerge the menacing face of the preoedipal mother, with all her powers of coercion. Compulsion and threat play a role in Elisa's faltering tale. The flood of aggressive emotions released by these projective fantasies in turn brings about a partial ego regression accompanied by disintegration of the faculty of speech, while the destructive tendencies are projected into the content of the fantasies. This time it is a white man. This way of dealing with aggressive impulses is like a reversible act. The ego regresses with a gradual loss of the speech function to the level at which the rudiments of language are just beginning to be mastered and at which the preverbal yearnings for omnipotence are still paramount. It is significant that in these situations the cruel events expressed in the aggressive impulses are always specified as having taken place "earlier," "years ago." One might conclude that what is referred to is that period during the second year of life when the Anyi mother withdraws her complete attention from her child, when she simply lets it cry uncomforted, and when there is no one to satisfy its emotional needs—that period during which the Anyi child must learn to cope with the tensions created by these needs without the contacts with its mother and the activity on her part that would help to mitigate and channel libido and aggression. It can be assumed that the child's experiences at this stage are bound to disturb the development of neutralized ego activities and the achievement of secondary processes.

But what is it that helps Elisa reemerge from this regressive deterioration of the speech faculty? When she succeeds in projecting the content of her aggressive impulses to past deeds done by old, evil men, she can reachieve identification with me. She can again see herself as the good, courageous mother-female, the provider of nourishment.

Realizing this, I deliberately meet her halfway in her attempt to achieve identification; I tell her the story of how the potato was introduced into Europe. She listens with evident delight. We are equals. Both of us are brave and good. Elisa is enthusiastic, and I have difficulty in getting her to go home.

The next time, though, Elisa comes to our compound. They tell her I am waiting for her at the tent, but she does not come.

The following day she appears at the appointed time but gives me no excuse for yesterday, merely saying that she supposes I was angry with her for not coming. Now she has reached the point where she is able to bear the thought of my anger without fear. She is even able to dissociate herself from a feeling of envy toward my second subject, Suzanne. Yesterday evening a jealous affair was the sensation of the entire village. Unlike Suzanne and the rest of the village girls, all of them up in arms against the adultress, Elisa declares the man to be the guilty one. And she begins to talk, passionately:

> *Elisa:* Here a woman works long and hard on her husband's plantation, she has children, and he meets a younger woman and goes off with her, divorces his wife and marries the younger one, and the first one is left with nothing because the plantation belongs to her husband. He forbids her to come to the plantation to get food for the children. When a family has nothing, or when a woman has no family to go back to, she's to be pitied.

Elisa speaks excitedly about the new law that is to introduce inheritance through the male line.

> *Elisa:* Now we've won—when a wife works for her husband, she'll always receive a piece of his land in return for her labor. Then she'll have her own plantation and won't be left without anything at all in case her husband dies or leaves her.

There is a pause in the conversation. A very pretty bird flies down and settles on a branch of the mango tree in front of us. I call Elisa's attention to it.

Elisa [scaring it away with a motion of her hand]: Now it's gone. Things are bad here, too many devils. The measles have carried off thirty-five children. It was the devil, who ate two or three children every day. And one can't give birth to a child here, either. There is an old woman, she took the flesh of her daughter and sold it; so her daughter died. As a matter of fact, my grandmother may already have sold my flesh, and I won't know it until I die. This old woman was in Abengourou, nobody saw her. She goes out into the fields, and when she comes back, she says, "I've seen my dead daughter, she wants her flesh back." And then the old woman takes the flesh of another child, so that the daughter won't demand the flesh of the old woman herself. One woman lost six children this way. She is the first divorced wife of the chief. She cried all the time and kept seeing her daughter. And the spirit has entered the body of the bird that calls "kiu kiu" and has already taken three children. The woman was changed into the bird. The chief used to have a fetish, and one woman had already almost died because the old woman wanted her flesh, so that she could give it back to her dead daughter. The chief put the question to the fetish, and the fetish accepted the sacrifice, and right away the woman who was nearly dead got up; she was cured. In the meantime, though, the chief has been to consult the healer in Dabou and since then he's thrown all his fetishes away.

During the pause that follows, Elisa's fears obviously grow. I ask her: "You mean it would have been better for the chief to keep the fetish, then he would have had a weapon against the evil women who sell flesh?"

The sudden fright in Elisa's eyes and the violent trembling of her body are pitiful to see, and I point out that all these flesh-eating witches had not entered her mind until I showed her the bird. I ask her whether she thinks that the foreign white Madame summoned the bird. Elisa says no, but she admits she is afraid.

Elisa denies any magical link between me and the transformed bird. But I don't quite believe her; I am too deeply impressed by the evident intensification of her fear since the bird's appearance and by the magically projective elements concerning the evil, flesh-devouring mothers. Surely these regressive fantasies reflecting her fear of women are an indication that she is afraid of entering an object relationship with me?

It could be that the gesture I made in calling her attention to the bird simply did not fit into the concept of the "new, better, more hygienic, and more sensible" order with which Elisa felt compulsively bound to identify herself in order to banish the old, anal-sadistic element of compulsion and the oral element of the devouring mother. By telling me about the flesh-eating witch-mothers, she tried first to vanquish her fear by articulating it—the fear created in her by the conflict between her attitude toward me, with its dominant component of phallic identification, and the anal-sadistic and oral ties that linked her with the pregenital mother. When I confirmed her suspicion that the chief who had gotten rid of his fetish could not help her either, her reaction was acute anxiety. Neither she nor the chief possesses a fetish, a phallus, with which to protect themselves; both are powerless. The danger looms that I may turn into the omnipotent, menacing mother.

On the other hand, it must be remembered that before the unfortunate appearance of the bird Elisa had demonstrated remarkable ego achievement in that she had countered a reaction of envy with an ego-adequate demand for justice (that every individual be rewarded for his labor instead of the system of matrilineal succession). Although she experiences anxiety, this time there is no accompanying linguistic deterioration—an indication that in spite of everything, our relationship has become more relaxed, that her ego is no longer driven to regress to meet a sudden emergency.

Elisa arrives punctually for our next meeting but sits on the campbed dejected and silent. She admits that she is afraid that something bad might happen to her or to her child. And, as a matter of fact, a great many women seem to die of tetanus here while giving birth.

> *Elisa:* My mother says that this sickness comes from a bird that attacks mother and child during the night.
> *Madame:* You're thinking of this sickness now because I showed you that bird yesterday, and you have an idea that there is something evil about the bird and that I have some connection with this evil bird.
> *Elisa* [smiling]: No, Madame. The evil bird lives in the forest and not in the village. It isn't this bird.

Outside we can hear the women singing and striking their sticks for the funeral ceremony. Elisa tells me that she didn't go there with them yesterday.

After a long pause, I remark: "Yes, I can understand that. When one is about to bring forth new life, one doesn't go to a funeral ceremony."

> *Elisa* [merrily]: No, the reason I didn't go was because in my condition I can't dance and drink all night long; it's bad for me.

It is strange that in my countertransference, in my desire to be close to her, to understand her better, for the second time I am attributing to Elisa magical projections she no longer has. She has reestablished her operational identification with the strange not-mother and gives me perfectly sensible reasons for her conduct, while I am still way behind her, still suspecting her of motivations dictated by magic and superstition.

Elisa tells me something about the life stories of her mother and sister and is able to express her resentment at social conditions convincingly and without functional ego regression: "Things used to be bad, and the chief is a very bad man." And she explains how the chief used to exploit his supreme power over her mother and sister.

"But now we have *indépendance,* and he can't do things like that any more" (she laughs); "now the chief has to go work on his plantations himself."

The chief, and the male in general, is evil. Elisa can now direct an ego-adequate aggression against this situation and counters it with her "new order." *This* is the positive identification with me.

The next day Elisa relates that the schoolteacher beat her yesterday evening. She had gone to his plantations to get some plantains, because her family had nothing to eat. She points out that it was her sister who had planted these trees while she was still living with the teacher; and she tells me of the sad love story between the two.

"And now the teacher won't let us go to his fields and collect food. But after all my sister used to work there, and I just went instead of her. She is not here, and the teacher beat me. And this evening old Dibi is going to rule between me and the teacher."

With a laugh, she assures me that she is not afraid, she intends to say just what she thinks.

Though the "ruling" has not yet taken place, Elisa declares defiantly that she will go to Abengourou if she gets no justice here.

I interpret for her the meaning of her identification with me, with the new order that for her symbolizes independence, justice, and a chance to change her environment. Basically, for her the identification with me means the predominance of her own phallicity over the old order that keeps her in bonds, the order that represents the predominance of the pregenital mother.

But by now Elisa refuses to give up this identification. Once again—even more clearly and with greater differentiation of vocabulary—she summarizes her concept of justice, that every individual must be permitted to reap the fruits of his labors.

Elisa's phallicity and her attitude of aggressive rebellion, which she is forced to emphasize more and more strongly in order to maintain a satisfactory relationship with me, have brought about her acting-out. She is conscious of a drive to take proud and defiant action against the former lover of her sister. In her sister's place, she now demands the latter's rights from the rival. She identifies herself with the social and economic claims of the sister, which are clearly justified, adopts an active role herself, and is able to combat her passive fears of being harmed by a witch by means of an active challenge to the male rival. She sees now that I can never become such a witch, coveting or seizing anything of hers; *she* is the one who covets and intends to seize something from a man, and in this she feels at one with me. Both of us demand the phallic power from the male—that is, we both demand justice, the man's plantations, the fruits of our labor, love, the trees, children. Her own mother now seems weak and dependent; she has no choice but to let herself be turned out by the schoolmaster; she wants no trouble. Elisa does want trouble!

A week later Elisa tells me about the court held by old Dibi, before whom she stood up for her rights, insisting that every person must be allowed to reap the crops for which he has labored. Then the teacher said to her, "If I ever catch you in my fields again, I'll cut off your head." To this she replied, "They won't throw away my head if you cut it off," whereupon the teacher wanted to know, "What would they do with your head?" Elisa replied to this, "They'd stick it up your rear!" The schoolmaster took this as an insult and threatened to sue her in the court at Abengourou. But he would never win his case in Abengourou, she explained, for he had forced children to work for him and had raped all his female pupils. "He sleeps all over the place." Elisa laughs loudly as she recalls the schoolteacher's fury.

After this recital, she tells me the story of an old man who was killed by the fetish of his farm workers because he had stolen coffee. At this point her story becomes confused, and her speech begins to deteriorate. Suddenly it is Thomas's father she is talking about, then somebody else, who refused to confess to three sins and had to die because of his refusal. Now her story becomes more comprehensible. She is telling me about the chief's wife, who had an injection in her leg, whereupon the leg rotted away and the wife died in Zaranou.

"Her relatives came and said, 'She was so good. It was death that killed her, and not some person. In her case it was nobody's fault, nobody has to pay.' The dead woman was so good. Her relatives simply asked for her bones and her property and took them home with them. The woman was very good. She always made sure that all the children, the adopted ones, too, were paid for their work. She took care of everything. Since her death, the chief can't find any more workers, and his children are leaving him."

Just as had been the case three sessions before, when Elisa was beginning to act out her conflicts, this time, too—after her phallic victory over the schoolmaster—she found herself unable to come to our next scheduled interview. As far as the teacher is concerned, what she is doing to him is tantamount to anal rape—"They'll stick my head up your rear"—and thus puts the final seal on his humiliation and castration. Quite possibly, Elisa was afraid that our talk might once again cast doubt on the victory she had just achieved.

The pattern is becoming clear: Elisa's ego, secure in the awareness of its identification with that of the powerful white woman, feels safe in giving rein to violent, phallic aggressive wishes. With her ability to express these wishes openly and to act them out, they are felt to be ego-conforming. When she is sitting together with me in the tent, though, when her recalling of those events no longer permits such massive emotional release, then she falls prey to a damming up of emotion, to a buildup of aggressiveness (the story of the fetish penis of the farm workers and its power to kill), which seem to endanger her ego coherence. The flood of emotions that threatens to engulf her brings about a regression, marked again most clearly by a disintegration of the power of speech. By renouncing this ego function, she comes perilously close to the sphere of omnipotence-impotence characteristic of her relationship to the pregenital mother image.

There is something remarkable about the rapidity with which Elisa succeeds in reevoking the image of the "good mother"—the good wife of the chief—in order to counter her fear of being helplessly abandoned to fate. "She was so good that her relatives said, 'It was death, and not a person, that killed her.'" Via her image of the good wife, Elisa reestablishes the positive identification with a good woman—with me, and her power of speech returns. This identification with a person whose role is clearly that of a "giver," a person who has no need to project aggressions of any kind, makes it possible for her to dissociate herself with astonishing rapidity from her desire to deprive the male of his penis and from the anxieties this desire engenders.

I have the impression that her efforts to sustain this image of the good mother for herself and for me are rather desperate. The evil ones remain the men, over whom she triumphs.

We have been invited to attend the festival of the female shamans in Yosso, and Elisa asks me whether she can ride with us. We have the whole car loaded with passengers, and we manage to squeeze her in too.

Elisa is the second client of the shaman who steps into the circle; her question concerns the outcome of her pregnancy. In contrast to the first client and all the following ones, who hold their heads bent, their eyes downcast, Elisa stands erect, her expression grim, almost tragic. The shaman, in a state of deep trance, takes dancing steps around Elisa, dusts her belly and back with powder, and then casts an egg to the ground. Then she murmurs something in Ashanti, which an old man later translates into Anyi. Our interpreter can understand only the gist of what is being said, namely that the pregnancy will end badly. During the ride back to Bébou, Elisa sits rigid with shock, not saying a single word.

When she turns up for our interview that same evening, she is still silent. Then she begins to speak:

> *Elisa:* The shaman says that if my fiancé doesn't come, I'll die. She says that I'm an ill-bred person and that I'm disagreeable with everybody. The men drag my name in the mud, they all do, because I always give as good as I get and don't just accept everything without answering back. I'm angry with my mother.
> [Pause.]
> My mother is continually throwing things up to me—she talks and talks the whole time against me. She prefers my older sister; she doesn't love me. Even my father used to tell her, "You don't love Elisa." I cry and cry all the time, and all my mother and sister do is reproach me because my fiancé doesn't send any money so that I have to eat their food. If my father were still alive, things would be different. My fiancé is in Daloa, he's a teacher there. My fiancé is my uncle, the younger brother of my father. When the father dies, his brother takes his place as far as the mother is concerned. But now I've slept with him, and it's just as if I had slept with my father. It's really my mother who ought to be marrying him. The chief said that since I'm expecting a child from him, I ought to marry him whether I love him or not. He is my husband. But my mother doesn't want me to marry him.

I ask her what she intends to do, and she replies: "I'm going to ask my mother's pardon. When my husband comes, he can take the baby and I'll stay with my mother."

What has happened to make Elisa surrender so completely to the shaman the phallicity she had demonstrated so clearly just the day before and to make her submit without protest to the shaman's pronouncement? At the end of the last hour, she was trying to identify not with the penis-robbing mother, but with the good, nurturing mother, the wife of the chief—in other words, with me—and I had noted at the time that her efforts were rather strained. It may be that the threatening castration anxiety had led her to fear for her child.

Her identification with me was not able to calm entirely the fears concerning the outcome of her pregnancy. Very probably, during her quarrel with her mother she did regress to the level of oedipal rivalry, but the resulting anxieties presumably manifested themselves in oral, hypochrondriac form.

Possibly, too, the fact that Madame was also invited to attend the spectacle in Yosso may have played a role. As one of the many people present I had been ranked more or less among the Anyi spectators. Thus the transference significance of the "alien, good order" was lost. During that earlier episode with the bird, I had noted a similar confusion in the transference relationship. In any case, like everyone else, I had been fascinated by the impressive spectacle in Yosso, where the wildly dancing shaman, the sword at her hip suggestively erected—with her whirling leaps and unintelligible screams—had presented such a convincing picture of a phallic witch. If even I admire the shaman, does that not mean that Elisa, too, must bow down before her sword?

The verdict of the shaman was grim. Three circumstances would have to be changed if Elisa were to be able to keep her child, and it is astonishing how acutely the shaman had analyzed the situation when she stated: that Elisa was too prone to revolt against both men and women, that she was poorly adjusted as an individual; that Elisa's mother had neglected, on some past occasion, to give the shaman an adequate present—the family was poorly adjusted; and that the man who had sired the child ought to come to Bébou—adjustment to the demands of society.

Up to that point, Elisa's lover and father of her child had not played an important role. Now, however, Elisa is being forced to come to terms with an entire complex of oedipal problems. The mother becomes the rival; she is against the marriage. According to Elisa, her mother does not love her, whereas her father did. Then the surprising discovery that the fiancé is Elisa's uncle, her father's younger brother. According to the laws of the levirate, a man is supposed to marry the widow of his brother, and this explains Elisa's feeling that she has slept with her father. The daughter's lover is the man whom the mother ought to marry now that her husband is dead. The mother is against the marriage of her daughter to her own prospective husband, and she threatens Elisa with death and castration. For, according to the shaman's verdict, if the fiancé does not come, that is, if the evil mother refuses to give up the prospective husband-father, Elisa's baby will die.

Lesbian shamans are a firmly established institution in the matrilineally organized society of the Anyi, an institution that fulfills the deep need of both women and men for spectacular demonstrations of phallic power, an institution born of this need and necessary because of it. When I became, during the course of transference, the good, nurturing, but unfortunately deceased mother of early childhood, Elisa turned to these representatives of the powerful mother with her questions: "Is it all right for me to be as I am now? Is it all right for me to screen over the deeper-rooted rivalry conflicts with my mother with my own competing male behavior?" The answer was: "You must not revolt as you are doing now; you must observe the traditional customs concerning gifts; and the man—the child's father—must come back to assume the role that is his due. You must fight out to the end the oedipal problems with your mother."

At our next interview, Elisa once more accuses her mother with passionate words of having acted wrongly. When the chief said that among the Anyi it was all right in certain circumstances for a girl to marry her uncle, the mother had not said a word and had pretended to agree to Elisa's marrying him, but as soon as they had returned home she had forbidden the marriage. The chief had summoned Elisa and declared, "Take the man as your husband. If you refuse to obey, you can leave and go wherever you like."

Elisa continued: "My mother and my sister do nothing but reproach me. They drag my name through the mud. Everybody is saying mean things about me, that I won't listen to my mother. But she doesn't say anything in front of the chief, it's only at home that she protests against the marriage. She says she'll turn me out if I don't listen to her and do what she says."

My question as to what she herself wants, whether she wants to obey the chief—that is, marry—or obey her mother and not marry, makes her pause for a moment. Then she replies, "I won't live with him. When my husband comes, he can take the baby and go away."

But she goes on right away, "Dibi says, too, that my mother should have spoken up before the chief, that she's in the wrong, and that the whole business is her fault."

It is apparent that Elisa is avoiding the oedipal conflict with her mother. Though she has demonstrated in her fight against the men how strong she can be, Elisa refuses to fight with her mother over a husband. She evades a showdown by resorting to the passive attitude of a victim and abandons both husband and child. Whether she wants him or not is no longer important: "He and the baby can go away."

Instead of fighting actively with the mother for her husband, Elisa lets the mother and the chief fight *for her*, that is, over her marriage. She is deeply disappointed at her mother's unwillingness to argue openly with the chief.

I have the impression that since our last hour together, Elisa has identified with the female shaman. She is keeping out of the conflict—letting her mother and the chief decide whether she is to marry or not. She is behaving like the shaman, who also stands aloof from events, and saying, "just go ahead and try to satisfy *me!*"

Two days pass without Elisa's appearing at her usual time.

When we meet again, she tells me some horrifying tales of death, murder, and mutilation. It is evident that she is unwilling to bring about a decision in the rivalry conflict with her mother. Instead, in her fantasy, she is creating a rivalry conflict between the mother and *me*. The two of us are now fighting for possession of her person.

Later Elisa tells me about how a female shaman dies: "A shaman dies when the spirit that possesses her releases her. When I was little, I always believed that shamans lived forever, that they couldn't die." Elisa laughs loudly. "I used to ask my mother whether it was possible for shamans to die, too." She laughs again. "My mother told me that they die just like anyone else." She laughs.

Then she describes how female shamans are trained, how they have to go through many terrible and painful ordeals in the forest, for three years. Again she laughs excessively. "They're only allowed to carry the plantains on their shoulders, not on their heads." The violent outbreak of emotion in her laughter shows that Elisa has mastered a magician's trick—when the spirit that possesses the shaman releases her, she will die.

Elisa has escaped from her dilemma by resorting to passivity and by projecting her own rivalry conflicts to her environment; now it is the others who are fighting tooth and nail. In this way she evades her own castration anxieties—it is the others who risk castration. She herself is like the shaman. Thanks to the "spirit that can release its body," neither the mother, nor I, nor the shamans represent a danger any longer. Elisa's relieved laughter indicates that she feels herself invulnerable and autonomous. The early, threatening object representations, with their omnipotence, which formerly had absolute and irrevocable power over her, are mortal after all; all she has to do is withdraw the spirit, eliminate the emotional cathexis, and they can be controlled; she can cope with them.

Elisa's secondary autonomous ego is now functioning in that it shows itself capable of a sudden turn to passivity, of withdrawing and thus saving cathectic energy. Instinctual impulses and desires, to which she had formerly given over her ego actively and in full measure, are now projected to the family, to the group, which is competing and fighting in her place.

This might be an appropriate starting point for the theory of the group ego. It may be that Elisa needs the group to act out her own tendencies and wishes; and, since these have now been projected, there is no further need to modify or neutralize them. One can well imagine that an ego of this type will always be able to restabilize its inner relative autonomy by means of these oscillations (abandonment and reorientation of cathexis). But the ego is dependent upon the cooperation of the group; it must be able to participate (by participative projection), passively and orally, in its own instinctual desires—as acted out by the group—and in the emotions engendered by them.

Apparently this turn was made possible by Elisa's identifying with the shaman, who—in this particular society—is endowed with genuine omnipotence. The shaman is closer to her than the white woman, with whose phallic power she is unable to identify on a lasting basis.

A week later Elisa seems almost merry. She mentions casually that her fiancé has come to Bébou to renew his identity papers—nothing more. An old woman goes by the tent, carrying a load of kindling. Elisa comments: "That's the witch who sells the flesh of so many children because she killed and devoured her own daughter. The daughter always appears to her when she's out in the fields and threatens her mother with the words, 'If you don't bring me flesh, I'll kill you and eat you.'"

At this point Elisa begins to relate the most hair-raising stories about older women, usually grandmothers, who "sold the flesh" of this or that person. The whole thing becomes rather confusing because she skips from one of these endearing old ladies to the next without identifying them by name. This time, though, there is no linguistic deterioration. She relates the following about one of these grandmothers: "Her son-in-law brought her an antelope because she demanded flesh, but she told him she didn't want antelope flesh—she wanted the flesh of her grandchildren because they belonged to her."

This brings Elisa to the story of a woman who turned herself into a bird and one who slipped into the skin of another woman to carry out her nocturnal forays after flesh. The shaman discovered who she was and demanded that she confess aloud and in public. But the woman refused, and people said that she was in the wrong.

I remind Elisa at this point that she herself had reproached her mother for not speaking up loudly before the chief and telling him what she really thought about Elisa's marrying. This time Elisa gives me a radiant smile and remarks, "Yes, Madame, that's exactly right."

She goes on unconcernedly telling me about dead and devoured children, which brings her to the following story about the son of her older sister: "When he was three years old, he was on his deathbed—he was swollen all over. A sorcerer gave him some medicine and said that if it didn't help, he would die. After three days the swelling had gone down, but people said that my mother [the child's grandmother] had already sold his flesh. My mother insisted that she would never eat the flesh of her grandchildren and went to a female shaman. The shaman had seen that it was another woman, who had slipped into my mother's skin and went out selling children's flesh and doing harm to people, and she advised my mother to grind up hot peppers very finely and to rub the powder into her skin. She did, and the very next day the woman that had borrowed my mother's skin came down with pains. And this way the shaman was able to point her out!" She laughs. "And the proof is very simple—the moment the child of the other woman died, my sister's son got up and was cured." She laughs loudly.

"There are women who turn into young men at night and sleep with other women" (she laughs); "they have a prick that reaches down to their knees." She laughs again. "But then after three days the women they sleep with get their periods. There was a woman like that in Yosso, and the ones she slept with never got pregnant. These women kill the children in the mother's body—the fact that they get their periods proves it."

Elisa had told me all this in her usual manner, her face averted as if she were talking to herself, turning to me only when she laughed. Now she suddenly turns to face me directly and continues: "Believe me, Madame, our women are far worse than our men. When men quarrel, one can always offer apologies and the affair is settled. But with the women it never stops! They talk and talk and keep on dragging my name through the mud, and there's never any end to a quarrel—never! They keep starting all over again from the beginning. The men are much better; you can rely on them."

Elisa's attitude toward me today is decidedly independent, yet friendly. Her narration of the witch stories seems to have brought her satisfaction this time (in contrast to the other time, when the stories she told after the appearance of the "bird" had caused her acute anxiety). All these tales strike the listener as fantastic descriptions of the representation of the preoedipal mother, the mother who regards her children as mere property. She can give them away or eat them, because they are hers to do with as she likes. But now, talking about people being transformed, Elisa laughs with pleasure: "and the moment the child of that other woman died, the other child got up and was cured." The emotional release of her laughter once again reflects a saving in cathectic energies. The many transformations Elisa tells me about with such evident enjoyment remind her of the triumph she felt herself when she was suddenly able to project her conflicting tendencies to the external world. The conflict of urges takes place *outside*. By means of this "transformation," the ego has managed to remain free of conflict. These sudden oscillations between active and passive, internal and external give Elisa a feeling of satisfaction because she is now able to control internal tensions and instinctual desires.

She now experiences pleasure in telling these stories, which reflect her ability to externalize conflicts. The recurrent theme of the witches that "borrow" the skins of others represents Elisa's own handling of conflicts, her relative secondary autonomy.

As for her attitude toward me, she feels that we are on an equal footing, and she is now able to find men better and more likeable than women.

During the next seven interviews, the last before our departure, Elisa tries in her own way to solve the problem that is becoming increasingly crucial for her—how she can achieve independence without leaving her mother. She is still vacillating.

On one occasion, to my surprise, Elisa brings Jacqueline, Anoh Michel's wife, along to our session. Jacqueline, carrying her baby of about seven months, squats down and remains for the entire hour, though she does not understand a word of French.

Elisa opens the conversation by saying, "You worked with my husband" (he had taken a Rorschach test for us); "he told me about it and he laughed because you didn't know it was my husband you were talking to." She laughs, too, then goes on, "There was a woman who didn't want her daughter to marry. The daughter got pregnant, and her mother begrudged her the child. But the woman sold and traded the flesh of other children. She didn't kill her own grandchildren, but other children in exchange."

The story becomes confused and turns into an entirely different one. Then, pointing at Jacqueline, Elisa says, "That's the story of this girl's sister. She couldn't get married until her mother died. Her mother didn't want her daughter to have a husband. That's about the same as with me," she concludes spontaneously.

I ask Elisa whether her mother is still against her getting married. She replies: "My husband offered his apologies to my mother—that is, first I did, and then he did. That was the day before yesterday, before old Dibi. My mother insisted that I belong to her because she pays for my food. But then Dibi asked me, and I said, 'When I happen to have one hundred francs, then I pay, and they all eat my food. I catch fish sometimes, too, and cook sauces that we all eat.' And then Dibi said that my mother had no right to hold me back. Then everybody talked a lot and finally Dibi said that now that I'm pregnant I should marry my fiancé, and the chief said that my mother had spoken falsely and only said at home that she was against my marrying, and never in public.

"We have offered apologies, and my husband brought a bottle of wine and some palm wine. The teacher apologized to me and admitted that he had been wrong to hit me, and he apologized to my husband right away, too. We needed lots of wine for all those apologies." Very shyly, Elisa now adds: "In November I'm going to join my husband in Daloa."

Madame: And how about your mother? Can you leave her here alone?
Elisa [with a touch of malice]: My mother still has her epileptic friend, Benzué. They say he's crazy. [She laughs gleefully.] My mother has been cooking for him lately. He drinks, and he's funny when he dances.

She laughs and goes on to tell me more about this odd gentleman. This time she translates for the benefit of the patient Jacqueline, who also bursts out laughing. Then Jacqueline's little boy suddenly looks at me suspiciously. This makes Elisa laugh some more—"The little boy is afraid of you," she says. Then the two girls, obviously very pleased with themselves, leave with the little boy.

At the beginning of the hour Elisa laughs with delight at having a secret that she shares with her fiancé but that excludes me and also her mother. As casting director, she assigns the role of mother to me and brings her friend Jacqueline along, whose baby she can leave to me, the threatening mother, thus purchasing her own freedom. At first the child was quiet. Then finally Elisa got it to display fear of me. And only at this point had her skillfully arranged drama of exchange achieved the desired emotional success; Elisa was able to express her malice toward and her triumph over her own mother, who is so against her daughter's marrying and having children. In the same way as she foists off a strange child on me, she hopes that her mother will be forced to content herself with the crazy epileptic as a magical substitute. This was the mood in which she made up her mind to go away with her fiancé.

Elisa fails to appear for her next appointment, and when I see her again she explains that she had gone down to the river because she wanted more fish. What she really means is that now *she* can have a husband as well, she no longer has to depend on me. She declares that she is not dependent on anyone and owes no one anything. She even tells me that her mother is in constant conflict with her older sister—not with her (participative projection). That this conflict is dormant at the moment does not deter her in her efforts to project the conflict with her mother away from herself and onto other persons. She develops the background of the conflict between mother and sister:

Elisa: My mother says it's not good for my sister to go with the schoolmaster—after all, she's not yet divorced from the chief and

she'll only get a bad reputation. But my older sister refuses to listen
to her and is going to Abengourou anyway, but everybody
there knows the chief, and she'll never get her divorce .... And my
mother says, "All right, go ahead and do as you please—leave me to
die alone." Then my mother bursts into tears, and I start to cry too and
my older sister cries, and we all offer apologies to each other. But my
older sister went away anyhow, and then my mother said, "All right,
leave your children here, you can go away and I'll just have to die
alone"; and then we all weep some more and talk it all over together
until .... And the schoolmaster, whose cassava plants had been set
on fire, also says that the people of Bébou are bad, so that no teacher
is willing to stay here for long; he himself intends to leave the village,
and the chief offered his apologies to the teacher over and over again.

With great ceremony, involving the offering of drinks, the exchange
of apologies, and a great many tears, Elisa repeatedly becomes reconciled with her mother, the schoolmaster, and her husband. In the
field of social relations, everything can be settled with the help of this
ritualized behavior—the offering and acceptance of apologies. But psychologically such a settlement only has the effect of a conjuration, a
banishment, similar to the defenses mobilized by obsessive-
compulsives. The internal conflict continues to exist. The mother that
threatens Elisa corresponds to an object representation going back to
the preoedipal phase of development. It is a part object; the conflict of
instinctual urges retains the character of a pregenital fixation.

Our coming separation disturbs Elisa greatly. She says to me: "Here
the women are often not kind to the children. They spoil a child until it
learns to walk—they give it everything it wants. And as soon as it can
walk, they push it away and leave it to cry alone. My sister just doesn't
care; her children don't mean anything to her. She never stops to think
before she goes away on a trip—it's as if she had no children at all. Her
children don't even know her—they only know their grandmother, my
mother, and they call *her* mother."

In this way Elisa is letting me know that, for her, the little child, I am
like the women she has told me about, like her sister. From now on,
she'll have only her mother to turn to.

Elisa is deeply moved when I show her that I understand how sad she
is about our separation. But she has found a way to cope with her
sadness and her desire to remain with me. She sternly condemns the
domestic quarrel between her friend Jacqueline and her husband Anoh
Michel. The reason for the quarrel was that Jacqueline had made friends
with our interpreter François and wanted to go away with him, one of
us strangers.

As Elisa sees matters: "Jacqueline is bad. She always has an eye out
for other men, and then her husband Anoh Michel is nothing compared

to them. When the other fellow, François, is here, she nags at her husband all night long. That's the way she is—she looks at François, who works for the whites, and can't see any good in her own husband. She told Anoh Michel that he wasn't really a man, that she liked François and wanted a divorce. And they talked and bickered—the same things over and over again. Michel came to me and complained that François was his colleague and, now, whenever they met, François would go out of his way to avoid him: 'That's because he's looking for my wife,' Michel said. But Jacqueline said to her husband, 'I wasn't born into this world to spend my life with Anoh Michel—I'm here for all the fellows.'" Elisa chuckles, then adds, "But that's not good, there's bound to be talk. Adultery normally costs fifteen thousand francs, but adultery with the wife of a chief costs a hundred thousand francs, plus one ox, four sheep, a case of gin, and another sixty thousand francs. That's what it costs to commit adultery with a chief's wife."

Elisa tells François that his purpose in coming to Bébou was to earn money. He ought to forget about high-flown emotions, for they could only lead to strife and tears.

Once again Elisa is projecting her own wish to go away with me to her friend, in whom she condemns it. In this way she dissociates herself from her own desires and actively adopts the role of the wise arbitrator in trying to reconcile the dissension and tensions in her friend's family. This restores her independence of me and enables her to face me on an equal footing and as an adult during the last hours before our departure.

Her relationship to me shifts—as to a transitional object—to my aspect as a representative of European medicine, and in the end she asks me for pills to cure an attack of malaria.

Elisa is expecting her baby very soon now. She informs me that she plans to stay with her mother until she dies. "As long as their mothers are alive, a lot of girls are unable to marry. They can only leave home when their mothers die." What she means is that now she must remain firm and ruthlessly demand her due, collect outstanding debts. She recognizes the situation for what it is and doesn't intend to do anything just to please someone else.

Under the strain of her approaching delivery and our separation, Elisa identifies with her mother. As a result she finds it relatively easy to accept the fact that I am leaving. She herself has become the mother who turns away from her child, in this case from me. She is resorting to one of the most efficacious and most important defense measures that the Anyi ego erects, namely, identification with the mother who abandons her child. In this way she is able to evade experiencing any loss and to secure for herself the phallic active role of the powerful mother. Elisa herself has become the "spirit that releases" the body it inhabits.

She intends to remain with her mother and, in so doing, emphasizes with her own pregnancy her identity as a mother in her own right.

And, indeed, at the time of our departure, Elisa is due to give birth to her first child very soon. Her baby will be her exclusive property, just as she was her mother's property and will remain so as long as the mother lives. Elisa, like her child, is expected to comply with the active demands and libidinal desires of the mother.

Elisa will no longer need her strong phallic strivings for purposes of revolt; in the beginning she will be able to gratify the libidinal components of her phallicity autoerotically with the infant and its care, in the same fashion as she has observed in other Anyi mothers. And she will be able to give expression to her exhibitionist tendencies in her social environment in the role of a proud mother with a baby at her breast. Her phallic aggressive strivings are fulfilled in her demonstrative support of the new order as opposed to the old.

It seems that precisely these phallic tendencies, which—in the beginning—Elisa was forced to stress so strongly in order to establish an identificatory relationship with the alien white doctor, have undergone modifications in the various vicissitudes of her transference to me. It may be that they lost some of their instinctual character and could thus be implanted in her ego in a more neutral and more rational form.

One can even imagine that, when she is older, Elisa—in spite of the handicap of not belonging to a distinguished family—might have a chance of becoming one of those imposing and, in certain respects, truly wise old women that the Anyi culture seems to produce so often. For the authority imputed to these women rests on their ability to reconcile strife and conflict within the group. They are characterized by their unshakable poise and by their willingness to adopt a decided, active position. And Elisa has clearly demonstrated the latter quality during the course of our interviews. Toward the end she made it increasingly clear that she is able to dispense with acting out her own conflicts when she can take over the role of stage manager within the group and thus contribute to bringing about solutions.

A few months after we left Bébou, we received the news that Elisa had given birth to a healthy son.

Madness in the Midst of Normal Life?

A number of magical phenomena—the belief in witches, the institution of the female shamans, the high incidence of messianic movements, and the belief in forest spirits—form part of the everyday life of the Anyi. If we are tempted to find this exotic, anachronistic, or primitive, perhaps we ought to ask ourselves whether it is any more normal to be dependent upon a psychoanalyst, a tax consultant, or the Dow-Jones index.

Elisa needs external instances; they help her cope with her internal tensions and her conflicts with the environment. On the one hand, she succeeds in mobilizing her mother, the village chief, Dibi's court of arbitration, and finally even the domestic troubles of her friend Jacqueline to solve her problems for her. On the other hand, at particularly crucial moments in her life she resorts to the traditional belief in witches and consults the female shaman in Yosso. In both instances she is able to act while remaining relatively passive and is thus less responsible for her emotions and acts; "it" is outside, the responsibility of society, while she feels happier and is able to function better— relative ego autonomy has been reestablished.

Dependency on the persons of the family and the village is supplemented by a second series of instances that have their roots in the realm of magic and religion. Here the roles of the individual persons are defined in accordance with a spiritual power attributed to them.

Elisa's dependence on external instances, particularly witchcraft and sorcery, cannot be taken as the sign of an immature or disturbed personality.[1] Social dependency is a universal phenomenon. Psychologically, in the Anyi culture as in ours, it follows the pattern of early childhood experience. Dependent behavior can be regarded as immature or regressive only insofar as it impairs ego autonomy. Not just Elisa, but all the Anyi we met resorted to magical or religious instances when the need arose. Even the skeptical and highly intelligent Chief Ahoussi had consulted the healer Edjro Josué.

This should not be taken to mean that spiritual institutions do not have any psychological or social function; they very definitely do. They are an indispensable component of normal life.

The need for witches, sorcerers, and healers—and their effectiveness—can be reduced to the following process: The ego autonomy of an individual becomes impaired, either as a result of the flaring up of a neurotic conflict or through an external influence that poses a threat to his security or entails frustrations. The normal environment provides no relief or is perhaps itself the source of the conflict; libidinal cathexis is withdrawn from the persons of the environment. A hunger arises for other, "better" objects, objects that stand in contrast to those of the family and the social environment. Priests, female shamans, and healers are "mediators"; they provide spiritual objects that can be cathected as the representations of God, gods, spirits, witches, all of which correspond to the objects of early childhood. Unconscious wish fantasies have given them shape.

The belief in witches is supposed to be only a little over a century old among the Akan peoples, and it is said to have grown enormously over the past few decades.

> At that time [1940], new altars mushroomed out of the ground over-night in Akim and other parts of southern Ghana. The turn of the Ashanti came much later, and the movement there had reached its peak in about 1956/57. During the last ten years [i.e., up to 1965], the movement in the south has burnt out with the same suddenness with which it had started—like a brush fire—and has been replaced by the new "apostolic" or "spiritual" Christian cults, whose members ex-perience states of "possession"—whereby it is assumed that it is the Holy Ghost that takes possession of them. [Field, pers. comm.]

The emergence of these new magical-spiritual phenomena has fre-quently been interpreted as a kind of psychic epidemic. It was assumed that something had occurred to upset the equilibrium of social life. The blame was assigned to the introduction of industrialized agriculture, or to the spread of venereal disease resulting from a relaxation in morals and the improvement of communications and transport. Society had drifted into a state of lawlessness, it was believed, and its institutions were gradually disintegrating. Observers were of the opinion that the new spiritual movements were symptoms of the estrangement of the individual in a decaying society. Africans themselves often share this opinion: "No wonder that the blessing of our ancient spirits is no more getting up to us. The thunder of the guns chased them; they don't like the sound of bells; when they want to come to our aid they are caught in the telephone wires. No wonder that the witches propagate enormously and that the power of our old magic loses its potency" (12).

Although a change in social customs may certainly be a sign that existing institutions are no longer functioning, it is probably wiser not to attribute such phenomena to damaging influences or to an overtaxing of social structures without further study. The rapid fluctuations alone should be sufficient warning against automatically assuming that an-cient traditions are sound and new ones merely inadequate stopgap structures. Just as projection to a witch brought relief for *one* person (Elisa), spiritual movements can be the expression of successful adjust-ment to new requirements.

All the social institutions summarized above stress and support the independence of the individual vis-à-vis the family (and the family neuroses it creates). They do not necessarily lead to a European way of life, however, but sometimes give promise of new possibilities for a collective African way of life. This is particularly evident in the messianic communities.

It is utterly pointless to evaluate magical acts in terms of the direct personal advantage they bring. If, at the moment the witch who wants to devour the little son of Elisa's sister is unmasked, the child recovers, this is white magic; if at the moment the witch is unmasked her own child dies, this would be black magic. A successful act of vengeance that does not entail any guilt feelings may be more satisfying than the most inspiring sign of favor from a god.

The spiritual instances of the Anyi all belong to the same category of beings; the spirits of the dead, the souls of witches on their nocturnal wanderings, the Akan gods and the purchased ones, and even the Holy Ghost of Christian dogma come from the same world and merge into one another. Though their forms may be different, they all have the same properties—they are powerful and cruel, and at the same time as greedy as the living or as frustrated desires. Only when they are invoked do they define themselves clearly, become recognizable, discrete, endowed with specific qualities, the embodiments of certain rules and requirements. The ritual in which the supplicant participates evokes spiritual forces out of the world of vague and unconscious desires, forces which then have a social and psychological effect. For this reason alone there is little to be gained from comparing the Anyi belief in witches with a Christian belief in witches and demons. The Anyi care little whether a certain person is a witch; it is only her magical misdeeds that lend significance to the doer. Once she has fulfilled her function, she is treated as an ordinary person once again.

The reestablishment of spiritual order has succeeded when individual anxieties are calmed, when the act of personification and the ritual involved have tamed the evil spirits. It is not that the consequences of an evil act are eliminated; nor is there any punishment for sins. What the Anyi expect is a pacification of society. This becomes possible as soon as the danger comes from without and no longer from within.

Everyone has ambivalent emotions toward the persons in his environment: "Even though your teeth are bad, you're always touching them with your tongue." This is why everyone is frustrated, filled with hatred, potentially a witch: "They shout 'a witch, a witch!' If you're not one, why do you turn around?" A woman will be careful to appear as respectable as possible, so that no one will suspect her of being a witch. And when people know that there is a witch involved, they can still feel safe because they know there are traditional remedies for dealing with her. This even applies to Jean-Pierre, who—side by side with his "healthy" attitude toward witches—suffers from a witch phobia.

Witches

If you put out poison for someone,
you're likely to get poison to eat yourself.

One of the greatest experts in the field of ethnopsychoanalysis (129) has associated the "deeply rooted fear of witches and vicious demons" with "oral cannibalistic" fantasies and attributed the latter to the long nursing period characteristic of some cultures. Among the Anyi, the nursing period is comparatively short. With them fixation on the oral phase takes place as a result of the highly satisfying rewards it provides, rewards that are suddenly replaced by traumatic experiences. In any case, Anyi witches are female as a matter of principle—mothers, grandmothers, their own sisters, or older sisters in general. Their victims, on the other hand, can be man, woman, or child: "No matter how horrible a witch's mouth is, she eats only on her side of the river and can't get across the water." In other words, a witch is dangerous only to the members of her own uterine lineage. This defensive device is safeguarded by the fact that one's own mother is hardly ever likely to be a witch; it is usually a woman more distantly related.

Although men naturally can also be the objects of oral aggression and paranoiac anxiety, the people of Bébou never speak of male witches. They fill the linguistic gap neatly by means of a fine distinction. They admit that men, too, can use poison, which of course then owes its effectiveness to the workings of magic. Thus they do no harm through their persons (since they cannot, of course, be nursing mothers), but through a medium—poison. The successful defense against them preserves the aggressive fantasy stemming from the oral phase; only the object from which the aggression emanates has been exchanged for another.

Ordinarily it is old women, or women frustrated in some other way, who become witches. A young woman, content with the life she leads, is never a witch. Witches fly through the air at night, often in the guise of weird birds, and they radiate a reddish glow. They have their tavern or "shop" at the top of a kapok tree, where they meet to devour the souls *(sunsum)* of the bodies they have seized, preferably those of young people and children. This meeting place is called a "shop" because witches often sell the flesh of their victims to other witches; twenty-five francs is the going rate. The victim does not notice immediately that he has been devoured. Then he slowly dehydrates, swells up or develops some other ailment, and dies unless a countercharm is applied in time.

Greed and envy motivate the witches. The reason they are so spiteful is that they are frustrated. The women who buy flesh from them are equally greedy and frustrated. "I don't want antelope, I want to eat the flesh of my children," as one of them said.

It is no wonder the price for flesh is so modest on the witches' market. For oral aggressive greed is the important thing, not anal possession. The sexual activity of witches is also destructive in character; it is rooted in the oral phase and represents the mother who possesses a phallus (which the child does not). Some witches have a long penis, down to their knees, and at night they sleep with women. As a result the ravished woman starts to menstruate and becomes sterile. Other witches have a venomous snake concealed in the vagina. These witches, too, are less interested in obtaining sexual pleasure than in ruining the sex lives of their victims. The frustration of love emotions suffered by the witches during their daytime lives has led to the regression to oral hatred and envy.

It has been pointed out in connection with the belief in witches that paranoiac behavior is normal in Akan peoples and that most "healthy" people have anxieties about being robbed or harmed that are otherwise found only in paranoia victims. In explanation of this, it has been suggested that these Africans have more guilt feelings, more greed and hatred to ward off than other peoples. We find it more accurate to attribute the prevalence of witches not to a greater quantity of oral aggression, but to a lower tolerance threshold; or perhaps to the fact that the process of defense is public and therefore more strikingly organized than elsewhere. It is an Akan belief that individuals with a strong personality soul (sunsum) never become witches, but only persons with weak souls.

We never happened to meet anyone who called herself a witch, though we were told that it is common. Amon d'Aby (3) reports the case of two women. One of them had a son by a white man and the other a son whom she sent to the European school. During the course of a quarrel, the first one shouted, "I'll eat your son!" to which the second one replied, "If you eat my son who writes like a European, then I'll eat your white son!"

When a woman turns into a witch, it usually happens at night while she is asleep, and as a rule she is seduced by another witch. She knows what has happened to her only as one remembers a dream, but she is regarded as fully responsible for any acts of witchcraft she may perform. For it is the acts that count; it is the acts that disrupt the existing order. No one is the least interested in the personal guilt of a witch; what is important is her sense of responsibility toward society.

Witches and their victims, defendants and plaintiffs, are inspired by a peculiar basic distrust (the opposite of "basic trust"), by a feeling of being unable to control their greed, hatred, and anxiety. Both sides feel themselves exempt from blame when the reason is determined. Then a restoration of equilibrium becomes possible.

This presumably explains why, in witchcraft trials, the accusation alone often sufficed to induce a helpless old woman to confess that she had killed so and so many children and made so and so many women sterile. Naturally there were exceptions as well, cases in which women accused of witchcraft refused to confess and remained firm in spite of beatings and torture, insisting that they hated no one and that the witch must be some other woman.

A witch's evil influence is terminated when she has confessed all her misdeeds and paid the necessary sums in compensation. Both practices can be traced back to the conviction that private, concealed (and repressed) aggressions are dangerous, whereas aggression publicly admitted is not. For this reason confession not only is a means of determining the facts in the case, it actually cancels the deed, provided that it is complete, that is, that no evil deeds are concealed. And the compensation paid, always extremely modest in the land of the Anyi (twenty-five francs, an egg, or a chicken), merely serves to notify society that "I was the one who did it." This conjures away the fear of the unknown and breaks the spell. And, if it is not already too late, the planned misdeed can even be averted.

Since accusations of witchcraft have not been accepted by the official courts for a long time now, and the traditional courts for this purpose are forbidden by the authorities under threat of heavy fines, in Alangourou the task of discovering which witch is responsible for a death or some other misfortune is almost always assigned to a female shaman. In principle, any older, wiser person could do this. But witches have the power to change their shapes, and that makes it extremely difficult to discover their identity.

The ability to "transform herself" is in fact the most important quality for a witch. In a good many tales about witches (told by Elisa and Jean-Pierre), the plot is based on successive transformations—from one person into a witch, some other person, or an animal, or from a witch into a person, an animal, and so forth, as if the process of shifting or transferring an anxiety-evoking aggressive striving from one being to another might lead to a relaxation of tension and ultimately to a resolution of conflicts. In fact this mechanism does lead to temporary relief of tension in the case of every neurotic transference; the resolution of the conflict follows as soon as a female shaman has unmasked the witch.

In the institution of witchcraft, anxieties and aggressions from the oral phase of development find an expression that is adequate to the needs of the ego and adapted to the environment. Greed and envy are projected. The witch, to whom these strivings are imputed, is the devouring phallic mother of the symbiotic phase. The uncanny transformations that form the basis of the witches' power, in other words that defense mechanism to which, psychologically, this power owes its creation (displacement and projection), can be countered by measures taken by the individual and by society. The identification of the witch and her confession correspond to a conscious working out; further transformations (displacement and projection) are rendered impossible. The remainder of the ritual serves the purposes of social adjustment and reintegration.

The Oracle of Yosso

If the evil consequences of witchcraft are to be countered with an effective ritual, persons possessing phallic qualities are needed. Identification with active phallic drive modalities in accordance with the childhood pattern of identification with the aggressor is one means of silencing passive oral anxieties and modifying greedy oral impulses. Among other institutions (chiefs, priests, healers), it is primarily the lesbian shamans who fulfill the need of both men and women for spectacular, active phallic power.

Only more meticulous comparative studies might be able to provide answers to the questions of why there are female shamans in some places in the land of the Anyi and not in others, and why and in what circumstances their role is assumed by priests or by male sorcerers. Such studies might perhaps be based on something like the following hypothesis: At present there is no female shaman in Bébou, whereas there are five of them in the small village of Yosso. Part of the reason may be that Chief Ahoussi, who has been ruling Bébou for about forty years, satisfies directly the need for an object exercising phallic power within the society (in part by his "purchase" and employment of a "fetish"), while during the same period the chiefs of Yosso have failed to perform this sociopsychological function adequately.

According to the general view, the aptitude for becoming a sorcerer or a female shaman is rooted in childhood. An Anyi fairy tale (38) is entitled "The Vicissitudes Experienced by a Mother Who Lacked Sufficient Maternal Affection," or "An Attempt to Justify the Profession of the Sorcerer." The plot is this:

"Old Mala had three sons. She loved the first two dearly, but hated the third one. One day she turned him out of her house. He went away and built himself a hut at the edge of the jungle. The first son became a planter, the second a woodcutter. The third son became a sorcerer...."

When a young girl becomes a shaman, the spirit seizes her suddenly; she has fits, trembles, screams, dances, or runs out into the forest. This usually happens to girls who come from a family of female shamans. If the parents are wise, they send such a child to live with a shaman for several years to be trained and initiated.

The village chief of M'Basso tells us about his daughter, who stole money and clothes and ran away from the home of her grandmother: "Even when she was quite small, we already knew that there was something wrong with her. She would often spend the whole day sitting in a corner without speaking a word. She made motions that no one could understand. They resembled the dancing of the female shamans. Then we knew that a sorcerer had touched her and that she was destined to become a shaman. But since we are all Christians in our family, we couldn't bear the thought of this. So we had her baptized, and afterward she became very ill. She very nearly died. Then we realized that, by baptizing her, we had tried to destroy the power she possesses. And that's impossible, of course. Later she was no longer able to become a shaman. It happens that way when such a child is baptized. When a man is a sorcerer, he feels the compulsion to dance in order to relieve his emotions. If he can't dance, he may go mad. His mind becomes clouded and he can't think any more. It's as if someone had laid his soul in chains. There's something that doesn't function properly from that time on. People like that can suddenly do the most impossible things—robbing somebody perhaps, or something even worse. There are even cases where they have committed murder. It's the same with my daughter. We're always having trouble with her."

The female shaman of Yosso whom we filmed during a major ritual—during which she used her clairvoyant powers to counsel and answer the questions of suppliants (including Elisa)—went into a light trance after her buttocks had touched the stool of the spirits. The trance state manifested itself first in a rapid, rhythmic shaking of her entire body. During the dance and during the remainder of the ceremonies, which lasted more than two hours in all, she remained in this state, from which she then emerged of her own accord and without visible effort. As soon as all the suppliants had been answered, she laid aside the ceremonial sword, put her shawl back on, and dried her body, which had perspired heavily. Then she chatted for a moment with her colleagues—two other female shamans, one of whom had danced together with her for a short while—and casually walked away.

The beating of the drums, only moderately rhythmic, functioned more as an accompaniment to the dance than as a stimulus. The shaman was already white, her body smeared with kaolin, when she appeared on the scene. The narrow stripes of white on her forehead and eyelids are supposed to enhance her clairvoyant powers. Her shawl, hip cloth, and the long chain of beads she wears are also white. Her clients can be identified immediately by the anxious rigidity of their gaze, while the other persons present look unconcerned and expectant, like an audience at a spectacle. The shaman's assistant, a nondescript, middle-aged man dressed in black shorts and a rather dirty jersey, brings the stool, the sword, and a cardboard box containing the kaolin powder that will be needed. The dusting of the forehead, breast, and arms with kaolin form the transition to the state of trance. It is indicative that the shaman must first lay aside the attributes of a respectable woman (her shawl and beads) before the phallic spirit will take possession of her. Then, however, she becomes properly uninhibited, struggling in a series of wild leaps with the spirit, who is concealed in clouds of powdered kaolin, intended to ensure his docility and cooperation. The Ashanti sword held at the level of her loins and erected almost vertically in front of her, the shaman rocks her pelvis rhythmically, seizes young girls and women and makes them join her dance; she grabs them roughly by the breasts and loins, and soon releases her startled but compliant victims, only to seize others in their place. Only when she turns to her female clients or to sick children does she display a dreamy regard for etiquette. On this particular occasion there do not happen to be any men among her clients. The shaman grabs a child by the arm and lays it down on the ground. She dances, then returns to the child. Without looking at what she is doing, she passes the sole of her foot, which she has dipped in kaolin, over the child's face and chest. She paints the abdomens of pregnant women with white lines and symbols. Then she mumbles her oracles to herself in "Ashanti language."

The spectacular symbolization makes it possible for the audience to identify and ensures collective participation. The uninhibited representation of regressive processes (trance, phallic aggressive and phallic sexual acts) makes it easier for the spectators to be carried away, for men and women alike are greedy for such experiences but are unable to bring them about without assistance. Participation, however, does not lead to collective regression; the trance of the shaman is a spectacle presented for the eyes and ears. The ethnopsychologist finds it particularly understandable that the utterances of the id should be presented in the historically traditional forms of expression (dance, Ashanti sword, use of the Ashanti language in a state of trance)—that the individually archaic should appear in the form of the collectively archaic.

But it is impossible not to see that the most important aspect of the entire undertaking lies in its "ego" components. Regression, symbolism, and magic are only the instruments that produce the effect on the individual and thus on society. The lines of force that intervene in the endopsychic process and in the life of the village (Elisa) emanate from the mumbled verdict of the shaman, translated by her assistant, from the expressionless monotone issuing from the mouth of this non-descript little man—in other words, from the secondary process. With every verdict, the shaman also sets the sum to be paid as a sacrifice. This integrates the client and his or her family into the economically defined areas of function (which also include the healer!); behavior guidelines are issued and punishments threatened. The reward that beckons is a relaxation of the conflict and—given back into the hands of the "patient"—an adequate control of anxiety.

The language employed by female shamans in the trance state, called "Ashanti," is the language of the spirits that have taken possession of them. The shamans themselves do not understand what they are say-ing, and even people who are acquainted with the Ashanti language understand only a few words. It seems to be an artificial language or a mixture of languages.[2] Because it cannot be understood, it is an appro-priate vehicle for transmitting messages from a world that, for the Anyi, is the very real world of spirits and for the psychoanalyst is the world of the unconscious. The messages can be read and understood only after their encoded utterances have been translated and interpreted.

The ritual of the female shamans in Yosso is a process closely akin to the pronouncements of the oracles of Delphi, the verdicts spoken by the shamans of the Mescalero Indians (94), and the interpretative psychotherapy of the Western world (psychoanalysis), all of which ad-dress themselves to the ego. As a psychological process, it differs fun-damentally from healing methods based on suggestion, such as the voodoo cults of Brazil and European methods like hypnosis and au-togenic training, which circumvent ego resistance and address them-selves to id functions. It is quite true that the trance of the shaman is supposed to convince the audience by means of suggestion, but the trance is only the first step toward the verdict. Thus it might better be compared with the interpretation done by the psychoanalyst, who also makes use of regressive empathy, than with the activity of a suggestor, who induces the regressive act in the patient in order to bring about a healing effect.

When we describe the dance of the female shamans as a healing process, we do not mean to imply that it has no other significance; one can investigate the same phenomenon from the standpoint of its reli-gious content, for example, or from the standpoint of its social func-tions. We have elected to use the term "healer" for the female shamans and various other instances that contribute to the recovery of a dis-turbed, sick, or suffering individual and thereby seek to improve his functioning within the society. The goal of the healing process is the restitution of the ego functions of the individual; this in turn leads to an improvement in or restoration of social integrity.

In contrast to these instances, there are naturally also social institutions that so far fail to take the individual and his ego into consideration, such as Western criminal law, for example, especially when a conviction leads to the death penalty. We all know how difficult it is to fit the legitimate demands of the individual—abolishment of the death penalty, psychotherapy for the criminal—into institutions such as this. The Anyi have hardly any social institution that does not include factors of healing, in the above sense, along with other functions. This was pointed out in the section on the institution of chiefship. But the Anyi, too, make a very clear distinction between "healers," who concern themselves with individuals seeking help, and other socially important institutions.

On the other hand, in the event of a disturbance or illness, "the question as to what particular constellation of circumstances has caused the illness of a specific person" is the main point of interest. The individual is the constant and not, as in Western medicine, the illness (1). Accordingly, the healer must investigate the individual, his social situation, his personal history, and his inner life, any one of which may lie at the root of the disturbance, if he is to devise effective countermeasures. For the Anyi, physical and mental ills—between which they make the same distinctions as we do, on the basis of the forms in which they manifest themselves—are the consequence of some situation in the life history of the individual. This view is fairly close to modern Western psychosomatic medicine. Among the Ga in Ghana, Field (16) recorded the complaints that led individuals to consult a shrine priest. Exactly as among the Anyi, she found that bodily ills are just as much a reason for the sufferer to seek help as mental anguish, misfortune in the family, failure in professional life, or the envy of neighbors and suppression by the powers that be.

The fact that the activity and the methods of the healers are so eminently oriented to the life history of the individual and to social aspects has tempted observers to contrast European psychotherapeutic methods, aimed at healing the individual, with the African methods, as collective resocialization procedures. It has been concluded that we shall never be able to understand or apply the latter, and that our therapeutic methods are completely unsuited to application to Africans because Africans are a different sort of people, with collective modalities of experiencing—in the last analysis, a more primitive people.

It seems far more to the point to concede to all therapeutic procedures the capacity to effect changes in society through rehabilitation of the individual, and then—for each method separately, whether African or European—to examine the individual measures in contrast with the collective ones, and the effects on the individual treated in contrast with the effects on society.

Psychoanalysis can serve as an example. It can be regarded, comparatively speaking, as a very one-sided individual procedure and has itself claimed that it refrains entirely from using collective suggestion and that it is not directed toward changing society in any way. We need only think of its endopsychic individual content and of the interpersonal uniqueness of the dialogue between therapist and patient. Yet the application of rational processes in the formulation of our interpretations and in the emergence of emotionally supported insights on the part of the patient stems from the intellectual heritage of the European Enlightenment and corresponds to the scientific thinking of our civilization; the placing of the principle of truth above illusory wish fulfillment corresponds to the ethical ideal of the Reformation. The desired effect of successful analysis, the improvement of autonomous ego functioning, must by definition result in a higher degree of adaptation to society. Thus this consequence of individual analysis must also be regarded as an effect on society, whether it leads to an integration of the individual into existing areas of function or to a modification of these areas. In other words, when the healing process is successful, it has collective consequences, regardless of whether the subject is rendered capable of tolerating his environment or sets about changing it in the role of a revolutionary.

The "witch doctor" of Bébou, a middle-aged Ashanti herbalist who has lived there for many years, is an extreme example of a healer who uses individual-oriented methods for individual-oriented purposes. He is consulted only in connection with bodily ills. He concentrates on the ailment that he has diagnosed and dreams of what remedy must be used in what fashion in this particular case. He searches the forests for the remedy he wants, finding the proper plant on the basis of his knowledge of botany, acquired during his years of training under a prominent medicine man, and gives the patient the remedy together with the instructions for its use that have appeared to him in his dreams. He is paid according to the success he achieves. There are not more, but rather fewer collective aspects than in European medicine.

Apart from certain connections between generally known pharmacological properties of the prescribed plants and the widespread view that in dreams one acquires "accurate and otherwise inaccessible" knowledge, the whole procedure is oriented toward the treatment of the ailments of individuals. When the remedy fails to help, or when some indication of a disturbing situation in the life history of the individual concerned has already appeared in his own dreams or in those of the medicine man, this is considered a sign that the patient must turn to a female shaman or to some other healer for relief.

The appearance of forest dwarfs, referred to as pygmies in Alangouan, is a classic example of how a collective belief can be exploited for the restoration of personal homeostasis. These dwarfs are designated as "spirits of a lower order" (28); in Ashanti they are called *mmoatia*. They are about 30 cm tall, hairy, and their feet point backward. They dwell in caves, but they also come into houses, where they cause all sorts of minor trouble—for example, they may steal the palm wine prepared by the family. This type of forest spirit can be found in large areas of West Africa, for instance in the Gao region and in Dahomey (Benin). A belief in spirits is certainly a collective structure. Their restitutive function consists in their appearing in the vivid illusionary fantasies and in the dreams of persons who are unable to cope with their personal problems. Sometimes they perform helpful acts, like the brownies in our fairy tales. But when an individual is in conflict with himself or with his environment—situations that cause guilt feelings and depression—he is frequently made aware of the situation by the fact that pygmies lie in wait for him in his dreams at night, pursue him, and beat him with clubs. The sufferer awakens with pains in his arms and legs. This is a sure sign that he is no longer capable of solving his problems by himself but must consult a "healer," thereby introducing a greater degree of collectivity into his personal sphere of conflict.

Messianic movements periodically find increasing numbers of adherents among the Anyi. The belief in a certain healer spreads throughout the country in epidemic waves, only to subside after a few years until the doctrine finds a new prophet. In 1966, for example, the "mediator" Edjro Josué seemed to promise healing for large numbers of people who were suffering, anxious, and in need. Insofar as such a phenomenon lends itself to psychological interpretation at all, his efficacy was based on a balance between the application of individual and collective means of influence—ideal within the framework of the present Anyi culture—and between the traditional and the revolutionary elements of his teachings.

7 Fantasy and Communication

Jean-Pierre N'da Assinien (Paul Parin)

Preliminary Interview and Jean-Pierre's Motives for Working with Me

Like our other patients, Jean-Pierre comes to me for analysis like a sacrificial lamb. Initially, his older brother Thomas had forced the young Pierre Kablan from Yosso to talk with me. This undertaking had been a dismal failure, since Pierre Kablan said hardly a word to me and successfully managed to get out of having to come back a second time. Instead, Thomas brought me Jean-Pierre—in the first place to restore his own self-esteem, his authority among his kin, and his prestige with us, the strangers, which he felt must have suffered from the first failure, and in the second place to be of use to Jean-Pierre's kin and to Jean-Pierre himself. With this plethora of motivations in the background, Thomas's efforts overshot the mark by a good deal. Before I had even been informed of his plan, he had summoned Jean-Pierre from his native village of Yosso (to which I drove every day anyway) to Bébou, had assigned him sleeping quarters in his own court, and promised him one hundred francs a day to work with me, payable at the conclusion of the project. Thomas had succeeded in increasing the kin of his court.

Nothing could be done to change these decisions made by the older brother. It would never have occurred to Jean-Pierre to question any of Thomas's orders. When I tried to suggest that what had been arranged was perhaps not very sensible, he looked at me uncomprehendingly. The only thing I was able to achieve during the first few sessions was to persuade Jean-Pierre—although he did not understand it, let alone accept it emotionally—that he was not expected to work for me all day, cook for me, or keep house for me, but merely to talk with me for an hour every day. He insisted that I give him a letter confirming his "employment" for his oldest brother N'da Aka, the real head of his kin, that is, the head of his home court in Yosso. Since I was already aware of the secretiveness and distrust of the Anyi, especially between family members, in all financial matters, I asked Jean-Pierre whether I should mention anything about his salary in the letter. He was unable to decide one way or the other and answered "oui, Monsieur" or "no, Monsieur" indiscriminately, but in the end he was relieved that I made no reference to what he was to be paid. During our third interview, which took place after his first trip back to Yosso, Jean-Pierre informed me that his older brother had said nothing about his employment, which meant that he gave his consent.

Although Jean-Pierre had not come to me of his own accord, he seemed to feel differently about the work he was to do than other subjects who had been "dragged" to me. He was more cheerful, less depressive than the others and was eager—in fact overeager—to perform his task well. Since he understood what I said only in terms of comprehending my French, but was incapable of expressing an opinion on anything, let alone accepting my interpretations, during the first two sessions (and frequently later on as well) he was like a robot with no will of his own.

I had the impression that he was glad to have made the move to Bébou. For a long time I assumed that there was some special conflict with his family, perhaps with the head of the court, the brother N'da Aka, that had led him to welcome an opportunity to leave Yosso. I never succeeded in entirely understanding the motivation behind this step, which was so important for Jean-Pierre and for the whole series of interviews. But at least the following emerged clearly: the tensely aggressive atmosphere in the court of his own kin, though it was really no worse than in any average family in any of the three villages and—as far as I could tell—no worse than in Thomas's court, where he was now living, made him feel that he would probably be happier in Bébou than at home. Subliminal, smoldering conflicts with his mother (in fact with the various classificatory mothers) could no longer bother him once he had left and once the mothers had given their blessing—that is, officially sanctioned their son's undertaking. Other conflicts with siblings and peers in his home village as well as mutual feelings of envy and distrust also became less tense. Jean-Pierre's irresolute submission to Thomas's authority—more precisely, his identificatory adjustment to Thomas's actively intervening will—was probably the primary reason for his move, but this would not have sufficed if the stay in Bébou had not been an ideal way out of an almost intolerable life and family situation for the young man.

Evasions of this kind are an opportunity for many Anyi—young and old, single and married, male and female—to restore their mental balance, though this is especially true of the young men. Sometimes, apparently, it is absolutely necessary to get away on some pretext or other, to take flight in order to avoid being overwhelmed by conflicting emotions or drifting into chaotic states, into melancholia, or into helpless alcoholism.

But from the very beginning, Jean-Pierre's decision—actually made for him—had an additional purpose. He was looking for confirmation of his own identity as an adult. Since leaving school in Abengourou and returning to Yosso a few years ago, he had seen and perceived himself as a widely traveled young man, capable of coping with life "abroad" in a larger village, even in a metropolis. A number of trips to Abidjan and Bouaké in the company of two of his brothers (cousins) had confirmed this feeling, and in his eyes the villagers had no reason to be surprised that this slender young man—always dressed in European clothes, his hair straightened in accordance with the latest fashion—who was often seen going about with a book or notebook in his hand and who only rarely went along to work on his brothers' plantations, was now living with the strangers and working with them in the "village of the whites" (as Bébou became in the eyes of Yosso's inhabitants as soon as we had settled there). For a long time, in fact almost until the end of the two months he spent in Bébou, this confirmation of his fragmentary and insecure feeling of identity was more important to Jean-Pierre than his personal relationship with me or with his new friend François, our interpreter, with whom he tried right away to establish a friendship based on blind identification.

Payment for the Interviews and Jean-Pierre's Relationship to Money

Except in a few instances that will be described later, the payment for our interviews, the money Jean-Pierre was to receive for his work, also played a role in his search for identity and represented one of the ways he could restore—or even newly establish—his self-esteem. The far greater sums he could have earned working on his brothers' plantations (either in Yosso or with Thomas's family in Bébou) held no temptation for him. Wages of that sort would have lowered rather than enhanced his self-esteem, not because work as a planter would have made him dependent on his brothers or their enterprises (this dependency existed in any case and was something that he could not avoid and that he accepted), but because the money received from the whites, the "fame and fortune acquired away from home," satisfied him by reconciling his concept of what he could and should be like (his ideal self) with his actual situation. Only much later, after he had succeeded in part in identifying with me, did the daydreamlike wish for a "European" way of making money begin to emerge, the fantasy that he might establish a transport company with his own truck. Till then he had never even considered looking for a job as a chauffeur; after all, he was employed by me. This aspect of his suddenly discovered self-esteem could not be disregarded even in a daydream. Thus the money he received for his interviews with me did not represent "seduction," nor was it perceived "anally" as the reward for an achievement; rather, it was seen as a tangible and symbolic compensation for the depressive feeling of being worthless, a nobody.

It is the need for such narcissistic repair that leads so many young Anyi to invent and cling to a daydreamlike fantasy of the gold that awaits them elsewhere, of a magnanimous patron who will some day reward them generously without their having to perform any manual work. Usually this wish does not come true even in their fantasies.

It is quite possible that for a long time Jean-Pierre had no need to produce and narrate such a daydream because the promised payment and the contact with me already represented its fulfillment. True, Jean-Pierre's thoughts were often preoccupied with money, but he did not expect anything more from me, so to speak. It was not seduction when I occasionally gave him an extra hundred francs so that he could go to a dance. At the end of our series of interviews, I had to go look for him to pay him the promised "salary." When I finally found him, he took the money without looking at it, holding the bills in his clenched fist like a talisman. When I disregard Jean-Pierre's conscious attitude, which did not seem to be influenced in any way by the promised payment for the interviews, and consider his fantasies about money, I can find a connection between the latter and his relationship with me at any given moment only during our first seventeen sessions. Occasionally he had fantasies in which he robbed me. He refused, however, to accept my interpretation to the effect that these fantasies reflected the payment for our talks and his greed to receive money from me. Later on I could note no further influence by the idea of payment on the process of transference; as in the case of seriously disturbed European patients, who pay for treatment but still feel themselves dependent on the good graces of the analyst, in Jean-Pierre's case, too, transference tendencies developed that led to his feeling dependent on me.

In Jean-Pierre's fantasies one can come into money by stealing, by gaining the favor of the great, or by sheer good luck, especially luck in gambling; money can be lost through bad luck, theft, robbery, envious evil persons, and especially through women. To earn money, as a remuneration for work performed, is unthinkable. Toward the end of our interviews, however, in a more relaxed mood, Jean-Pierre tells me that he once earned quite a lot of money selling snails he had gathered himself. Naturally, since this is only an activity for girls and women—that is, an essentially female way of making money—he did not consider it an occupation. He had done it, so to speak, in his female identity; the connection with a strong passive homosexual trait in his character was obvious. When he told me about the snails, he added immediately that of course men could not do that, because if they did they would lose the money they earned right away through theft or some other means. Only women, he assured me, were able to keep money earned in this fashion. Nor had Jean-Pierre ever considered another of his abilities, this one with phallic narcissistic cathexis, namely his skill at soccer, as a possible way of earning money, though the subject of professional athletes who suddenly acquire fame and fortune is a popular one among Anyi youths—as it was, for example, with Adou Agnimou, who was not very good at soccer himself.

We can now look more closely at my previous statement that payment for the interviews was not "seduction." This money did not have the effect of placing Jean-Pierre in a position of demanding and frustrated dependency on me as the nurturing (maternal) object. Narcissistic gratification outweighed by far any gratification I could offer as an object. The object of the narcissistic gratification is an imagined, omnipotent, idealized parent or mother image, over whom one has no influence and from whom one may expect, but never demand, satisfaction. When this image fails to provide the hoped-for gratification, the reaction is not rage or some other form of frustration aggression, but rather depression, and the change that takes place is not in the object (object representation) but in the self. Accordingly, the need to be given money seems to stem from the oral libidinal phase. The "repair" of self-esteem seems to be brought about by the magical powers of the giver or of the money, that is, to correspond to the omnipotence of early childhood. The attribution of phallic power to money (and likewise the theft and robbery fantasies) indicates that this source of happiness (or rather this defense against misfortune) consists in a phallic repair of the impotent child, and that happiness is usually expected more from the overpowering phallic mother, the mighty father, than from the nurturing breast. The satisfying substance itself is anal. The money I had promised Jean-Pierre was the anal penis of the omnipotent mother who is impervious to influence, presented to the powerless child who is in need of complementation of the self.

Early Transference Reactions and Regressive Attitudes

Jean-Pierre's prevailing attitude toward me at the beginning of our talks was that of a completely docile tool or a robot. I made the following note the day after our first interview:

> I find Jean-Pierre in Yosso, where he had gone to pick up his luggage, two small suitcases. When I ask whether he wants to drive back (to Bébou) with me, he nods. I tell him that I'll sound my horn before my departure from Yosso to let him know I'm ready to leave. When he hears my horn, he comes up to the car and stands there, irresolute. I ask him where his luggage is. He points to the house. I ask whether his brother is bringing his luggage. He says no. He continues to stand there motionless until I tell him to go get his suitcases. Then he runs into the house, brings them out, and puts them in the car. During the drive to Bébou (on the way I pick up a few villagers returning from the fields), I have to suggest every little motion to him, tell him when to open the door, where to sit, how to help load the plantains the villagers have with them.

Yet during the first hour Jean-Pierre is by no means in a depressive, brooding, or apathetic mood. He makes an occasional spontaneous remark, sometimes he smiles.

Occasionally he becomes confused, for example, when I schedule our daily hour for half-past three, or when I want to discuss some necessary concrete arrangements for our work, and especially when I remain silent and leave it up to him to open the conversation.[1] At times like these he looks and acts as if he were simpleminded or mentally deranged, or as if he understood no French. During such moments of confusion, he is extremely tense, rubs and cracks his knuckles, fidgets with his feet, eagerly accepts the cigarette I offer him, but is then unable to smoke it properly, as though he hardly has the strength to draw on it.

During the first two hours I find it difficult to keep from succumbing to the suggestive effect of his condition and treating him as if he were sick and not responsible for his actions. I realize, though, that these moments of confusion always happen when I "come in too close," when my presence or my intervention places too great a strain on the organization of his defenses. The contact with a stranger, whose behavior does not conform to his expectations, evokes paralyzing anxiety in him.

Even so, during the first hour it becomes evident that he perceives me—in one form of transference—as an all-knowing and powerful stranger, someone who can fulfill his every desire, but whom he can neither trust nor influence. Deception seems to him the only way of countering such authority.

In an attempt to help him relax, I ask him about his schooling. He describes his schooldays clearly and with evident enjoyment, seizing the opportunity to demonstrate some of his academic achievements, but he can neither understand nor accept the fact that I do not know the local abbreviations for the various types of schools and examinations (for example, CEP=Certificat des Etudes Primaires/Certificate of Primary Studies) and must ask him to explain them to me. He takes no notice of my questions and goes on talking as if I were already thoroughly familiar with the entire system.

Immediately afterward, when I ask how old he is, the extent to which he associates me with the strict authorities of his schooldays becomes even clearer. First he says he is fourteen, then seventeen. After I have gone over with him the life histories and ages of some of his siblings and it turns out that he must be at least nineteen, he absolutely refuses to admit that he may be twenty or twenty-one (the latter is probably correct). When Jean-Pierre was going to school in Abengourou, his older brother, with the help of perjured witnesses, had had his age recorded by court decree as much younger than it really was and had repeated this one or two years later. This is currently the standard procedure among the Anyi for circumventing the regulation that fifteen-year-olds who have not yet completed their primary studies are excluded from further school attendance. In Jean-Pierre's case it did not work; he had to leave school in 1961 (according to what he says) or perhaps a bit later and return to Yosso. All in all, he seems to have attended school in Bébou for three years and in Abengourou for four or five years. Objectively he knows, of course, that I have nothing whatsoever to do with the schools or the authorities and that his work with me is not dependent upon his being any certain age. Emotionally, however, the transference of his school experiences to my person prevails. During our later talks it becomes obvious that this is based on his tendency to see in me an all-knowing, omnipotent, and unmanipulatable person, a derivative of the "idealized parent image." This has already been mentioned in the above discussion of Jean-Pierre's salary for the interviews. A powerless person can influence this type of partner only by means of magic, and magic here includes the court decree fixing Jean-Pierre's age. From this time on, the lies and deceptions he resorted to with me were not intended to secure him tangible material advantages. They were simply magical means that Jean-Pierre employed when he felt himself particularly powerless and incompetent.

Actually we can distinguish three quite different, successive modes of behavior in what I have described so far, the third of which I should like to call transference reaction.[2] The first is the behavior of a robot without a will of its own; the second is the stage of confusion caused by anxiety and emotional strain and accompanied by a breakdown of language comprehension and performance; and the third is the act of projection to an all-knowing and omnipotent being.

Since these modes of behavior on Jean-Pierre's part were endangering the successful continuation of our talks, I resorted to an artifice during our second session. I tried working out a genealogy with his assistance.

This activity placed our work on neutral ground, in an area that was of interest to both of us. I was able to assume that my partner, like any Anyi, would know all about his own kinship ties, since such knowledge is indispensable for anyone who is to handle contacts with his relatives properly and in accordance with traditional custom. I myself had a direct interest in familiarizing myself with his genealogy, since dealing with the Anyi with the proper classificatory designations is rather confusing for a European.

When Jean-Pierre was not cooperating sufficiently during our work and merely answering my questions with "yes, Monsieur," I could now successfully suggest that I was bound to make mistakes without his help. Then he would begin to help me immediately, correcting my work—starting with the spelling of proper names and smiling when I wrote something down correctly.

Our work on the genealogy had the effect of a transitional phenomenon (Winnicott), which made it possible for the one partner to maintain an interpersonal relationship by means of the libidinal (or aggressive) cathexis of an object or—as in this case—an activity also cathected by the other partner, without feeling anxiety, impotence, or other unbearable emotions engendered by the direct confrontation with a threatening object.

At the beginning of our fifth interview, when I was better acquainted with Jean-Pierre, I tried the same artifice again and asked him to complete the genealogy with data about his cousin in Abidjan. After a few moments his initial bewilderment and mute confusion had disappeared. In fact he even told me spontaneously that he liked it here in Bébou; this was his very first direct and positive expression of emotion. After this he gradually began to talk to me about his relatives.

Jean-Pierre's Kin

First he spoke of his brothers. He has no younger brother in his immediate family. As far as he is concerned, brothers are always older brothers—his own, like the aforementioned oldest brother N'da Aka, as well as his cousins, including Thomas Assoua, who had first brought him to me, and others, particularly the one who lives in Bassam. Such brothers must be obeyed implicitly; one can remove oneself from their sphere of influence by various maneuvers, or one can identify with them, especially with their enviable qualities, perceiving these qualities as one's own. During our talks Jean-Pierre showed no special fondness or dislike for any of these brothers. Emotionally, they were equal in status, and it was only the characteristic qualities we happened to be talking about at the moment that made it possible for me to tell which brother Jean-Pierre was referring to. When he said "my brother" he often meant two or more at the same time—for example, the prestige of the cousin in Abidjan, the wealth and reputation of the cousin in Bassam, and the dignity of Thomas Assoua in his capacity as chief of a court in Bébou.

It was pretty much the same with his sisters, except that they were not distinguished from one another by attributes, but simply by which one of them was cooking for him now, which one had cooked for him previously, or which one had otherwise taken care of him. The youngest sister, N'da Bourou, however, who is married to the medical orderly in Zaranou, seems to possess Jean-Pierre's special affection. He occasionally mentioned her by name and sometimes would even say, "Bourou gave me something to eat" when he really meant that he had eaten with his older sister Thérèse.

Jean-Pierre's real mother, Akouassi N'guessam, with whom he lived before he moved to Bébou, and her two half-sisters seem to mean equally much to him—as far as I could tell from our talks—at least as regards his statement that they were all in agreement with his leaving Yosso, or when he says, for example, that it is difficult for an Anyi to leave home because of his desire to stay with his mother.

Jean-Pierre mentions his father of his own accord, without my asking about him. He tells me, "My father was seized by the devils. The female shamans told my mother about it." The father had died suddenly one morning while at work on the plantations. There was no one present at the time. Jean-Pierre cannot remember his father's death, which took place about the same time as the birth of his youngest sister. He himself thinks his father caused his own death by going out into the forest on a day it was forbidden, so that the evil spirits had no choice but to kill him. To him this method of committing suicide, by delivering oneself up unprotected to witches and spirits, is the natural fate of fathers who have allied themselves with a woman.

For a young European, who at the age of twenty-one is still very dependent and not yet secure in his identity as a male, it would be natural for some of his inner conflicts to be directed at the persons who make up his immediate family and who have played decisive roles in the conflicts of his childhood. This was not so in Jean-Pierre's case. We are omitting nothing essential from our account when we say no more than the above concerning his living relatives. However, this should not be construed to mean that he did not inform us of these conflicts, or that his relationships with these persons were free of tension.

Etiquette and Object Relations

Contacts and conversations with members of one's own family are governed by the same rules of courtesy as those with strangers or slight acquaintances. One speaks little, one does not complain, and one does not express one's affection, concern, animosity, or distrust. At most one may utter an admonition or, when someone has gotten into a difficult situation, may say "Voilà ton arrivée" ("See, that was bound to happen"); or one may recite a warning proverb. Certainly there is no one who can invariably adhere to this etiquette. Playmates and siblings speak much more naturally with one another, as do people in love. Etiquette rules are often broken during a quarrel or under the pressure of some other emotion.

The application of the etiquette rules enables Jean-Pierre to introduce relatives into the conversation as the representatives of specific roles, thus denying the emotions he may feel toward them and the conflicts he may have with them. Western cultures offer an analogy in the form of social affairs regulated by protocol. At a diplomatic reception, for example, one pays less attention to the wife of the Chilean military attaché than to the wife of the Russian ambassador, even though one may find the former much more congenial. This is simply a way of preventing personal feelings or conflicts from disturbing social contacts. During his talks with me, Jean-Pierre almost always took advantage of this possibility of reducing the members of his family to the status of role representatives.

He was not quite successful, however, in his attempts to make our interviews follow what he considered appropriate ceremonial rules. For here the rules were different; above all, he was supposed to tell me "everything," and the things I wanted to know were precisely the things one does not usually express. An exchange of material goods was out of the question. To make up for it, he introduced a kind of "dictation ceremony" and held fast to it as long as he could. He would tell stories that I took down in shorthand. Whenever he saw that he was going too fast for me, he waited for me to catch up. When I stopped writing, he would resume his narrative. When I didn't write anything at all, he became confused. This ceremony established itself from our third session on; later we gave it up temporarily from time to time, but it was only after about the thirtieth session that it could be dispensed with entirely over a fairly long period. I could tell from the disruptions in the ceremony and from the varying consistency in his need to resort to it that this stereotyped behavior gave him a feeling of security. It can best be described as a transitional phenomenon similar to the artifice with the genealogy that I had used in the second interview.

Jean-Pierre's dealings with the persons of his environment, however, were marked to an extremely high degree by the images experienced in early childhood. His object representations of adults bore clear traces of the emotions and conflicts characteristic of the environment of a small child, but the object representations that emerged during our interviews corresponded rarely and only vaguely to real, living persons, least of all in the case of his closest relatives. He spoke of people and treated them, their relations with one another and with him, and their personal qualities as if they were figures in a fairy tale. People out of the past, whom he knew only by hearsay, deceased persons, spirits, witches, magicians, and sorcerers, foreign laborers, the always slightly uncanny strangers from the north, and even Jean-Pierre's own friends, acquaintances, relatives, teachers, and foster parents were always the embodiments of a significance he himself attached to them; in comparison, the fact that some of them were also real people was of little importance. The rules of etiquette sufficed completely for Jean-Pierre's day-to-day contacts; that he perceived these people as different from what they really were was not an insuperable obstacle in his dealings with them.

The Turning Point in the Third Interview

During our third hour together, a change of atmosphere took place, a change in transference behavior and ego functioning—in short, a shift in Jean-Pierre's entire relationship with me. At the beginning of the hour, he still stands around rather forlornly. His new friend François, toward whom he no longer feels any distrust now that he is reassured that François cannot take away his "job," has had to lead him to my tent.

When he informs me that his family had reacted with silence to his departure from Yosso, I praise the advantages to be gained from evading a direct confrontation. He speaks of François and of the nature of contacts between friends. One can talk seriously with them, one can be silent, one can chat. If one of them should become too personal, or abusive, one stops speaking to him. Once more I praise the virtues of evasion as a means of averting the outbreak of potential conflicts. Jean-Pierre begins to talk about money, of which he has none and which the foreigners, particularly the whites, have in such abundance. I reply with an account of how, with cunning and skill, one can borrow money or find oneself a rich patron, and I explain that one can achieve satisfaction and security in roundabout ways.

With my new attitude I strengthen him in his evasive, secretive behavior and in his readiness to cheat, and I range myself on the side of the instinctual desires. I do not interpret the refusal to give in to them as resistance, but stress the positive aspect that, even so, he can gain some measure of satisfaction. I cast doubt on what we term mature ego functioning and minimize the dangers emanating from the external world and the superego, which seem extremely threatening to him.

And while I am still talking, Jean-Pierre seizes the initiative for the first time. He interrupts me and all of a sudden begins talking about something apparently quite different. Much in the same fashion as someone who plucks up his courage to deliver an address while another speaker is holding forth on the platform; he just may be able to shout him down. Naturally, I stop speaking immediately.

Jean-Pierre begins: "Once upon a time there was a thief. He was a friend of mine. And this friend went along with someone else"—is the someone else Jean-Pierre perhaps, or a third person?—"to Bouaké. There the two of them stole a car. Then they ran it into a tree. The police found them and took the friend to jail. The thief took the other man with him and said that *he* was guilty. So the police didn't know which of the two was the thief. They were never able to find out. He was accused of theft. He couldn't manage to talk his way out."

The hearer has no idea which of the two was the thief, or who accused whom. At the beginning of the story, Jean-Pierre's linguistic performance is very bad, hardly understandable. I wait in the hope that I will gradually be able to understand him better.

Now it is quite clear what I should interpret. He is unable to ward off the assault of instinctual urges, and his ego cannot cope with them well enough to express them clearly. I have to come to his aid (auxiliary ego) and show him that I—as his listener—do not reject, condemn, or punish his greedy or aggressive wish fantasies. I remark that it is very difficult for both of them. Nobody will believe that the thief's companion is innocent because, after all, he *was* along with the thief; most people will believe the thief when he denounces the other man: "Rogues of a gang on one gibbet must hang." Right away Jean-Pierre's mood becomes cheerful and his French excellent. He points out the moral of the story: "The best thing is to put them both in jail; then they won't steal any more. They'll finally come to their senses."

The originally fantastic tale now turns into a genuine story. A former friend of Jean-Pierre's (the thief, perhaps?) ran away from home and went to Aboisso. He has no job, begs for his food in restaurants, and sleeps in the street with the men who load coffee sacks. He has no respect for his parents. When his father goes by, or his mother, he looks the other way. He won't take advice from anybody. He has become a regular bum.

Identifying with morality, Jean-Pierre himself has become a model of respectability, functions better, speaks more fluently, and achieves control over his aggressive impulses. As he gradually stops speaking, his story petering out rather than coming to an end, it is easy for me to intervene by appearing to question authority: "Maybe it was the father who was at fault. If he had given his son more money, he might not have become a thief."

Jean-Pierre replies to this with a new version of the same story. This time the two fellows were not even arrested by the police. The theft remained undiscovered. A friend of the father's found out about it and told the father. Then the father reproached the son for going about in such bad company and said that he had become a thief himself. The father thrashed him and denounced both boys to the police, saying that they should both be locked up.

Jean-Pierre fails to take in my second defense of the thieves. He condemns that "bum" once again. He wasn't really a bad fellow, conceded Jean-Pierre, just dumb, and he hadn't learned any occupation either. Later, perhaps, after he'd had enough bitter experience, he might turn out all right.

I had introduced the "father as aggressor," who was then conjured into the second version, where he was perceived in all his cruelty and lost his power to frighten.

Jean-Pierre's behavior and mood have changed entirely. His voice is now firm, his French fluent and understandable. He is in harmony with morality and with me, and for a short while he is better able to deal with the reality of our interview.

The First Fantastic Tales and Transference Fantasies

Jean-Pierre continues immediately with another story, this one about the cruel white despot Monsieur Duplis (as he calls him), who operated a gold mine along the road between Bébou and Yosso during the time of the Pétain regime. The brutal punishments meted out by the white man to his workers and to persons he suspected of stealing his gold are described vividly and in great detail—he would whip them, for example, or force his victims to stand for hours with baskets of stones on their heads, and so on. Monsieur Duplis had not employed village people or given them any chance to earn money, but had hired foreign workers instead. Later, when he had all the gold packed in boxes and shipped to his own country, he himself died on the way home, and his whole family also died out.

This story can be assumed to be a transference fantasy. When he speaks of the white foreigner, Jean-Pierre means me; the villagers had indeed complained that we "gave no work" to local Anyi. Jean-Pierre himself had envied our interpreter François his job with us, and he also envies our servant Yoro, who is a foreign laborer. Most Anyi assume that the frankly given information about what we are trying to accomplish is a lie, invented to conceal our plans to mine gold in their country and carry it away. The story about Monsieur Duplis is common knowledge. Jean-Pierre's embroidery of it gives it the character of a fantasy. The component of cruel impulses emanating from his unconscious apprehensions (and possibly wishes) is unmistakable. It is obvious that my partner, who cannot even bear confrontation in an everyday conversation without regressive disintegration of his communicative and integrative ego functioning, would not be able to tolerate an interpretation revealing that, unconsciously, his story had been directed against me. I do nothing to disturb his defenses, but I intervene—as before—on the side of his thirst for vengeance, saying merely, "It served the white man right that he died, and that his family didn't profit from the gold either. An evil fellow like that deserves to die."

Jean-Pierre feels himself confirmed. He speaks more directly, expanding his story to include his own experience, at the age of seven, as a victim of the private police force maintained by Monsieur Duplis. On the basis of a false suspicion that he had stolen some meat, they had put Jean-Pierre and an old man in prison, and then the policemen had eaten the meat themselves. When he returned to the village, Jean-Pierre had warned the old people, "There's no point in trying to protect yourselves from the white man and his police; they're stronger than you."

This remark helps me to understand the abject, robotlike obedience to which Jean-Pierre repeatedly succumbs. Protecting yourself against someone stronger than you is not only dangerous; it also goes against common sense (reality principle) and the accepted rules of life (superego). I have no further comment to make.

It is clear that Jean-Pierre, approximately twenty-one years of age in 1966, cannot have been put in jail in 1945 as a seven-year-old child. Later on—not only during this interview, but until the end of our sessions—stories of this kind prove to be a mixture of his own memories, things he has heard from the villagers and from his friends, and fantasies. It is the fantasy element, stemming from the unconscious of the storyteller, that determines the emotional tone and frequently the content as well. That personal memories are also involved, experiences from early (and in part later) childhood, is most clearly recognizable at the point where I enter the story as the object of transference, either directly or thinly disguised.

Jean-Pierre cannot distinguish at all—and usually I cannot tell with certainty either—that component of his tales that is based on memories, and thus stems from the preconscious, from the component that reproduces internal experience from early childhood. Apparently his ability to assess reality is inadequate from time to time. While he is telling these stories, his ego is oriented inward, so to speak, to enable him to conjure hard-to-control instinctual urges and anxieties into his tale. When he addresses himself to me more directly, his imagination falters and the defense process grows stronger and manifests itself in the form of resistance.

During our thirty-eighth interview, a poisonous snake slithers into the tent unnoticed by Jean-Pierre, who at this moment happens to be troubled and absentminded. I call his attention to the reptilian visitor, and Jean-Pierre, who has been lying curled up on the cot, his thoughts wandering, leaps up all of a sudden, grabs a mango branch lying in the tent, kills the snake with a few well-aimed blows to the head and neck, picks it up with the branch, and—is suddenly paralyzed. He has no idea what to do with the corpse and, just like a robot, stands there waiting for my orders. I declare, "This dead snake can't stay here in the tent, it would start to decay and attract all sorts of insects." Jean-Pierre remains motionless. Only when I add, "We'd better throw it outside in the road" does he hurl it out of the tent; then he sinks back onto the couch. It is evident that the confrontation with reality has forced him to react quickly and appropriately. His ego functioning is not nearly so efficient in his relationship with me, as the object of transference.

Ever since our third session (i.e., since I have stopped making the defense process impossible with my interpretations), escape into fantasies, with its effect of denying the transference going on, has enabled Jean-Pierre from time to time to descend from the stratosphere of fantasy-distorted fairy tales and legends in telling his stories to the firmer ground of less distorted memories and even of his present life.

For example, he continues the story of the gold-mine owner in a more idyllic vein, describing the ponds that Monsieur Duplis had had excavated, in which Jean-Pierre often went fishing as a boy and still does occasionally. A rainbow arched into the pond, the heavens made it fertile. . . . Comforted by the thought of sumptuous fish dishes, he returns to the tortures inflicted by Monsieur Duplis. With undisguised pleasure he describes how the white man ordered his victims to be undressed and held fast, then worked them over with a whip; his description leaves out none of the grisly details—the weals, the torn skin, the bleeding extremities and genitals. The lust he finds in his narration seems to be masochistic rather than sadistic. When he comes to the end of his tale he assures me earnestly, "The white man had a pistol. He would have shot anyone who tried to defend himself. Not even the old village chief could do anything to stop him."

I begin to speak of fear and point out what a good thing it is when the enemy is so powerful that one cannot hope to defend oneself and thus is not obligated even to try. In these circumstances one avoids having to fight out conflicts to the end and need never experience fear. I deal with the (masochistic) turning of sadistic aggression to the self in the same way as I had dealt with the earlier forms of defense. In other words, I praise a defense that at least permits some gratification of drives and reduces anxiety. I note that it was the memory of oral gratification that introduced the transition to masochistic pleasure, but I do not formulate this observation in my interpretation for Jean-Pierre.

Jean-Pierre is now downright cheerful and, on occasion, even waxes ironic. He tells me that the new village chief was petrified with fear while the villagers were carrying him on his official stool to his inauguration ceremony.

That Jean-Pierre is now capable of feeling superior to a father figure shows that the conjuring of such figures into his stories has been successful and that his ego has experienced relief. Even the masochistic turning of aggression to the self has become temporarily unnecessary as a defense.

He goes on to tell me that once, as a child, he himself had found a gold nugget and held it in his cupped hand. People said he had stolen it and locked him up. His own mother, he related, used to go down to the Manzan River and wash gold in secret, hiding whatever she found in her hair. One time she was caught and went to jail for it.

In my answer I point out how one can resort to deception to conceal the booty, thereby fooling the authorities, and still gain an advantage for oneself. One can also make life difficult for those in power and, in certain circumstances, even kill them.

At this point Jean-Pierre, in no uncertain terms, begins to berate Monsieur N, the present village chief in Yosso, complaining that he is stingy and selfish and that he hires outsiders for the best-paid jobs in the village.

In my interpretation I call Jean-Pierre's attention to the fact that the village chief Monsieur N, the gold-mine owner, and the father of the young thief who denounced his son to the police all resemble each other; I point out that fear is actually a good thing because it enables one to save oneself in time and to avoid danger.

A Chapter in a Family Romance

Jean-Pierre has become extraordinarily lively and is positively bursting with a desire to talk. He speaks about his teacher in Bébou. At the time he was still attending school here, the teacher used to make his pupils work on his coffee plantation. When they came to work late, he beat them, and when they had forgotten their bushwhackers, he made them dig holes in the ground with their bare fingers. Jean-Pierre adds that this plantation now belongs to our friend Chief Ahoussi, who harvests three (sometimes he says thirty) tons of coffee a year. And he glories in his obviously lustful descriptions of how the teacher—a man from Senegal, that is, another stranger—mistreated the children.

The gratification and thus the reinforcement of his ego is so strong that he now tells me about a genuine schoolboy trick that he and his playmates once perpetrated. There was to be a particularly difficult written test in class, and the teacher had threatened to thrash all those who made mistakes. Thereupon an impudent, obviously wide-awake boy had called out, "There! Up under the ceiling [of the classroom]! There's a snake!" Everybody ran outside, and the teacher ordered that a fire be made in the classroom to drive out the snake. It goes without saying, of course, that the test had to be postponed.

When I express my appreciation of this trick, Jean-Pierre is still not satisfied. Deeply regressing to his masochistic pleasure once again, he feels frustrated until he has a chance to embroider his tale of the beatings more fully. He relates that every week the teacher would order a whole load of rope from the city to beat the boys with (we too drove into the city once a week to do our shopping).

Incidentally, the parents had by no means stood up for their children; on the contrary, they had told the teacher to give them a good thrashing. This could very well be true. But it provides the transition to a sequel, related in a highly personal fashion but certainly greatly distorted by fantasy, in which the teacher is introduced directly into Jean-Pierre's own "family romance."

"The teacher," he continues, "was my sister's husband. He beat her, too, even when she was pregnant. He injured her breasts. One time I was with my sister in her room and there was a knock at the door. I thought it was some friends of mine and called out an insult as a joke. The teacher came in and found me with my sister. He grabbed my hands and feet, picked me up and threw me down on the floor, twelve times one after the other, and then he beat me. I was seriously hurt— there, you see." And he points to a barely visible scar about two millimeters long on the underside of his arm. "They didn't take me to the hospital. I had to keep on going to school."

These scenes with beatings and whippings make it clear that what we have here are "oedipal" fantasies—the teacher is linked with the father, and the sister (Jean-Pierre didn't say which sister) is his wife. Masochistic, primordial-scene fantasies from early childhood, in which the small boy who wants to stay by his mother is attacked and punished by the furious father, are intermingled with memories of his schooldays. Initially the masochistic pleasure he feels seems to stimulate him. He hates the teacher. Gradually, though, the teacher becomes a less threatening figure; he didn't really mean it that way, he just wasn't quite right in the head. Later, after he had been transferred to another village, the teacher came back several times to visit Jean-Pierre's family, and everyone was glad to see him.

Once the teacher is rehabilitated, another white man takes his place as the anxiety-evoking figure. In a story that might have taken place within the last few years, a white man whom Jean-Pierre rows across the Camoë River accuses him unjustly and threatens to beat him. But a second, good white man appears upon the scene and takes his part. Our hour is over. Jean-Pierre is completely relaxed and is speaking excellent French.

As we are leaving the tent, he suddenly asks me for a headache pill, saying that he had had a headache the night before.

The situation of analysis, the demand that he talk freely, had thrown Jean-Pierre into a state of passivity, paralysis, and impotence. This state changed during our third hour together—he was suddenly able to express himself. This change cannot be accounted for only by his having become accustomed to me and to the situation. It was precisely the regression encouraged in the analytical method that had produced or intensified the resistance described.

My attitude and my intervention did nothing to break down his defenses. Thus they diminished his anxiety and permitted him to find gratification in his fantasies. He succeeded in avoiding direct aggressive statements and in shifting the conflict to substitute objects. The narration of fantasy stories is comparable to dreamwork. Under the guidance of the (temporarily strengthened) ego, the magical conjuring away of aggressive desires is feasible. These desires corresponded to the most varied phases of libido and aggression development. Particularly strong was the masochistic component, which not only impressed me as gratifying and—even in the oedipal primordial scene fantasies—not genuinely threatening; but it was also shifted to "whites" and to other objects resembling my person and thus did not have to be repressed. Desires for direct oral gratification emerged. Under their influence, at the end of the hour a new form of transference developed—that of oral demanding dependency.

I have described this third interview in such detail because it was typical of a great many others, both in its course and in its atmosphere. Naturally, during later sessions there were numerous fluctuations and modifications in the content of Jean-Pierre's fantasies, in the type and order of appearance of the instinctual urges they stimulated, and also in the functioning of his ego.

It was only gradually—and even then only fragmentarily—that I was able to pick out from the entangled thickets of his wildly imaginative fantasies memories that can be treated in the same way as "screen memories" in European patients, namely, as the distorted reproduction of genuine experiences. Using some of these memories as a basis, I shall describe in the following sections certain phases of Jean-Pierre's childhood and adolescence that were of decisive importance in his development.

Childhood Experiences: Abandonment

"When I was very small, I used to go out to the plantation with my grandfather. There were fires burning all over the place [to clear the ground]. I was so small that I couldn't even talk yet, or just barely, but I helped with the work. They set the fires in such a way that I was nearly burned together with the trees. There was almost no way to escape. They were not paying any attention to what they were doing. My big brother told me he thought I had already left, and I was really still there. Later on they organized things differently; the workers lined up in a row and set fire to the underbrush in a straight line. There was a pangolin caught between two fires. He was burned alive."

This experience, which Jean-Pierre related to me in our thirty-ninth, or next-to-last hour, when he knew that I would soon be leaving, seems to summarize as a "screen memory" a good deal of what he experienced as a toddler. Though he is small and weak, he has to work in order to be with his family. He is neglected, abandoned, and exposed to terrible danger. The grandfather, the head of the family, pays no attention; the older brother sets the fire, but he apologizes for his carelessness. Later on, too late to do Jean-Pierre any good, they improve things. As it was, he barely escaped becoming a meal for a cannibal, like the tasty little pangolin. There is no nurturing mother to be seen.

Again and again in his fantasies, children are given away, sold, stolen. He never revolts against these circumstances; at most he finds that it is wrong for fathers to sell their children for too little money. Evil foreigners, usually *atakora* (as he calls people from the northern part of Dahomey), force the children to work, beat them mercilessly, do not take care of them or give them anything to eat, and in the end—when the children have died—devour them instead of burying them or at least sending their bodies back to their parents.

Jean-Pierre related the following experience during our ninth interview: "I was ten, or maybe a little bit more, when they gave me away to my grandfather [uncle] in the land of the Attié. There there was no water. There was no way you could wash. And if I don't wash every day, my skin itches and I feel miserable. I saved the money they sometimes gave me for my work and hid it away. One day I said that I couldn't go out to the fields because I had a stomachache. Then I left and went back home.

"They eat a lot of cassava there and it was too much for my stomach and I really had pains in my belly. This time, though, I just said I was sick. Then I took my money and I got on the bus and went home to my mother. Oh, my mother was glad to have me back. She told me that I had been right to leave when I explained to her that there wasn't any water there. She said, 'Where there is no water, my son must die.' Later, much later, my grandfather came to visit us and told me that I had grown a lot. I said that was because I was able to bathe every day."

This brings us to a discussion of how mothers take care of their children, and Jean-Pierre says: "Yes, as long as she's still carrying it on her back, the child is good for the mother. She has to nurse it, that's true, but she can show herself with the baby in the village. Later, when she's not carrying it on her back any more, it's no good to her. What can she still do for the child once it's that old?" (He indicates the height of an approximately four-year-old child.) "If it's a girl, she can carry a baby on her back herself, or she can fetch water. But boys of this age can't do anything useful; they're not really good for anything. That's why the mothers are not interested in them any longer. Why should they keep on bathing them? Let them do it themselves!"

Consciously, Jean-Pierre does not blame his mother (or the Anyi mothers in general) for having neglected him after he had been weaned or for the loneliness and anxiety that he had experienced. He obeys his mother and feels that he owes her respect, or at least that—in keeping with the rules of etiquette—he is obligated to obtain her consent for all important actions and to ask her forgiveness when he has angered her; and the same applies to the other mothers, his maternal aunts. His reproaches are directed instead at the grandfather, the father, or the family elders, who ought to have taken over the nurturing role of the mother.

Lasting traces of the nurturing behavior of Jean-Pierre's mother toward her son even after weaning, during the toddler stage (and such behavior is typical of all Anyi mothers), can be seen in his insistence on personal cleanliness, his pleasure in eating, a certain anxious concern over his "handsomeness," and especially a deep-seated hypochondriac anxiety concerning the content of his bowels and his physical vitality, which may be greatly diminished in a sudden state of collapse (from which he always recovers quickly, however).

The emotions associated with abandonment frequently evoke passive cannibalistic fantasies in Jean-Pierre, in which he perceives himself as the pangolin that was burned alive or as the children who are stolen and devoured. We explain this as a regression to his own greedy devouring desires in childhood. Measured against the developmental steps that followed, these desires were gratifying, and this has led to a fixation. They are revived by every new instance of frustration (being abandoned). At the same time, the demarcation from the mother is incomplete. By turning against the self, Jean-Pierre is able to retain both the wish impulse (to devour) and the object (the mother); the latter, however, is experienced as a pursuer (female or male), and the experience is accompanied by a paranoiac feeling of anxiety.

Further analysis will show that Jean-Pierre's relationship with his mother was frequently seriously disturbed in other respects as well. His present relationship to real mothers is based on very little more than the empty observance of the rules of etiquette and is entirely isolated from his own emotions and fantasies. Jean-Pierre was not one of those children given away by their parents at an early age. When he entered school he came to Bébou, where he lived—probably—with one of his older sisters, the one who was married at that time to the "cruel" schoolmaster. For a short while he lived with a great-uncle in the land of the Attié. He spent the remainder of his schooldays in Abengourou, first in the home of a foster mother, who—allegedly—taught him to steal, and later with another, "good" foster family.

Thus his move from Yosso to Bébou, to be able to talk with me every day, represented not only a flight from his tension-laden, unsatisfactory kin to the court of his big brother (cousin) Thomas Assoua, but also an active repetition of the process of passive abandonment. Every time Jean-Pierre accompanied me to Yosso in the forenoon to pick up something from home, to discuss something with his mother, brothers, or sisters, or sometimes even without really knowing himself why he wanted to come along, there was a repetition of traumatic experience. He came to his kin with an unfulfilled yearning for warmth and affection and encountered suspicious reserve and coolly polite etiquette. Optimistically, he would be eager to get back to Bébou in the hope of finding, either in Thomas's court or with me, some vestige of the happier times he had experienced with his foster family there. This hope foundered repeatedly as a result of inevitable frustrations, and once again the following morning his still unsatisfied greedy dependency drove him back to his own kin, to Yosso.

His despondency after these trips was determined, of course, by a number of factors. For one thing, he had watched me treat the sick and take movies in Yosso. He tried to ward off his envy of the objects of my attentions and his fury at my infidelity by being especially servile. It seems to me, however, that this and other happenings are not so conducive to explaining the compulsive repetition of those joyless trips to Yosso as the abandonment motif described above.

The Oedipal Conflict

Jean-Pierre's imaginatively embellished memory of sitting in his sister's room as a small boy and being thrown on the floor twelve times and beaten by her husband, the cruel schoolmaster who also beat and maimed the sister, was interpreted above as a primordial-scene fantasy. This is one of the forms in which Jean-Pierre expresses the oedipal theme, a theme that occupies his mind almost to the exclusion of all else.

In his earliest conscious memories (which he describes during our thirty-third interview), the intruding, anxiety-evoking third figure appears in the guise of a black monkey. This is only after he has succeeded in distributing the frustrations suffered at the hands of his mother between his sister and his mother in such a way that he can now recall his mother with clearly positive emotions.

In a relaxed mood, he begins the conversation:

Jean-Pierre: Women don't want boys. When a woman bears a girl, she smiles with delight, but when it's a boy, she is silent.
Parin: As long as they're nursing, mothers like boys just as much as girls.
Jean-Pierre: Yes, that's true; but later on, when the child is bigger, they nag the boys. When a woman hits a child that doesn't belong to her, people warn her that she'll break its bones, and if she breaks its bones, she won't have any money to have it taken to the hospital. It isn't hers. They tell her she can't do whatever she likes with it.
Parin: How was that when you were a little boy?
Jean-Pierre: Mother was out at her plantation. They were planting corn. I was with my older sister. Instead of helping with the planting, I was pulling the little shoots out of the ground. My sister beat me for that, and I was sick for five days. She told me about it. She promised that she would never beat me again. And she kept her promise—she never did.
Parin: Those are all things that people have told you. Do you remember this period of your life yourself?
Jean-Pierre: The very first thing I remember is connected with planting corn, too. I had put the seeds too close together in the soil, and later my mother had to pull up half the plants. They were crowded too close together, and the pickers wouldn't have been able to squeeze between them during the harvest. I remember that I put six seeds in one hole, too.

At that time we had a lot of meat to eat. My mother would say, "You don't have to eat it if you don't want to." I didn't like meat. I enjoyed fish, but there was just too much meat.

One day my mother told me to keep an eye on the cornfield to make sure that the monkeys didn't get at the plants. Suddenly I saw a black monkey. I thought to myself, I've got to get away. I told the others [other children] that I was going to the hut. I thought the monkey would kill me. I was scared. They got my father and told him what was happening. He went and got his rifle and six cartridges. The monkey was just eating a cassava root and scratching itself, and it looked at us. [Jean-Pierre imitates the monkey's actions, scratching himself and looking at me in horror.] Then they killed that monkey, and the other monkeys ran away.

They brought the dead monkey to the village and sold it. We don't eat monkey meat. A monkey is too much like a person. Other people eat it, though, and they say, "These people are good to eat. They're very tasty."

The fright that overcame little Jean-Pierre at the sight of the harmless black money, which did not scare the other children away, can be interpreted as follows: I am guarding the field of my mother, and thus my mother herself. An intruder appears on the scene. I am afraid because I want my mother for myself. The real father, not the dreaded oedipal father, comes to the rescue and shoots the intruder. The intruder shot by the father, however, is the little boy himself; while telling the tale, he identifies with the monkey. His aversion to eating meat means: I do not wish to kill my father. People find that human flesh tastes good. In this "oedipal" screen memory, the fear of being killed and eaten himself, originating in the "oral" fixation, stands for castration anxiety.

The entire process of oedipal development is marked by intense castration anxiety. The threatening objects and the nature of the danger involved will vary, depending upon the level of regression being experienced. In fact, one can say that phallic, competitive oedipal impulses need only be hinted at to make them immediately evoke some form of anxiety, which—almost without exception—leads to regression to earlier phases of libido development (particularly to anal-masochistic strivings and oral greed).

"A boy gets hit on the head" is a frequently recurring motif. During our fourth interview Jean-Pierre tells me about a boy who stole some cake and was caught by the watchman. The watchman forced him to take off all his clothes and discovered the cake, which the boy had concealed between his buttocks. The watchman then hit him over the head with a hammer to punish him. Normally Jean-Pierre lies on the couch stiff and unmoving while he is talking; this time he mimics the boy's actions as he relates the story.

On another occasion, a young man had forced his way into the house of an elder. He was discovered—he had intended to rob the old man or to sleep there (?)—and in fleeing banged his head hard on the door frame or was hit on the head by a pursuing policeman.

In the fantasies and stories I term "oedipal," forbidden, incestuous desire is represented by forbidden, greedy eating, by thefts of food, money, or other objects, or by breaking into a house or dwelling. The culprit is invariably a young man, a son, a "little slave," often a friend of the narrator. The more unreal the stories are, the more remote in space and time, the more unmistakably adultery, rape, or the kidnapping and seducing of women take the place of stealing and breaking and entering, and the more clearly the victim is a cruel or weak father figure.

The threat emanates from the "father" or the "mother" or from both. And the female is the more dangerous of the two. She kills, poisons, maims, and above all seduces—which is what sets the whole drama in motion. Sometimes, for good measure, she even avenges herself on the "seducer," undressing him and leaving him to be mocked in his nakedness, or punishes him cruelly, as by rubbing his skin with pepper and leaving him out in the sun to suffer excruciating burns. (This burning sensation is mentioned repeatedly in connection with situations in which the sufferer feels ashamed of something he has done.)

Anxiety is brought under control in the content of the narrations chiefly by means of alternating identifications with the threatening objects, a process that was apparent in Jean-Pierre's memory of the episode with the monkey. The boy suddenly places himself on the side of the older man, then sees himself as a woman or girl and avenges the older man himself, while the intruder becomes an evil foreigner or a sorcerer. In the end the narrator always identifies, so to speak, with the morality represented by the old man or the mother; maliciously he repeats the verdict "It serves him right"; next time he'll think twice, now he's dead or maimed and has learned his lesson. This malice would have to be classified as masochistic were it not that the figures in the stories are not the real persons involved. As long as the incestuous culprit is someone other than the narrator and the parent imagoes are represented as displacement substitutes in other object representations, Jean-Pierre seems to be working through his oedipal conflict in much the same way as a European who identifies with the authority of his parents. In its main aspect, however, the outcome of the conflict is different; Jean-Pierre has not attained the autonomy of personality that we find in Europeans with a comparable outcome of the Oedipus complex.

Before turning to the consequences of the oedipal conflict, let us note (in abridged form, from the thirty-fifth interview) just how Jean-Pierre habitually expresses such fantasies. After homosexual fantasies have called forth anxiety in him, he suddenly changes the subject and starts to tell a coherent story, the one hundred thirty-third such tale since the beginning of our talks.

Jean-Pierre: I heard about a Mossi today in Yosso. He's a peddler, but he's not satisfied with that job. He wants to become a foreman with the woodcutters. A woman who has just had her first child told this [to her husband]. The peddler had said that he wanted to sleep with her. But the peddler said that wasn't true. So they called the woman, and she said, "He threatened me, he said he would kill me if I didn't sleep with him." After this they beat the Mossi. The husband wanted to kill him with his bushwhacker, but he was able to escape into the forest. So they just took all his property. The husband said he would cut off his legs and arms, and his head, too. People are saying that he was only able to save himself because he can run so fast. [Jean-Pierre himself is a fast runner; he plays left wing on the soccer team and has earned the nickname *Je suis rapide*, "I'm fast."]

When I comment that that sort of thing could happen to Jean-Pierre too, that he might some day covet someone else's wife, he takes no notice of my remark and continues with his story.

Jean-Pierre: The chief of the Mossi said he couldn't care less—let the man do as he pleased. The Mossi [who fled] still hasn't come back from the forest.
Parin: Maybe he'll come back to get his things; otherwise he'll lose them.
Jean-Pierre: No, his friends will help him. They'll convey his apologies to the husband.

According to custom, this would be the proper way of settling the affair. That does not seem to calm Jean-Pierre's anxiety, however, or to satisfy his morbid interest in the matter. In great detail he describes just how the husband sharpened his bushwhacker and how he threatened to kill the Mossi with it.

Parin: But one can defend oneself against an attack of that kind.
Jean-Pierre: No, not the Mossi. He didn't have a machete. In fact, he didn't have anything. All he could do was run away. That's why they all laughed at him, because there wasn't anything he could do.

It turns out very frequently that, behind these cruel visions of killing and maiming, the culprit has nothing, is completely powerless, and is thus the butt of ridiculing laughter.

I express my opinion that the Mossi himself was to blame for his unpleasant situation because he was too weak and defenseless to have permitted himself to do what he did. Now Jean-Pierre is greatly relieved. After all, there is not much danger that anything will happen to the Mossi if he comes back to the village to pick up his things. It is the disgrace, however, that keeps him from returning.

Again and again Jean-Pierre displays shame when his castration anxiety has been overcome. Sometimes it seems as if humiliation and disgrace are more violent emotions than even the fear of being mutilated; or perhaps it is simply that these feelings of displeasure that are

closely associated with the individual's self-esteem cannot be so successfully projected to other objects as castration anxiety.

Jean-Pierre goes on to tell me about the sermon on morality that he
preached to the people who had told him the story. He had told them
that the Mossi was definitely in the wrong; one ought to leave a married
woman alone. And this does not only correspond to his superego; with
me, too, he plays the role of the virtuous young man and has warded off
his castration anxiety. He continues his report:

Jean-Pierre: The husband was in a rage and said, "Here we took in
this young foreigner as if he were one of our own kin. My wife has
been cooking for him for a long time. And now he wants to have her
for himself."
Parin: It's not good to look for a wife in the family where you eat your
meals. A woman who cooks for you is like a member of your own
family, and you're not allowed to sleep with her.
Jean-Pierre: Yes, Monsieur, the chief of the Mossi said that he would
throw all his things away, but his friends have offered his
apologies . . . .

As the tale continues, a good many things become twisted. The chief
of the Mossi, who in the first version was completely indifferent, becomes an avenger; he and the husband [of whom there is no further
mention] blend into a single person. And now, instead of this person's
being determined to hack the Mossi to pieces, it is all the villagers who
want to keep everything he left behind when he ran away. He is no
longer to be castrated, but is to be robbed of his possessions, his anal
power. He can save himself only by appealing to a powerful Anyi for
protection.

Here I interpret for Jean-Pierre: "You are worried about what will
happen to you some day when you leave Bébou and return to Yosso.
You already go back from time to time, but only under my protection,
and then you have nothing to fear."

In response to this, Jean-Pierre begins to elaborate the psychology of
the case. He believes that the Mossi's comrades had had it in for him for
a long time. They would even kill him. "For he's rich; that's the reason." The wife has long since entirely disappeared from the story. The
Mossi's desire for her has been replaced by the others' envy of his
money.

He gives me some additional examples: a man who was rich and was
poisoned; another man who had a beautiful wife and his friends killed
him to take his wife away from him.

After my last remark, Jean-Pierre had turned to face me; he lies there
prostrate, squinting up at me.

I summarize for him: "People get killed when other people envy them. The woman the Mossi wanted is not important at all. What's important is his money, which the others want for themselves. The woman was just a pretext."

Jean-Pierre sinks back, much relieved, and says, "That's right," then launches into two long stories about how a wealthy, successful man was envied by others. In the first one, the murdering thieves are Djoula laborers, that is, still human beings, while in the second it is the spirit of the Manzan River itself, a half-maternal, half-paternal, uncanny, and powerful figure that has taken the place of the oedipal father.

Now that Jean-Pierre has succeeded in warding off his castration anxiety by identifying with morality, his story becomes more obviously oedipal in character; the coveted wife becomes the nurturing mother figure. I interpret this shift as incestuous, and this brings on a regression that is typical for Jean-Pierre. The sinner is to be not castrated, but robbed ("anal castration"). And the avenger is no longer the rival, but the chief. The only way to escape his wrath is to secure the protection of an even more powerful person.

This dependency corresponds exactly to Jean-Pierre's attitude toward me, and I say so quite frankly. Oedipal rivalry no longer plays any role. It has been replaced by envy, first the sibling envy of friends, then the envy felt by the poor and weak toward the rich and powerful, and finally the envy of the mighty spirits toward the tiny, impotent human being.

The regression takes place at two levels. The object (target) of the envy is anal property, and the instinctual impulse becomes oral in character. The person who is envied, and who is to be robbed, is first a chief and then the son, and finally the sexless, mythical spirit envies the small defenseless human being and destroys him. One seems to recognize the omnipotent phallic mother from that phase of childhood during which the toddler had to submit helplessly to the daily enemas she administered.

In the last example, the castration anxiety has been warded off successfully. It is not transferred. Jean-Pierre continues talking eagerly, becomes more confiding and more lively, and is finally so wrapped up in his tale that I have to interrupt to tell him that our hour is over. On the other hand this regression is also conducive to reorganizing the entire oedipal situation, to replacing it by a preoedipal (anal) relationship, and to projecting the resulting anxieties. In Jean-Pierre and other Anyi, the projection to traditional anxiety figures proves again and again to be a successful defense. It is only when such figures are secondarily cathected that they become threatening, secondary phobic objects.

But what happens—or happened in later life—to the oedipal urges? How can we reconstruct Jean-Pierre's development *after* the oedipal phase? His fantasy concerning the boy who is hit on the head because he steals or breaks into the house of the old man and covets the man's wife suggested that Jean-Pierre himself would attribute his frequent linguistic and intellectual lapses, in reality symptoms of hysteria, to a blow on the head, thus lending a masochistic or reproachful nuance to his description of the successfully accomplished castration. This interpretation seemed all the more plausible since the Anyi—like us—consider the head to be that part of the anatomy with which one performs cognitive processes, and since, for them, beheading is symbolic of castration. Subsequently, however, I was forced to admit that my assumptions were erroneous, that they had been determined in part by my own countertransference. Although Jean-Pierre continued to display occasional massive linguistic deterioration, confused thinking, and recurring moments of complete mental blankness, he nearly always perceived himself as being unusually intelligent. He did not connect his linguistic and mental lapses, of which he was not entirely unaware—at least he knew about his speech blocks—with a possible defect in his intelligence, let alone with a blow on the head that he had suffered in reality or in his fantasy. If he had any "intelligence complex" at all, it was his conviction that he was more intelligent than he really was, and that he was succeeding in enhancing his otherwise very vulnerable self-esteem by speaking of his own intelligence and cunning. My hypothesis had been based on a premise common in European psychopathology, that sudden stupefaction can result from hysteria and can be linked with castration fantasies. For a long time I was reluctant to abandon my theory, since it kept me from having to recognize the embarrassing fact that I suddenly no longer understood my subject—and had no idea why.

Bed-Wetting

That his castration anxiety was accompanied by an intense feeling of shame made it seem likely that Jean-Pierre had been—or perhaps still is—a bed wetter.

Our sixteenth session began with a story about how three female shamans had assaulted a young man, pulled down his trousers, and threatened and mocked him. This is followed by tales in which a thief is able to save himself by his swiftness (Jean-Pierre himself is a very fast runner), and finally by a story concerning a small boy who stole and lied.

> *Jean-Pierre:* This boy was a bed wetter. A lot of Anyi are. In Yosso there are a lot of young people that wet their beds, and even some grown-ups that still do. They can't help it. Naturally they are ashamed of themselves. But they don't do it on purpose.
>
> A bed wetter is punished like this: They place him between two bamboo poles, bind them firmly to his body, and then place certain leaves on top. When these leaves get wet, they cause a rash that burns terribly. When I was here in Bébou [attending school], a boy being punished like that once slept next to me. They had made a bamboo bed for him and even shamed him in front of everybody. But even after this he wet his bed four times in three days . . . . This happens when you eat too much before going to bed and drink a whole pitcher of water. People wet their beds because they're too fond of eating and drinking. That boy died a few years ago, by the way.
>
> *Parin:* You also wet your bed in your sleep when you dream.
>
> *Jean-Pierre:* Yes. The Anyi have a remedy for it that other peoples don't know about. You squeeze plantains to get the juice, then mix the juice with hot chili peppers, and take it as an enema. That's the best medicine for it . . . .
>
> [Again he speaks of being ashamed, and I adopt a tolerant and understanding attitude. He continues:]
>
> When I was still a little boy, I used to wake my mother at night and tell her my sheet was wet. She wouldn't give me a clean one, so I would move over to a dry spot and promptly wet it again. Then my mother gave me this remedy. Two strong enemas a day. That was very good. I stopped wetting my bed.
>
> After that my mother started giving all my sisters and brother two enemas every day soon after they were born. None of the younger ones ever wet his bed.

When Jean-Pierre accepted the excuse I offered, that people wet their beds when they dream, he was able to confess that he himself was a bed wetter. He does not consciously perceive the enemas as a punishment, nor will he admit that he was ever ashamed; "after all, he was still a child."

It is clear to me that his bet-wetting represents a regressive resolution of the oedipal conflict such as can be observed in some European children as well—urethral instead of phallic gratification, appeal to the mother, conflict with the mother alone instead of with the rival-father, shame instead of castration anxiety. In Jean-Pierre's experience, the enemas play the same role as the authority of the father in Western cultures; introjected, they serve to prolong the authority responsible for molding the individual into a social being.

These and other accounts of bed-wetting invariably follow stories with oedipal content concerning thefts, and just as invariably they lead to other stories of the same kind. On this particular occasion, Jean-Pierre is completely relaxed and tells me, with obvious enjoyment, of the abuses and beatings a "young Djoula" had to suffer; but he expresses equal pleasure that the Djoula was finally able to escape and even avenge himself, thanks to his ability to speak cleverly and convincingly. This time Jean-Pierre's speech is unusually fluent and uninhibited.

During our twenty-seventh session, I am especially successful in interpreting the oedipal theme, which Jean-Pierre discusses in endless variations. When I stop speaking, he remains silent for much longer than ever before on such occasions. Then he begins to speak, at first in a very low voice, then more and more animatedly, of how he himself has stolen from his friends, from the owner of a movie theater, and even from his foster mother.

Without any transition whatsoever, the hero is no longer Jean-Pierre himself. At night a certain boy had urinated secretly on his foster mother's clothes, so that there was a huge scandal, and the boy's father had to come and pay for the damage and take his son back home. Though Jean-Pierre tells the story as if the boy had committed this act on purpose in order to be able to finally leave school and return home, he refuses to accept this interpretation. "No, the boy was just afraid. He didn't dare to go outside, out into the open, at night; that's why he had to urinate on the clothes."

He goes on in a very subdued voice. He himself had lived with the same foster mother, and he had stolen from her, too. This sounds to me like an admission that Jean-Pierre himself is the bed wetter who is afraid to go outside at night and wants his father to come and take him home—all the more so since, this time, he is unable to conjure the conflict into a new story. From this point on till the end of the hour, his French is totally incomprehensible, his manner of speaking confused, and his voice very low; all I can understand is something about the fear of being punished (for stealing, for wetting his bed?).

When I declare our hour at an end and leave the tent, Jean-Pierre follows about ten meters, instead of the usual two, behind me. He is completely lost, gazing at the ground or up into the air instead of at me, as he usually does. When I hold out my hand to say good-bye, he is staring obliquely at the sky; he misses my hand, stumbles, and nearly falls.

The Renunciation of Phallic Aggression (Rivalry) and Submission to the Father (in the Guise of the Chief)

Since the very beginning, Jean-Pierre has hinted several times during our talks that he never intends to marry. The conscious reasons he gives for his decision remain unclear; I am inclined to see the deeper-seated reason in his exaggerated fear of women. When I mention this, he reacts—as so often—with a story, this one about a dispute between young people and an old man, a chief. His eyes shining, he describes how the old man, whom he considers to be in the right, incidentally, is beaten by the sons. Soon, however, the chief emerges victorious, and the "young men" are punished and beaten up. He goes into great detail in explaining to me everything that has to be done to restore the dignity of the chief—the workers who had taken sides against him have to atone by sacrificing a sheep and by paying compensation to the chief, the rich man.

I attempt to defend the rights of the young men, and at first Jean-Pierre agrees with me. He admits that there are evil, depraved chiefs who sleep indiscriminately with Anyi and Djoula girls. He soon changes his mind, however, and says that even if there really should be bad chiefs, they would mend their ways immediately if they were warned by the village elders. In other words, he is advising the use of official channels rather than revolt. The reason is clear. "A young man would have no way of defending himself; he can't speak up in his own defense." He goes on to explain that there is nothing to prevent the young men from bringing their case before the dignitaries; in serious cases, in fact, they are expected to do so. None of their kin could speak for them—neither a brother, a father, nor a mother. But the whole thing is impossible. A young man is incapable of speaking convincingly.

Monsieur N, the half-caste, has been the village chief in Yosso for two years. He has behaved in a way that is absolutely contrary to custom. First he seduced a sixteen-year-old girl (a "sister," i.e., cousin, of Jean-Pierre's) and soon thereafter took the girl's even younger sister as a concubine. For such an act, which is tantamount to incest, he ought to express his remorse publicly and atone by sacrificing one sheep. But there was no one in the village who dared even to suggest to Monsieur N that he was violating traditional custom. Each elder had a different excuse for not calling the chief to order, though in fact it was evident that the latter had no real power. The villagers had already realized that their chief had no intention of hiring them for jobs in the newly opened lumber-processing plant; thus, financially, they could expect no advantages from him. And since the whole village was afraid of being visited by misfortune if the chief continued his immoral behavior without making atonement, the dignitaries reluctantly decided to take up a collection and to pay the sum required for atonement themselves. So they paid on behalf of their erring tyrant. The chief had no idea that he had done anything wrong and did not realize how much the whole village was suffering under his rule. But the kin of the young girl were forced to leave the village, some of them moving out to their field huts and others going to join relatives in other villages. The girl who had been seduced was sent away to live with relatives.

During the course of the twenty-third session, the one during which Jean-Pierre tells me of these events, it turns out that his older "brothers" have sided with Monsieur N. If there is no other way of avoiding the misfortune, then at least one ought to make sure of not losing the potential advantages to be gained by demonstrating one's submissiveness to the chief. The brothers had remonstrated with Jean-Pierre, reproaching him for moving to Bébou to work for me instead of continuing to wait for a job with Monsieur N. For the first time, Jean-Pierre speaks more or less frankly and openly about his reasons for coming to Bébou. He wanted to be dependent on a better chief than the disappointing Monsieur N. By the end of the hour he is displaying an independence that I have seldom seen in him before; he asks no special favors of me, does not come to our consulting hour, and does not even ask me for a ride to Yosso for the next day.

The insight into his act of submission has resulted in ego reinforcement, not in regression.

In the twenty-sixth interview, a few days later, Jean-Pierre is able to formulate his attitude more consciously. At the beginning of the hour he tries to identify with me completely. He speaks of the foreign laborers, whom he admires and despises at the same time. In this connection he regards me as an Anyi. The Djoula, he says, are persevering; they can take up a lost cause and start all over again. An Anyi would never do that; he would become discouraged and do nothing. Then, too, the Djoula always fight with sticks, while the Anyi use only their fists. This is why they usually get the worst of it. It just doesn't occur to them that it's possible for them to use a stick too.

In the grip of a feverish and erotic identification, he returns to a topic he has mentioned several times before—forced labor during the colonial period. He describes the tortures inflicted by the foreign overseers, the sufferings of the people of Yosso and of his own mother. Yet, to my surprise, in the end he sides with the torturers, the whites, and declares that all these tortures were necessary to make possible the achievement of technological advances such as scissors to cut one's hair with and beautiful textiles to be made into clothes. Only to the women, who did rebel occasionally, is he willing to concede a certain triumph over their torturers, and in this, as in his submission to the whites, he is identifying not only with me, but also with his mother.

After my interpretation, to the effect that the Anyi of the colonial era had had to suffer tortures similar to the ones he had suffered in school in Bébou, he is silent for quite a while, then starts to relate a new tale of adultery. This one is concerned with foreigners. The injured husband, and especially his brothers, are eager to kill the adulterer. When Jean-Pierre soon gets completely confused, I remark that he apparently is not sure which is more dangerous—when a wife betrays her husband, or when the adulterer is threatened by the husband's brothers. That's no different with the Anyi than with the Djoula, I point out. The brothers of an injured husband would go out after the adulterer in both cases.

Jean-Pierre straightens up at once with the comment, "The Anyi say that, I know, but they wouldn't do it. They declare that an adulterer ought to be beaten, but they don't beat him. At the most, they beat the wife, and the adulterer has to run away."

Now I remind him of his story of the chief who offended the entire village by seducing two sisters, which is really worse than adultery.

Jean-Pierre: That's different. Naturally, you can't beat a chief. He can do whatever he likes. If an Anyi, or even a Djoula, hits a chief, he is fined an ox, or at least a sheep. Of course a chief shouldn't do things like that. But he can. Nobody can stop him.

Jean-Pierre is perfectly calm, and his French is getting better and better. He is engaged in reestablishing the great father-chief, who is in the right because he is stronger. And why? Because he can speak better. He holds the floor. A Djoula can do nothing against him, for a Djoula is unable to speak. An Anyi wouldn't even try to speak. He would never say anything against his chief.

I remind him of his own kin, and the wrong the chief had done them. And now Jean-Pierre maintains that the chief had not done anything to them after all and that he himself knows nothing about the affair. He is filled with enthusiasm at the thought that his Anyi chief, with whom he now identifies, has always been in the right and will be proved right in court because he can speak better, because he is richer, and because chiefs are always right in any case. And when a man like that takes a woman that doesn't belong to him, it's not adultery—he just takes her, that's all.

Submission to chiefs and to other father figures is in conformity with a persistent predisposition. Identification with the aggressor can also take place with objects that are not intended for this purpose either by traditions or by family organization. This outcome of the oedipal conflict can be observed most clearly when there are rivalry aggressions involved, aggressions that Jean-Pierre never attributes to himself, but that he follows with avid interest in strangers or in persons long dead.

Our thirty-ninth session, during which Jean-Pierre speaks of naughty and lazy children who refuse to do what their mothers tell them and of young people who let the old work in their place, makes it abundantly clear how closely the reestablishment of a strong and severe father corresponds to a need in Jean-Pierre, a need that cannot be termed only a need for punishment—for a stern external authority can protect him from the consequences of the jealous rivalry aggressions that paralyze him. He declares that the fathers of all these children and young people are to blame for everything; they ought to have given them a good talking-to, and if they still refused to obey, should have beaten them until they learned obedience. That's what he would do if he were their father. If you don't tell children what they are supposed to do, you have no right to be angry later on when they don't turn out the way you want them to. If a father doesn't take the trouble to bring up his children strictly, there's no reason for them to work for their parents.

The Preoedipal Mother is More Dangerous Than the Oedipal Father

While the outcome of the oedipal conflict outlined above is accompanied by a high degree of anxiety and leads to submissiveness, it cannot be regarded as a particularly unfavorable, or even as a definitive turning point. In fact, in Jean-Pierre's case I observed that every time he succeeded in overcoming his fear of the rival-father in one way or another, he fell prey to even more intense fear. His fear of women emerged behind his fear of the male rival, so to speak. His fears of being hit on the head, of being killed, or driven away—which we have classified as castration anxiety—were innocuous compared with his fears of being seduced by women, of being debauched, poisoned, devoured, and finally castrated for good measure.

At our sixth interview, Jean-Pierre had already related a long and adventure-filled story about a youth who set forth to seek a wife. This youth was constantly helped by his friends, who gave him food and drink, but nevertheless, while he was still on his journey, before he had succeeded in bringing his wife home, he died a miserable death by poison, given to him by an evil witch. An evil witch—and one can't be sure that it was not the bride herself, or perhaps the young man's mother. But, on the other hand, the mother was determined to kill herself, now that she had lost her son.

At the end of his story, Jean-Pierre commented as follows: "When you marry, that's not good. You shouldn't marry as long as you're still so young and inexperienced. You shouldn't take a wife. That leads to no good."

Jean-Pierre's teacher—not the cruel schoolmaster, but the one who taught him after that—was a bachelor and warned his pupils to avoid marriage at all costs; there was no need for them to imitate everything they saw other people doing. Jean-Pierre had remembered these words and made up his mind to heed them. It's not good to marry. Jean-Pierre becomes quite cheerful while telling his tale. He points out the terrible dissension that Ernestine had brought into a marriage (a topic the whole village was talking about at the time). Jean-Pierre certainly did not intend to marry, not ever, or at least not for a long time; when it comes to marriage, a young man gets the short end of the stick. But his conscious attitude offers him no protection against the fear that women evoke in him.

During our tenth session, Jean-Pierre tells me about a young man who tries to settle a quarrel that has broken out between two women. One of them cuts off his thumb. An old man comes up to him and says, "Who told you to get mixed up in this quarrel? Women are hard-hearted, and they don't stop to think what they're doing. If you hadn't interfered, that wouldn't have happened to you. When a man gets involved with women, he has to pay for it." Jean-Pierre continues:

> Yes, Monsieur. I can remember a lot of cases like that. If you start a fight with a woman, she's apt to grab her pick or a bushwhacker and kill you. One woman put out her husband's eyes that way, and there are others who have maimed their husbands with bushwhackers. They hack off a finger, a leg, or an arm, or they put out an eye.

He launches into a description of the most incredibly brutal acts performed by women. No murders, though—just maimings.

Parin: Then the fear of women is greater than the fear of men?
Jean-Pierre: Yes. That's because women don't think before they act. And they don't stop to think how the case will turn out in court. And because they don't stop to think of that, their hearts are hard, and they rush at you with a machete and injure you. I'm really much more afraid of women than I am of men. If you fight with a woman, she'll kill you. Friends are better than women after all. Yes, much better. As long as you stick with your friends, you don't run any risks. There's not even any danger of a fight.
Parin: You've told me that you don't intend to marry. Perhaps that's because you are afraid of women.
[Jean-Pierre denies this, but goes on talking.]
Jean-Pierre: Once there was a woman who married a young man

about my age. They hadn't been married two months when she
began to fight with her husband's mother. She took an empty gin
bottle and hit the old woman over the head with it. Her head was
injured. [He points to his own temple.]

Here is not Jean-Pierre who is hit on the head, which would have been
natural in the case of fear of a male rival, but the mother of the young
man. Actually, this story contains two messages. The first is fairly close
to reality: daughters-in-law fight with their mothers-in-law. The
second is more in keeping with Jean-Pierre's anxieties: you can never
tell what a woman will do.

This by no means helps to conjure away the danger that threatens
from women. Jean-Pierre constantly adduces new evidence of just how
dangerous women are; they are stronger than men, and stronger than
their husbands when they're married.

Jean-Pierre: An Anyi wife would never cook just one rat or just a few
snails. She needs a whole pile of snails or several rats at a time. If her
husband brings home less than she needs, she hits him and says, "If
the meals I cook are not good enough, it's your own fault. If you want
to eat, go to your mother. Let her cook for you. I won't." Lots of men
lose their courage and don't go home to their wives at all any more.
They raid the traps out in the savanna and cook whatever they find,
and grow poorer and poorer, while their wives devote themselves to
business, get rich, and—when they feel like it—take lovers. Women
like that are worse than witches. And most of them are like that.
   If a man takes a second wife, then he's not so dependent on the
first. But in the long run it doesn't help. The two wives start quarreling. The man tries to mediate, and they both turn against him. Either
he loses both of them or—worse still—they're stronger than he is.
   [Therefore:] When a mother says to a young man, "I won't have
that girl in my house!" if he's wise, he'll listen to her. The young girls
are the worst. They're always wanting new clothes and money.
They'll ruin any man. Once a girl said, "My father was a planter, but
I want to marry a government minister." And she couldn't even talk
properly. A minister wouldn't have her. She wouldn't be able to
stand living with him anyway. Ministers only want educated girls. A
minister would send her home. Ministers always have money.
Planters don't, though. The husband is ruined.
   The men say that our women don't know their duties. They can't
even cook. It's better to marry an old woman; she's glad to get a
husband, and she'll take good care of him. All the young ones can
think about are shoes, money, and more money. They take everything we own. And when we have nothing left, they say, "I don't
want a black, I don't want a farmer. I want a minister or a chauffeur
or somebody important."

The longer we talk, the more frequently women appear in the role of seducers. In Jean-Pierre's life story this notion is firmly anchored in his experience with the first foster mother he lived with when he was going to school in Abengourou. According to him, she forced him to steal for her, thus leading him and his friends into thievery and exposing him to all the cruel penalties imposed on him by chiefs, old men, and policemen. Once again, the "oedipal" stories and fantasies come out much more clearly, the further removed they are from Jean-Pierre's own person. Even that taboo act—a young man sleeping with two sisters—is now the fault of the women. The latter are brutally beaten, to be sure, but the man is killed.

It is a recognized fact that a man's neurotic fear of "women" can always be traced back to preoedipal development. Yet we describe Jean-Pierre's fears in this respect as an outcome of the oedipal conflict. This is because of the increasingly more obvious role of sexual seduction, because the fear of the castrating woman (as mentioned above) often manifests itself immediately after the aggressive conflict with an overwhelmingly powerful, punishing rival and, in fact, replaces the fear of the rival.

The things a woman can do to one are more cunningly conceived and more cruel than the things one must expect from men, chiefs, or policemen. Jean-Pierre relates the following: A man stole some coffee. After the theft was discovered, they first beat the thief and then made him load the coffee he had stolen on his head and led him through the village to be mocked at by all the inhabitants. Then came the women: "They rubbed pepper over his face and in his eyes, and the sap of a plant like a nettle. Then they stuffed poisonous taro into his mouth—if you eat it, your stomach swells up and bursts—and said to him: 'If you ever do that again, we'll make you eat this taro!'"

The thief is the oedipal thief. Behind the avenging father lurks the mother who provides poisoned food. The castration anxiety triggers oral dangers and becomes oral anxiety. Sometimes the victim is undressed and put to shame; sometimes he is cast into a state of paralysis and, having been jealously deprived of his possessions, is robbed of his vitality. During our fortieth and last hour together, Jean-Pierre tells me about a young man who has become unhappy living away from his native village. He had taken a wife of whom his mother did not approve. And this wife brings him bad luck. He can't go home because his mother refuses to forgive him his disobedience. He falls ill, his arms and legs covered with sores that burst open and gradually consume him. It was his mother who sent him this sickness. Jean-Pierre shows definite signs of anxiety as he is telling this story. When I remind him that our work will soon be finished and that he will have to return to

Yosso, he admits that he is not certain his mother really had no objections to his coming to Bébou. He'll have to wait and see, he says, whether she will take revenge on him for having preferred to work for me instead of for her kin.

The Witch Phobia

Women of the type populating Jean-Pierre's fantasies are what we call witches. Among a people that recognizes witchcraft as an established institution, a danger is banished, or at least becomes controllable, when it is known to emanate from a witch, that is, when it is known to come from without and not from within and thus can be countered by traditional methods. Nevertheless, Jean-Pierre suffers from anxieties one can only describe as a witch phobia.

During our fifteenth interview, Jean-Pierre—in a relaxed and cheerful mood—reports that during the forenoon the female shamans of Yosso had danced and demonstrated their magical powers. He had been among the spectators.

Jean-Pierre: There's a young Baoulé who lives in Yosso, and when he's drunk he often boasts that he can cast a spell just as well as the shamans. This morning he came to the tent where the shamans were getting ready for their dance and made fun of them. They grabbed him and tore off his clothes so roughly that he had to go back home through the village all bruised and naked. He covered his genitals with his hands.

Jean-Pierre laughs maliciously. He says that the Baoulé just kept on drinking and boasting, and adds: "The shamans were right, of course, but I'd never have believed that they had the strength to do what they did to that young man."

The shamans warned the villagers that they would finally have to hand over the sheep they owed for the death of the chief (about three years before). They reported that his spirit had already threatened to start a bit of killing in the village if the inhabitants didn't pay up soon.

Eagerly and with amusement, Jean-Pierre tells me about other verdicts—no less ominous-sounding—delivered by the oracles. Then he describes the female shamans and their habits in exactly the same fashion as the witches of the Akan peoples have been described countless times during the last hundred years.

Jean-Pierre: At night they open up their shop in the top of a kapok tree. The shop is invisible to ordinary people. They fly through the air at night; a red light shines around them. They seize young people and kill and eat them.

Parin: Does that mean that they die?

Jean-Pierre: Yes, but not right away. Some of them dry out. There's something wrong with them inside. If they don't do anything [countercharm], they're sure to die. That can happen to anybody.... [His story becomes confused at this point, and I am unable to follow.]

Parin: Are you afraid of these women right at the moment?

Jean-Pierre: No, I'm not. I have nothing to fear because I'm not a sorcerer myself. They can only do things to people who are devils themselves. That young Baoulé isn't afraid of them either.

[As he continues his narration, the female shamans are transformed into small, weak, but wicked creatures. He himself has never seen any.]

Some people set out traps for witches—holes that they fill with water and sand and some kind of medicine. If you dig these holes in the places where they dance at night, it's easy to catch them. The medicine is probably the same one they put in their eyes to make them see better [i.e., become clairvoyant].

It is evident that Jean-Pierre feels no fear at the moment; in fact, it amuses him to think that one can capture witches as if they were game. Subsequently, he tries another form of conjuring—with success. He relates one of his fantastic tales.

In olden times there was a man who went out to the fields with his wife and child. He worked there till about half-past three. His wife wanted to go back to the village. Her daughter wanted to pick more plantains. Along came a wind and blew down a dry branch. It fell on the daughter and killed her. The father carried the dead child into the village on his back and brought her to the chief. The villagers wanted to ask the oracle whether it was really the branch that had killed her, or maybe some person. The shamans said, "It was the devils; they changed themselves into wood and took the child." But the chief asked the man, "Why didn't you give your daughter to the shamans while there was still time? What good is she now? She's dead. They wanted it so." That man lived in M'Basso. He had nine children. Four of them are still living.

And Jean-Pierre tells me of the terrible fates of the other children, of the parents' grief, and the consolations offered them. He concludes: "There's no point in weeping. If it's dead, it's dead. You can forget about it. Even its brothers and sisters stopped mourning it."

He finds a similar solution in an extremely long tale during our twenty-eighth session, a tale in which a witch changes shape again and again, first killing a young man out of jealousy, then wanting to devour his wife, until the chief finally intimidates her with the cruelest possible countermeasures and threats. He adds: "Witches like that eat only little children or very old people"—in other words, not Jean-Pierre.

In spite of all this, Jean-Pierre does not dare leave the house at night. When he has to urinate during the night, he needs someone to go outside with him. Right now he has found a five-year-old boy who accompanies him so that he can relieve himself.

It is only with reluctance that Jean-Pierre speaks of these anxieties. When I try to interpret his fears for him, he does not understand what I am talking about. His speech deteriorates. By the time he recovers, he has dropped the subject and forgotten it completely. The customs governing dealings with witches—how they can be caught in traps or rendered harmless in other ways—all this is forgotten the moment he himself experiences fear of them. Toward the end of our interview series, he denies that he has ever been afraid at night, except as a child. Then, though, he was very scared. He relates that his wicked grandfather once forced him to sleep in an abandoned house; the grandfather had tied up him and another boy who was to sleep there and who was also scared, and then whipped them both with a length of rope. He elaborates this "memory" enthusiastically, and his fears are gone again—for the time being. As in the "primordial-scene fantasy," the switch to masochism has made the anxiety unnecessary.

Although we did not succeed in finding a complete explanation for Jean-Pierre's present phobia, or even in influencing it, we do have two clues as to how it may have originated—the first from childhood, and the second from puberty.

Our eighteenth interview produced the following tale:

When I was little, people used to shout at me a lot. Not now, though. Now I'm an adult. When I was little, I was often afraid, too. I couldn't sleep alone. I thought a witch would come and get me. When I was alone, I was scared of witches. They gave me a room where I was alone. But I never stayed there, I always went to sleep with my playmates.

Now I'm not afraid any more. But at that time I used to cry out in my dreams. It was this way: I dreamed that when I went out of the room, they'd be lying in wait for me there. They'd grab my feet, lift me up, and drop me into a hole. That was my dream, and that's why I screamed during the night.

That dream always came after I had knocked down a broom. When you throw a broom away, they throw you away, too—my mother told me so. Because there are certain things you're not supposed to do, and if you do them anyway, then they grab you and throw you down. If you don't do them, then you don't have dreams like mine.

Then I wanted to try it out once more. So I did something my mother had forbidden. And I had the same dream again and screamed in my sleep. When I slept with my playmates, though, I never screamed. Sometimes, when I'm sleeping, something falls on top of me. It grabs me by the throat, and I can't breathe. It's like death. He grabs your throat, too.

That's why I'm afraid and don't sleep alone even today. Especially when it's dark. During the day I don't mind sleeping alone.

The guilt feelings about his disobedience as a child, which Jean-Pierre now regards as the cause of his nightmares, indicate that unconscious guilt feelings help to maintain anxiety dreams and the witch phobia connected with them. The dreaded punishment in the first dream recalls the scene with the schoolmaster, interpreted as a primordial-scene fantasy, in which the teacher finds the intruding boy in his sister's room, picks him up, and roughly throws him on the floor. It is conceivable that anxiety dreams reflect a primordial-scene experience—the father wants to have intercourse with the mother, grabs hold of the little boy asleep at her side by the feet and carries him into another, dark room, closes the door, and goes back to sleep with the mother. Anyi fathers have a habit of taking babies by the feet and whirling them around in the air as a game, as if they intended to let go of them. Most babies seem to enjoy it. Older children burst into howls or go stiff with fright when a grown man seizes them and picks them up in this fashion.

Jean-Pierre's incubus dream, in which he is being strangled and thinks he is going to die, would then represent a revival of the excitement he had felt while watching intercourse between his parents, an excitement accompanied by a fear of punishment and of the cruel event.

These assumptions are substantiated by the fact that the presence of his friends and his identification with them are the most effective means of defense available to Jean-Pierre when he is confronted with the problem "man and woman." Thus, while we trace the anxiety dreams and the witch phobia they engendered back to a fear of the father in the primordial scene and regard them as an expression of oedipal guilt feelings that have not been adequately worked through, we have found another source of phobic anxiety in his homosexual urges. These urges emerged during puberty and adolescence and go back, as a rule, to preoedipal fixations. They can be better understood as a coherent psychic complex, however, if we take the oedipal conflict as a starting point.

Gender Confusion and Homosexuality

In relating memories from his childhood, Jean-Pierre often speaks of a little boy, obviously himself, and then—without being aware of the transition—begins to speak of a little girl. This occurs most frequently when he is talking about bed-wetting, but occasionally in other connections as well. The situations that give rise to his gender confusion are not uniform; sometimes Jean-Pierre seems to envy the girls their greater closeness to the mother; sometimes it seems that he is using this switch as one of the measures to ward off the castration anxiety that threatens to overcome him. During the thirty-sixth interview, at a stage where he is far better able to express his "adult" opinions, he makes it quite clear that he considers women more efficient, more powerful, and stronger than men, not only within the framework of fantastic, cruel, semimythical happenings, but also in daily social life. And he points out that the only success he ever had in earning a livelihood had been achieved in a female role—gathering and selling snails.

Jean-Pierre: Men only *think* about how they could earn money, but they don't dare start a business because they're afraid of being robbed. Women buy and sell, one thing after another; this way nobody steals from them. They're always on the lookout for a chance to trade and barter. Men don't want a trading permit. They simply haven't the courage . . . .

When I had to leave school in Abengourou, I began to collect snails and sell them. I earned two thousand francs that way. I wanted to give half to my foster mother, but she would accept only two hundred francs and told me to keep the rest. I spent the rest of the money on a length of cotton. I took it home with me, and it's still there today.

At first my foster mother didn't want me to go out into the forest. She said there were robbers out there, and that they would kill me. I said, "I have my bushwhacker, I can defend myself," but she replied, "You might lose your way, you can perish out in the forest. Don't go, it's too dangerous."

But I went anyway, and it was really fine. In the evening after five, when the rain is over, they start to come out. You can collect snails for a while, then cut a palm for the sap, and while you're waiting for the wine to be ready you can collect more snails. There are so many that you can pick and choose. You take the biggest ones and leave the small ones alone.

Parin: It's that season again right now.

Jean-Pierre: That's right. Now that the mangoes are ripe and falling off the trees, the snails feed on them all night long, and all you have to do is pick them up from under the mango trees. That's how the Attié do it.

And he relates how the Attié come into the territory of the Anyi and the Anyi first try to drive them out, then catch them in traps and bring them before the chief because they are not allowed to gather snails here. They talk their way out, however, and offer their apologies. Then they are permitted to continue collecting snails. And the Attié use their snails sparingly. They eat them the whole year. They use only one snail when they make soup. The Anyi eat theirs all up right away. The Attié share things. All the kin help each other, in gathering snails and in sharing their food. That would be impossible with the Anyi, he says; with them each person has to do everything by himself. "Me—I've stopped thinking about it. Our women get rich, I can't."

Jean-Pierre has no intention of returning to his former successful trade in snails. One reason is certainly the fact that snail-gathering is regarded as a "female" occupation. This is the conscious reason. Unconsciously, he is afraid—he would be alone, he might be attacked, he might get lost. "I wouldn't be sure any more whether I'm a man or a woman." The women are strong and successful; the men stop to think of the consequences and don't dare to do anything. These are not only socially accepted patterns, they are also reparatory fantasies that protect Jean-Pierre against the anxiety that appears whenever he becomes active. The depressive fantasy "I might get rich some day yet, with a stroke of good luck" safeguards him—and many other Anyi—against the need to take action and against an all-too-intense feeling of frustration. The uncertainty in Jean-Pierre's gender identity goes back to an identification with the mother of early childhood in her role as a sexual object; this identification is one of the prerequisites for the fixation on homosexual desires. In his case such desires have emerged only gradually, accompanied by increasingly acute anxiety.

During our seventh session, Jean-Pierre speaks of the spirits of the dead that roam around the village "taking," that is, killing, people, especially young people, unless they are sufficiently propitiated and sated with sacrificial offerings. This brings him to stories about how the chiefs of olden times used to take slaves with them into their graves, and he describes—with grisly relish, thus without fear—how slaves were hunted and strangled at night in the cemetery. But this is not the end of the topic; it turns out that Jean-Pierre himself suffers from an acute fear that a dead chief, perhaps the chief from Yosso who had died three years before, might drag him out to the cemetery and kill him if he returned to Yosso. At that time, this neurotic fear was apparently one of the main reasons for his moving from Yosso to Bébou (where he enjoyed the protection of the whites).

In our twenty-first interview, Jean-Pierre's fear of being dragged along to the cemetery by the dead shows up in a dream. He opens the conversation as follows:

Jean-Pierre: Sometimes [in a dream] you see one person, sometimes several. Sometimes you know them, sometimes you don't. These people laugh at you, make fun of you. Then they try to grab my hand, and I hide it behind me. I won't give it to them. They'd kill me. This is the dream that I had two nights ago. I was still scared when I woke up at eight in the morning.

Parin: I give you my hand when you come for your interview. Last time I came by to pick you up. That pleased you, but at the same time you were apprehensive about our talk.

Jean-Pierre: Oh, no. Last night I had another dream. I saw dead people. They said that they would come to meet me. I laughed. Then they said I should come with them, and I said, "I don't want to." They said "good-bye." I was very much afraid and I repeated, "I don't want to." Then they went away.

That's a dangerous thing. The mouth of one of the dead persons was all red. It was open. They took hold of my head with both hands. Sometimes at night you can hear them screeching—"Oh, oh!" Then the people sleeping in the same room can hear them too.

Parin: The dead people were the whites. You're afraid of me.

Jean-Pierre: Oh, no. I recognized them. They're all people who are already dead. Two women and two men [like our research team]. I didn't tell anybody about it. I didn't want anyone to think I was sick, having dreams like that, and take me to a doctor to be treated.

Though it is perfectly clear to me that I am this dead man who frightens him so much and try to explain this to him, he refuses to accept my interpretation. The hour is soon over. During the next few days there are no interviews, and when we meet again the topic has been forgotten for the time being.

Jean-Pierre cannot seem to get it out of his mind, though. Once he tells me, as if it were something that really happened to him, that when he was in Abengourou (at the age of about twelve to fourteen) the schoolmaster had sent him and some of his friends out to the fields on the day a chief was to be buried. If the boys had not been warned, and if they had not been clever enough to take a detour around the cemetery, they would certainly have been seized, strangled, and thrown into the chief's grave. During our thirtieth hour together, he speaks of the masked dances performed by the foreigners. The masks are very powerful. To placate them you have to let them rob and steal. If a woman crosses them, she is doomed to die.

Since Jean-Pierre's fear is obviously growing more intense, I interpret for him, explaining that, as a foreigner, I seem like a mask to him, and he is afraid of dying, like a woman. He hardly listens to what I am saying, and he pulls at his fingers nervously.

Jean-Pierre: No. It's the women who dance with each other. They're the really wicked devils. They dance all together; no man is allowed to join them. He would fall ill immediately or fall down dead. They'd kill him on the spot. Those dancers are horrible to look at; they're completely naked.

All of a sudden he refers to the terrible dancers as "the boys" (*garçons*). When I call his attention to this he explains, "They're girl-boys. They look just like the others, there's no difference." He lapses into confusion, stares at me, and—throughout the remainder of the hour—responds only with "yes, Monsieur" whenever I try to get through to him to free him from his anxiety paralysis. During the thirty-fourth interview, he tells me about a young man who met a sorcerer in the forest and had to fight with him:

> Suddenly he heard a noise. He loaded his rifle. Then he heard the sorcerer growling. It was one of those very tall ones. He was sitting high up in a tree. The young man fired his rifle right into the sorcerer's face—twice. His blood spattered everywhere, and it was completely white. Then, when the young man set out for home, he couldn't find the path any more. His brothers made a racket so that he could locate the path. He just followed the noise.
>
> When he got home he discovered that the flesh of his hands had rotted away. His mother sacrificed a sheep for him. He bathed four times [purification ceremony]. But his body turned white all over. He had slept too long with the witches in the forest.

The sexual theme and the punishment for the symbolically represented homosexual acts (the rotting hands—he had slept too long—his body turns white) are quite clear. But it is not until our thirty-sixth interview that Jean-Pierre relates a memory that enables me to connect his fear of homosexual experiences with his life story.

He has just been talking about soccer. He is a very good player himself, and he enjoys the respect of his teammates. His self-esteem has been enhanced by the discussion, and now, with a sly smile, he relates the following:

> In Abengourou, while I was still in school, I met a sorcerer. This is the way it happened. I had hurt my foot while playing. And this man was among the spectators. He took me to the hospital to have my foot bandaged, and after that he continued to take an interest in me. Later he gave me an amulet and told me that if I wore it, I would be able to play well again. [He shows me the chain he wears around his neck, with a pendant of European workmanship.] Yes, it does help me. When I'm wearing it, I can run fast and hit the ball properly . . . .
>
> This man looked out for me. He was fond of me, that's why he gave me the amulet. Then he told me I should go with him to the cemetery at night. I was supposed to sleep there. He was going to sleep next to me. I was afraid, and I never went with him.
>
> He told me that the amulet will work only as long as I don't sleep with a woman. He said that I should never sleep with a woman, otherwise it would lose its power. He said that I should just come to

the cemetery and sleep there with him. Then he would give me an even better medicine.

I interpret this for him: "You wanted to go with him, but you were afraid. That's the reason why you've been dreaming ever since that the dead are taking you with them into their graves, and that they lie down on top of you and want to sleep with you." Jean-Pierre nods in agreement. I add: "And that's also why you don't want to go with girls. As long as you don't, you're being faithful to him."

This time Jean-Pierre disagrees and stresses the point that he had had the medicine with him when he and his team had played so well in Abradinou, a village situated in the depths of the forest and extremely uncanny to him. (This soccer match is one of his proudest memories.) He goes on to say that in Abradinou he had dreamed of two eggs being broken into a pan, whereupon he was absolutely certain and bet with his friends that they would score two goals—and they did. Full of enthusiasm, he now admits that the reason he feels so happy when he is playing soccer is that there are only boys, and no girls. When there are girls watching, he says, he always feels very embarrassed.

During the thirty-ninth interview I succeed in establishing a connection between Jean-Pierre's fear of being sacrificed and his experience with the so-called sorcerer. Again he tells me about such a sacrifice, the victim this time being a Yakouba. I remark that these stories, which may have really happened a long time ago, seem so plausible and real to him because of his experience with the sorcerer. He assures me earnestly that human sacrifices do, indeed, take place, and he describes with almost voluptuous pleasure how they lay one tree trunk across the neck of the victim and another across his legs and literally trample him to death. I repeat that he is still afraid of being accosted and seduced by the sorcerer and of not being able to defend himself. He laughs in embarrassment and says:

> *Jean-Pierre:* No, it wasn't that way at all. He was just a rich man who happened to like me. When he left Abengourou, he asked for my address. Maybe he'll come back some day . . . .
> He once said to me, "When you're in the cemetery with me and we dedicate the new amulet, you mustn't make a sound or turn around. Spirits with red mouths will come, and you must let them do whatever they want with you. Otherwise you will have to die."
> *Parin:* Those are the spirits with red mouths out of your dream. As a boy you had to stand still when the man wanted to try something with you. Otherwise, he would kill you, as he threatened to do.
> *Jean-Pierre* [beaming broadly and showing no sign of fear]: But the man didn't threaten me. All he said was that the spirits were so

dangerous. Before he went away, he bought clothes for my friend and for me, and even gave us money. We thought the money would vanish out of our hands the minute he was gone, but it didn't. We looked at it carefully, again and again. Then we spent it.

The "Alter Ego"

The following questions seem justified: Did Jean-Pierre develop a "transference" to me? Did I become a person (object representation) for his unconscious strivings (love and hate) who was capable of involving his emotions? Was I a person from whom he expected gratification of his desires, or one from whom he expected rejection and harm?

From the very beginning, Jean-Pierre has his assigned role. He is compelled (for internal and external reasons) to talk to me. He is the speaker, as long as his ability to speak remains intact; I am the listener. The situation might be compared to an oral examination in school or to the ceremony governing the delivery of the "first and second news." There is no need for an object-oriented, all too intimate relationship; in fact, this is to be avoided. I set up a genealogy. He corrects me. Our common interest in a project (transitional phenomenon) supplements our relationship and helps prevent any too directly object-oriented strivings from making themselves felt. Through the interpretations I have been giving him since our third interview, I have become more or less a function of his own self. I represent an "auxiliary ego" that helps him master his conflicts.

His demarcation from me, as from some auxiliary function of his ego, is incomplete. He is not forced to accept my interpretations or to reply to them. When I insist, he fails to comprehend. He often replies "yes, Monsieur" or "no, Monsieur" at random, as if he had not understood me, or—even more frequently—he denies that my assumption is correct. This is the case even when his expression, a change in his mood, or the nature of the topic that occurs to him next clearly show that he has accepted the interpretation and has admitted and integrated into his consciousness an urge just warded off (for example, my interpretation of his fear of being assaulted homosexually). His conscious rejection of my comments is not accompanied by hostility. In my opinion, he resorts to rejection in order to differentiate himself from me, to avoid a fusion with me, or to keep himself from being overwhelmed by the power of suggestion.

In the sense that I am his "auxiliary ego," he is mine as well. When I am taking down his stories in shorthand, he pauses whenever necessary so that I can catch up. When I have finished recording what he has already said, he goes on. When I lay my notebook aside, he falls silent. When I stop taking notes entirely, he replaces our "joint" activity with postures or gestures, now imitating me, now reflecting my movements as if he were my mirror image. On such occasions he feels that he has to smoke if I happen to be smoking, but he is unable to ask me for a light and draws on his cigarette when I draw on mine, though his isn't lit. Or he leans back when I bend forward, or vice versa.

Explanations and interpretations have no effect on his behavior. He understands that I do not need to record every single word that he utters, but he nevertheless succumbs to his compulsion to follow my lead exactly in this respect.

When his self-esteem is reinforced, as it frequently was after an interpretation, especially toward the end, the behavior described above subsides. During the thirty-seventh interview, for example, I succeed in making it clear to him that he is afraid of not being sufficiently intelligent to find a new job and a new livelihood when I leave. He immediately starts talking about soccer, a subject where he feels sure of himself and thus superior. Our discussion becomes very animated, and there is not the slightest trace of the dependency I have described. Then comes the confession that, as a schoolboy, he had met that homosexual lover whom he calls the sorcerer. Abrupt changes of subject like this occur frequently, though sometimes, of course, the opposite is true. During our twenty-second session, for example, he is in a relaxed and easy mood and quite spontaneously expresses the wish to own a car like mine. Then, very briefly, he is overcome by intense anxiety, perhaps because he immediately perceives his wish as "impossible" and feels frustrated, or because he is afraid I may reject him. I interpret his desire for a car and his fear of rejection. He seems to take no notice of my interpretation, but he immediately resumes his stereotyped behavior.

Omnipotent/Impotent Objects

The symbiotic dependency described above, in which I am Jean-Pierre's "alter ego," does not prevent him from perceiving in me from time to time a good or a bad figure—or, more precisely, from projectively endowing me with the attributes of such figures. It is easy to tell, too, that pregenital forms of transference are involved. In the first place, these projections are dictated by one or another instinctual urge or by anxiety and correspond to a momentary narcissistic need and thus are not cathected with object libido. Probably they do reflect earlier experiences, but instead of retaining the features of real persons, they display those of fantasy figures. In the second place, the figures are not endowed with maturely differentiated qualities, but rather have a power that is so unreal and archaic in nature that it is immediately obvious that it must go back to the ideas of early childhood. Omnipotence and impotence alternate rapidly—Jean-Pierre is quite capable of humiliating figures he perceived just a moment before as overwhelmingly powerful, of suddenly transforming them into others, or of abandoning them entirely, and his self-esteem undergoes corresponding changes. In our third interview, for example, I was suddenly briefly equated with the cruel white gold-miner, to whom Jean-Pierre submits masochistically. Sometimes I may appear to him like a village chief, inviolable, the possessor of wealth and magical powers, or I may be like his first, cruel schoolmaster, or like his wicked foster mother, or like his second, kind schoolteacher, or like his second, good foster mother; and sometimes (as in our fourteenth interview) I am like the stern doctor who can see through his patients' deceptions. Only rarely, and then only briefly, am I represented as a figure well versed in Anyi customs and powerful or dangerous, for example, as a magician, sorcerer, witch, or even healer, and these projections are withdrawn almost immediately.

It is not the lack of a sense of reality or the exaggerated aggrandizement or belittlement of the figures concerned that makes it possible to recognize such "transferences" as structures of projective omnipotence. After all, I really am the friend of a number of Anyi chiefs and am closer to them than my patient will ever be; I could be a teacher; I am a white man; and I am incomparably richer and more powerful than Jean-Pierre. It is only Jean-Pierre's own attitudes toward these figures that make it possible to distinguish these forms of transference accurately from more mature forms.

This may become clearer if we recall Jean-Pierre's attitude toward the payment he was to receive for our interviews. He regards this money as a talisman. When he wants money, he is unable to demand it of me. Once he needed one hundred francs to attend a dance. When I guessed his need and gave him the money, he was thoroughly nonplussed for a moment, until he soon denied the whole transaction and I once again became a "fantastic" figure in his eyes, a figure from whom he might expect to receive, among other things, immeasurable riches.

More Constant Objects

Sometimes I have the impression that Jean-Pierre's transference objects, the figures he perceives in me, are taking on more definite shape, coming to resemble more and more closely the dreaded father of the oedipal phase, the anxiety-evoking mother-witch, a nurturing parent figure, or an older brother. But the cathexis of these more sharply delineated, clearly recognizable objects is never sustained for very long; it changes in accordance with the emergence of aggressive or libidinal desires. The (narcissistic) needs to experience pleasure and to avoid displeasure are constant; the objects, however, are inconstant.

The oral demanding dependency on a powerful, nurturing, sexually only vaguely defined figure, which we have described as the patron relationship in other Africans, recurs frequently. But not even this relationship can survive repeated frustration. Instead of being transformed into an aggressive demanding dependency, the whole relationship is abandoned. Nor is the object exchanged for another (as a "displacement substitution"), as in the patron relationship. Objects cathected with oral libido, such as the "nurturing mother," are abandoned just as inevitably and just as suddenly as any others.

During our fourth interview, Jean-Pierre asks me for shotgun cartridges—not for himself, but for a friend who has nagged him into asking me because he has a chance to borrow a gun from a third friend. I have no cartridges, however. Jean-Pierre does not mention the matter again. In our sixth interview, he says that he would like to come with me to Switzerland, and in the sixteenth session, he would like to have me as an older brother. All these wishes are quickly abandoned—for no apparent reason. The whites are good, you can trust them, expect and obtain advantages from them; the blacks are wicked, they poison your food (twenty-first interview). This alloplastic identification with a positively toned dependency is dropped just as quickly as the identification Jean-Pierre demonstrated during our twenty-fifth interview when he experienced not me, but my colleague Dr. Morgenthaler (whom he referred to at first as "your brother" and later as "Papa Frédéric") as a wealthy, Arabic-speaking, and thus learned father who provides generously for his son.

Judging from these transference reactions, object cathexis is extremely fragile, anything but constant. Accordingly, it is not surprising that the development of a genuine transference neurosis could not be observed, at least not at an early stage. For a neurosis of this kind requires more constant object relations, which develop as a rule from the oedipal conflict.

At least one anxiety-producing fantasy became attached to my person, however—the fantasy of being sacrificed to a dead chief or being killed by a sorcerer in the cemetery. The analytical elaboration (including dream interpretation) revealed an unconscious desire to be homosexually seduced by me and elicited the memory of the experience with the "sorcerer," presumably repressed up to that time.

The therapeutic gain achieved by this elaboration of transference is not lasting. During our next interview, the thirty-eighth, Jean-Pierre *is* still capable of making plans for the future, however. He is thinking of becoming a chauffeur and identifies with me, with the paternal authorities I represent, and even with my role as a doctor, inquiring for the first time about another of my patients, Benzié the alcoholic. He concedes that Benzié no longer drinks because I have cured him. Then he goes on to speak of the greed and laziness of the alcoholic, of his defiant refusal to work at all since the women, the mothers, won't offer him what he originally demanded, and comes to the following conclusion: "Yes, he is unhappy and alone. When he is very drunk, at night, he weeps aloud to himself and cries out for his dead mother. He would like to go away with her, to the land of the dead, because she left him too soon and went there."

After this he speaks of abandoned, damaged, and miserably unhappy children, blaming their mothers for their state, and enhances his own self-esteem by telling me a story in which one such mother is revealed as stupid and helpless, while he himself understands arithmetic and wins out over her. He keeps me overtime with his story, then takes his departure cheerfully and apparently in the best of spirits.

His feeling of independence lasts only a short time. (He knows we will be leaving in a few days.) About ten minutes after the end of our hour, he comes back and plaintively informs me that he aches all over and is very ill. With an expression of suffering, he opens his eyes wide and looks up at the sky, then hugs his shoulders to show me that he has pains everywhere. Since I am just about to drive off, I tell him that I can't stop to treat him now and ask him to come back in two hours, toward eight that evening. He does not show up again until the following morning; he is cheerful once more and says he feels only a little pain.

Once the homosexual transference has been interpreted, Jean-Pierre's independent autonomy is of short duration. Talking about the unfortunate, resentful alcoholic who has been abandoned by his mother helps him a little. His own terrible feeling of abandonment and his abject dependence on me are expressed in a psychosomatic reaction.

Then I interpret for him, pointing out how much he needed me, particularly after the end of our previous hour, and explaining that he had no choice but to become ill, in order to gain a bit more attention from me. It is at this point that he relates his childhood memory of how—neglected by his family—he had nearly been burned to death in the brushfire, almost roasted alive like the pangolin.

Thus the pregenital form of alter-ego transference, in which I represented a supplementary function for him, presumably had its basis in his dependency on his mother, which ended so soon in frustration and terrifying helplessness. This summarizes my interpretation of the course of our interviews just before their conclusion.

Identification as a Transference Defense

While other Anyi (Adou Agnimou, Elisa) entered into identificatory relationships with their analysts that turned out to be so stable that they could hardly be shaken by interpretations and even covered up deeper-lying conflicts, Jean-Pierre proves incapable of establishing such an identification with me. It is true that he already possesses some attributes of "Europeanism" in the more or less alien roles he plays in his home village as "an educated man," "a widely traveled man," "a soccer player," as well as in his mode of dressing and in his speech. Nevertheless he finds it difficult to identify with qualities and attitudes he observes in me and is unable to integrate them well.

An attempt in this direction can be seen in his friendship with François, which Jean-Pierre entered into with ill-considered haste and which was constantly breaking down and being renewed; at times Jean-Pierre was able to feel himself an equal of François, my Anyi assistant.

Whereas the initial disturbance in Jean-Pierre's identificatory relationship with François could be traced to feelings of envy and rivalry, his later ties to him were so superficial that no cause for conflict could arise. In fact, these ties were no closer than those existing between Jean-Pierre and the companions of his fantasies, the little boy who accompanied him when he had to go outside at night, the members of his soccer team, or his school friends. His efforts to apply European value standards to himself as the driver of a car or the custodian of morality and thus to equate himself with me in this way were also feeble. His constantly fluctuating identification with the aggressor—often an aggressor that was projected to me at the moment—were equally unstable.

On the other hand, Jean-Pierre manages quite frequently to contrast himself with the Attié, through his feeling of identity as an Anyi, and with the inhabitants of other villages, as a native of Yosso, and he can also perceive himself as a member of his family and as a loyal supporter of his older brothers. It is these confirmations of his personal identity, which—though based on identification with persons and ideals of the environment—are always reinforced when self-perception and external perceptions coincide, that made it possible for Jean-Pierre to confront me from time to time in a more independent, more mature frame of mind. Thus they were by no means an obstacle to transference.

Countertransference

The impression Jean-Pierre makes on me is far less that of a depressive individual than that of a fearful one, in whom instinctual anxiety cannot be entirely warded off by projection. I continually have the feeling that I have to "free him of his anxiety." Yet he is not afraid of me; I am unable to provide any effective transference interpretations. I try my luck with ego interpretations in order to diminish his anxiety. Since I often have the impression that he does not understand what I am saying even from the standpoint of comprehending the language, and since he usually fails to respond to my interventions and very seldom reacts directly to them, an unsettling feeling of helplessness begins to take possession of me. Moreover, with every more intense manifestation of his mirror-image or robotlike behavior, which represents a kind of primary identificatory relationship or fusion, I sense a need to defend myself against being placed on the same level with his helpless personality. At moments like this I feel very alien, or Jean-Pierre suddenly seems to me mentally deranged or feebleminded.

The above remarks (based on the twelfth session) stand in contrast to later ones (twenty-seventh session). By this time I understand Jean-Pierre better; he no longer seems so disturbed. But now I feel the urge to "put him in order," to give him some backbone, some sort of strength. The fault lies in the defective development of the phallic phase in Jean-Pierre and in the disappointment of my own identificatory expectations; the problem is rooted in our differing cultures. We are accustomed to expect a different outcome of the oedipal conflict in a man—a higher degree of phallic masculinity than is tolerable or normal among the Anyi in an average man (i.e., not a chief).

Strangely enough, I do not feel repelled by Jean-Pierre's cruel or disgusting stories. Obviously they have the character of polymorphous-perverse fantasies, like the tales children tell each other while they are playing with puppets. This points to the regressive level of experience, all the more so as the impression Jean-Pierre ordinarily makes is by no means naive or childlike, but rather taciturn and sly. Sometimes, however, when his anxieties cease to plague him, he seems like a bashful boy of prepuberty age who would dearly love to be able to boast of having played some wicked tricks, but who is so timorous that no one would ever credit him with sufficient devil-may-care impudence.

I have already mentioned that Jean-Pierre consciously avoids frankness and that, for him, deception is the only proper method to use in dealing with his analyst. In these circumstances I consider dreams to be unintentional, authentic communications of the subject. The conscious censor, otherwise so efficient, has been replaced by the unconscious one.

A Selection of Dreams

All in all, Jean-Pierre related eleven dreams, seven of them in the eighteenth interview, three in the twenty-first, and one in the thirty-seventh. I have already dealt with his anxiety dreams, which are no different than those of European patients.

Four of the dreams related during the eighteenth interview are unusual in that, viewed superficially, they resemble the wish-fulfillment dreams of small children. The first was as follows: "In my dream I'm holding money in my hand. I close my fist and hold the money tightly. When I wake up, my hand is empty. I tell myself I'll always remain poor. I'm sad." In his dream, he tries to deny his wish to receive money from me as from a homosexual seducer. Instead of experiencing the anxiety that this wish would evoke in him, he experiences the emotion of disappointment. He is able to hold fast to his wish only when he is sure that there is no chance of its coming true. The last of the four dreams is this: "Last night again I dreamed about a car. It was a [Peugeot] 404. Those are the best cars. I got in and drove off in it."

Again, the feeling of disappointment that in reality he has no car of his own. He describes how he was once permitted to try driving a car and promptly landed in the bush beside the road. This is why he must never try it again, he says, and besides he doesn't want to any more—it's too dangerous. There is an unbroken chain of associations linking this conscious attitude with his thoughts in the dream: "Because my wish will certainly never come true, it is all right for me to wish unconsciously that it will." Many Anyi have "conjuring" dreams like this one. Characteristic, and significant for purposes of interpretation, is the depressive emotion that accompanies the apparent fulfillment of the wish.

Some Other Ego Peculiarities Observed during the Interviews

Jean-Pierre is utterly incapable of making or keeping appointments for a specific time or place. Any direct request or question throws him into a stupor. He replies either not at all or with a random remark, usually "yes, Monsieur" or "no, Monsieur," and then takes some action or other, by chance.

This stupor, which also occurs during our talks whenever he has to cope with some emotion or other, represents a regression in the service of the ego. When he finds escape in one of his fantastic tales, even while he is engaged in telling it I am often able to observe how his babbling—best compared with the "word salad" produced by schizophrenics—gradually becomes understandable speech and signals the restoration of linguistic communication.

An analogous phenomenon—but one never displayed by any of our other Anyi partners—was Jean-Pierre's habit of occasionally repeating his own sentences four or five times in stereotype form, like a phonograph record playing the same groove over and over again. On one occasion (during the thirtieth interview), this happened when he got carried away by fantasies of cooking and eating and I asked, "Isn't it a disgrace for a man to have to cook his meals himself?" Probably he felt threatened by a diffusion of his already insecure gender identity. Gradually he began speaking normally again and identified with a man who scolds a young girl and gives her a good thrashing to teach her her duties in the household. A few minutes later he is talking confidently and in his best conversational tone.

In order to maintain a certain continuity in the interviews, it proves useful to make the sessions a binding ritual; I have already described the dictation ceremony, which turned out to be a helpful symbiotic ritual, often marked by mirror-image behavior on Jean-Pierre's part.

Toward the end of our stay, it was interesting to note the high degree of empathic identification during the interview sessions—for example, when Jean-Pierre would shake the tent to get rid of the red ants, using exactly the same motions as I usually did (identification with gesture). Sometimes I happened to slap a mosquito that settled on my leg. Jean-Pierre promptly slapped his own leg, although there was no insect there. One time he even slapped his right thigh, as I had just done, while letting himself be bitten by an insect that had settled on the arch of his left foot.

I regard Jean-Pierre's practice of always carrying something in his hand when he comes for his interview as a symptomatic action. He feels an inner need to cling to this object, whatever it may be—his sunglasses, a book, a brightly colored advertisement for some medicine or other, a long straw, a broken cigarette lighter, a page out of a magazine, a stalk of papyrus he has removed from my car; he needs this object as a completion of his self. On one occasion, when he happens to look more than ever like a little boy, he carries a broken toy; another time, when he is totally absentminded, he has a piece of cloth in his hand, from which he continually pulls threads. The European origin of most of these objects may have some identificatory significance; what is even clearer, in any case, is that he brings with him what he himself lacks, a symbolic phallic component of the self, a narcissistic supplementation of his body ego.

As soon as he begins to feel more self-confident, other symbols start to replace the objects listed above. Not until our ninth hour together does he appear in African dress. When he talks about love or about music, he has no need of an object. After his attitude toward the village of Yosso has lost its tenseness, he alters his hairdo and is not carrying anything when he appears for our interview.

It is striking that, after the interview sessions, his movements are awkward and unsure, like those of a blind man; he has difficulty in walking, stumbles, and bumps into trees. All this never happens when he has "something" in his hand to supplement his body ego.

Interpretations and Defenses

During the third session I had managed to get a conversation going with Jean-Pierre by resorting to a special kind of interpretation. In addition to designating his resistances, I tried each time to stress my understanding of the way my partner was seeking to avoid unbearable experiences (emotions and conflicts). This procedure, utilizing the analyst as a kind of auxiliary ego to enable the subject to work through the instinctual urges he has warded off, can also be employed with European patients suffering from serious regressions. With Jean-Pierre, too, it helped to maintain the emotional rapport between us and led gradually to a relaxation of his tensions.

During this process it became evident that, in addition to unusual regressive forms of defense, such as the disintegration and restoration of the speech faculty, all the defense mechanisms known to us from the analysis of European neurotics appeared as well—projection and various forms of identification, drive reversal, displacement—with magical forms, such as undoing, playing the most important role. Denial was more prevalent than repression, and regressions (from anal to oral instinctual modalities, for example) more common than stable reaction formations, though the latter could also be observed.

It was usually easy for me to guess what was going on in Jean-Pierre's inner life. That I remained extremely cautious for such a long time was due not to a lack of understanding, but rather to the fact that an interpretation, even though it later turned out to have been accurate, too often led to a momentary confusion of the situation. Jean-Pierre would change the subject, cease to understand what I was talking about, answer questions I had not asked, or begin to fantasize some tale or other, and only the content of a later story would prove that the interpretation had made an impression on him. When I finally became more daring and began (in the thirty-fourth interview) to interpret everything I would expect a European patient to be able to tolerate at the conclusion of successful analysis—in other words, when I no longer permitted myself to be misled by Jean-Pierre's immediate regressive reactions—the success of which I had thus far caught only glimpses was fully confirmed in my patient's greater openness and freedom from anxiety.

It is natural to ask just how my partner Jean-Pierre differed from a European subject with predominantly pregenital instinctual fixations and preoedipal conflicts. Was it the instability of his object cathexes, the rapid fluctuation in forms of defense, the ease with which he was able to oscillate regressively and progressively between anal and oral instinctual qualities, active and passive goals, aggressive and libidinal desires?

It was probably a combination of all these factors—in short, a personality that, though often deeply impressed by my interpretations, still refused to be defined. Jean-Pierre's inconstancy was so great that a serious psychosomatic breakdown, a state of abject dependency, could subside within a few moments; so great that he was capable of transforming a greedy oral striving with relative ease into an anal masochistic pleasure. He never appeared to me to be free of conflict. To be sure, he repeatedly experienced me as a lasting object representation, but with interruptions and now in one way, now in another. To put it briefly, the constant factor was made up of an extraordinary ego flexibility, an instability of fixations, and an ability to withdraw cathexes.

In the beginning it seemed to be only the external framework, the social role, the rules of ceremony, a mythical faith and a magical ritual, that lent Jean-Pierre's ego a measure of constancy. During the course of interpretation, an ego was revealed that was temporarily failing to fulfill almost all its functions. Sometimes reality control broke down, and often the ego appeared to be losing its autonomous functions entirely; an inundation with polymorphous libidinal and aggressive strivings was followed abruptly by rigid, perfunctory identifications with a restrictive morality. Nevertheless, insights were possible. On many occasions my patient gave the impression of being mentally disturbed, but in terms of overall personality he was incredibly capable of adjusting to a life that was deficient in gratifications and in the security offered by the affection of one's fellows; Jean-Pierre was dependent almost exclusively on his fantasies for the satisfaction of these needs.

Careful questioning of the deputy chief of Yosso, an intelligent and thoughtful man who had known Jean-Pierre since boyhood, revealed that the general opinion of the village inhabitants as regarded Jean-Pierre could be accepted as valid; this young man was considered an exceptionally intelligent and honorable person, normal in every respect.

Language and Art

A god gave me the power to express what I suffer.
                    Goethe, Torquato Tasso

Jean-Pierre often relates his fantastic stories in the first person, thus declaring them to be authentic. The tales of the Nigerian poet Amos Tutuola (152) are told in the same fashion. Their charm lies in the contrast between their prosaic, almost banal everyday language and their fantastic content. The reader experiences pleasure because his perceptive and critical ego is stimulated without having to make an effort to reject the message from the unconscious. Jean-Pierre's stories have some of the same appeal—as long as he is in control of his linguistic performance. His partial regression in the service of the ego makes him a poet.

But as soon as other ego functions are affected by the regression, when his mode of expression becomes unclear or when his speech deteriorates, the regression can no longer be regarded as serving the ego. The listener has the agonizing feeling that he is just barely failing to understand. He must lend the narrator his own reparatory functions, so to speak, in a monumental effort to recapture for the comprehending ego the seemingly senseless babbling issuing from the unconscious.

In the telling of myths and fairy tales, the reciting of proverbial wisdom, and the singing of songs, the integration Tutuola achieves by the relevance of his tales to external reality can be provided by the familiarity with content and traditional form shared by performers and audience. The two groups enter into a relationship with one another that permits them to regress together. Fantasies stemming from the unconscious are brought alive with no danger of a breakdown to the ego.

With the exception of Suzanne and Brou Koffi, all our Anyi interview partners were afflicted from time to time with a breakdown in linguistic performance. They would begin to speak confusedly, to mix up words and concepts, while intonation and mode of expression remained unchanged; sometimes their voices would become lower. The utterances they produced were reminiscent of the "word salad" of schizophrenics. After an interval of varying duration their speech would become understandable once more. In some instances they would be aware of the breakdown in communication and would reformulate what we had not been able to understand. We observed that speech deterioration can also occur when an Anyi is speaking his native tongue.

Suzanne was able to avoid linguistic disintegration by withdrawing into proud silence, and Brou Koffi simply stopped speaking and lapsed into an offended pout.

The direct cause of a breakdown in speech is always some intense emotion—anxiety, shame, pain, grief, joy. The affects themselves are warded off; the individual neither experiences nor expresses them. The listener is forced to guess at them. It is not necessarily a specific conflict that is responsible for the disturbance; it can be anything that triggers an intense emotion.

The conditions under which the Anyi acquire their language skills have left their mark on the speakers. Even adult Anyi find it impossible to express a definite "no," the indispensable core of an individual's expression of language and of his own will around which—in Western cultures—fluency of verbal expression develops. Among the Anyi, custom decrees that the primary function of language is communication within the framework of the rules of etiquette. Interpersonal communication on an emotional basis is avoided.

The deluge of emotions characteristic of the years of early childhood, and the scornful rejection experienced by the child who tries to express his feelings, explain why a deep feeling of shame warns the adult against any attempt to do likewise. In this respect the warding off of emotion is akin to that observed in European patients who equate an emotional outbreak with a lack of sphincter control and thus avoid it at all costs.

As long as they themselves remain unmoved, the Anyi often refer to love and pain in their letters and even enjoy discussing emotions. The moment they are affected, however, a defense mechanism goes into action. Their language, which has never been of any help to them in learning to curb emotions or to make them more aim-inhibited— abilities that European children acquire through the dialogue with the mother—temporarily loses its communicative function.

Both the pattern and the origin of the disturbance are reminiscent of the phenomenon observed in schizophrenics, for whom speech communication within the family has been reduced to a symbolic semantic system that is meaningless to an outsider. These patients have never learned to exchange information in accordance with the rules of the secondary process (93). The Anyi child lives—not always, but every time he is overcome by emotion—in a family in which words are not a vehicle of communication.

Even undisturbed linguistic performance is often imprecise and vague. This cannot be accounted for either by a defect in the Anyi language system or by inadequate mastery of French. Speech is deliberately kept noncommittal in order to evade a potential conflict. An Anyi may say, for example, "Somebody said a wife was unfaithful"; what is meant is "Mr. X said his wife had been unfaithful to him."

Clarity and preciseness are not desired. Oral communications are treated like statements to be made "on the witness stand." Anything that is said might later be turned against the speaker in the form of reproaches or mockery.

Inasmuch as speech disturbances are based on social anxiety, the ability to speak well depends to a great extent on who the listeners are.[3] Most difficult of all, of course, is to speak well before a large audience or before persons of high rank. And competent speakers are held in correspondingly high esteem—that is, speakers who are never at a loss for words and are capable of fascinating their hearers so completely that there is no break in the process of communication. They speak slowly, accompanying their words with gestures but only rarely with facial expressions.

Since time immemorial the spoken word, so very fragile and so difficult to mold into a living message, has carried great weight. The Akan kings never spoke in public. They had their spokesmen for this purpose; an Ashanti king, incidentally, usually had twelve. The spokesman was the bearer of the public word; as such he was required to have perfect mastery of his language. There were many spokesmen who served as prime ministers, or as judges representing the king. The king occasionally referred to them as "my husband" or "my mother." Through their services he was spared the ever-present potential disgrace of a linguistic faux pas. As people said, "There are no inferior kings, only inferior spokesmen."

Splitting the royal role into a representative of the dignity of office and a herald of the royal word proved useful in preserving the hierarchical power structure. That magical and religious reasons undoubtedly also played a role does not preclude a psychosocial interpretation. In a matrilineal society, in which the phallic-active development of the male is inhibited, but in which specific social functions require precisely such phallic-active capabilities, ways and means were found to compensate for the inadequacy of individuals by an appropriately pragmatic role distribution.

When one stands up for one's views in public, before a court of arbitration or in a political gathering, but also even in a personal discussion (which is governed in any case by rules of ceremony), a well-chosen proverb or saying can carry conviction. Countless Akan proverbs deal with the body of experience gathered through the ages and the moral principles derived from it. We have emulated, so to speak, the use the Anyi themselves make of these proverbs in that we too have quoted them on occasion to emphasize the generally recognized truth of a given statement. Our interpretation of linguistic disturbance might well be accompanied by the saying "There is nothing so painful as shame" or "When the tongue stumbles, it is worse than when the foot does." Very frequently these proverbs allude to social value standards. In the saying "When a poor man finds wisdom in a proverb, the wisdom is lost," one valuation is corrected by another. Finally, there are proverbs that appear to contradict accepted values completely. In spite of the obligation to offer hospitality, one finds such sayings as these: "If you are wealthy, always keep the gates to your house closed" and "Because she invited friends to dine, the crab has forfeited her head" (i.e., the friends have eaten her out of house and home). In Bébou one of the proverbs we heard most often was a French one—"The bird builds his nest bit by bit." People recite this to help them curb their own greed or impatience. It has nothing to do with morality; it simply expresses a need of the ego and not a part of the content of the superego. It can be said that proverbs always give expression to a generally valid truth, sometimes to a norm that is highly valued by society, sometimes to a principle that governs human relations in spite of and in contradiction to all existing norms.

The uses of proverbs and sayings are manifold, but they are invariably pragmatic. The Anyi themselves say, "There is no proverb unless there is an opportunity" (to apply it appropriately). From the psychological standpoint, reciting proverbs can be regarded as an ego performance, in which an ego that breaks down in verbal communication provides itself with a substitute. Accordingly, the persons most frequently selected as arbitrators, witnesses, and dignitaries are men who have a large repertoire of proverbs and know how to use them effectively—just as men of wisdom and experience would be chosen for such offices in our Western cultures.

The same proverbs and sayings that lend weight and validity to public speech are also pressed into service in the most important form of artistic expression among the Anyi—poetry. A proverb takes on new meaning in a song. Art is not life itself; it is set apart from life by specific forms and rules. Yet its function is to enable both the artist and the audience to experience directly. One of the rules is that every new song composed must be based on a familiar proverb or saying.

For example, the following song, composed by a young man in Bébou, was inspired by the saying "You can love the honey wasp when it is far, far away" (because then you think only of the honey; otherwise, when it is nearby, you kill it because it stings).

There are men
Who want to kill me.
I live in loneliness, far, far from men.
But I live.

A young girl hears my song.
I should not sing.
My song can find no favor with her.
I should not sing in her presence.

I am like the honey wasp—
When I am far, far away,
Then people love me.
When I am here,
They have no love for me any more.

Art is solely what is communicated, that inner process in which others are enabled to participate. The whole village is delighted when a youth appears with his guitar or when it is announced that old Louise Ya (Thomas Assoua's aunt) is going to sing the old ballads for the whites. Forms and rules are not sufficient to protect the singer's vulnerable inner life from the affective reactions—the enthusiasm or the criticism—of his public. The social group must come to his aid. When the women sing, men are merely tolerated; they stand or squat at the outer edges of the circle. When the singer is a young man, the other young men flock about him closely, while the girls remain outside the circle. When they try to push their way to the front during the intermissions, the young men shoo them back with mocking comments. They simply laugh and continue to criticize the performance. The singers egg one another on, shouting between stanzas:

Keep better time when you beat your drum, Koffi!

Tap the glass more lightly, make it sound like a bell!
That's the way! Thank you, Kwame!

Don't sing as if this were a funeral, my friend!
We're singing to make people happy!

For months we have been living next door to Jacqueline Amoikona, the lovely granddaughter of old Denda and the great-niece of Chief Ahoussi. She often talks and jokes with us and sometimes asks us for medicine. Her pains always appear just before she makes a sudden decision to go away for a few days. She goes shopping for silk head scarves, which she offers for sale in Bébou. We assume that she also has a lover whom she visits in the city. She has never spoken of her personal life. It is only when her daughter comes home from school in Zaranou for a few days that we find out that Jacqueline is divorced and has a child. Before we leave, though, she wants to sing for us. The following is part of one of her songs:

A young man has come
And taken her as his wife.

He brings her parents three bottles of gin, or four.
But he gives his bride no clothes.

She is the little daughter
Of old Denda.

She is lovely to look at,
She wears all her jewelry
For the young man
Who is her husband.

She is the little daughter
Of the king, Ahoussi.

The young man says he wants her,
But his thoughts are not of her.
In the morning he goes out into the forest,
And late that evening he is gone.

This particular song has twelve stanzas, and Jacqueline sings us five long songs during the course of the evening. Their melodies evoke memories of Gregorian chants. Movingly, she describes her fate. A young girl could never "say" what she feels, but in her song she is poor, alone, unloved despite her distinguished birth. Beauty, toil, and work have availed her nothing. She has realized—and feels—that she has been abandoned, that there is no one who loves her. Fate is to blame—for her mother and her grandmother, squatting among the listeners like witnesses carved of stone, are unhappy themselves. The family is not to be blamed.

It is moving, and a bit disconcerting, to find that the art of the Anyi opens up an entirely new world, a world that is otherwise closed to them. Words, which can so easily be stiff and lifeless, flow with vivid grace; love and pain delight and sadden the listeners, and melody unites these reserved people in a common enjoyment.

The songs of the Anyi are not the product of religious or magical tradition. It is the magic of art itself that emanates from them, the age-old miracle that the artist can satisfy the deepest needs if he knows how to give his fantasies appropriate form. We feel no urge to try to explain this art. But we can attempt to understand how it achieves its effects and what the inner processes are that make artistic experience possible.

We assume that Jacqueline had long wanted to be closer to us. Like all men and women, she feels the need to communicate and the need for sympathy. But only in her songs can she express her innermost feelings without experiencing shame. The translation of these feelings into the accepted form and the communicative power of the accompanying

music absolve her ego of responsibility and delegate her personal conflict, her pain, and her yearning to collective experience.

Psychologically, the uncanny power of the singer is based primarily
on the fact that, with his song, he achieves a completion of the self. He
is able to admit intense emotions without feeling shame and to display
a phallic exhibitionistic mode of behavior without suffering castration
anxiety. A sense of narcissistic completeness and integrity is necessary
if one is to display one's self to public view. A musical work has the
significance of a "completion phallus" (112, 128), which can reabsorb
the erotic cathexis of the self in case the external world should refuse to
accept the emotions that have been expressed. The Anyi have lost their
narcissistic completeness during that childhood phase of helplessness
that they have never been able to work through satisfactorily. When the
phallic phase seemed to offer a chance of repair, the threats that accompanied it doomed phallic narcissistic cathexis to similar failure and
forged a link between the wariness toward emotions and castration
anxiety.

In Western culture the most important prerequisite for artistic
activity—in other words for creating fantasies that promise
perfection—is a personality capable of permitting "regressions in the
service of the ego." And this is a capability that can be attributed to all
Anyi. Even in the situations of everyday life, their ego cannot dispense
with the flexibility it provides.

One can theorize on the reason why music and poetry are the art
forms preferred by the Anyi—possibly because they represent a talent
capable of uniting the words of the secondary process with the world of
emotional experience. Musicality is a roundabout way to the achievement of body cathexis, a way that may derive from being rocked by the
mother during the long period of infancy and that may have managed to
establish itself unimpaired in spite of later traumatic anxieties and fail-
ures. In contrast, the mastery over words comes only later, when the
most decisive traumas have run their course. It is conceivable that the
two capabilities are preserved despite the fact that they are later en-
dangered, and that they unite to create the talent mentioned above.
Dance as an art form would require a better cathexis of the body as a
whole, and sculpture or painting a better development of manual skills
than the Anyi are able to acquire during their first years of physical
independence.

Strangely enough, many Anyi who are themselves incapable of expressing an independent opinion, let alone a criticism, or who can do so
only in the general form of paranoiac anxieties and projections, are
knowledgeable connoisseurs, consumers, and critics of art. Even Jean-
Pierre, who would normally prefer to die of shame and embarrassment

rather than express an independent judgment—not to mention an aggression—directed against a fellow being, was able to criticize and comment on any song he heard, giving his views on the voice of the singer, the beauty of the verses, and the song's emotional content. Both men and women would wait in eager anticipation for Jacqueline to unpack the newest, brightly elegant silk scarves she had brought from the city. The women would try them on, one after the other, and spend hours making their selections, while the men, who just a short time before had been afraid of addressing a woman, even their wives, directly, would argue excitedly about color schemes and patterns and about the esthetic and erotic value of the newest creations in fashion.

In matters of art and taste, the Anyi display great sensitivity and critical judgment. The beauty of a work of art must be confirmed by consensus if it is to bring its creator the completion of the self he needs so badly. Then, however, the work can stand for itself, a source of deep enjoyment. Artists and art lovers alike may accept it with delight or reject it in disapproval; their normally inhibited empathy can be given free rein without the danger of their becoming involved in emotional dependency relationships. The claim for perfection has isolated the work of art from the artist and from the public. Fantasy crystallized in artistic form has become an ideal object.

8 Metapsychology

The Prerequisites of Metapsychological Description

A theoretical description of psychological development and its outcome—namely, the psychic apparatus of the Anyi, whom we investigated with the tools and methods of psychoanalysis—cannot be based on the simple comparison "This is the way we are, and that's the way they are." That the observer is inevitably involved in his own psychology, that he is dependent upon the acquired standards, judgments, and prejudices of his own cultural community and of his own class ideology, is bound to distort and mutilate what he sets out to investigate. Only by applying the abstract conceptual world of metapsychology, with its theories, hypotheses and conjectures, can he succeed in reducing psychological life—intangible and resistant to comparison in its individual and cultural uniqueness—to simple fundamental processes. Structures, functions, and developmental steps can then be evaluated in comparison with those of other individuals from a different environment.

It must be realized, of course, that psychoanalytic theory, which itself is incomplete and in need of constant revision and which—by its very nature—can never claim to possess the same degree of inner coherence as a philosophical doctrine or even a hypothesis in the exact sciences, is bound to be even less consistent and less complete when it is applied to the Anyi. We are fully aware of the gaps and the questionable conclusions, even though they may not be specifically pointed out.

It is tempting to describe a conflict manifesting itself in society and to designate the individual as the locus at which the conflict—after the socialization process has been completed—makes itself felt. The result of such a procedure would be a model of human behavior determined by the more or less successful adaptation to the society in which it appears, that is, by whether the socially "correct" behavior has been learned more or less satisfactorily. Psychoanalysis has relatively little to say concerning such learning processes, since it views cultural adaptation as a more complex process, in which the conflicts, attitudes, and demands of a given society constitute the "average expectable (or nonaverage expectable and thus atypical) environment" (144) under whose influence the developmental steps take place. The environment is the source of the psychic structures, with all their typical functional possibilities, which often become manifest only when they are disturbed. Adaptation to the environment and to internal needs can be regarded as one of the principles that determine individual developmental steps, conflicts, and behavior patterns, but it must not be considered an end in itself. If it were, any theory of individual psychology would be superfluous, and so would any explanation of why not all members of a given social group behave in accordance with the accepted standards of adaptation, and of why cultures are not static, but rather dynamic, changing structures.

The society of the Anyi is characterized by particularly striking contradictions. The cohesion between brothers and sisters and all other members of the maternal lineage stands in contrast to the power and prestige structure of the masculine world of chiefs and dignitaries. The heritage of ancient kingdoms against the background of a democratic, twentieth-century republic; the archaic-aristocratic attitudes of warriors and hunters in industries producing for the world market; the right of ownership of one's own children, without any stable nuclear family structure; a skeptical sense of reality that nevertheless submits with impunity to the mystical and magical; the haunting beauty of the rain forest that harbors disease and danger—all this and more gives rise to the tension-laden equilibrium through which the Anyi move. Alien and unique, skeptical, ironical, and intelligent, the Anyi glide through their world. Depressive, immersed in their fantasies, withdrawing into a stupor akin to stultification, past masters at decadent enjoyment and gifted with incredible mental agility, unbelievably isolated and absolutely dependent upon each other, they have discovered the secret of leaving everything in abeyance. They can remain aloof and yet be active participants; they can do one thing, and they can do its opposite; in rapid alternation, or even simultaneously, they can participate and withdraw, love and hate. Their character corresponds to the conflicts contained in their environment; it internalizes conflicts without resolving them by compromise, and it has developed the ability to be "not only/but also" in situations where "either/or" would be bound to fail.

Genetic Considerations: The First Phase of Childhood, up to and Including Weaning

Before dealing in detail with the dynamics of these structures, it is advisable to look first at the development of the personality. From the very beginning, the development of the ego is marked by a dichotomy. The Anyi mother, a highly perfected instrument for the satisfaction of the infant's instinctual desires, retires into the background at the very moment when the maturing of the child's native abilities makes him incapable of gratifying her own instinctual needs any longer; she leaves the initial shaping of all those dialogic abilities that go beyond mere action exchanges (138) to other persons and to the still undifferentiated ego of the child.

The vital function of the mother as the infant's partner in the dialogue of needs and their gratification is ideally fulfilled in the beginning. She provides a reliable supplementary auxiliary ego. But she fails when she reaches the point where she must detach herself from the child in order to offer him an "additional autonomous ego" (Loewenstein). Actually, her active participation in the steps of his development would be extremely important.

> For example, it seems to make a difference to the timing of speech development and the quality of early verbalization if a mother, for reasons of her own personality structure, makes contact with her infant not through bodily channels but through talking. Some mothers find no pleasure in the growing infant's adventurousness and bodily unruliness and have their happiest and most intimate moments when the infant smiles. We have seen at least one such mother whose infant made constant and inordinate use of smiling in

his approaches to the whole environment. It is not unknown that early contact with the mother through her singing has consequences for the later attitudes to music and may promote special musical aptitudes. On the other hand, marked disinterest of the mother in the infant's body and his developing motility may result in clumsiness, lack of grace in movement, etc. [104].

Those forms of exchange that require active participation by adults, and thus a certain distance between the partners as well as a "tension-free instinctual field" (91), are not practiced with the mother. During infancy, dialogic exchange at a distance occurs only with persons who contribute little or nothing to the child's demarcation of objects, simply because they are not constantly present and thus are only a minor source of gratification for him. The majority of these forms of communication probably do not begin to develop until after weaning.

All the greater is the influence exerted on the baby by the mother's moods. That this is indeed the case "was known in psychoanalysis long before such infant observations that depressive moods of the mother during the first two years after birth create in the child a tendency to depression (although this may not manifest itself until many years later). What happens is that such infants achieve their sense of unity and harmony with the depressed mother not by means of their developmental achievements but by producing the mother's mood in themselves" (104).

In the case of the Anyi, the depressive moods, dreamlike in their intensity, with which nursing mothers try to counter the danger of an unbearably painful loss of their babies, seem to have contributed to the general predisposition to depression that is so typical of this people. In addition, mothers who are unable to resist the temptation to gratify their own instinctual needs autoerotically with their babies encourage the latter to remain at the level of the originally sensual affects accompanying physical stimulation and gratification.

In the European child, the hands and eyes begin to become independent of the mouth at an early date. Touching, feeling, and looking take over the libidinal and aggressive characteristics of oral part drives, acquire a relatively high degree of autonomy, and become components of the developing ego. The exploration and investigation of the mother, and later of the outside world, take the place of biting and sucking. The child's main interest is no longer his own body; his goal at this stage is no longer exclusively the stimulation of erogenous zones (134).

In the Anyi child, the close link between all his activities and his bodily sensations seems to persist longer. His exploration of the outside world remains longer within the dangerous vicinity of direct bodily gratification and the discharge of drives. The act of looking, which interposes a distance between perception of an object and stimulation of erogenous zones, begins at a much later stage.

The first phase of life for the Anyi child is marked by a direct and—barring accidents—undisturbed gratification of his instinctual drives in symbiotic unity with the nursing mother. This unity is all the more intimate since the mother enjoys the relationship autoerotically and makes no attempt to prepare the baby for greater independence. (She herself anticipates the inevitable separation from her part child in the form of fantasies.)

Yet, at the same time, the baby is by no means excluded from the rest of the society. On the contrary—any child who is still being nursed by his mother or carried on her back immediately becomes the center of attention. And this attention often has a touch of voyeurism about it; in the baby, the viewer is admiring an erotic attribute of the mother. The older they are, the more the children enjoy this kind of attention. As social beings they experience a high degree of narcissistic gratification along with their first centrifugal, asymbiotic activities.

Weaning, and with it separation from the mother in her capacity as a constantly available instrument for the gratification of all the child's needs, takes place as soon as the child becomes "independent," during his second year of life. The sudden change comes at a time that is particularly decisive for the development from infant to toddler. "The practicing period culminates around the middle of the second year in the freely walking toddler seeming to feel at the height of his mood of elation. He appears to be at the peak point of his belief in his own magic omnipotence, which is still to a considerable extent derived *from his sense of sharing in his mother's magic powers'* (124).

Neither direct observation of the children nor reconstruction of the experiences of adults induces us to assume, for this period in the life of the Anyi child, development of the self that is essentially any different from that described for European and American children. "The sixteen-to eighteen-month level seems to be a *nodal* point of development. The toddler is then at the height of what Joffe and Sandler [120] have termed 'the ideal state of self.' This is, I believe, the complex affective representation of the symbiotic dual unity, with its inflated sense of omnipotence—now augmented by the toddler's feeling of his own magic power—as the result of his spurt in autonomous functions" (124).

If we disregard for the moment the direct traumatic effect of weaning and the emotional withdrawal of the mother, which makes itself felt in abandonment reactions and affective overstimulation, this step and the subsequent second phase of childhood for the Anyi, namely, the phase of the child "who can run, but not run away," have lasting consequences for the demarcation and cathexis of the self, for object relations, and for dealing with reality. The transition from a deeply satisfying symbiosis to a relationship between two distinct individuals is not a gradual one. In the European child, beginning with the critical age of eighteen months, the process of individuation leads to a diminution of magic powers.

"In the next eighteen months, this 'ideal state of self' must become divested of its delusional increments. The second eighteen months of life thus are a period of vulnerability. It is the time when the child's self-esteem may suffer abrupt deflation.—Under normal circumstances, the senior toddler's growing autonomy has already begun to correct some of his delusional overestimation of his own omnipotence. During the course of individuation, internalization has begun, by true ego identification with the parents" (124).

The development of the Anyi child follows a different course from this point on. Instead of gradual awareness of the abilities and limitations of the self and a secondary narcissistic cathexis, there is narcissistic withdrawal and precocious autonomy. Since the mother has not prepared the child adequately for the process of demarcation, he finds it difficult to recognize her as a being separate from himself, to establish her as a libidinally cathected object representation. Instead, introjection and the projection of nondifferentiated split-off part objects take place, and the first identifications with the aggressor appear.

The irrevocable frustration of such an intensely satisfying exchange would be unbearable for the child if there were no way for him—or for the mother—to combat it. The mother keeps the child close to her, except for the time necessary "to make him forget his desire to drink at her breast." She prepares his food but does not feed him. And, above all, twice a day she administers enemas, which are followed by baths. Later she begins to address verbal commands to the child. In other words, she continues to perform a number of actions intended to guarantee the bodily well-being of the child, at the same time doing her utmost to provoke in him the cathexis of her person as a powerful, aggressive, violating figure. This may well contribute to the fact that frustration aggression not only is directed inward in the form of depression (malign regressions), but also is projected outward. Nevertheless, it can be assumed that this leads to a damming up of aggression, accompanied by anxiety and a feeling of impotence in the self, which leaves lasting traces and a predisposition to further changes in ego orientation, in self-cathexis and in the drives.

The still unfinished ego of the child would be unable to cope with the cessation of the earlier intensely emotional attention given by the mother if he could not resort to a withdrawal into hallucinatory satisfaction. The child is forced to revive the earlier fusion with the mother in his imagination, to embark upon large-scale narcissistic regression. Suddenly frustrated greedy desires, which no longer find an external object, are cathected with a conglomeration of gratifying and frustrating experiences, sensual as well as painful, internal and external perceptions that we must recognize as the nucleus of the grandiose self of the adult. Its libidinal cathexis is similar to the "primary narcissism" of early infancy. This perception of self is based, of course, on the body ego, especially on the perception of hunger and its satisfaction, the sensations associated with the care of the body surface, and the first sexual excitement. For the rest, however, either the self is a part or an extension of the mother, or—conversely—the mother is felt to be a part of the child's own person. In accordance with the law of omnipotence/impotence, the handling of these two possibilities is left to magical manipulation.

Narcissistic regression is the first consequence of the independence forced upon the child. Cathexis is withdrawn not only from the mother, but also from the other persons making up the environment. As a rule, in the beginning the ego is not able to find and cathect substitute objects. But at this point the child experiences his first lasting identification—the identification with the aggressor, namely, with the mother who abandons him. Abrupt "oral" abandonment is an instrument available to all adults for the resolution of interpersonal conflicts. As far as the ego structure is concerned, this process is the development of the mechanisms of cathexis defense and recathexis out of the enforced denial of object dependence (127).

Parent figures are still indispensable to the child, primarily to help him satisfy or master his instinctual needs. Thus part objects, which are—and can be—demarcated only imperfectly, but which are invested with omnipotence, are transformed into what we call in Europe "idealized parent imagoes." Not only is the child dependent on these, he dominates them at the same time. He projects them outward and can participate in them (participative projection) and identify with them (projective identification). Thus armed, the child faces the task of mastering reality—in which, for the most part, he has to find his own way—and of dealing with the coming developmental conflicts inherent in the maturing instinctual phases.

Genetic Considerations: The Second Phase of Childhood

We have described the way the Anyi child, instead of gradually becoming acquainted with his human environment and aware of his own limitations and abilities, creates a fantasy world in which he is omnipotent and in which he manipulates his objects so that he achieves gratification of his needs and, above all, completion of the self. That he can withdraw into this world at will and be protected in it from anxiety, frustration, and loneliness makes the further developmental steps possible. But from this point on a dual course can be observed. On the one hand, the child retains the fantasies deriving from the interrupted symbiotic phase, most of them belonging to the primary process. On the other hand, emotional experiences and learning processes lead to more complete demarcation of the self, to a realistic assessment of the environment, and to the development of the thinking and experiencing patterns typical of the secondary process.

The mother's emotional withdrawal not only leads to frustration and enforced narcissistic regression on the part of the child; at the same time, the independence forced upon him stimulates his ability to cope with the persons and the material things of his world.[1] Cognitive development, in particular, is encouraged. The children are mentally precocious. Thinking according to the rules of the secondary process, empirical reasoning and logic, criticism and skepticism become finely differentiated. The foundation for the proverbial intelligence and the coolly calculating skepticism of the Anyi is established.

There are a number of reasons why this development does not include the relationship to objects or render superfluous the need to resort to the fantasy world of omnipotence. Above all, at this age not even a child with well-developed cognitive ability is able to modify or achieve his exorbitant demands without the guiding and restraining help of his mother. If he tries to reach the moon, it must be demonstrated to him that he is capable of reaching as far as the footstool—and he must be given recognition for this achievement. During the second phase of childhood, the Anyi child receives neither explanations nor recognition; such guidance is conspicuously lacking. Instead of giving recognition, his environment—previously so kind and friendly—now rewards him with scorn and mockery. The development of bodily skills lags behind that of cognitive processes. The child's narcissistic gratification is interrupted by a chain of defeats and mortifications leading to a lowering of his self-esteem. Cathexis of the self is slight, and its demarcation remains blurred. In contrast, the cathexis of the idealized parent imagoes is all the higher. At the same time, however, these are disappointing; their behavior deviates so much from that of the real parents that they cannot be internalized in order to be subjected to ultimate correction. The approach to them continues to be the same as was appropriate to the split-off part objects—introjection, projection, and magical manipulation.

The image of the omnipotent-symbiotic mother, however, is augmented by another feature, one that derives from her compelling commands and from the experience of anal stimulation and violation through the daily enemas. From this time on she appears in the child's fantasies, anxieties, and desires as anal penetrating and sadistically dominating, without, however, forfeiting her reparatory-supplementary qualities or her role in gratifying oral greed. Cathexis remains ambivalent. These mutually contradictory experiences permit the development of neither a positively libidinally cathected object representation nor an anal demarcation or anal defiance capable of being sustained for any length of time; the ego does not contain a resolute "no," nor does the object world offer any clearly defined hate object. Although the experiences of the anal phase produce strong and, in part, pleasurable stimuli, leading later to an addiction to enemas, they do not provide satisfactory narcissistic cathexis of the overall body image. The self does not achieve demarcation. In most cases, an anus-penetrating maternal phallus is internalized as a permanent introject.

The development that follows entails such strong frustrations that constant recourse to the primary process, a revival of omnipotence and symbiotic part objects, is necessary. The relationship to these objects is the same as in the phase in which they originated. When intense desires emerge, they are directed to supplementary idealized objects that promise a gratification of needs. When such gratification is not forthcoming, the bad introject is projected to the external world, and paranoiac anxiety is the result. If, on the other hand, a narcissistic mortification is experienced, the injured ego needs to be repaired. The need to supplement and complete the self leads to increased fantasies and to the depressive feeling of deprivation.

The Anyi child does not envy his younger siblings the mother's breast so much as the mother's person; thus it is understandable that sibling rivalry is not particularly intense. The mother either appears in the child's fantasies as a supplementary object or is eliminated entirely.

The phallic phase is marked by the recurrence of the child's attempts to achieve stable narcissistic cathexis of his own person. But his body cathexis, having been subjected to the strange manipulation of the enemas during the anal phase, is not sufficient to permit him to achieve complete differentiation of the body image, nor does his castration anxiety, reinforced by sadistically interpreted observations of primordial scenes, permit the development of phallic sexuality. The male child's penis has not yet been stably cathected with narcissistic libido by the end of the crucial oedipal development phase, leading to wish fantasies for supplementation by means of a phallus received from the symbiotic mother. This resembles the penis wish experienced by some European women, who expect completion of the self from their children or their husbands.

Moreover, in his immediate environment the Anyi male child has no ideal models of phallic masculinity, unimpaired and deserving of admiration, with which he might identify. In spite of this lack, some of the idealized introjects are now modified. The broader human environment, its values and its customs, allow identifications that—although no longer capable of assuring stable self-esteem—do permit the construction of an ideal self and the development of a feeling of identity. The child begins to acquire social skills and attitudes secondarily cathected with narcissistic libido; these are unmistakable features of the Anyi character.

Adults whose egos are not adequately equipped to permit them to rely on their object-oriented emotions in dealing with other individuals learn the rules of etiquette that enable them to maintain the appropriate distance. The ritualization of these skills seems to consolidate the individual's awareness that he is functioning successfully, an effect that grows stronger the older the individual becomes. The desire for prestige, which may be oriented at various periods toward personal status, the possession of gold, of objects of beauty, of women or children, is capable of providing narcissistic gratification. And, finally, the pride of many adult Anyi in their descent from a renowned family or in the importance of their role in society seems to confer upon the self the cathexis that could not be achieved during the second phase of childhood. But when something goes wrong, when contact with another individual is disrupted, when etiquette and assigned roles break down, the extremely unstable cathexis of the self becomes apparent. Narcissistic mortification is the most normal and most frequent emotional reaction. And yet there is no narcissistic injury. Directly and simultaneously, the grandiose self arises out of the ashes, omnipotence regained again manipulates the environment, participation in the nursing mother, and the fulfillment of all lustful and aggressive desires have been reestablished through fantasy.

Summary of Narcissistic Development

As a result of the abrupt change in the behavior of the mother during the child's second year of life, early childhood can be divided into two phases; this division, for the time being, does not take into account the developmental phases of the libido. The first corresponds approximately to the symbiotic phase of the first eighteen months (according to Mahler, 124), during which the mother's attentions to the child are intensive and designed to maintain symbiosis. The second phase, covering the "second eighteen months" and continuing into the latency period, is characterized by the almost complete emotional withdrawal of the mother.

The feelings of a mother for her child are decisive for his self-esteem and thus for the demarcation and cathexis of the self. Consequently, this duality of phases in the course of the mother-child relationship is bound to have far-reaching effects on narcissistic development; these effects are summarized below.

Because the mother's nearly total withdrawal catches the child unprepared, it encourages in him early independence and recourse to his own resources. Nevertheless, individuation is hampered in a number of respects. Because the acquisition of bodily skills lags behind both the development of independent cognitive processes and the demands of reality, and because the child's environment offers him no friendly, helpful objects, but reacts to his appeals with scorn, he has to accept a good many mortifications and humiliations of his self-esteem. The narcissistic cathexis of the self is impaired. Instead, what remains is the grandiose symbiotic self, cathected with undifferentiated—perhaps primary-narcissistic—libido; idealized part objects, or part objects cathected with destructive aggression remain available and can be manipulated at will. The alternation between fantasies and reality-oriented action, between omnipotent/impotent experiences and object-oriented libidinal and aggressive strivings, plays a decisive role in contacts with other individuals and in the preservation of individual homeostasis.

One cannot maintain that the adult Anyi are committed to the pleasure principle, nor can one say that their ego has fully accepted the reality principle; the two functional principles exist side by side. The logical-empirical intelligence of the Anyi is supplemented by the magical manipulation of reality, that is, the secondary process is supplemented by events of the primary process. Their fantasies are an indispensable source of gratification. The Anyi possess the ability to function, simultaneously or in rapidly oscillating alternation, on two developmental levels of the self, of their object relations, and of the way they deal with reality. When they experience narcissistic mortification, they can restore their self-esteem with the help of fantasies of omnipotence. This ability is part of the apparatus that safeguards their ego autonomy.

Flexibility and Elasticity of the Ego

If we regard the ego as a dynamic structure with the task of mediating among psychic structures, we must admit that it is extremely flexible.

The functions that guarantee its relative autonomy are many and varied, present in wide selection, and—so to speak—broadly conceived. On the other hand, most of them are relatively weak and unstable, necessitating frequent reorientation as well as simultaneous functioning on more than one level of organization. Regressions to earlier, in fact to the earliest, stages in the development of the entire apparatus are permitted in order to ensure appropriate performance (regression in the service of the ego). Even then, loss of single important functions can be tolerated if a specific task can thereby be carried out effectively (disintegration of linguistic communication in the service of a defense against emotions, for example). In the normal environment, at least, this does not entail a lasting impairment; the elasticity of the ego is safeguarded.

From the economic viewpoint, ego organization of this type precludes any rigid cathexis. Defense mechanisms in particular, which require a stable countercathexis of the corresponding instinctual representations (repression, reaction formation), are rarely part of the standard equipment of the ego.

Thanks to the regression to the grandiose self described above, narcissistic injuries can easily be compensated by narcissistic elation or by the gratification of object-oriented instinctual desires; conversely, the frustration of instinctual drives can be compensated by narcissistic gratification. In this way a lasting impoverishment of gratification is generally prevented.

These circumstances presuppose special handling of the instinctual demands of the id by the ego. These demands are constantly being rerouted, reoriented. Strong and even violent aggressions can be held in abeyance; they become a part of the individual's fantasies and are subjected to the influence of a series of defensive processes, so that they are never discharged in a manner harmful to the environment. Libidinal desires can be handled by gratifying them as polymorphous-perverse strivings deriving from any stage of fixation. Through participation, the ego can vicariously enjoy gratification in the external world, abandon the object concerned, become its counterpart, and experience the opposite gratification in a new, fusionlike identification.

By means of this alternation, the drive can be mastered and instinctual anxiety relativized. Nevertheless, the ego stands in continuous need of defensive devices against emotions. The instinctual impulses, which are continually being activated and reoriented, are governed by means of intense anxiety signals to which the ego is highly vulnerable, since its demarcation from the environment was accomplished originally under the impact of acute fear of loss, of separation anxiety, and of paranoiac persecution anxiety. Since flexibility is a basic prerequisite for all its functions, the ego must guard itself at all costs against being flooded with anxiety or being paralyzed by it. But all other affects as well—grief, pain, joy, and so on—were so firmly rejected by the childhood environment that any expression of these emotions would in turn give rise to a feeling of shame.

Relations to Objects and to the Environment

The need to reorient cathexis in order to deal with instinctual desires precludes the maintenance of any stable object cathexes. One might express it by saying that there is no longer any "basic trust"; for it has been destroyed by the mother who, after a period of supplying all the child's needs, abandoned him suddenly and too soon. A latent distrust, an intuitive recognition of the unreliability of human relationships dominates the individual's contacts with others. Again and again, we found the following verse by Bertolt Brecht coming to mind:

> And he took what they gave him for his need was great.
> But he asked (for he wasn't a fool)
> "Why do you give me shelter? Why do you give me bread?
> Woe is me, what are you plotting against me?"
> [Bertolt Brecht, *Three-Penny Novel*]

Nonetheless, the ego derives a dual advantage from the unstable cathexis of object representations; it does not need to adjust to objects that promise only slight gratification, and it has freedom of action in such contradictory social situations as polygynous marriage, conflicting loyalties toward persons of the mother's and persons of the father's lineage, homosexual and heterosexual relationships.

For such individuals, love may well bring passion and enjoyment, but not contentment. The tension physically apparent in countless nervous symptoms proves how difficult it is to control the emotions. The expression on the adult Anyi's face reflects his realization that the unclouded happiness experienced in the feeling of togetherness with his mother as long as she was nursing him can never be recaptured. Perhaps the expression of ironic, rather than tragic resignation that distinguishes almost all Anyi men and women from other Africans may even be intended to express their ability to simply abandon their partners or their lovers, just as they themselves have been abandoned.

Interaction with the social environment provides the ego with stabilizing functions that serve as an effective defense (group ego) and that in turn help to promote adaptation to the environment. Furthermore, even the individual superego, whose aggressively cathected preautonomous nuclei are a threat to equilibrium, is bolstered through the collaboration of society (clan conscience). And, finally, even the perception of the self, which tends to be enhanced by traditional ideals and to derive a certain stability from the feeling of identity in being an Anyi or an Anyi from a respected family, supplies the support needed to enable the individual to cope with social reality. However, the role played by the environment in the economy of the ego and in the formation of the superego can be defined only after we have outlined the organization of defenses, the typical resolutions of conflicts, and the identifications and autonomous functions that shape the ego.

The Array of Defense Mechanisms

The definition and description of defense mechanisms was the starting point for the development of modern ego psychology. In order to describe the ego of individuals from an alien culture, it seems advisable to apply the methods of this branch of psychology. Through a change in function, defense mechanisms gradually become responsible for the majority of secondary-autonomous ego functions; their dynamics can be formulated abstractly, and they appear immediately in the form of resistance at the beginning of every exploratory interview utilizing psychoanalytic techniques. The array of mechanisms itself does not seem to vary from one social structure to another so much as does the preference for different mechanisms in each case, the order in which they are applied, their effectiveness, and thus their adequacy. The situation is similar to that encountered in comparing individual subjects. The mechanisms employed may be the same; what is typical or idiosyncratic is the way they are organized.

Still, the differences that do exist in the array itself are informative. Forms of defense used with success to master those dangerous impulses for which the ego is no longer the scene of conflict do occur, but they cannot be sustained for long. Repressions, as "primal repressions," that is, the content of fantasies that have never been verbalized, are readily acted out or at least dealt with in fantasies under the appropriate circumstances. There is such a thing as an amnesia that erases the memory of unbearable childhood experiences so that they can be recalled only in the form of allusions in screen memories, but this type of amnesia is remarkably easy to cure, as is reflected, for one thing, in the fact that when the erased memories are recalled, the subject is not in the least astonished at them. And, finally, repression may sometimes occur when it is no longer possible to deny the emotions. In some of our Anyi subjects, feelings of apprehension about the coming separation and sadness at the thought of our leaving at the end of our stay occasionally led to repression and conversion to bodily ailments, until these affects had been replaced once again by other defense reactions such as re-orientation of cathexis (oral abandonment of the frustrating object), recourse to passivity, or regression to less object-oriented modalities and gratification through a displacement substitute.

Hardly any reaction formations in response to anal strivings could be observed in our Anyi subjects. In the character of the village chief, Ahoussi, reaction formations seemed to play about the same role as the formation of the obsessional character in European subjects; it was for this reason, and not as a result of his experiences with white persons, that we found him more "European" than all the other Anyi we met. When we consider that, although strong anal constraints are applied, there is no sphincter training in the usual sense of the word, the conse-quences are clear—retention (as opposed to release) is neither desirable nor feasible as an expression of protest against the physical effects of the daily enemas. Nor can there be any devaluation of excrement or a re-sultant need for personal cleanliness as a reaction to the pleasure of playing in it. (The delight the Anyi feel in bodily cleanliness has its origin in the sensual pleasure afforded by being bathed by the mother. It is reinforced by a fairly low aversion threshold, which has nothing to do with defensive reaction formation.) And stubbornness apparently cannot develop in spite of the authoritarian compulsion and often sadistic treatment to which the toddler is exposed. Commands and punishments are too inconsistent to create a lasting counterreaction, and—in addition—because of the constant frustration of their need for an anaclitic object, the children are utterly incapable of giving up ob-jects they need so badly.

Although the ego is forced to get along virtually without rigid de-fenses, we definitely are not implying that the Anyi are more or less defenseless against any and all instinctual impulses, or that their egos need no defenses. Not only do they produce en masse vehement denials of their own thoughts and feelings and of a vast array of external per-ceptions, but they insist on clinging to these denials even when it requires massive curtailment of other functions. This is illustrated by the fact that Jean-Pierre sat through forty interview sessions without agreeing to a single one of our offered interpretations, or that our inter-preter François, when asked to make a note of something, replied on numerous occasions that unfortunately he was unable to because he had left his pad and pencil at home—though he was holding both in his hand at the time. Emotions of all kind are denied as a matter of princi-ple. When Ahoussi felt affectionate concern for his ailing sister Denda and said "I tremble," the very next minute he was worrying not about her health, but about how much money her funeral would cost him, cheering himself up at the same time with the thought of how much the mourners would have to contribute and of the fact that they would all be forced to attend the burial festivities whether they wanted to or not. To be sure, the following day he took care not to ask his sister about her health, so that he would not be forced to start worrying again.

Such evasions in major and minor matters, most of them reversible ego restrictions and displacements that often lead to substitute gratifications, are very frequent. Displacement to a minimal detail, as observed in our obsessional neurotics, is only a special case. Occasionally we had the impression that the waking ego of our partners was dealing with love and hate objects in exactly the same way as a dreaming ego, especially since other characteristics of the primary process—condensation, expression by the opposite, reversal—sporadically seemed to find their way into normal cognitive and defensive processes.

Other simple mechanisms originating in the oral phase of ego development suffice to provide adequate defense; in Europeans we hardly include them among the defense mechanisms either because they are ineffective for us or because they require a complex reorientation of the entire ego. In the Anyi, however, these devices are quite capable of warding off a precisely defined internal danger; instead of greedily demanding to receive something for himself, the Anyi can spontaneously and actively give to someone else. Thomas, for example, mastered his envy of, and feeling of rivalry toward, his older brother by means of passive submission, and immediately afterward he was able to assume an active role as his brother's protector. Sometimes even the active and immediate renunciation of something one is passively anxious to have is possible.

These techniques have little to do with magical omnipotence; they effect a partial, often reality-oriented change. The prolonged (for European standards) and profoundly satisfying nursing period permits the maturing ego to develop these simple but adequate defensive attitudes during the oral phase of organization. Both infant and mother profit, for each gives the other something of value. This is perhaps more evident among the Anyi than in our culture. The mother is well aware of the satisfaction she derives from the infant (as in Suzanne's case, for example), and in return she provides not only for his care and his rearing, but also for the gratification of his sensual needs. In any case, these mechanisms can easily be distinguished from those that originate in the oral phase of libido development and become fixated during the "second phase of childhood."

It is during this second phase, in the harsh school of almost fatal psychological trauma, that the repertoire of mechanisms on which the ego of the Anyi can rely is assembled, and this period also marks the beginning of the dual-phased, or even multiphased course of personality development that makes it possible for the Anyi to function simultaneously on various developmental levels. We can safely describe the most important of these levels as regressive, as long as we bear in mind that they are precisely the ones needed to guarantee behavior that takes reality into account and is thus acceptable to society.

It is certain that the first lasting identification with the mother who abandons her child is not established in the ego in a single, brief process as a direct response to the mother's withdrawal. It must be remembered that the toddler remains in his mother's vicinity and is constantly trying to recapture her affection; thus he has ample opportunity to become acquainted with the person who has no scruples about depriving of the endearing name "my child" the child who, day and night, was in contact with her body, shared her warmth, moved when she moved, and nursed at her breast. The child has become a material possession, entitled to a certain modicum of care, just as pets are in our culture. Replaced by a younger sibling, the toddler can be given away or offered as a pledge for certain family or financial obligations. In any case he still appears on the credit side of the ledger of the lineage in which his mother is a shareholder. He cannot run away on his own; thus far her possession is safe. If he dies his mother will deny her grief, for—reliving her own childhood experiences—she has already withdrawn from him and need only complete the self-mutilating operation she has begun.

We have made a point of emphasizing this state of affairs, which lasts for several years, throughout the entire "second phase of childhood," because in our opinion an ego apparatus that is so elastic, so consistently available, and so useful even though it was acquired under the compulsion to "identify with the aggressor" does not come into being unless it is developed and assimilated along with maturation processes, with integrative and differentiating processes in the ego itself and in trial encounters with the object world. Such processes need time; they cannot take place in the atmosphere of despair engendered by the experience of separation from the mother, in the hallucinatory world of megalomania and fusion fantasies. Suzanne is quite capable of abandoning her beloved Paul, soon even Syrien, and even Madame, to whom she feels closest of all during this phase of the interviews; and old Ahoussi would have no difficulty in abandoning all his wives, children, and dignitaries the moment they no longer pleased him. "When the spirit leaves her, the shaman dies." Elisa laughs when she thinks of it. Any conflict with other persons can be broken off; libidinal and aggressive cathexes from every phase of development can be reversed, simply cease to exist, and the object so recently coveted or hated is viewed with complete indifference. The loss leaves no narcissistic scar behind. Now freed, the libido enhances the grandiose self in the form of narcissistic cathexis; the self becomes as powerful as the abandoning mother of early childhood, and the result is a temporary manic inflation of self-esteem. Now the individual is capable of renewing contact or may simply look for a new object. The limitations of the defense process do not lie in the process itself. Yet the ego of the Anyi does need helpers. His internal tensions are far too great for him to be able to bear the isolation that results from abandonment. Perhaps his most intense feeling is the longing to regain in this world that lost paradise of comfort and safety, a melancholy yearning for the unclouded and sensually satisfying togetherness—and oneness—of the symbiotic period.

Thus abandonment, a useful instrument in major reorientations in life, is usually only a short, intermediate step within the organization of defenses, designed to let the ego recover its balance, to give it a moment of object-free autonomy before it enters—as it must—into new dependency.

We seem to have characterized the ego as independent, and the self as differentiated and complete. This was not to gloss over anything, but rather to point out that lasting identifications formed in the early phase of individuation do contribute to mature defensive measures (and to the self-esteem of the adult).

Apart from this, the boundaries of the self continue to remain open, and the ego must rely on a defense that we can safely call magical and that can be compared with psychotic mechanisms insofar as gestures, fantasies, and internal reorientations suffice to manipulate reality or—more precisely—to give reality a different sense, a different emotional meaning, a different relationship to one's own person, and to alter this relationship according to internal needs and not to external perceptions and experience. The recurring constancy of two processes, which we call participative projection and projective identification, their effectiveness in maintaining or reestablishing the autonomy of the ego, and their usefulness in the environment—all of which was substantiated during our analytical interviews—justify their inclusion among the normal defense mechanisms of the Anyi.

Participative projection may be defined as sharing, by empathy, fusion, or incorporation, the qualities of magic power projectively imputed to an object by the subject. The goal is not only to provide a defense against feelings of impotence and frustration, but also to enhance the cathexis of the self and to enlarge the person of the subject. Brou Koffi transforms the white doctor into a powerful magician, participates in his power, and immediately experiences a heightening of his self-esteem. Anyone who purchases a "god" abroad enjoys a similar advantage. For Suzanne, the white Madame embodies a better husband, one who drives the hated rival away. Thomas invests the white man with the power to compete with his older brother; for him, too, the rivalry conflict is robbed of its tension—it is two other people that are quarreling, and he himself can participate in the power of the victor. The Anyi are like conspirators who delight in the success of their schemings. And they do not even have to stir up intrigues; this is taken care of by the endopsychic process of participative projection.

This process differs from simple projection by virtue of its dual objective—not only to externalize evil or the bad object, but to participate in its power at the same time. Our explanation for the all-pervading animistic tendencies is that the introjects are abolished from the ego together with the evil desires they inspire, but that the subject urgently needs instances to supplement and support his ego. The process differs from simple identification in its instability and fragility. If the object's omnipotence, which the subject shares, cannot be sustained, the entire process is immediately annulled. The mechanism might also be characterized as a projection in which the subject abandons the projected object (following the pattern of the mother who abandons her child) and then, in a second step, identifies with it as along as this permits a completion of the self. In any case, there is no paranoiac anxiety.

Projective identification is closer to paranoiac projection and delusion formation. Oral aggression, for example, may be projected to a witch. The subject can borrow magic powers for his own use and render the witch harmless; otherwise he will be afraid that she may devour him or poison him. It is this mechanism that is responsible for the superficial observer's impression that the Anyi suffer from delusions of persecution. For witches can be conjured up, and even if one lives in mortal terror of such spirits, that may be better than having to discharge the emotions concerned with members of the maternal kin in person.

If the child were not so pampered during the first, oral phase of childhood, the anal violation, which is not experienced as such until the second phase, would not have such grave consequences. The enema pipe, the phallus of the mother intent on rape, is experienced as *the* persecutory part object. As long as it is outside and represents a menace, the desire to have it inserted grows; what can no longer be obtained orally, by sucking, must at least be administered anally. Once the persecutory object is inside, however, with its entire destructive cathexis, it is subjected to immediate reprojection in order to ward off anxiety.

Both mechanisms are transitions to actual identifications; the first more in the sense of a fusion or supplementation, the second from the need to absorb something satisfying, admirable, or useful from the partner. As a defense against anaclitic desires and other preoedipal strivings, intensive identifications with phallic-active attitudes are repeatedly established. In the eyes of the Anyi, a stranger who refuses to comply with the rules of etiquette is invested with enormous phallicity—Morgenthaler, for instance, when he refused the gift of fish, and Edjro, that rebellious alien man of God. Furthermore, men feel the need to identify with an active, energetic father and women with a kind, dependable mother who takes good care of her family. That these identifications and others like them are extremely unstable is explained by the course of the oedipal conflicts. It has been pointed out that identification or fusion with a phallic-aggressive father in the Anyi society would inevitably lead to conflicts with the maternal lineage, which demands submissiveness and passive dependence.

We do not, however, wish to create the impression that identifications have no role in structuring the ego of the Anyi. Both girls and boys identify with the attitudes, activities, and desires of the mother, whose role is to care for the home. For the girls these identifications probably constitute a fairly firm basis for behavior, and this in turn is partly responsible for the fact that in general the women are superior to the men in energy and efficiency. The boys, though, have greater difficulty with these identifications. Because of their assigned roles in society, they will have to give them up unless they happen to become chiefs or heads of their courts, that is, persons who are expected to possess both paternal and maternal (homemaking, food-providing) attitudes. In a different sense, certain identifications that are concerned with a single trait and that in themselves do not shape any structures may play a role in structuring the ego. The identification with the mother who forcibly administers enemas is reflected in a later addiction to enemas, injections, and the like, and—in a still later form—in a tendency toward masochistic fantasies of being beaten. However, the ego also acquires action potential. The violating object remains outside in part and in part is projected to the external world. The act of violation is practiced on the subject's own initiative; he acts it out in his fantasies instead of submitting to it passively. In fact, the ultimate result of identification with the intruding object may be the subject's domination of the act of violation by acting out everything himself, with no need for a compelling object, the mother of the anal period.

Culture-Specific Metapsychology

At this point, before we concern ourselves with the process of defense—that is, the way defenses are organized—and examine in greater detail its influence on the development of drives and the handling of objects so that we can derive the typical resolutions of conflict and the resultant culture-specific psychic phenomena, we ought to reconsider for a moment just how metapsychological explanations come about and what purpose they serve. Psychoanalytic theory is always derived from an understanding of the unconscious mind of a specific individual. With the help of abstractions and generalizing hypotheses, it can be applied to help the analyst understand the next subject more easily and more accurately. During the course of the process, the theory itself is subjected to correction. If we continue long enough along this path of forming hypotheses, we shall be rewarded by arriving not only at an understanding of individual subjects, but also at a model of the structure, dynamics, genesis, and so forth, of a group of persons. So far we have been acting on the assumption that this process of theory-building is far advanced as regards the Anyi. There is greater justification for this assumption in connection with the development of the self and the formation of defense mechanisms than in any other field—not because observations in these other fields are less conclusive, but because they lend themselves less readily to abstract formulation and because they are far more decisively influenced by individual variations. Since metapsychology does not permit a separation of phenomena that are universally human from those that are specific to their cultures and those that are strictly idiosyncratic, yet at the same time assigns the main responsibility for psychogenesis to the environment, we too are unable to establish clear dividing lines. Since we shall continue to speak very generally of "the Anyi," the reader is asked to bear in mind that our data are based on a vast number of individual items of information, but from very few persons. Thus we have characterized as "culture-specific" whatever can plausibly be attributed to the influence of the Anyi environment; in the last analysis, the demarcation lines separating culture-specific psychological traits, those that are common to all mankind, and those that are purely individual must remain blurred.

Preoedipal Development of the Instinctual Drives

The oral phase of drive development is accompanied by fairly complete gratification of needs and by sensual stimulation. This process of gratification may be interrupted on occasion by chance events (bodily ailments), but never by a rhythmical or otherwise predictable change in the attentions of the mother, such as may occur in the granting and withholding of affection or in "hygienically" regulated child care. Stimulation of the sucking apparatus continues long beyond the first teething period, the mother allowing the baby to bite her breasts. In addition, deeply satisfying tactile or kinesthetic stimuli are provided by the mother, or rather exchanged between mother and child in the form of direct skin contact and during bathing and grooming. The genitals are not excluded, nor are they singled out for special attention. On the other hand, the daily stimulation of the anus by chili-pepper enemas begins during this period. That the child is rather pampered in the gratification of these physical and psychosexual urges cannot be explained by the scope of the stimulus alone. Even more important is the fact that the mother needs the child above all for her own sensual gratification and is careful not to introduce any dialogic communication (such as smiling at the child, looking at him, playing with him, or talking to him) that would involve interposing a distance between herself and the child and thus between the child and the immediate gratification of its needs. Both are practical consequences of a specific emotional attitude on the part of the mother; whether the child is male or female, she experiences it as a phallic completion of her own self, enjoys this in the form of hallucinatory fantasies, and—after a period of adjustment in the case of the first child—begins to achieve a sensual satisfaction in caring for it. During the period of adjustment the young mother is taught by her mother how to take care of a baby. This is necessary, since from the very beginning the baby's secondary—or rather primary—significance as a sex object interferes with the new mother's ability to learn to care for it. It is also understandable that the mother makes no effort to educate the child by means of dialogic communication to become an independent being. For then she will lose it not only as her child, but also as the phallus that confers completion, pleasure, and prestige. In other words, she does nothing to pave the way for her own castration in the child.

As far as the child is concerned, this means—as we have explained above—that his differentiation and individuation are made more difficult and that a permanent symbiotic inclination is established. Drive development and the approach to objects are particularly affected.

Oral instinctual impulses and the libidinal desires they later engender, especially sexuality in the strict sense of the word, retain a tendency to demand immediate discharge. Unlike other daydreamers, these people find it extremely difficult to postpone fulfillment of their desires, to wait for pleasure—in fact, to wait for anything. Not just the ultimate frustration of a desire, but even a delay in its gratification produces extremely unpleasant affective tension. It is important in this connection that among the Anyi, though the discharge of pregenital and genital impulses is occasionally threatened and is thus cathected with anxiety signals, it is by no means forbidden or taboo. Just as there is no compulsory sphincter training, there are no restrictions on the child's interest in watching sexual activity or in playing with his genitals. In other words, immediate gratification is permitted; a postponement may entail the danger of a threat from without. Probably the most important contributing factor in the prolongation of the oral urgency of instinctual demands is that the mother makes it virtually impossible for the child to develop aim-inhibited, affectionate, and aim-diverted impulses capable of modifying drive processes. There is one exception: oral exchange, the acts of giving and taking, evolve into a form that, later on, is rechanneled to help promote thinking in terms of oral justice. There are European patients whose easily injured sense of justice is highly developed and comes into play in connection with very personal questions and with the rules of etiquette, especially at table. These persons tend to react to unjust treatment with helpless rage. And in their case, too, the investigator will find that their mothers dealt with their children's greedy desires by demanding sensual gratification in return for their care.

The Development of Preoedipal Object Relations

If the individual is to deal successfully with objects, both the maturation of the functions of differentiation and perception and the inevitable frustrations must counteract the pull exerted by symbiosis. Alien objects—in the beginning by definition all objects that are not the child's mother—give him all those things that she withholds. They admire him, are sometimes affectionate with him, look at him, play with him, and even talk with him. Even during the last few months of the nursing period there is probably a beginning of that division of object representations that later results in the Anyi's having a completely different relationship to objects that are close to him and offer gratification of his drives than to alien objects that have no connection with these drives. In the case of the latter, that is, the exponents of the broader social environment—whether they are prestige figures, strangers, or representatives of other roles—the Anyi have no difficulty in building up relationships based on the rules of etiquette or dictated by reason and intelligence. Such relations are disrupted only when frustrations (particularly narcissistic mortification) occur or when instinctual desires impinge upon them. The division as such does not result in endopsychic conflicts.

The conflicts between the initial image of the mother as a part object gratifying the child's needs and her later representations from the postweaning period are all the more intense. It is difficult to say just what happens during this period, not only because such early forms of object relations are in any case encountered in the adult only in the form subsequently evolved during the oedipal conflict, but also because the transition from the first to the second phase takes place under highly traumatic conditions.

From any standpoint, however, we ought to expect that the sudden weaning of the child, together with the emotional withdrawal of the mother, would create a particularly sharp demarcation line between the two phases of psychic development, perhaps a deeply satisfying oral phase, followed by a frustrating anal phase. In any case there is bound to be an inclination to regress from the second to the first.

In fact, regressions to the "most recent level of satisfying experience" are numerous and persistent. They result not only in symbiotic inclination but also in manifold oral fixations. But the situation is still more complicated. On the one hand, overwhelming unpleasurable feelings lead to grave narcissistic regressions, in which oral modalities are no longer pleasurable but are cathected with acute anxiety; the most common adult phobias, for example, are connected with experiences from the oral phase such as the fear of being left alone, especially at night or in a forest, or the fear of being devoured, poisoned, disemboweled, desiccated, or mutilated. On the other hand, the attentions of the mother during this period—anal violation and verbal commands—are experienced not only as unpleasant, but—quite soon—as gratifying as well. Basically, passive wishes are not being frustrated, but are being satisfied in another manner. Since the anal product is not devalued, but is still something the mother wants, the passive strivings from the earlier period are carried over into the new object relationship. The association of feces with gifts and gold, which for us, too, is an early anal, orally colored construct, remains valid. The acts of eating and smearing are inextricably linked in customs dealing with the preparation of the most important foods (*fufu*, palm oil, shea butter, snails).

It is significant that anal violation takes place without any anal sphincter training. A retention of feces is just as impracticable as an outright "no!" or an expression of defiance. Aggressions elicit no response. No object differentiation is possible. (We might mention briefly that the specific course of the anal phase probably explains why the Anyi are extremely poor in organizing, differentiating, and in fact even accurately perceiving the dimensions of time and space.)

During the second phase of childhood the handling of objects is fraught with contradictions and conflicts. The most obvious feature is the symbiotic inclination to experience objects or parts of objects as an extension of the self. In addition, apart from entire objects (such as the mother who withdraws), there are also countless part objects to deal with; none of these is clearly differentiated from the self. Most of them are part of the need-gratification phase—the breast at which the child feeds, the mother's skin that warms him, the water that cools him, the enema tube that gives him power and pleasure, and on the other side of the ledger the woman who devours, the food that kills, the anal violation that the child is powerless to stop and that kills. The ambivalence would be intolerable if the child had to suppress his intense feelings of aggression toward these pain-producing and frustrating objects. Instead, he wards them off by the projective mechanisms described above. No ambivalent tension arises; aggression remains outside. Occasional guilt feelings, or rather the depressing feeling that the individual himself is to blame for everything, make themselves felt in later life as preautonomous superego nuclei, reflecting the child's own impression that he himself, in his omnipotence, is responsible for many of the frustrations he experiences.

Other objects assume more definite shape—younger siblings, for example. Envy is rarely violently expressed and does not lead to lasting aggressiveness. It is replaced by a constant fear of being robbed or deprived and is absorbed into a general skeptical feeling of distrust, a feeling that other people have or are given (usually by the fates) more money, more food, more luck than they. On the other hand, envy leads to a demarcation of the self—it's someone else who gets it, not me. And this demarcation no doubt contributes to the circumstance that older siblings who take care of the younger children are loved in accordance with the anaclitic model.

And, last of all, there are strangers to be dealt with. At that period this category includes all persons who are not part of the immediate household unit. Since the child as yet has no rules of etiquette to help him, and since these formerly kind and friendly persons are now cold, harsh, and scornful, he experiences fear at the sight of any stranger and is overcome by a panic anxiety that drives him to seek the vicinity of his mother or an older sibling or, occasionally, to revert directly to stupor.

These strangely precocious, isolated, often seemingly dull-witted children strike the observer as being totally without will. They immediately abandon all defiance as soon as they notice even a superficial sign of attention from the mother. They do not cling to her or clamor for affection, but they take their sexual gratification and their food when and how they can. Once in a rage, they let themselves be incited to attack playmates of the same age, just as in a cockfight. They allow themselves to be teased as the victims of sadistically inclined adults or played with like toys by teenage girls. They have very few activities of their own, and almost no creative ones. Yet they enter the next conflict that the maturation process holds in store for them with a vividly developed fantasy world. The onset and course of the phallic phase and the outcome of the oedipal conflict are marked unmistakably by the object relations mentioned above or by oral-anal drive fixation. In this respect they resemble European patients with primarily pregenital fixations.

The Phallic Phase

The environment, that is, the external world, does nothing to hamper or restrict the maturation and exercise of independent motor activities, the exploration of the environment, or the cathexis of body feelings, which proceed in part under the guidance of the muscular apparatus and in part under that of the urethral and genital erogenous zone and which can be summed up as the developmental process leading to phallicity. In fact, it appears that the environment actually encourages this development. During the first phase of childhood, the baby is given ample opportunity to learn to crawl, to sit up (with early and intensive help from adults), and to walk—at approximately the same age and just as proficiently as European children. During the second phase, any purposeful, externally directed activity can only be of advantage to the child, who can expect little help from his environment. He is not forced to learn to control the urinary sphincter. Boys and girls are allowed to masturbate as much as they like, and they make abundant use of it to compensate for frustrations and to ward off aggressive tensions, anxiety, and loneliness.

Girls and boys are treated just the same. The Anyi say that, according to traditional value norms, the mothers prefer girls because they can keep them at home, while they have to relinquish the boys sooner or later to the world of men. There is a verse that the young men sing:

If you're a boy,
That's fine.
For it's hard
to produce a son.

During that phase of childhood (third and fourth year), however, this difference hardly makes itself felt. For, quite irrespective of which sexual role this being whom they possess will be expected to play later on, the mothers and the environment—neither of which place any obstacles in the toddler's way when he begins, during phallic development, to become actively aware of his sex and the differences it implies—give the children hardly any more help in this respect than they do in the other important steps of this period. In the beginning, phallic development is left up to the child's own activity and to his inherited and acquired aptitudes.

Cognitive processes and fantasies are apparently least dependent upon outside help during this period. From this time on, active phallic strivings become an integral part of all games and, later, of daydreams.

Boys and men dream of aggressive deeds; both sexes dream of prestige, sexual conquests, physical beauty, jewelry, and beautiful clothes.

The development of intelligence is largely the development of "defensive intelligence." We assume that the ego, confronted by a flood of intense emotional demands, mobilizes certain cognitive processes that have the advantage—in the beginning, anyway—that they can be isolated from external and internal dangers. A similar phenomenon has been reported for European adolescents (103). This is perfectly possible, for the Anyi have no taboos on sexual exploration. And for this reason the children (like the adults later on) are not motivated by curiosity; they are quick to grasp human weaknesses, intrigues, and danger, and they can argue logically and convincingly, but they have few additional interests. It may be that early mastery of the sitting posture, as in our "sendentary" Western culture, is a precondition that conduces to the Anyi child's endeavoring to comprehend the world through cognitive processes rather than actively moving out into it as, for example, the children of the Dogon do.

There is still another contributing factor in the case of the Anyi—that at the beginning of phallic development the child receives hardly any help in acquiring physical or language skills. Toddlers are not provided with toys of any kind, nor do they invent any for themselves. Older children will not play with them at this stage, and the grown-ups ignore them. The physical clumsiness of the toddler is surpassed only by the even greater clumsiness displayed by the adults in dealing with all technical appliances. Women are an exception, at least in the fields of child care and homemaking; there they learn the necessary skills by imitation, by identification, and by instruction toward the end of the second phase and the beginning of latency. The regularity with which adults manage to burn themselves, to cut their left hands or their shins with their bushwhackers, or to stumble and fall leads one to conclude that as children they were never taught during play how to handle things, and that they have deliberately avoided venturing far enough into the material world since childhood to "learn by experience" before it was too late.

If not even a positive narcissistic cathexis of the muscular apparatus can be achieved, it is bound to lead to difficulty in recathecting the erogenous zone from the anus to the genitals. The intensive stimulation of the anus produces sensual pleasure, admittedly associated with anxiety and pain, but nonetheless intense, and it is offered to—in fact, forced upon—the child by a beloved being, the desperately longed-for mother. The toddler's mingled fear of and desire for the enema reflect this clearly. We know that later on an addiction to increasingly harsher enemas develops, but we have no information as to whether anal coitus (either homosexual or heterosexual) is practiced. Coitus a tergo is a form of sexual intercourse sanctioned by custom, but it is by no means the only form.

Whatever course genital evolution may take, the cathexis of the phallus is left to autoerotic activity.

The women are better off in this respect. Passive anal pleasure can be channeled more easily to female than to male genitality. Cathexis of the phallus that the woman receives from the man, and from there to that of the child she bears, is perfectly possible—with an admixture of the anal. The remaining phallic-active tendencies may appear later, at the time of puberty, and not only in the form of delight in one's own beauty and a positive addiction to beautiful clothes, which can be observed in Europeans as well. With the Anyi, phallic tendencies may also be discharged with an anal sadistic component as represented by the enema tube or, in sublimated form, as the aggressive phallic acts inherent in the role of the woman in the maternal lineage. In spite of their passive anal preparation, it is possible for Anyi girls to cope with their lack of penis. They do not develop penis envy during the oedipal conflict, but instead master their lack of power, their anal subjection, and their anatomical structure later on by acquiring phallic attitudes and a fantasy penis.

The men never succeed in achieving phallic erotic cathexis of the body as a whole. Phallic sexuality remains narcissistically oriented, threatened by acute anxiety, and vulnerable, and as a lasting consequence of the difficulties attendant on its origins it never gains primacy over the other pregenital impulses. Not only is it accompanied by hypochondria and enema addiction; it frequently needs an acted-out or imagined stimulus in order to function. It should be noted here that the masculine roles offered by society are absolutely indispensable. They are ritualized and reinforce the self with a supply of phallic narcissistic cathexis; this effect is due partly to the ritualization of certain behavior patterns and partly to identification with the prestige enjoyed by the male.

The Oedipal Conflict in Boys

Ego maturation under the influence of the stimulus provided by phallic development regularly entails a reorientation toward the persons of the environment that leads to inner conflicts. The child enters the oedipal situation. Libidinal desires now tend to be directed outside and to focus on a specific person. Any third person intruding in this relationship is felt to be a disturbing factor and is frequently made the target of aggressive drive components. In general, the behavior of the objects of sexual and aggressive instinctual impulses gives rise to acute anxiety (castration anxiety) that compels the child to find a temporary solution to the oedipal conflict. Seen from without, this marks the beginning of the latency period. It is possible to isolate the characteristics of an oedipal conflict specifically typical of the Anyi. Let us begin by reconstructing the process in the Anyi boy.

The object representation to which sexual strivings are directed, the "oedipal" mother, acquires the features of the gratifying mother of the nursing period. This probably takes place right at the beginning of the phallic phase, and not only through later regression, when difficulties and dangers begin to appear. After all, the mother, associated with gratification experiences, is the only object the child has ever experienced as desirable. The child reverts to the mother-infant dyad. The object representation of the coveted mother corresponds better to the boy's more mature desires if the real mother, who abandoned her child, has been replaced in the meantime by an older sister or some other woman entrusted with his care. When this is the case, the emotions are new—not ambivalent to start with. The object, in any case, is not a sharply differentiated one; its purpose is to restore the participative and need-satisfying union once experienced by the child, but it must not have too clearly defined a shape of its own.

The relationship to a beloved object selected through oral regression actually excludes a third person (92). The child has a tendency to avoid the interloper and to deny the existence of rivalry or rivalry-engendered aggressions.

The external conditions of Anyi life would frequently be conducive to complete disregard of the father as a rival. Many parents are divorced, and there are a great many mothers who do not live in a common household with the fathers of their children. Even when the father does reside in the same household, he remains an outsider to the lineage and has no role as an authority figure in the matrifocal group that forms the child's immediate environment.

One may well ask oneself why, in these circumstances, a boy is ever confronted at all with the problem of rivalry, and one will probably conclude that the reason lies in unavoidable and ubiquitous psychic maturation processes that coincide with the circumstances with which the boy is now confronted. Within the wider range of social functions to which the boy is now gradually being introduced, the phallic masculine component is valued highly as an expression of prestige and power. The son is not able to derive self-esteem from his partial identifications with the mother and other female persons because female activities within the household are no longer considered appropriate to his role. And he is finally compelled to face the fact that what his mother really values and desires is not the submissive, manipulatable child, but the man in his significance as a sex object and as an exponent of prestige and wealth. As a result, the phallic male to whom the mother is drawn is idealized and envied by the boy. The image of the father, as the mother's preferred embodiment of phallic power, is highly cathected, but it has virtually no uniformly integrated significance as the image of a kind and dependable, or even a strict and respected, father.

The tendency to evade the emergence of a rivalry conflict continues to exist, owing to the symbiotic nuance present in oedipal love. Dual conception of the triad is all the more plausible since there is an over-estimation (idealization) of the representative of phallic power but no mature object cathexis of the father. These specific factors account for the fact that the Anyi boy is not forced, as boys in our society are, to identify with the father and eventually to introject his most incisive qualities, his authority, in order to be able to cope with the rivalry situation, in which he cannot in any case hope to be the victor. Refusal to recognize the existence of rivalry conflicts is one of the compromises that help to resolve oedipal conflicts. Important and effective as this attempted solution is, it is not the only one.

The phallic libido is unmistakably sexual, and only to a small extent aim-inhibited or otherwise transformable. The tendency toward aggression, mobilized in the anal phase and carried over, is great, and so are the anxieties that accompany this aggression. External conditions only apparently eliminate disruptions of the dyad. Many other typical oedipal compromises can be observed. The life-styles of most Anyi and their indulgence in fantasies suggest that it is common for the child to watch sexual intercourse between his mother and his father, or some other man; and this experience very frequently evokes extreme anxiety. We must not forget that, although no one seriously tries to prevent children from observing sexual activity, they are not given any verbal explanations of what they see, and they are laughed at when they ask questions. The sex play preceding intercourse often has frighteningly cruel overtones. The mother's lover is a man with whom the child ordinarily has no contact, or at least no affectionate contact. He does not even have any significance as an authority figure, which would at least permit a lasting realistic cathexis as a figure inspiring fear. Consequently, observation of sexual intercourse has the traumatizing effect on the child of watching the "primordial scene." The intruder is experienced as a housebreaker and a murderer, and sexual activity is associated with fantasies of oral, anal, and genital violation, mutilation, or annihilation. However, the notion that it is the woman who tears off the man's clothing, castrates and devours him, or bites off his penis is just as common and gives rise to even more acute anxiety.

These impressions no doubt explain why such terrifying castration anxiety develops in children who are not brought up repressively as regards sexual matters and who do not evolve clearly defined desires to kill the oedipal rival, for which they would have to fear retaliation. The fact remains that in boys castration anxiety takes the form of a fear of being castrated by the woman; this fear is more intense than the fear of rivals and is experienced regressively as a fear of being killed, sadistically abused, penetrated anally, disemboweled or devoured orally, poisoned, or abandoned, and thus left to die. Sometimes this regressive series is run through very quickly; the fear of having the genitals mutilated is followed by one or two or several of these steps from the anal and oral phases. The further back these regressive stages go, the easier it is to cope with them. For example, the fear of being devoured or poisoned by a witch can be warded off by projective identification. The fear of witches in itself functions as a kind of last refuge for the defenses against anxiety; in this form it is even possible to cope with castration anxiety without appreciable consequences for the psyche.

We cannot pinpoint any *single* event or psychic turning point at which the oedipal conflict of the Anyi "is resolved," nor can we designate any *single* typical outcome. It would be more accurate to say that, throughout life, conflicts arising out of the oedipal constellation can be revived with relative ease and then must be reworked according to the original pattern, and that several outcomes that parallel and supplement each other are the rule, both in dealing with objects and in molding the self.

In our Western culture, the introjection of the father's authority is the most important step to establishing the superego. With the Anyi, the traits of the oedipal rival and the demands made by the persons originally responsible for rearing the child, together with the aggressions directed against both, are partly internalized singly, but in part they remain outside or are at least accessible to projection. They are distributed among various organizations of the group, among traditions, customs, and rituals. A sexual prohibition is not generalized but—in keeping with its genesis—remains linked with the original incestuous object. The horror of incest, which derives psychologically from this period, must be integrated into the exogamy rules whose purpose is to guarantee the cohesion of the kin. Other important aspects of conflict resolution are left up to society. These are embodied in the structures we call clan conscience.

All object relations colored by the oedipal conflict can be regarded as comparatively unstable. The most long-lasting are those established to older sisters, who, although they functioned as mother substitutes, at least did not give rise to any greedy sexual impulses directed to their persons, and who in most cases played no role in anal training. These persons, whom the boy loves tenderly and who regularly turn up later as rivals to his wife, are the recipients of most of what we think of as love for the mother figure. In the sublimated guise of sibling loyalty, they give the boy something of the dual relationship of early childhood that was inevitably destroyed by (anal and) oedipal sexualization. For the Anyi these persons come closest to the concept "mother" because they differ so completely from the real mother in their instinctual meaning.

If all other later relations to female objects are unstable, we must consider that, because of the family organization and living habits of the Anyi, many toddlers have to change all their related objects quite frequently, and sometimes even have to exchange their own mothers temporarily or permanently for foster mothers. This naturally weakens the tendency to enter into lasting relationships. Then, too, many adults have few valences free for object relations because they are continually engaged in fantasies to help them achieve a "projective adjustment to reality." The women whom the young men finally select as sex objects or wives often enjoy the state of being in love as idealized in their fantasies and provide their men with phallic pleasure, both sexually and because they are their property. This is especially true when the women are beautiful or come from distinguished families. Faithfulness is a matter for the kin. The important thing is that the subject keep his ability to withdraw from the relationship entirely or in part, and he is enabled to do this by the pattern of abandonment that he himself has experienced. For social reasons, Anyi men must be capable of leaving their wives without suffering too greatly, and a relatively unstable object cathexis is an advantage in a system of polygyny and frequent divorce. For the psyche the defense mechanism of reorientation of cathexis is virtually indispensable; in the oedipal conflict the image of the sexually desired female is inextricably associated with the idea of being subjected to her, of being robbed or poisoned by her. The women demand too much of their men—they exploit them beyond endurance, they are mean to them, and in the end they leave them; this is a truth that is deeply rooted in the emotions. The last of these dangers can be obviated by taking a second wife, because women are considered to be so jealously inclined that they would refuse to give up a man to a rival.

As a rule the true mother or mothers (the corresponding generation of the maternal lineage) will later assume an important position among those prestigious persons from whom one can win approval and a certain self-esteem if one behaves properly. They become externalized components of the ego ideal, so to speak; if one enjoys their approval, one has a good clan conscience. Since they are the representatives of the powerful lineage that refuses to give up its sons and never abandons them entirely, later on—after oedipal fears have been overcome—they often win back a part of that basic trust that they may have given to their sons in early childhood.

Lasting introjects are formed out of important experiences with the preoedipal mother, out of her seduction and anal violation. These undergo modification during the oedipal conflict but are not given up. The powerful female phallus, which can at least be relied upon to violate even if it refuses to nourish as a breast, is symbolically invested with object character when it is projected to a chief who must be submitted to or a god who must be obeyed. If one traces the nucleus of these projections back to their point of origin, one can safely state that all men remain true to the mother as long as they live. There is an expression they use in Bébou when something unexpected happens: "Since I was brought into the world, nothing like that has happened to me!" An Anyi derives the normal course of life directly from the moment of birth, as if he realized intuitively that his mother is his fate.

We could hardly link the preoedipal relationship with the revived, compelling mother with the oedipal crisis if the image of the mother really remained where it originated. As it is, however, the mother image—in a number of forms—is attributed to paternal instances. During the course of its transformation in the oedipal phase, it changes so drastically that it can be recognized only with the help of analytical investigation.

The ideal oedipal father is the one who remains outside, who can either be isolated from or reexcluded from the family, the father who permits his son to enhance his self by partaking of the father's qualities and who then has no function as a rival placing obstacles in the way of the son's return to the lineage of the mother or the court of his uncle. This is the way it was in the myth of Osei Tutu, and this is the way the Anyi still prefer to resolve their oedipal conflict. They try to split up the father into his individual features and to master him in this fashion, so that they can evade rivalry with him yet at the same time develop into active aggressive males endowed with sexuality, prestige, and wealth. The rules governing inheritance through the uncle facilitate this. The uncle is not endowed with any of the qualities of the father; he is not a father substitute. As a result, the idealized father image can be retained unimpaired. In Osei Tutu's case, this was the third father figure, the shaman, the one who gave him the golden stool. The people of Bébou are not so fortunate. Most of them have been disappointed by their fathers, but they continue to dream of finding better ones.

Identification with an active phallic father is never entirely successful; Brou Koffi and Thomas Assoua, for example, have a constant wish to identify with their impressively masculine fathers. Since they cannot succeed directly, they try indirect methods (by performing certain rituals, for instance). One would think they would have to abandon these identifications or deny them, since they bring them into conflict with the other men of their environment and since their castration anxiety makes rivalry unbearable. Internal factors, however, seem to be stronger.

The active phallic traits of the father are assigned to an ideal figure evolved relatively late. Parallel to this, there are always identifications with a father who abandons his family, who deserts his love objects. In their behavior as lovers and fathers, adult Anyi repeat not only the unreliability of their own fathers, but also the internalized experience with the mother at the end of the first phase of childhood.

For some men (Anoh Michel, Adou Agnimou, Jean-Pierre), the "negative outcome" of the oedipal conflict, in which the boy renounces his own phallic role, offers himself as a love object to the father he fears, and thus adopts a "feminine" attitude, is just as important as the competition among a number of various father identifications. The process is the same as that observed in European patients with latent homosexual tendencies; the transference to the analyst and even the neurotic paralysis follow the same course. Actually, this fixation is incontrovertible proof that an oedipal triangulation does develop. The homosexual transference could be clearly identified and, after it had been interpreted, the symptoms of neurotic paralysis disappeared. From this point on, however, differences were noted. The paralysis seemed to have its roots not so much in the patient's inability to be unequivocally male as in the fact that fixation on a male love object made it impossible for him to oscillate back and forth in regard to his object relations and his own sex role. And finally, the subject's shift of passive libidinal, and frequently also masochistic, desires to the male was not accompanied, as it is in our culture, by simultaneous renunciation of his identification with the female; in fact the latter becomes even more clearly manifest—except that the love object in the identification is no longer the father, but rather the violating, phallic mother. The "negative outcome" was not primarily an attempt to escape the father's aggression or to unite aggression against the father with an affectionate relationship with him, but rather an attempt to achieve anal violation at the hands of the father instead of the mother.

At the conclusion of the oedipal conflict, the normal attitude toward the father or the male is characterized by rapidly alternating and mutually supplementary partial identifications. The boy's sexual identity remains undefined. Parallel to passive anal and active phallic instinctual impulses, there is a tendency for him to deny that he possesses a penis. The restless search for new identifications can be interpreted as an expression of the boy's penis envy. When Ahoussi concludes that people function best under constraint, he is referring to an inner need of the Anyi—the need to find a chief or master who enjoys prestige and power so that they can submit to him and introject his power, but who also has sufficient motherly qualities that they can rely upon his continuing to maintain the compulsion and not depriving them of the phallus. The harsher the god who accepts one's services, the better; for such gods intensify their servants' active potential and assuage their hunger for objects.

The outcome of the oedipal conflict fails to leave the Anyi boy with a clearly defined male sexual identity or with object constancy. Instead, it leaves him with a second important instinctual fixation, in which phallic-active desires are intensely mobilized and easily renounced, exchanged for anal desires or combined with them. In this respect the tension-laden relationship between the parents in a matrilineal society is reminiscent of those marriages in the Western culture area in which children are hampered in developing their sexual identity because neither parent is willing to grant the other the child's affection (126).

Aggression

Aggressive tensions and acute anxiety are typical of the culture-specific personality of the Anyi. Their aggressive fantasies are persecutory in nature; thus we have used the term "the normal paranoiac character" of the Anyi.

Aggressive strivings are more frequently projected to objects than discharged in an object-oriented way. Ambivalence tension is slight, which means that aggressions can be directed to the same object together with positive libidinal impulses. The defense mechanism involved is not repression, but rather projection, conjuration, denial, or reversal. The fear of reprisals follows the pattern of magic; it is not subject to the retaliation principle, "an eye for an eye," but usually to the law of "all or nothing," which expects total annihilation in response to a minor attack.

In the Western culture area, even aggressions originating in the oral phase and susceptible to paranoid projection regularly assume an anal-sadistic or phallic competitive quality in normal subjects as soon as they come to be discharged through the ego. Aggressions resulting from a later fixation and thus less liable to be projected exhibit the same characteristics but can usually be subdued by sufficiently strong defenses (repression) or by suppression. Once in the ego, aggressions are held back and focused on an enemy (even those originating in the oral phase) through the combined action of an ego function acquired during sphincter training and one stemming from the phallic component of ego formation. Separation from the object and retentive internalization go back to anal conflicts, while the ambivalence tension and object-focusing can be traced back most clearly to the oedipal conflict.

The aggressive fantasies of the Anyi sometimes reflect oral instinctual phases (hypochondria and the fear of being poisoned) and are sometimes anal-sadistic in content. Phallic competitive aggressions appear only in rudimentary form even in fantasies and dreams. The modality of aggressive instinctual impulses is primarily oral. Their strivings can be shifted easily and have no tendency to focus on a single object, on the self, or on an external figure. A buildup of aggressive cathexes is hardly feasible. An internalization of aggression is avoided; strivings remain versatile, are projected to the outside world, reabsorbed into the ego, shifted from one object to another, and find expression sometimes in the form of aggressive wishes or fantasies, sometimes as a fear of possible magic consequences or as an archaic sense of guilt and need for atonement. This oral quality of aggression can be traced back to specific aspects of ego formation and of object relations. Instinctual fixations on the dividing line between the oral and anal phases permit the subject to regress to an oral discharge of aggressions, which can be adjusted to comply with social norms and is accessible to manipulation by magic (thus harbors no real danger) even though the aim of the drive involved has become an anal-sadistic one. In this case the objects are interchangeable part objects. They are so closely related to the frustrating mother that it is no wonder that witches are nearly always sought among the matrilineal kin. By the same token, strangers—as members of an "outgroup"—are exempt from suspicion. But not even the second important instinctual fixation, on the dividing line between anal and phallic phases, enables the subject to focus aggressive impulses on a specific object or to project them once and for all to the external world. Inasmuch as the child is given no sphincter training but is forced to experience anal violation and utter submission, there can be no phase of defiance. In other words, object differentiation remains incomplete, and a categorical "no" on the part of the child, to express his opposition to the enemy, is out of the question. At least in Anyi males, phallic strivings are inconsistent and influenced by acute castration anxiety. Even by the end of the oedipal conflict, the ego has not acquired the ability to counter rivalry with aggression. The desire to eliminate the rival yields to the desire to submit or to externalize him by projection.

The tendency to come to grips with the cruel and hated object in the outside world is slight. Anxiety compels the ego to seek another means of release. It is not capable of building up a countercathexis, but—thanks to its flexibility—it can have recourse to omnipotence fantasies and thus quickly achieve a victory that in reality would demand lasting aggressive cathexis of the hated object and would entail a certain danger.

If a society is to function smoothly, aggressions must be handled in a way that will not harm its members, but that does not require either internalization or repression.

The Oedipal Conflict in Girls

The course of oedipal development in girls is considerably simpler, and the outcome is more clearly defined. They enter the phallic phase with just about the same preoedipal experiences as the boys, but they have a number of advantages.

The withdrawal from the compelling mother and the focusing of emotions on the male/father is not achieved completely. Like the boys, the girls are frightened by the oedipal father and thus turn away from him, not so much because they are in despair at not having a penis themselves as because he has disappointed them. The girls, too, cling to an idealized father image, but the image is rather vague. Later on, when they begin to lead normal sexual lives, they accept the male as sufficiently desirable in his capacities as the exponent of prestige and the provider of pleasure and wealth that they are willing to leave the world of the mothers and the women at least for the moment and to remain with their mates even though they may be disappointed in them. The men, to be sure, must constantly continue to demonstrate that they actually do embody the desired qualities, and they must supplement their personal worth with valuable presents to their wives or mistresses; otherwise they are deserted, no matter how many "fatherly" qualities they may possess. The women's wish (quite contrary to custom) to be the only wife or the first wife seems to be based less on a desire to usurp the position of the mother than on a determination to be less dependent on the man as a love object than they once were on the mother.

Anyi girls tend to direct violent reproaches and aggressions toward the mother as a rival. This hatred has two specific characteristics. In the first place, it contains preoedipal aspects in that it reflects the experience of being violated and abandoned. In the second place, in spite of the rivalry situation, fear of the mother or feelings of guilt engendered by aggression do not play a significant role. This can probably be explained by the fact that the girls—in contrast to the boys—in resorting to the preoedipal identification with the phallic mother (the aggressor), are able to identify permanently with the phallic character traits of the mother and with her corresponding role in the immediate and more extended family circle. Adult girls and women (unlike the men) can afford to become aggressive toward their own mothers or similar figures without experiencing great fear because they are able to return quickly and without serious effects to the equal footing established by identification. Thus it happens that the young women can repeatedly discharge their feelings of rivalry toward the oedipal mother and still defuse the conflict fairly soon.

Castration anxiety appears in this process only as a fear of being left alone and defenseless, or of being orally abused, devoured by a witch, sold, or poisoned. The loss of the penis does not seem to be blamed on the mother. This is not because the Anyi culture lacks the overvaluation of the male as compared to the female genitals, but because the girls have already received and introjected the symbolic substitute provided anally by the mother. Nevertheless a kind of castration experience persists, as can be deduced indirectly from the importance attached to the child; although in the beginning pregnancy gives rise to hypochondriacal oral anxieties, the child is regularly cathected as a "completion phallus" (112) that brings not only public prestige, a relevant part object of the girl's own and thus a defense against incompleteness and dependence, but also sensual gratification.

The value attached to the male penis is less than that attached to the child. The child can complete the mother's self; the penis cannot. Since, after all, only *one* partner in a heterosexual couple can possess the penis, the mother accepts her baby as a substitute and is independent of her husband for a time, "until the baby is able to walk," when she will have to turn to him once again.

We possess little information on genital sexuality. We can assume, however, that the girls' reorientation from the anal zone to the vagina would be easier to achieve than that of the boys to the penis. In any case, we have no reason whatsoever for assuming that the women are afraid of the men or their penises; the female phallus is the more dangerous one, and the male penis is only sporadically important.

At the resolution of the oedipal conflict, the girl (unlike the boy) is able to develop sexual identity—as the phallic female and mother—and this is doubtless why puberty is less problematic for her. Her anxieties can be mastered more easily, though they still contain preoedipal components. Her love objects, too, are inconstant; the male, in particular, receives very little of the transference of an idealized father figure. But the girl is better able to handle rivalry with other females.

The difference in outcome of the oedipal conflict in boys and girls, a difference that is even more sharply accentuated during puberty, affects both self and objects. The world of representations is composed of different elements for males and for females. On the other hand, the two

most important stages of instinctual fixation (on the dividing lines between the oral and anal and between the anal and phallic phases) are the
same for both. Our description of ego structures, which we have
characterized as flexible and elastic, need not take into account any
further significant differences. The female ego, however, has frequently
acquired greater relative autonomy (130, 131) than has the male ego.

The Ego's Defense Organization in Operation: Elisa

Typical childhood conflicts and a number of more or less autonomous
defense mechanisms are the prerequisites that permit an investigator to
describe a culture-specific system of defenses. Yet such a system cannot
be formulated in abstract terms; it constitutes a highly idiosyncratic
psychic structure, although certain typical features are found in all the
Anyi we met. To illustrate these, let us summarize the interplay of
defenses that emerged during the interviews with Elisa.

This young woman identifies with the independence of the whites,
with a phallic power implying activity and completion of self. She finds
herself incapable of maintaining this identification, however. The
group (her sister and the latter's son) must come to her aid. A brief
acting out in the identification with the group restores autonomy
sufficiently to permit Elisa to identify with a "giving mother." Her
earlier anxiety, warded off, gains entry into the ego but is immediately
projected outside as devouring greed. Elisa succeeds in renewing her
identification with the "new, good order." Phallic aggression is acted
out and takes on a sadistic nuance in the "raping" of the teacher. This
establishes the identification with the penis-stealing power of the anally violating mother. The rivalry aggression thus mobilized creates
anxiety, which this time is not experienced but leads to a deep regression of the ego (with linguistic disintegration), to fantasies, and to
passiveness. Regression proves its value as a flexible defense. The ego
emerges from it immediately, reinforced by a new identification with
the "good wife of the chief." But this elastic restitution does not suffice
to enable her to deal with the oedipal conflict with the mother, revived
by Elisa's situation in life (as the child of the mother's virtual husband).
The female shaman to whom Elisa turns (as the representative of the
group) structures the conflict even more sharply and offers a solution.
When this solution proves impracticable, the conflict is evaded by refuge
to passiveness, then immediately projected to the group. This projection is participative in character: the persons of the group do not
appear as persecutors, but they must act out the conflict with one
another instead of Elisa. When Elisa herself threatens to be drawn in
once more, she withdraws the cathexis and—following the pattern of

the mother who abandons her child—abandons her love objects. The conflict is mitigated. There is a heightening of Elisa's self-esteem. She is active again and begins to direct the course of events. Her conflict is acted out by another couple in the group. This aids projection. The conflict has now been rendered so harmless that Elisa is in a position to participate in a solution she has not had to work out for herself. When her analyst departs soon afterward, she finds it surprisingly easy to give her up by identifying with the mother who abandons her child.

The Topographical Point of View

The flexibility of the ego, which impresses us structurally as a rapid alternation of defense processes and which can best be described in genetic terms as an inclination to temporary regressions, has strange consequences when one views it topographically, separating the conscious, the preconscious, and the unconscious. Paradoxically, the unconscious seems to be closer to the ego than the preconscious. This impression was reinforced during our interviews with the Anyi, when subjects, quite consciously and in only slightly altered form, would relate in the form of fantasies experiences and recollections they had warded off just before. The inclination to symbiotic forms of relations and the participative and projective defense mechanisms open the way for unconscious desires to enter the conscious ego. The process is related to the regressive linking of the sleeping ego with the unconscious, which is familiar to all of us from our dreams and can be compared with the regressions of the creative artist in the service of his (waking) ego. But here the dream to be dreamed and the work of art to be created are life itself, with its anxiety-engendering and disillusioning human relationships.

The easily ascertained laws governing unconscious thought processes dominate the scene only in part; not even among the Anyi can fantasies replace real life, and, apart from acting out unconscious strivings, they think and behave extremely rationally, according to the laws of the secondary process.

Conspicuous as is its access to the unconscious, the ego is just as impressively strong in its defenses against preconscious impulses. The phenomenon is thoroughly familiar from analyses of European patients who, even under the influence of transference fantasies nourished from the deep unconscious, are unwilling or unable to give the analyst certain consciously accessible information concerning their persons or to express any emotions because pride, shame, or the dictates of courtesy forbid it and because the ego, particularly in a state of partial regression, is dependent upon the observance of certain consciously governed limitations. In similar fashion the Anyi rely upon their social roles and their rules of etiquette; they remain aloof, refuse to speak at all or to speak about certain things with certain persons, whether their wives or their analysts. These attitudes not only govern their approach to objects; they also serve as barriers against preconscious processes, especially against the acknowledgment and expression of emotions.

Ego Autonomy and Emotional Defenses, with Special Consideration of the Defenses against Anxiety

Since the absence of anal retentiveness and anal reaction formations obviates defiant regressions and protest behavior, what impresses the observer as defiance is in reality intended to be provocation: "Let me feel your aggression so that I can submit to it or perhaps even identify with your sadistic or phallic assault." But not even the phallic narcissistic independence of ideal masculinity can ever be sustained for very long, above all because it releases castration anxiety. Where there is no defiance and no phallic independence, the individual perceives his own dependence and weakness in feelings of shame.

Thus there is a kind of pride that gives the ego's autonomy a boost so that it can cope with this feeling of shame. When one actively renounces a thing that one passively would like to be given, the narcissistic mortification emanating from an awareness that one does not have it and is not going to get it is blocked, and the unbearable feeling of shame does not arise. Pride prevents neither identification with the group nor the secondary participative gratification of frustrated desires—quite the contrary! It is precisely persons from distinguished families who have strong identifications with traditions and ideals, and every Anyi—not just a chief—has it within his power to avoid feelings of shame by identificatory internalization of the demands of the roles assigned to him and by the observance of fixed ceremonial rituals. He has no need to "lose face" or to see his name "dragged through the mud." His pride keeps him from remembering that as a child he was exposed to scorn and mockery in the "second phase of life," at a period when—seen from without—he was utterly helpless and—seen from within—his still incompletely structured ego was being flooded with violent emotions. It is unthinkable for an Anyi to admit he is ashamed, and most of the time he probably manages to avoid perceiving shame.

There is an almost equally strong prohibition against expressing anxiety. Fear is not warded off for the sake of a social ideal, as it is among European men of certain groups (young athletes, for example, or officers in the military). Phobic anxiety does occur (Elisa, Jean-Pierre), and hardly any attempt is made to conceal or deny it. Most of the time, however, anxiety defenses function automatically, on the boundary of the ego. The case is similar with other emotions—joy, pain, grief. The only emotions permitted are a depressive feeling of skepticism, discouragement, and hopelessness, a deep-seated distrust toward one's fellows and toward the future, and the anxieties engendered by hypochondria.

As regards anxiety and these other emotions, one can assume that they—like shame—must have been acted upon by effective defenses during the period in which the abandoned child was a prey to a veritable flood of affects, simply in order to permit him to go on living. (It is quite likely that numerous small children are unable to cope with these painful affects and actually die of them.) This has characteristic consequences for the ego. First, emotional defenses do not follow the pattern of drive defenses; they are as rigid as the latter are elastic. Second, there are countless ways to drain affective arousal. Nevertheless, unconscious anxiety responds readily and invariably gives rise to strong repercussions so that, as in Elisa's case, the oscillating alternation of defenses seems to be regulated by frequent and effective anxiety signals. Only for a short time does she experience conscious anxiety, but like all Anyi she has to cope with it constantly and is accustomed to obeying her anxiety signals whenever her inordinately flexible and elastic ego is confronted with the dangers of her object world and the world of her drives. Because she fears her neighbor and herself, she is capable of surviving.

Diverted affects are easy to identify. "Nervousness" expresses itself in stiff and unnatural body postures, in ticlike movements and uncontrolled "skipping-over" behavior such as rocking, drumming, wringing the hands, cracking the knuckles, scratching, and spitting. Anxiety is reflected in an embarrassed smile or a clearing of the throat. Suzanne seems able to express her emotions most directly; her small son Syrien serves as her channel of expression. She herself is relieved and feels no compunction about letting him express what she feels. When anxiety threatens to invade the ego, regressions are mobilized to deflect the emotion involved. Since it is the verbal expression of emotions that is most strongly blocked, the faculty of speech not infrequently is suddenly and temporarily inhibited. This process serves to ward off castration anxiety when rivalry aggressions have been mobilized. But the same phenomenon, linguistic deterioration, can also be triggered by other emotions, even pleasurable ones. Anxiety must be denied even after it has passed; even the memory of it is unbearable. This is why the Anyi never permit themselves to show their relief after recovering from a serious illness; this would be tantamount to admitting in retrospect the seriousness of the danger and their fear of it.

The urgency of emotional defenses is responsible for a typical characteristic of many dreams; within the manifest dream they contain a wish fulfillment that has been divested of any negative emotions— disappointment, anxiety, and so on—by a process of splitting. Dreamwork permits an apparent fulfillment of the wish, provided the emotion is separated from it; the dreamer is consciously aware of the possibility of failure. The wish is sacrificed, so to speak, to ward off the emotion. (This appears to be in contrast to the maturity examination dreams described by Freud, in which the negative emotion is linked with success and the dreamwork retains the wish.) On the whole, the dreams of the Anyi are not essentially different from those of Europeans.

When the deflection of emotions and other defenses are no longer effective, and not even denial will help, there are other possibilities. One way out, surrender to the anxiety/pleasure of masochism, is surely instilled in the Anyi child by means of the daily enemas; Jean-Pierre and Adou Agnimou always found that masochistic fantasies relaxed them. It can happen that, in spite of regressions, acting out, fantasies, and recourse to alcohol, emotions may still be directed to a good external object. When the pain of separation threatens, emotional defenses collapse and the result is psychosomatic breakdown (Suzanne, Anoh Michel, Jean-Pierre). Or perhaps the subject's vague feelings of malaise and weakness in connection with one of the many ever-present ailments that plague him may suddenly become acute. The body breaks down rather than let the emotion take over—a frightening form of expression in persons who had previously almost never allowed themselves to give in to an emotion.

Body Ego and Hypochondria

These breakdowns are evidence that for the Anyi, just as for us, the evolution and cathexis of the body image must be regarded as one of the most important—perhaps as *the* most important—bases of ego formation. Before we go on to sum up the culture-specific mechanisms that preserve ego autonomy, which we term "group ego," it may be advisable to describe the development of the body ego and some typical autonomous ego functions. In other words, we shall investigate just what materials the fortress is made of and what equipment it has at its disposal; only then shall we turn to the question of just what relief it can expect to receive from the outside world. (Introjects, identifications, and their relics represent the defenders of our fortress; the defense mechanisms are their weapons.)

The later cathexis of the body has its roots in the first phase of childhood. Eicke-Spengler (96) has this to say concerning the childhood of

European patients suffering from hypochondriacal syndrome: "[They] showed a narcissistic hypercathexis of bodily functions. They were vain, reacted with anxiety to the slightest physical indisposition, and were ashamed of their imperfections since the beauty and the intactness of their bodies played a major role in their feeling of well-being and their self-confidence." In an environment in which the child is viewed as material property and his external beauty and perfection represent a definite value, this is no wonder—all the less so as beauty is the only quality in the second phase of childhood with which the child may, on occasion, be able to attract the love and attention of adults.

Among the vast majority of the Anyi the pleasure in good food and, above all, good drink has remained intact and finds expression in a highly sophisticated cuisine and in gourmet appreciation of its achievements. Modalities of rhythm and movement are later modified and distorted (in contrast to other African peoples). Anyi men are rather poor dancers; the women are better. Their dance posture, body bent forward, pelvis held stiffly toward the rear, and feet moving in short, tripping steps, goes back to the combined anal fear of and longing for the enema. Most striking is that the Anyi have only one dance step for men and women alike—namely the female step; it is as though the girls' superior body cathexis during the phallic phase had preserved in them something of the rhythm they had experienced while still being carried on their mothers' backs. Extremely important is skin contact, a physical sensation that leads to perception of the symbiotic security of the mother/infant dyad and later to the differentiation of the self from the mother and the external world. In spite of this, fondling is avoided, even during sexual intercourse. Even toddlers and children of school age try not to touch each other, and it is only in aggressive encounters that the child feels someone else's skin against his own. Anyi in a group photograph remind one of "distance-keeping" animals (seagulls). The photograph of the Assoua kin is similar to many a Victorian family portrait in which body contact of adults is enforced by space and channeled into ceremonial postures. The experience of being abandoned at the end of the second phase of childhood seems to have lasting consequences, as if the person were determined that it will never be permitted to happen again. The narcissistic cathexis of the skin persists, however, and the regular bathing of the child and the care of his smooth skin are among those rare attentions that the mother does not discontinue. Without exception, personal cleanliness becomes a source of well-being for the Anyi child, for he is able to associate positive memories with the knowledge that his body, at least, is well demarcated. This also obviates any necessity for commands to keep themselves clean; they acquire the habit "automatically." There are fenced-in washing areas behind every court. In regions without abundant water, so they say, the Anyi would die. The village of Yosso was founded when a hunter thrust a twig into the ground to mark off his bathing area; according to legend, the twig grew into a mighty tree, which still protects the village. Beautiful clothing, as a logical extension of the body surface, is accorded an importance that cannot be explained merely by its secondary phallic narcissistic cathexis as an expression of vanity and a status symbol. The constant airing and rewinding of the toga not only is an expression of exhibitionistic gratification, it also permits constant enjoyment of the cooling breeze and sensuous awareness of the body's contours.

The widespread hypochrondria, with its ever-present anxiety that there is too much in the intestines and too little coming out, or the other way around, can be traced back further than the period of anal training with enemas, though the latter does seem to be responsible for the typical content of hypochondriacal anxiety. During the anal phase, when the relationship with the mother is exceedingly inadequate, regression and narcissistic withdrawal take place. Anal experience modalities are replaced by oral ones. Under the influence of the infant's intensely narcissistic body cathexis, the "object and self representations which cannot be assimilated by the child's ego because they are too intermingled become manifest in the body ego as split-off components, together with their respective instinctual cathexis, particularly when there is a surplus of non-neutralized aggression" (96). If the situation is complicated by neurotic conflicts, sensations of personality disintegration and bodily hallucinations may develop instead of hysterical symptoms. Cathexis shifts from the body ego to its split-off components. It was interesting to observe how quickly and easily these symptoms—which in our culture are regarded as indications of a grave distortion of the ego—disappeared as soon as projection of the aggressively cathected part objects became possible. All that remained in the way of psychogenic somatic symptoms was the hypochondriac's anxious inclination to monitor his body signals and the addiction to the pleasure-bringing ritual of the enema, which had developed into a repetition compulsion. The desire for physical treatment, which in adult Anyi is most likely to be directed to uncanny persons (white people, strange medicine men, charlatans), can be traced back to the wish, "If you refuse to violate me, than at least let me drink at your breast, and take care of my body."

The image of this aristocratic, handsome, and proud people, with their stately gestures and the graceful folds of their togas, does not correspond to the development of their body ego. It is only their identification with their social roles, and with the phallic exhibitionistic elements the roles demand and permit, that gives shape to the body ego (and a boost of secondary autonomy to the ego structure). A few of the chiefs (in Alangouan, however, only Ahoussi de Bernard) and many women from distinguished families never lose their "bearing." All the other Anyi are inadequately identified with the phallic components of their roles and constantly suffer that loss of bearing that is so painful to the observer, relapsing into physical clumsiness and lethargy. The cathexis of the body ego is too weak to cope with the strains of daily work performance, let alone an assault by instinctual desires. When a young man is courting his girl friend, his magnificent bearing is certain to be marred by embarrassingly clumsy physical gaffes; and an elder, the picture of dignity as he sits on the high seat of the arbitrator and begins his speech, is bound to relapse into ludicrous stuttering from time to time, unless he employs a spokesman.

Autonomous Ego Functions

The study of cognitive functions and of autonomous ego apparatuses was not included in our investigation. Although the Anyi culture is unmistakably a "sedentary" one (80), the structures and dynamics of their cognitive processes seem to differ from our own. One reason may be the relatively late release of the tension inherent in instinctual urges, one of the prerequisites for the playful development of cognition. Once this point has been reached, however, magical thought processes can be better integrated into the Anyi intelligence than into the thinking of Europeans, thanks to the Anyi's already highly developed empirical-logical pragmatic system.

Particularly striking is the way the Anyi deal with time and space. At first, Europeans are bound to have the impression that the Anyi have no sense whatsoever of time. Just as a toddler has no definite schedules for nursing, eating, or emptying the bowels, just as the adult's daily routine is determined by the need to go to work only four days out of seven, and just as the tropical year fails to provide clear divisions among the four seasons, the Anyi need neither calendars nor clocks; they do not know how old they are, or the ages of their children; and they make use of only nine temporal adverbs, the seven days of the week and one each referring to pastness and futurity—and even these last two are "open"; they can refer to time long past or to an extremely remote future.

This imperfect ritualization of the passage of time and the resultant lack of perceptual tools capable of structuring the feeling for time differently (and, as we would insist, better) is wholly in keeping with an ego that is constantly forced to master the present within the framework of past conflicts and then resorts to depressive fantasies akin to daydreams in order to assure itself some modicum of gratification. To prevent such fantasies from leading to a delusional misinterpretation of the present and to make sure that they can pass the test of reality, it is best to relegate them to the future; but in that case their content must remain more or less vague. The same process can be observed in European utopians.

The shimmering bluish green wall of jungle perceived through a curtain of low-lying patches of fog can hardly provide the experiences needed for structuring the feeling for space. "Familiar" space, on the other hand, that is a room or a courtyard, is all the more sharply contoured, its boundaries all the more clearly defined. The street map of a village like Bébou resembles that of Manhattan. But despite the inexactness and vagueness of the Anyi's notions of more remote space, it is noteworthy that the ego's handling of objects positively demands the division of space into a narrowly defined, manageable area and an essentially impenetrable, indefinite one. Otherwise it would hardly be capable of sustaining the concept "out of sight, out of mind" that helps it to cope with separation anxiety and frustration and to ward off object-oriented aggression. "When you're here, I see you; when I can't see you, you're not here." When love or hate objects, living or dead, vanish into unstructured space, they can soon be forgotten as nonexistent, then recathected as spirits, enemies, or ideals, according to the requirements of fusion or the projective needs of ego economy.

The continuity of an activity or a conversation is often interrupted by a sudden overpowering weariness. It seems, at least, as if an Anyi cannot help stopping what he is doing, retreating into himself or into fantasies, or turning to some other activity because he is simply too tired or too bored or too offended to go on. Anyone watching the Anyi at work on their plantations is apt to conclude that they are either utterly exhausted or under the influence of drugs. And anyone demanding an intellectual effort of them, such as translating a song, for example, will soon succumb to despair unless he resigns himself to the fact that his informant must repeatedly go back to the beginning of each stanza because he is incapable of sustained concentration. With almost all of the 130 subjects tested, we found it impossible to carry out the usual inquiry after administering the Rorschach test because they were simply incapable of making a second effort. Violent quarrels usually subside after a few minutes and then flare up again after the participants have had a chance to rest. This tendency to tire so quickly bears only superficial resemblance to psycho-organic exhaustion. The ego loses—or rather deliberately forfeits—one aspect of its functioning in order to make room for others: for fantasies, projective manipulation of the partner, defense against various signals of displeasure. The pattern of an Anyi's performance recalls the "absentminded professor" of Western anecdotes. In the middle of a conversation, or in the middle of a meal, he may forget where he is and turn to the contemplation of matters that are of greater importance to him than what is going on around him. The group takes this peculiarity into account; established etiquette assigns the ego—in small portions—tasks that enable it to avoid too-intense concentration on external objects or on reality, in short, tasks that do not interrupt its narcissistic equilibrium for too long a time. What at first glance appears tồ us to be offended withdrawal and low stress tolerance proves upon closer study to be a personality trait that is by no means felt to be disturbing in the Anyi culture.

Mastery of the rules of etiquette ensures an adequate level of self-esteem, which is constantly being confirmed; it also aids the individual in concealing his inner life. For the ego, it fulfills the function of establishing, by verbal means, the proper distance between partners who are emotionally not quite certain just how they stand with one another. Because of this, it is an integral part of the group ego.

The Group Ego

We have established this concept as (1) a particular way of functioning that is valid for the entire ego, and (2) a series of particular ego functions that depend upon the participation of a group for their effectiveness and their retention. The group concerned must have a certain structure, and its members must react in a specific fashion. The characteristic overall functioning of the ego is merely the precondition; the particular ego functions are to be regarded as manifestations of the group ego.

Thus our interpretation is different from that advanced by Federn (102), who coined the term "group ego" in the first place on the assumption, based on culture genetic reconstruction, that members of earlier and more primitive cultures possessed no individual, differentiated ego, but rather an ego with an "extended ego boundary" that included the group as well. An ego of this type would be basically entirely different in structure from the ego of Western culture, and with the Anyi there was no valid justification for such an assumption.

The structure we call group ego can also be observed in Europeans. We need only think of a European scholar who returns home with a feeling of deep satisfaction after participating in a scientific discussion with colleagues in his own field, and to whom occasions for such discussions are essential to his feeling of well-being. We can state that his feeling of well-being stems from the gratification of aggressive and libidinal desires that can find their way into his ego only in "neutralized" form and only under these conditions. The prerequisite, that is, the way of functioning valid for the entire ego, is that the ego must have developed the ability to find gratification—deflected from its goal and subject to the secondary process—in the discussion, provided that (and this would be the manifestation of the group ego) there exists a group whose structure allows for scientific discussion and whose members possess egos with very similar abilities.

Thus the group ego is not an essentially different psychic structure, nor is it an added structure—as if each Anyi had his own, differentiated ego and a group ego in addition to it.

In psychoanalytic studies of African peoples, however, description of the group ego has proved to be a practical approach, either because the human environment is really more important to them than to us in enabling the ego to function with relative autonomy, or because their dependence upon the environment is more obvious to us than in the case of European subjects, whose dependence the analyst, after all, shares. The two explanations are not mutually exclusive.

Among the Dogon, an empathic understanding of their fellows and a readiness to enter into and withdraw from affective identificatory relationships without suffering emotional tension is a general quality of the ego, which we attribute to the vicissitudes of oral relationship modalities—to the maturation of oral ego qualities. On the basis of this general prerequisite, certain permanently established forms of identification may come into play, as a manifestation of the group ego, guaranteeing the ego its autonomy and, to some extent, also regulating association with the objects of the environment (80, 82, 85, 87).

In the Anyi, too, the general prerequisites for group ego functions originate in the oral phase of ego formation. We might mention that the group ego of the European scholar mentioned above is also able to function only by virtue of the ability to participate orally in a group that has cathected with libido something its members have in common. Though the group ego always presupposes oral relationship modalities, it is not restricted to these. As an aspect of ego structure that is set apart solely by its relations to the environment, it shares the development of the ego but can develop completely itself only if the child remains in an appropriately structured environment up to the preliminary resolution of the oedipal conflict, that is, up to the latency phase.

The general predisposition to enter into identificatory relationships is one of the preconditions of any group formation (107), but this does not adequately define the group ego—as becomes immediately apparent in a comparison of two group egos. The Dogon alternate between identificatory relationships such as those with an older and a younger brother, then exchange them for a quite differently structured identificatory equality with a member of the peer group. Their response to a compelling authority figure, in the so-called patron relationship, is passive receptive; they are unable to derive increased ego autonomy from such a figure and are more than likely to turn away from it, offended and frustrated. The Anyi identify with the phallic or the anal compelling qualities of their own traditional authority figures or of imported ones and thereby gain increased activity potential and, above all, an enhancement of ego autonomy. They find it well-nigh impossible to achieve a lasting identificatory relationship with companions who have the same status as they do; nor does their ego autonomy derive any direct benefit from their own position on the hierarchical scale of brothers. At most they find themselves able to submit passively to an older brother, as they would to a chief, or to manipulate a younger one sadistically—which does bring gratification but does not diminish dependence either on drives or on the external world.

We regard the general flexibility and elasticity of the Anyi ego as the most important internal precondition for the functioning of the group ego. The flexibility can be maintained because neither object constancy nor a rigid and lasting drive defense develops. The elasticity, reflected in the inclination and the ability to reestablish a disturbed state of equilibrium, is based primarily on the circumstance that object cathexes are easily abandoned for narcissistic ones and vice versa (recathexis [127]). This is possible as long as emotional defenses are strong enough to counteract paralyzing anxiety, shame, and depression.

The external precondition, the existence of a specifically structured group, develops gradually during childhood out of the transformation of the mother/child dyad and the complementary relationship of the baby to the admiring adults making up his social environment, and later during the process of integration into the spheres of social functioning. In keeping with the most important instinctual fixations at the dividing lines between the oral and anal and the anal and phallic phases, the activity of compelling and nourishing/protecting figures (the maternal lineage, the chiefs) as well as of phallic prestige figures in the human environment is necessary to the group ego. The manifestations of the Anyi group ego are traits originating in defensive processes as well as other directly acquired traits based on components of social roles. Both categories enrich the ego's store of secondary autonomous functions and, in case of need, are integrated into the organization of defenses.

In Elisa we saw the group ego in action on three occasions in connection with defense organization—first as a transitory identification (with her sister and her little nephew, who had cut his toe), second as a projection (during the visit to the shaman), and third as a participative projection, when the group takes over to work through her conflict. In all three phases it is clear that the defense can be successful only if the objects of the external world behave in accordance with the defensive needs of Elisa's ego.

Aggressive tendencies can be processed particularly well by the group, whose acting out of aggressions, in which the individual concerned participates, contributes to controlling instinctual impulses. The individual's conflict is first relieved of its aggressive components (in somewhat the same way as a virus may be weakened during passage through the body of another host), after which the aggression can either be cast off entirely or made available for other purposes. If the group reacted with counteraggression, remained indifferent, or otherwise responded inadequately, the group ego would forfeit its autonomy; the same would be true if the aggression were aimed directly at the object rather than being projected to it.

For the ego, ideal figures in the environment serve as mediators, from the village chief and Edjro, the God-appointed mediator, to Dibi, the shaman, and any other individual who may be called upon to act in that capacity. A mediator possesses (or, by means of projection, is invested with) both paternal and maternal qualities and can thus accommodate different libidinal desires. He is able to remain passive in aggressive conflicts, for it is not his quarrel. The individual who calls upon him for help runs no risk of either becoming entangled in a fight (reality) or being made to feel guilty (superego). When the individual no longer can do so, the mediator can still have it both ways.

Beginning with symbiotic empathic insight and the induction of emotions in other persons, a series of ego functions emerges, more sophisticated with each phase of development, that are capable of operating to maintain relative autonomy only when the environment reacts in the proper fashion. These are participation, participative projection, projective identification of oral dependent and oral aggressive tendencies, anal-passive identification with the aggressor, and identification with phallic attitudes and traits. Any impairment in the flexibility and elasticity of the ego puts the group ego out of action, as does a change in the environment.

It should be emphasized that the term "secondary autonomy" refers solely to the structure known as "ego" and not to the individual as a whole. The ego is continually subject to the influence of the id, the external world, and the superego, and indeed is dependent upon receiving "stimuli" from all three of these instances. Rapaport (130, 131) speaks of an indispensable "nutrition" needed by the ego to maintain its relative autonomy. A description of the group ego necessarily stresses the part played by the environment, which creates the impression of dependence (not of the ego, naturally, but of the self). The ego flexibility whose derivation we have outlined above is essential if the individual is to adapt himself quickly to the various methods of dealing with various persons and groups. It is quite irrelevant whether one speaks of "regressions in the service of the group ego" or prefers to stress the defense against cathexis and the process of recathexis of previously important representations of the object world as the individual's own achievement. The second version has the advantage that it helps to explain why some group ego functions may occasionally be interrupted or replaced by others without even any temporary sign of overall regression.

An extremely important ego function is identification with the social role. In the Western culture area we are accustomed to assigning this to the ego-identity, or possibly to the ego ideal and ideal of self. It is questionable whether this is always accurate. For these instances are fairly stable structures, and even among normal Europeans, people who have found their identity and acquired inner maturity, ego functions are often largely dependent upon the social role assigned at any given moment. This is very striking among the Anyi. Brou Koffi can feel like a chief one minute and be functioning perfectly, only to suffer a psychological breakdown the next minute because he has to relinquish the role temporarily; he regains his identity and efficiency as soon as he can act the role of chief again. This fluctuation has nothing to do with active or passive behavior. Anoh Michel, Jean-Pierre, and even Suzanne demonstrate undisturbed ego functioning in roles requiring passive behavior, only to go completely off the rails the moment they no longer feel themselves identical with their roles, even when they become active. The more intensive the demand is for behavior commensurate with the role, the better the ego functions.

In summary, we might say that the ego of the Anyi functions as a group ego mainly when it utilizes participative projection and projective identification for purposes of defense, when it has its conflicts acted out "in the outside world" by the group, and when it absorbs, autoplastically and as a secondary autonomous function, the identificatory attitudes associated with the social role assigned.

It may be the large share of the group in important ego functions that enables the Anyi ego to function normally despite the fact that it is equipped with mechanisms that we find almost exclusively in subjects suffering from serious psychological disorders. On the other hand, certain other mechanisms that are standard equipment for the normal European ego would make it extremely difficult for the latter to get along with the human environment of the Anyi. An Anyi who behaved in European society the same way as he behaves in his own would be just as conspicuous and abnormal as a European in Anyi society.

Let us look at the patients in the Bingerville Insane Asylum[2] as a paradigmatic illustration of a borderline phenomenon of group ego. These patients are given maximum protection against projectively externalized objects and, as mentally disturbed persons, have maximal projectivity to the persons of their lineages, without being able to correct these projections through day-to-day contact. In other words, they know exactly where the aggression they are not permitted to experience comes from and can participate in it just as much or just as little as they need to. Their group ego is eminently successful in providing defenses against aggression.

One could think of numerous potential disruptions in this state of affairs. If the walls of the asylum were to vanish, the patients would be at the mercy of imaginary pursuers, just as normal Anyi would be at the mercy of their aggressive conflicts if they no longer had etiquette to fall back on, palm wine to drink, or the option of simply going away. A projection of aggression to persons outside the kin could not follow so easily the pattern of their inadequate demarcation from the symbiotic object. On the other hand, if we were to assume that it is not maternal relatives that have become pursuers, but strangers, participation in the externalized conflict would be made much more difficult. An identificatory bridging of the split, that is, identification with projectively cathected object representations, is a feat that even normal Anyi can manage in the long run only within the matrilineal lineage (or possibly within some other social system at family level).

The Clan Conscience

Not only the Anyi's ego, but also his superego, is dependent upon a human environment that is culture-specific in structure and populated by specific figures; it functions, in a sense, as a "clan conscience."[3] The explanation for this phenomenon given by many Anyi and also accepted by European psychologists (56) is only superficially simple, namely, that the clan, the village, or even one's own ancestors demand obedience to the rules of behavior they have established. This demand is internalized in the superego. Any violation is punished in the form of guilt feelings or anxiety. Submission results in a good clan conscience.

This explanation is incorrect. For modern Anyi it is more like a rationalization. Their conscience—and even the unconscious component of their superego—rarely contains the injunction that they must be loyal to the spirits of their ancestors; if such an injunction exists at all, it is one that can be disobeyed with impunity. Rules established by the environment must be obeyed, primarily because of urgent ego needs; for the psyche, however, violation results not in guilt feelings, but rather in shame and in a fear of external consequences.

Reconstruction of the oedipal conflict has shown that introjection of the authority of the father, that is, internalization of the superego demands of the frustrating parent of the same sex, cannot—for the Anyi—be the decisive step in the construction of a relatively autonomous inner authority that Freud assumed it to be for Europeans. On the other hand, observations of normal European children have revealed that, in their case as well, formation of the superego proceeds step by step over a fairly long period, and that inner authority only gradually becomes independent of the authority of parent figures and parent substitutes. In many European patients it can be demonstrated that introjects that are cathected with aggressions as a result of preoedipal conflicts remain stable throughout life, and that they cannot be combined to form a coherent instance, or superego, or be integrated into the ego; these introjects are what we term preautonomous superego nuclei.

In the Anyi we can assume that the formation of the superego is a dynamic process, as it is in Europeans. A conflict with love objects develops—as a result of frustration, for example—and these objects are cathected with aggressions. Thus the ego is forced to choose between object-oriented and narcissistic interests. The latter are the winners. To protect itself from the consequences of aggression (fear of being abandoned, castration anxiety), the ego gives up the external objects and replaces them with introjects. Object loss is avoided at the cost of internalizing the conflict. The disappointing external object has been replaced by a superego nucleus cathected with aggression.

This process begins at an early age, is most intense during weaning at the end of the first phase of childhood, and is apparently repeated again and again with appropriately cathected objects, particularly during transition from the anal to the phallic phase of drive development. It is typical that there is never a second massive concentration of internalization, which would serve to combine the individual introjects containing the commands and prohibitions acquired through experience into a uniformly organized instance.

Throughout an individual's life, part introjects, cathected with intense aggression, continue to play a role more or less reflecting the phases in which they originated. If the ego experiences a desire that runs counter to their commands, the resultant anxiety has the same destructive oral, cruel anal-sadistic, or phallic castrating nuance as during the original phase. It is the function of the group to create opportunities for the individual to reexternalize the introjects if possible and to integrate the contradictory commands of the preoedipal objects into a coherent system of rules that he can rely on. Clan conscience, then, is the term we have applied to superego functions of the individual in which the participation of the group is essential. Among the Anyi those particular components of the clan conscience that help to relieve the ego of unbearable anxieties and guilt feelings or their archaic precursors are more important than those that establish new restrictions for it.

The objection that in reality this is a description of ego functions is easy to counter. And, admittedly, clan conscience is more difficult to distinguish from the ego than is the European superego. But, just as in our case, the difference becomes clear in the orientation to instinctual desires. The Anyi ego distinguishes (consciously and unconsciously) between "I'd like to" and "I ought to." The need for punishment and parapraxia intended as self-punishment are extremely common. Anyi folk wisdom even recognizes a psychological symptom that indicates that an inner conflict (between superego demands and libidinal or aggressive instinctual desires) is becoming unbearable, and the individual must do something to get rid of his feeling of guilt—namely the appearance of anxiety and persecution dreams. The pursuers are usually spirits, pygmies, strange men coming from the bush, or the black bush-cow.

Early formation of superego nuclei has still another consequence, one that is responsible for the inability to bear guilt-anxiety and the need to externalize it. The introjects are not corrected to bring them into line with reality but retain the character of overidealized, omnipotent figures. Their positive, benevolent aspects cannot be linked with their punishing or destructive ones because there is no alternation between love and frustration for educational purposes. The gratifying ideal figures are incorporated into the grandiose self and the imagined ideal of self.

The frustrating parent imagoes inspire anxiety and form the superego nuclei. Thus the superego does not have two aspects—a commanding, forbidding one and a rewarding one. To put it another way, the Anyi sometimes suffer unbearable qualms of conscience, but they never have a clear conscience. Instead, they have fantasies of being happy; when these are insufficient, social prestige, wealth, and power are supposed to provide the necessary compensation.

The individual figures and groups the clan conscience needs are appropriate figures of the environment, who are psychologically more manageable than the idealized parent imagoes. These are the chiefs, female shamans, and healers, and—where these happen to be lacking—messianic figures and alien priests and healers, mediators, arbitrators, and judges, and finally the maternal lineage with its mothers and older sisters, who even today watch over the good behavior of each individual and who impose attainable external laws on the ego when it threatens to succumb to annihilating internalized aggressions. When harmony with exaggerated inner demands cannot be achieved, observance of the rules of etiquette, the legal system, and traditional clan and tribal laws can provide a satisfactory feeling of self-esteem. Existing clan or personal family taboos have been taken over by the legal system, which in turn passes them back to the individual, who lacks a self-contained. superego system. Brou Koffi, for instance, makes use of an ancient taboo to suppress his tendency to drink too much, and old Kablan, in Yosso, relies on a promise he once made to the previous village chief.

The clan conscience of the Anyi is largely lacking in the basic emotional ties to the society that the Dogon, for example, have. When a Dogon fails to follow his clan conscience, the elders, whom he reveres and upon whom he feels psychologically dependent, are sad. And this must be avoided at all costs. A little of this delicate external regulation of conscience can be found in the relationship between many adult Anyi and their mothers or older sisters.

To compensate for this lack, the Anyi—in addition to what we have just described as clan conscience—have a number of quite uniform inner rules that they have acquired through identification. As a result, their superego can be divided into one compartment that closely resembles the European superego and one that—as the clan conscience— requires a higher degree of participation by the social environment. There is one closed system of internalized rules that deals primarily with curbing externally directed brutal aggression, specifically with prohibitions against directing uninhibited aggression toward older persons. The content of these rules need not surprise us. Every form of superego development, ours included, has precisely that *content* suggested or demanded by the society involved. As regards the Anyi, we can assume that identifications with the superego of their ideals, especially in the later phases of childhood and during puberty, all reinforce the realization that these ideal figures are constantly trying to curb the direct expression of aggression. This is a point at which the need of the group coincides with that of the ego. Perhaps the feeling of identity—"an Anyi doesn't do that sort of thing; an Anyi has too much dignity to get mixed up in a fight; an Anyi is too delicate and fine to behave brutally, as the Djoula do"—gradually has an integrating effect on this identification-acquired attitude, even though no uniformly integrating overall internalization of a system of rules was possible in the oedipal conflict. That older boys and girls sometimes fight with one another to relieve their aggressive tensions, but that adult men and women are never brutal, even when intoxicated, tends to substantiate this.

Many sayings and proverbs contain rules and maxims that are immediately recognizable as superego components. But the way they are applied in a vast variety of situations is always regulated by ego activity: "When my own opinion is insufficient, I appeal to the general consensus." It is conceivable that the repeated checks and curbs experienced in this way may lead to a secondary identification with the values of society and to further development of the equipment and organization of the superego.

Feeling of Identity and the Ideal Self

There is no need for us to deal in detail with the feeling of identity. With the Anyi, as with us, it comes right after physical sensations contributing to the body image as the most important stabilizer of self-esteem.

Psychological identity is always based on experiences in the real world. Only through the endopsychic process of selection and integration are these experiences molded into a form that can be made part of the self (99) and, from that point on, can produce a feeling of identity.

The typical formulation of Anyi identity, its seemingly negative content, sometimes makes it difficult for us to understand just why such "unfavorable" experiences, why precisely this aspect of a social role, or why that particular value system should confer self-esteem. Seemingly paradoxical identity components of this type are common; it is important to an Anyi not that he has received his name from his father, but that he can drop this name almost at will. It is not the fact that he is physically healthy and fit that lends strength, but rather the knowledge that the Anyi, as a people, would be doomed if they worked as hard as the Djoula. The awareness that one is an Anyi, that one belongs to this and to no other people, is not infrequently a component of the feeling of identity; more widespread is the feeling of belonging nowhere at all—as Brou Koffi put it, "I don't belong anywhere; I myself am a stranger here [in my family, in my village]." In exact compliance with custom, Brou Koffi is the heir and successor of his maternal uncle.

These experience modalities, which in most cases would be anything but conducive to bolstering the individual's feelings of identity and self-esteem in our world, make narcissistic cathexis easier in the world of the Anyi. (The evolving of a feeling of identity is invariably a matter of narcissistic cathexis, regardless of whether the feeling is based on real experience or on experience distorted by fantasies of megalomania or micromania.) However, the identity feelings of the Anyi, as described above, correspond in part to the self-perception of the abilities of the ego—namely, the abilities to withdraw from a relationship at any time, to get along without the brutal acting out of aggressions, and never, not even within one's own family, to feel bound by emotional ties. Neurotic disturbances of the feeling of identity appear only when the outcome of inner conflicts is contrary to culture-specific realities.

The difference between the Anyi and the European can be observed in its pure form, so to speak, in connection with the content of the ideal self. Whereas our ideal is to achieve, theirs is to enjoy a fortunate lot in life. Instead of striving to become something, their ideal is to be something. For the Anyi, passiveness, which in our culture has predominantly negative connotations, is in itself neither good nor bad—like activeness. The ideal self evolves without any anal focusing of aggression, without urethral ambition, and without phallic oedipal focusing of the libido on specific objects. An ideal self of this description can seem worthy of emulation to us only if we happen to find the goals of our own social structure questionable. Since their social structure bears no resemblance to ours, those components of the Anyi self that are derived most directly from the environment cannot be the same as ours.

9 Ethnopsychoanalysis: The Study of Man within the Framework of His Society

Ethnopsychoanalysis is the product of a confrontation between psychoanalysis and the social sciences. The Anyi, as the subject of our report, are the scene of the confrontation; the anthropological description of their world will illustrate ethnopsychoanalytic views and investigating procedures.[1] While Western civilization is inexorably undermining, transforming, or destroying most other cultures, our own feeling of discontent with our culture is becoming more and more acute. We are constantly wondering whether there may not be, somewhere in the world, better sociopsychological solutions than we have been able to find—a way of bringing up children to be freer, happier persons who have no need to discharge their aggressions in murderous, suicidal wars, who do not sacrifice their children, do not hate their parents, and do not feel compelled to stultify their love life. We are constantly searching for social institutions that place less restraint on the individual and are more in keeping with nature than ours are. Indeed, a great deal would be achieved if we could learn to understand alien peoples better and if we could manage to prevent the dangerous secondary effects of the cultural change brought about by the Europeanization of peoples in Africa and elsewhere.

In Bébou they have a saying, "It's not the hunter who eats the meat." In other words, the hunter hunts at the behest of the chief or the clan and must distribute his booty in accordance with his social commitments. This saying expresses neither galling envy nor hopeless resignation. In fact, it is used when one is relieved to be rid of obligations, when one is well out of it. As ethnopsychoanalysts we present our booty—our methods and our results—for inspection; we do not eat it ourselves. It is not our place to decide whether it is fit for consumption or whether it is nourishing enough to satisfy the consumer's hunger.

At the present stage, the answers the ethnopsychoanalyst can find are still assumptions and hypotheses. This lies in the nature of the method, not in its relative newness. Each new finding confirms, refutes, or modifies one or more earlier ones, until the network of hypotheses gradually coalesces into the core of a theory.[2] Very few assumptions can be verified statistically. When we state that male Anyi, irrespective of their social position, go through a fairly long period during adolescence when they are utterly incapable of working, this can be verified with the help of sociostatistical methods. The characteristic psychic development to which we attribute this phenomenon is not susceptible to substantiation by statistics.

The method we use is similar to psychoanalysis—and to all other branches of science that, because their ultimate goal is objective accuracy, must accept the fundamental incompleteness of their explanations and the need for subsequent correction. In the psychoanalytic method, the entire psychic structure of the analyst is involved initially. With the help of empathy and identification, understanding is achieved. This necessarily subjective process is accompanied, and ultimately replaced, by additional cognitive processes. With the aid of metapsychological concepts and abstractions, the analyst seeks to come closer to objective explanation. In exactly the same way, ethnopsychoanalysis aims not merely at direct understanding; its purpose is to find explanations (98, 113).

The Anyi, equipped with the traditional mentality of an elite class of warrior marauders and hunters, make their living today by "industrial" agricultural production. The traditions and dreams of their splendid past impair their economic efficiency. This is a statement based on understanding and can be neither proved nor refuted. Our own explanation requires further evidence. Such evidence, in brief, is the following. In reality, probably very few Anyi dream of the mythical past of their people, even though their feeling of national identity is linked with these traditions. Nevertheless, the organization of their social world, which affects psychological development, embodies factors that make it constantly and vitally necessary for them to hope for a happy coincidence, to act out their power aggressively (in reality or in fantasies), and to enjoy prestige, both their own and that of their families. These experience modalities shape the social and economic reality of the planters in such a way that they tend to treat foreign workers like captured slaves, their coffee harvest like the spoils of war, and money like a title of nobility or like a snail that they may pick up in the jungle and then toss aside.

Any attempt at psychoanalytic sociopsychology encounters two obstacles: first, the difference between the approaches to research in psychoanalysis and in the social sciences, and, second, the very real limits of the researcher's ability to view his own society and its institutions dispassionately—to appraise social reality with the necessary objectivity. Ethnopsychoanalysis has developed a methodological procedure to deal with each of these problems.

The first can be solved through bringing closer together the two branches of science, which overlap only in part. Not only do psychoanalysis and the social sciences make use of different methods, their interests are also differently focused (115). By using intensive rather than extensive methods and by studying individuals within the framework of their cultures, it is possible to achieve at least some overlap; "Psychoanalytical sociopsychology ought to be clinically differentiated individual psychology. This does not mean, however, that metapsychological categories and clinical techniques can be applied directly to socio-historical contexts" (145).

Since social factors have no causal relationship with psychological factors, their influence cannot be measured directly. Nevertheless, social processes do have a selective effect. At every stage they influence both psychological development and the selection of specific tendencies from among various possible ones (115). A description of external events during childhood does not suffice to predict later development, since the latter is determined by internal, in part unconscious experience. Only a psychoanalytic reconstruction of the combined effects of individual and social factors can lead to accurate interpretation of the former by reference to the latter.

The second obstacle sociopsychological investigation inevitably meets is our inability to view our own social reality objectively and accurately. Ethnopsychoanalysis copes with this obstacle by stepping back and looking at its subject from a distance. It makes a virtue out of necessity by viewing the differences among peoples as an experiment whose conditions have already been set by nature. The social structure of the Anyi seems more transparent to us than our own because it is smaller and perhaps less complex, and because we are in a position to observe it from outside, so to speak. But the method of studying an alien people in order to understand our own problems better has still more fundamental justification.

The newborn child is a being that is extremely malleable and not yet fixed in a specific environment. Specialization is achieved only during a long period of childhood spent in interaction with the environment (socialization). The differences between persons belonging to various groups (classes, tribes, or peoples) are so great that they can be equated with the differences between zoological species—so great, in fact, that humankind can be divided into numerous pseudospecies (101). The distance between us and the Anyi is sufficiently great that we are able to perceive the mote in their eye when we no longer notice the beam in our own.

Naturally it would be incorrect to conclude that all peoples who are different from us are similar to each other and must thus necessarily be primitive. This error is likely to occur when we approach alien peoples from the viewpoint of our own emotional needs and our acquired thought patterns. When we look at the faces of our fellow men through the astigmatic curvature of the cornea we have evolved, they all seem to be distorted in the same fashion. To see more clearly what they really look like, we need a corrective lens.

Brou Koffi, the village chief of M'Basso, who has been spending an hour each day with Morgenthaler for some weeks now, thinks he finally understands just what the white doctor is up to—"I understand. You want to learn more; that's why you came here. When you return, you will know more than the others, and this will give you an advantage over them. That's the way it is with us, too." Brou Koffi's reasoning stems from a need to identify. He believes he has discovered the emotional motivation of the whites. If the doctor indeed intended to use his greater knowledge to earn money and thus to enhance his social prestige, then Brou Koffi would have understood him correctly. But if Brou Koffi had perfectly comprehended the motivation underlying our research work, a motivation stemming from the ideal self, he would have said instead: "I understand. Research and knowledge are the same thing for you as an unusually beautiful embroidered toga is for us. It's not that it keeps us warmer than any other toga would. We show it to everyone. It is a matter of indifference to us whether or not we are envied for it. For the wearing of such a toga is so important to our self-esteem that we would be willing to undertake an arduous and expensive journey to obtain one."

Brou Koffi's subjective reality differs from ours because his social environment differs. We are inclined to accept the idea that the reality principle never becomes exclusively effective; magical thinking plays an accompanying and supplementary role. A second—and different—counterpart to logical-empirical reasoning in accordance with the reality principle is the manner of perceiving the social reality based on the attitudes, stereotypes, and value criteria of the society concerned (117). This social aspect of reality is dependent to a high degree on the social structure involved. That the ability to perceive social conditions accurately is so limited, that the gap between subjective and objective reality is so great in this sector can be explained most readily by the realization that the individual's relationship to the human environment has its origins in his emotional needs and is governed by them throughout his life.

Through experiencing gratification and frustration, every child learns not only how his material external world is organized, but also which aspects of his human environment are regarded as reality and which are the prevailing values whose acceptance and observance will be prudent and will guarantee satisfactory adjustment. There will be time later on to test, and perhaps to discard, the assumption that things are the way adults want them to be or believe they are. But there are serious obstacles to this process. If the adult is to perceive his environment more independently, he must necessarily question important components of his own self based on internalization of the attitudes and values of his environment (the "superego represented by the parents," for example) and give up gratifying identificational relations, while at the same time retaining sufficient ego autonomy to enable him to come to terms with the altered external social world. We demand of scientific thinking that it achieve an objective understanding of reality in this respect as well.

One cannot even venture a guess; one can only give expression to a feeling that our Western culture has not succeeded so far in moving closer to such a realization of self. On the contrary, it seems that the expansion of the culture area, the changes in the methods of production, the multiplicity and complexity of social relations, and the accelerated shift in values and effective institutions have tended to restrict our ability to comprehend and interpret the human environment despite the proliferation of sources of information. In contrast, we find the psychosocial interrelationships of the Anyi to be more transparent and their social structure better adapted to the individual than our own. We had come to the same conclusions in our studies of the Dogon. We have emphasized that the viewpoint from which we examine an alien people is bound to lead to these conclusions, in spite of and because of the fact that our understanding of our own society is so imperfect. There is justification for asking—though the question is impossible to answer—whether the Anyi may not be less alienated than we are. We can, in any case, rejoice in the transparency of psychosocial inter-relationships in their world.

The political structure of the Anyi is organized in accordance with two principles. The decentralized, stable order of the matrilineal lineage contrasts with the centralized chiefship, which is subject to change. The integrative forces of the matrilineal lineage are balanced by the individual-centered and hierarchical paternal power.

Each individual must establish a secure place for himself in the structure of the people or tribe. Only on the basis of this fundamental dependence can he move freely through all the social relationships that confront him, and only on this basis can he rely on the functioning of the group ego and the clan conscience. Since the lineage never entirely relinquishes any of its members, this need is satisfied as long as the lineage order remains stable. At the same time, there is a need for hierarchical authorities possessing power and prestige and exerting compulsion—the chiefs, arbitrators, and priest figures. Their functions enable the individual to develop an outward-directed and sometimes aggressive activity. From the psychological standpoint, these authority figures unite paternal and maternal traits in one person. The individual is able to identify with them and to participate in their aggressive and phallic qualities. Experienced as sexually neutral, they fulfill the needs of both sexes; their role can also be assumed by women (the female sha-mans). They function not continuously, but intermittently; one turns to them in case of need. When the political order disintegrates, when there are no more chiefs, social life deteriorates. Society tries to find a sub-stitute or to invest new figures with their qualities (messianic move-ments).

This tension-laden balance in the political structure has its counter-part in many other social institutions and customs, above all in the matrilineal family structure out of which, historically, the political structure developed. A matrilineal family is never simply a mirror image of the patrilineal one. The maternal lineage, to which the chil-dren belong, is not merely a counterpart of the paternal lineage. The Anyi family system consists, rather, of a multitude of spheres of social functioning that overlap, compete, and supplement one another. These spheres—sometimes singly, sometimes in combination, and sometimes all together—correspond to what we term family. One can say that this system distributes, regulates in a number of ways, and defuses the conflicting interests of the lineages.

This is the social environment in which the Anyi child is reared, and the society of the adults is correspondingly structured. The son, who inherits not from his father but from the brother of his mother, and who thus moves from one court to another and from one village to another, at the same times moves from one pole to another within the social order. His human environment changes, but his affiliation with the lineage remains constant; as a result, he is reintegrated into a hierarchical system. After marriage, the wife can move in with her husband, the husband with his wife, or they can live in separate households (duolocality). Polygyny and monogamy are practiced alternatively, and divorce is common. This by no means reflects an absolute lack of rules. The differentiation of the bipolar order offers a number of possible courses of action; their practice, however (like the system of inheritance), presupposes a psychological aptitude in the individuals concerned. The Anyi of Bébou possess this aptitude; in fact, it is difficult to imagine that they could live as satisfactorily as they do if their possibilities were more limited.

During his first years of life, the child grows up in a so-called matrifocal family, that is, in a nuclear group whose central figure, emotionally and socially, is the mother, while the father remains in the background or does not appear at all. Matrifocal family groupings of this kind are also found in our social structure as isolated cells, and they are common among the patrilineal polygynous extended families found in other West African societies. They are not specific either to the Anyi or to matrilineal organization as such. As far as psychological development and personality formation are concerned, the "absent or weak father," though regularly occurring and important, is not the only consequence of the matrilineal order. The specific course of the "second phase of childhood" (from weaning during the second year to the latency period)—the violating, anally stimulating, and emotionally frustrating role of the mother, which is typical of the Anyi but by no means necessary in a matrilineal system—is of equal importance. Taken together, these two factors make the development to manhood far more difficult among the Anyi than is the development to womanhood. One might say that the psychological development of male children is inhibited and channeled to fit the needs of the social order.

Among the external events affecting the child the relatively early weaning following an intensely gratifying (though unilaterally manipulatory) nursing period and the "anally" colored possessiveness of the mothers (as representatives of the lineage) toward their children are equally decisive for later social relationships.

The personality of the Anyi, female as well as male, is marked by characteristics that we describe as flexibility and elasticity of the ego. With an admirable talent for accommodation, the result of oscillating and alternating adaptational devices, they manage to find their way successfully among the various spheres of social functioning. They shift rapidly from one social role to another yet are dependent upon their environment for the assignment of these roles. They are not very successful in adjusting to changes in social and economic conditions; yet they manage to cope with them by subjecting them to their own mercurial temperaments, now submitting, now withdrawing. Above all, from early childhood on they have learned to give up and to exchange both love and social relationships. Their social order forces them to do so; their personality makes it possible. In psychological terms, the constancy and stability of their character—the homeostatic ability of their personality—are due above all to the fact that narcissistic cathexis easily compensates for a loss in the realm of object-related cathexis. Their flexibility may be described as an avoidance of object constancy and of a stable system of defense against instinctual demands.

The matrilineal family, the resultant organization of the state, and the social order represent the external framework, a framework rich in conflicts and tensions. The modal psychology specific to their culture guarantees not only their idiosyncratic individuality, but also an impressive degree of flexibility in their social adjustment. Despite tremendous historical and economic changes, the forces of cultural change have not yet resulted in a fundamental disruption of the social order or, with it, in the creation of a different external framework. There are sporadic signs of an active rejection of Europeanization (as in the new emphasis on the traditional laws of inheritance). Far more numerous, however, are instances of the syncretic integration of Western customs and institutions. The emotional forces effecting this process can be studied in countless individual features of Anyi life. The final outcome is still uncertain. We have no way of predicting when or how a restructuring of their society and its representatives may come about.

The most decisive outside influence, the introduction of the use and exchange of money and of an "industrial" agricultural production system has led to an odd form of economic syncretism. Except for a few rudimentary beginnings, there has been no development of a capitalist class society.[3] Although the Anyi (almost all of them during the past twenty years) have become potential large-scale producers, retaining ownership of the means of production, and although they have a horde of foreign laborers (so far virtually unpropertied) at their disposal, in the long run the surplus value produced does not accrue to the propertied class.

In the heyday of their power, based economically on predatory wars, i.e., on the capturing and selling of slaves, the Akan states of the eighteenth and nineteenth centuries did not possess a genuine feudal structure. In other words, though slaves might be captured, sold, or killed, the product of their labor did not accrue to their owners. A number of social institutions acted as safeguards against the formation of classes. In addition to fulfilling its normal function of ensuring a minimum level of subsistence by organizing hunting, food-gathering, and rudimentary agricultural activities, the "government"—based on the principle of an aristocratic hierarchy—was eager to acquire wealth and power through marauding raids and wars. But it was the custom to incorporate the captured slaves into the victorious ruler's kin by social integration. This increased the size of the clan and enhanced its power by increasing its ownership of persons; but the fruits of this slave labor accrued to the clan only after the slaves had been made an integral part of it, with all the rights and reciprocal obligations thereby implied, and thus could no longer coalesce into a separate, exploited class.

The similarity to present-day conditions is striking. Now there exist legal provisions and economic practices that make the foreign laborers almost automatically members of the ruling class and the rivals of their employers. Monopolization of ownership of the means of production is no more than theoretical and symbolic, since their usufruct can accrue to anyone who is willing to work the land. A traditional credit system, under which money is not lent against interest, but only against security in the form of debtor's slavery, has developed a form that works against the establishment of a credit system based on banking principles. As a result, the laborer must be compensated directly and indirectly by a share in the ownership of the active means of production.

This development is not the result of a particular sensitivity of feeling in social matters. The Anyi would prefer to enjoy the advantages of a privileged class. But it is possible to demonstrate the psychosocial developments responsible for the present "anticapitalist" attitudes of the dominant class. The anal training that finds its culmination in a sedentary, gold-based culture is carried out in such a fashion that a gratification of retentive desires cannot develop.

The establishment of reaction formations against anal loss, which play such an important role in our ego equipment and psychosocial sphere, never takes place. It is for this reason, too, that anal-sadistic tendencies, present to a high degree in both sexes (fixations of instinctual drives), cannot be satisfied retentively—by means of expropriation or the formation and exploitation of capital. The only possessions that have emotional value, that guarantee satisfaction and freedom from fear, are the children, the persons owned by the lineage. As long as this is true, in consequence of the influence custom exerts over psychological development, one finds selective attitudes that make themselves felt in the social sphere and especially in the structure of the economy. Greedily as the individual may strive for gold and financial wealth, so as to be able to enjoy the prestige due a wealthy man, he feels no reluctance whatsoever in assigning to the lineage the right to hoard and increase this wealth—a right that has no emotional content for him. In renouncing all strivings toward stabilization, which can only be a source of uneasiness for him, he projects them to the larger group of which he is a part. It is not improbable that it was the same psychosexual fixations, in the form of psychosocial tendencies, that—nearly two hundred years ago—prevented the Ashanti nation from becoming a "European" feudal state. What the future will bring, however, remains an open question. If one postulates that the other characteristics of the Anyi remain unchanged, then a profitable modern plantation economy could develop among them only if they were permitted to remain exponents of an external paternalistic-maternalistic social order, instead of each being forced to become a capitalist in his own right.

Social conditions and peculiarities in economic structure are not the first things to strike the European when he reads about the ancient Akan peoples or meets the Anyi of Alangouan. At one time cruelty and terror seem to have prevailed there. Today, directly behind the facade of a dignified system of etiquette, there lurks the atmosphere of distrust and fear that justifies the title of this book.

When one hears that practically no death taking place in the region is attributed to natural causes, that all are due to the cunning machinations of some person or other, or that the action of evil witches is the most serious vexation in the daily lives of the population, one cannot help concluding that this society has not succeeded very well in coping with human aggression (125).

General impressions of this kind are seldom entirely true or entirely false. Here we are trying to find an answer to what the Anyi do with outward-directed aggression and whether they follow the pattern of collective scapegoat formation—that is protect their own group by hating the outside group. The latter question is inevitable, because of the paranoiac character of the collectively valid notions we call the "normal paranoia" of the Anyi. Similar attitudes have had disastrous consequences in our own culture (123), and for this reason alone we are bound to be curious about the course taken by these tendencies, so unsusceptible to the control of reason, in a people that appears particularly vulnerable to them.

It is bound to come as a surprise that the Anyi have never developed a collective hatred of the whites who suppressed them for so long, and that, as individuals, they regularly exempt them.from their paranoiac fears, even though they frequently use the threat of "the white man" to control children. Even the foreign workers, who are economically feared and consciously regarded as dangerous interlopers and competitors, have failed to evoke any appreciable collective resentment that might be equated with xenophobia. Observations of this sort become increasingly common as one gets to know the Anyi.

The social effects of the Anyi "normal paranoia" are different from the presumable effects of a paranoiac attitude in a European community. But up to a certain point every persecution delusion is based on the same psychology; an omnipotent aggressor has been incorporated into the individual (introjected) so he can be coped with. When this process fails to bring the needed relief to the ego, the enemy is projected to the external world. There, though he is still experienced as a threat and a source of anxiety, he can at least be combated.

Not only do the projected aggressive fantasies of the Anyi often have a different content from those of Europeans, they are also the product of a different development. The objects of aggression are usually members of the maternal lineage. Hostile strivings remain mobile, they have no tendency to focus on an object, and a damming-up of aggressive emotions (chronic craving for revenge) can develop only rudimentarily. Since the Anyi, by resorting to fantasies of omnipotence, can very quickly gain a victory that in reality would take a good deal of time, effort, and hatred, there is little tendency to combat the cruel object in the external world. These warriors incline to quarrels, not to acts of violence. While they can easily act out aggressions in their fantasies, exchanging one enemy for another in rapid succession and banning them into one form or another, any collective action would restrict their flexibility. It is not the function of the group to unite individuals for the discharge of aggressions. Yet the group is necessary so that each individual can cope adequately with the tensions engendered by aggression (group ego, clan conscience). The actual configuration of the screen of projection—who the real enemies are and how they behave—is rather irrelevant.

In keeping with the aggressive tensions, anxiety is ubiquitous. It warns the individual of inner danger, but also of thieves and robbers, strangers and spirits. The Anyi are afraid of the rain forests in which they live, of their indispensable kings, and of the great mother whose property they are. They try to get rid of their fears without yielding themselves up entirely and without fleeing like cowards. Their social environment makes it possible for them to discharge their aggressions in relatively harmless fashion and to mitigate their anxiety by projection and by conjuring, by compensation, substitution, and arbitration. In these circumstances their dependence upon appropriate behavior by their fellows is great, and the mechanisms of projection and conjuring are irrational. Although the persecutor is usually a member of the individual's own group, the consequences for the community as a whole are slight. The procedure reflects social common sense. After all, when a woman accused of witchcraft makes an imaginary confession and pays her fine of twenty-five francs, less damage is done than if a murder were to be committed or a war to break out.

In spite of their srong paranoiac tendencies, the Anyi do not follow the collective scapegoat pattern. Like any other psychosocial regulatory mechanism, their normal methods of handling aggression may become inadequate and break down when the strain is too great or too one-sided.

In our Western culture, the internalization of aggression, mastered during sphincter training, and the habit of focusing it on an object, learned during the oedipal period, are the reasons even the healthy individual has no choice but to focus paranoiac hostility on a common external enemy whenever it occurs. The principle that aggressive tendencies acquired later (anal sadistic or phallic competitive ones) must also be suppressed until they can be directed to external goals with the approval of the conscience or the group largely dominates not only the socially desirable performance of work but also the previously suppressed feelings of hostility. The economy of sociopsychology demands that our enemies, or the pursuers from whom we flee in our paranoiac anxiety, should be only symbolically dangerous—extant, but at the same time weaker in reality and living outside the group or capable of being separated or excluded from it. This corresponds to our so-called reasonable political and national interests.

Our subjective failure to recognize social reality makes use of these formulas and others like them. They are an unconscious part of the self, which—during the socialization process—has learned to accept the "achievement principle" and to deal with aggression in the way described above. Collective aggression has at its disposal the organizational and technological achievements that we—in just as culture-specific a manner—have worked to bring about. We have the choice of either continuing to follow our pattern and annihilating ourselves in ever more efficient wars, or electing to question the stereotypes, values, and rationalizations of our culture. But this is not a real alternative. The ideology and structure of our Western society have been subjected to searching criticism on countless occasions. But the necessary emotional recathexes and changes in psychological structure, no matter how significant they may be for the individual, are a partial process for the group, which as an overall entity continues to obey the deep emotional need to wage devastating wars, a need that is determined by a multitude of factors. The psychosocial regulatory potential—at least in our Western world—is so great that an improved perception of social reality alone is hardly capable of leading to an appropriate change in our handling of aggressions. On the other hand, a certain insight into the way developments are interlinked may be a favorable precondition to such change.

Today we rarely feel the need to believe in a witchcraft intent on evil. Thus we can readily recognize the "normal paranoia" of the Anyi for what it is; more than that, we can also find a more or less plausible explanation for it. Although we know incomparably more about Western psychology, we find it more difficult to draw sociopsychological conclusions within the framework of our own culture.

It seems a fairly simple task to develop a psychological theory to explain the efficiency the Ashanti and also the Anyi formerly demonstrated in war. If, in olden times, the need to identify with the compelling authority of the chief in order to participate in his aggressive activity was as great as it is today, then the figure of a warrior-king alone would have awakened in his subjects that courage in battle that has consistently evoked such admiration from the British, down to the ethnologist Rattray. Whenever they went forth into battle, the Akan kings acted on the orders and in the interests of the matrilineal lineage. And even today the lineage is still the guarantor and the embodiment of the clan conscience. A number of historical facts suggest that even at that time the individual had no way of directing his aggressions outward. If the king fell on the field of battle, his army collapsed. His death dissolved the identification with him and thus deprived his warriors of their borrowed aggressive potential. A defeat often led to the king's suicide. This was the only form of suicide acceptable to the Akan; the king had failed to defend the interests of the lineage and had thereby forfeited its approval. His clan conscience, which in war had demanded the otherwise impossible discharge of aggressions to the outside world, now demanded atonement; hostility now had to be directed inward, against the self.

There is a song sung by the young men of Bébou; they call it their dancing song:

Everybody knows me now.
On the day when I die,

When I lie in my coffin,
Nobody will know me any more.

Those who used to call me by name,
Now that I am dead,
Don't know my name any more.
You have forgotten my name!

On the day when I die,
They will carry me to my grave
When evening comes,
Quickly, when evening comes.

It is a strange feeling for life that can choose death and oblivion as the themes of a dancing song. Yet these verses also express a bold awareness of reality that refuses to let itself be deluded about the character of human relationships. The truly impressive power of survival inherent in the Anyi cannot be attributed to their culture making them happy. But it does enable its members to get along "appropriately" with their human environment.

Traditional customs are not given up as long as their practice lends identity. To have a "name," to belong, enhances a person's self-esteem and is a sign that he can rely on a society structured to meet his needs. When his name is forgotten, a vital aspect of his personality is lost.

European psychology finds itself in a dilemma. On the one hand, it views the individual as a historical being, formed by his environment. On the other hand, it would often like to endow this individual with an ego that decides freely and independently of the environment and of its own drives and acts for the good of society. To resolve the dilemma, psychologists have assumed that culture can develop only when there is renunciation and suppression of individual drives; both of these, renunciation and suppression, are characteristic of our traditional methods of education and our way of life. Only the ego that has conquered its drives and freed itself from the environment, they have argued, could become capable of genuine social achievement at the end of a process of maturation, development, and individuation.

The psychic structure peculiar to the Anyi suggests another view. In their case, as in ours, all cultural achievements emanate from derived instinctual drives that are "filtered through the ego." In the ego structure, which is the only one of the instances of the psychic apparatus that dominates access to reality, the drives undergo modifications. Among the Anyi, psychological urges dependent upon the various levels of ego development act on the human environment. Their ego has retained an astonishing degree of flexibility. In the adult it can revert to the most varied stages of development and still function normally within its soci-

ety. The various instinctual fixations and defense mechanisms correspond to socially appropriate modes of behavior and performance. Described from this point of view, the society of the Anyi is based not on a
suppression of drives, but rather on every expression of drives that is
integrated into the life of the society.

To put it more generally, the pursuit of psychosocial inter-
dependencies will always come upon the ego in those functions relevant to the culture, but the pattern of that culture will depend on the
course of ego formation specific to the group and on the characteristics
of the personality structures developed in its society. The "suppression
of drives" so characteristic of the Western world—in other words, the
anally influenced resolution of the Oedipus complex—the sexual
taboos, and the focusing of aggression, is a special case that finds expression, from the standpoint of the ego, in heightened social achievements.

It is difficult to avoid the impression that the society of the Anyi is
marked by inherent contradictions, that the personality of the Anyi is
complex and laden with tension. Just as there are people who are full of
conflicts and others who are well adjusted, there may well be forms of
society that are characterized by greater or lesser harmony.

In part the impression mentioned above springs from the ethno-
psychoanalytic way of looking at things. It operates on the premise that
all psychological development is based on the working through of conflicts, and that every society, even the most homogeneous, contains
conflicts between groups and institutions. This model has no room for
"ideal" individuals who have no conflicts or for societies that have
solved all their problems.

In comparing the structure of Anyi society with that of other
societies, much depends on the criteria applied. If one were to apply the
criterion "class conflict," disregarding all other points of view, the Anyi
would have to be regarded as ideal, since no such conflicts have so far
arisen in their society. If one is interested in finding out how appropriate the matrilineal system is in terms of the prevailing economic
structure, then one will be bound to run into contradictions that are
difficult to reconcile.

On the other hand, when the goal is to compare individuals operating
within the framework of their own society with members of other
societies, the researcher will find that there simply is no criterion that
can be applied equally well to members of different cultures. Such concepts as "sensible," "moral," or "socially desirable" behavior are likely
to mean different things to every people, every group, and every class.
Happiness and contentment are words that can be defined only
subjectively.

When no attempt is made to compare or evaluate, the characteristic features begin to emerge. The Anyi avail themselves of nature's abundant gifts with as little effort as possible. They prefer to avoid the perils of their material environment rather than to try to diminish them. Throughout the course of their history they have met the pressures put upon them by other peoples by absorbing as many of the oppressors as they could and then simply retreating into their own way of life. Their approach today is exactly the same. They are capable of dealing with great aggressive tension without waging war and of remaining a master race without exploiting others. Inside the group they are incessantly involved in quarrels, but they have a sophisticated legal system to settle their disputes. The price they pay is the constant need to deal with anxiety, to renounce affluence, and—instead of employing fieldhands— to treat their progeny as material possessions.

Anxiety and aggression are intensified rather than mitigated during psychic development. Ways of dealing with them are learned in a random alternation of externalization and internalization so that neither paralysis nor socially inimical acts of aggression need develop. Whatever is lost in the way of activity potential seems to be compensated for by an active intelligence.

The matrilineal system does not mean either that the maternal and paternal lineages are antagonists in a conflict of interests or that a stable balance has become established between the two lines of descent. Instead, there is polarization, in which the maternal lineage and the women provide and embody a stable system of rules, while power, prestige, and representation in the outside world are the prerogatives of the masculine world. (This "separation of powers" is reminiscent of the political subdivision into legislative and executive.)

The spheres of functioning within the family and in political and other social institutions are closely related to one another—not, however, as simply overlapping social organs, but at the cost of a differentiation at a number of levels. Tensions and contradictions appear in the relationships between the groups of men and women, particularly in the sexual domain, between generations, between individuals, and in the sphere of the psyche, as conflicts among a vast number of desires. In social situations there are ritualized rules of etiquette and clearly defined role assignments to bridge the contradictions. These institutions serve collective just as much as individual needs, and they are supplemented by secular, therapeutic, and religious instances and rituals that are themselves social institutions but that serve the needs of individual homeostasis.

In dealing with inner tensions and contradictions, the Anyi personality operates according to the "not only/but also" principle. It can function on various developmental levels at the same time or in rapid succession, can compensate for mortification and frustration in the external world with imagined gratification, and can switch back and forth between areas of social functioning and even between contradictory wish impulses without losing its coherence or its inner autonomy. To accomplish all this, of course, it must forfeit rigidity and singleness of purpose.

The Anyi cannot afford to let themselves become involved in long-lasting love relationships. One of their most characteristic sayings is "Follow your heart and you perish." Neither the social order nor the self, which does not even determine definitively its own sexual identity, could tolerate a tie to a love object that excluded others. The renunciation of any expression of emotion, which has nothing to do with asceticism but a great deal to do with self-respect, separates them from their neighbors, with whom their communication is subliminal.

Despite all their flexibility and suppleness, the Anyi are capable of maintaining their equilibrium on a long-term basis. This stamps them as independent individuals with unique identities. Their arrogance not only reflects the contempt they feel for this all too imperfect world; it is also intended to express their conviction that only within the framework of their own world can they be what they are.

Notes

Chapter 1

1. We use the term "chief" to refer to the head *(caput)* of a lineage, a court, a village, or a people (chiefship), and "king" when we wish to stress the traditional or political aspects of the institution of chiefship. The French *chef* and the English *chief* have established themselves in the ethnological literature, while the German *Häuptling* ("chief, chieftain") has a decidedly pejorative connotation.

"Eldest" and "elder" are the elders of the family or kin. These are married men who serve as the chiefs of a court (a dwelling community) or of a subgroup within the kin. The Anyi have no village elders who form or preside over a council. The "dignitaries" derive their rank and function from the king and, as a group, form his council of advisors.

2. The classical ethnological publications on the Anyi, from Clozel (10), Delafosse (13), and Tauxier (42) to the more modern works of Amon d'Aby (2, 3) and Mouëzy (30), and the accurately researched, sociologically and economically oriented studies by Köbben (25), Dupire (14) and many others, present an

outline of the main aspects of history, culture, and economic life. For comparison and supplementation we were also able to consult numerous sources, older as well as more modern ones, dealing with other Akan peoples, such as the works on the Ashanti by Rattray (31, 32, 33), Busia (6), and Abraham (1), and on the Akim and the Ga by Field (15, 16), to mention but a few.

We had a stroke of luck with a number of written records. The souspréfet of Abengourou was kind enough to make available to us from his archives a copy (made in 1928) of an original manuscript more than a hundred pages long prepared by Chéruy (7) in his capacity as commandant de cercle (district officer) in 1911/12 for his board of supervisors. And Monsieur Memel Foté, of the Faculté des Lettres (School of Humanities) in Abidjan, had just completed a hundred-page sociological study on the life and work of the healer Edjro Josué, which proved an indispensable aid in our psychological investigations.

Chapter 2

1. RDCI = Rassemblement Démocratique de la Côte d'Ivoire (Democratic Union of the Ivory Coast), the national unity party, describes itself as a member of a movement common to several West African nations, the RDA = Rassemblement Démocratique Africain (African Democratic Union).

2. Our reasons for not describing the society and personality of the Akan in terms of their conceptual world have been supplemented by a number of comments on structuralism. This was not in order to present our views on this philosophical system—this book is hardly the proper place for such an undertaking—but to stress that we are not adherents of the system, even though we describe and compare "structures." Nor is our method based on the phenomenological approach, which today is often contrasted with structuralism. In our opinion, both theories imply a narrowing of research to comply with the exigencies of a system of philosophical thought.

3. Adamson-Hoebel (44) has described the legal system of the Ashanti as a typical example of primitive criminal law. Taking Rattray (32) and Busia (6) as his main sources (as we did, too), he lists the punishable offenses and the often extremely cruel corporal penalties the Ashanti kings were empowered to impose. His verdict of "primitive criminal law" is based on his social theory of linear evolution. The following appears on the dust jacket of the German edition of his book: "[He] has described the legal systems of five primitive societies, their forms of social organization ranging from the rulerless Eskimos to the Ashanti, whose organization is military and strictly hierarchical." According to his theory, the ideal is Roman law, and thus the Western systems derived from it, and—as a matter of fact—these systems are far more similar to Ashanti than to Eskimo law. Inasmuch as we consider the application of the theory of linear social evolution—which comes originally from biology—unjustified, there is no need for us to apply the criterion of greater or lesser resemblance to Western legal systems, or to summarize the formal similarities existing between Akan and Western criminal law. What we are dealing with here is an entirely different social system, which has evolved an entirely different legal structure for itself, a structure that—naturally—is the product of a historical development and that deserves to be investigated on its own merits, not on the premise that it must somehow turn out to be similar to European systems.

4. It would exceed the scope of this investigation to attempt to determine whether the administration of justice as practiced by the Akan is "better" than that found in Western cultures. A body of law is the repository of rules that reflect, or should reflect, a collective concept of justice and that should be incorporated in abstract form into the superego of the individual. Without doubt, the Akan system is more flexibly adapted to the sense of justice *and* the emotional needs of the parties concerned; it is far closer to personal experience. At the same time, judicial verdicts are bound to be left in the hands of the participants, with all their human weaknesses, to a greater extent than in a system in which "objective" justice prevails, guaranteed by an "impartial" panel of judges. The concepts of guilt, atonement, and forgiveness are not compatible with the Akan legal structure. In Western nations and in Africa alike, the idea of providing a deterrent to punishable offenses is implicit in the administration of justice, but its practical efficacy is difficult to assess. The fear of punishment seems to have little influence on persons who, either constantly or at some crucial moment, are willing to or feel compelled to disregard social value systems; this is just as true in the West as it is in Africa.

5. A more complete system of concepts concerning the soul can be compiled from the literature dealing with other Akan peoples (1, 12, 15, 33, 69). According to these sources, there are four kinds of nonmaterial components in the living being:

1. *Kra, okra* = "life soul," which lives on after death, and which has seven forms depending on the day of the week on which the individual was born. Linked with it is:
2. *Mgoya* = blood of the maternal lineage *(abusua)*, which becomes the individual's spirit *(saman)* after death.
3. *Sunsum* = "personality soul," which departs from the body during sleep and can be attacked by witches.
4. *Ntoro* (genetic term) = the "ego inherited from the father," which is absorbed by the *sunsum* at puberty.

Only human beings have *kra*, not animals. It is the most important factor of the personality, the embodiment of (psychic) fate. Like fate, the *kra* operates automatically; it gives the individual strength and an identity of his own. When the *kra* departs from its abode, the individual falls ill and finally dies. The *kra* has been compared with the id.

Sunsum also means "a second person." It is the basis of the character, is malleable and teachable. The *sunsum* has been compared with the superego.

Chapter 3

1. According to his identity papers Thomas Assoua is twenty-two years old; judging from his life history he is certainly older, possibly between twenty-eight and thirty.

2. The most important stipulations of the law of inheritance are the following: The inheritance passes from the oldest brother to his younger brothers, and it is only when the fraternal line has died out that the "nephew," that is, the oldest son of the sister, inherits; the inheritance then passes from the nephew to *his* younger brothers, and so forth. Daughters can inherit from their mothers in direct line. Otherwise the law of inheritance is extremely complicated and provides for every conceivable possibility. In all cases, however, the classificatory siblings of the maternal line come before the children of the sister of the legator.

Chapter 4

1. In Senegal this inability to make up their minds whether to live or die is attributed to very special children called *nit-ku-bon* (72). This term defines their spiritual and physical qualities and subjects dealings with them to a special ritual. The symptoms by which such a child can be recognized correspond to those described by Spitz (138) in severely frustrated infants and toddlers in danger of dying from the effects of emotional deprivation. The prescribed method for dealing with these children is to provide them with satisfying contacts with their environment in spite of their reluctance and thus to make it possible for them to go on living. The Anyi have no comparable traditional institutions; all their children, so to speak, are potential *nit-ku-bons*.

Chapter 5

1. We were not able to observe any obvious differences in personality development between Anyi who had attended school and Anyi who had grown up without the benefit of schooling. In Bébou the school has long been an integral part of village life—as an institution, not as an instrument for transmitting education. Frequently, failure to complete school was an obstacle to becoming a planter. On the other hand, young men who had never been to school at all experienced exactly the same difficulties in finding their place in the world of adult work; the only difference lay in the reasons they gave.

Naturally, our chances of studying Anyi who were unable to speak French were very restricted. Thus any conclusions drawn from a comparison of Africans with and without formal education would require especially careful verification.

Chapter 6

1. A European surgeon who is a practicing Catholic and performs complicated operations requiring a large team and complex technical equipment must rely on spiritual instances as well as upon a highly organized professional environment. This cannot be taken as an indication that he has a more immature or a more disturbed personality than a physician who is an atheist, believes only in science, and operates alone because the surgery he performs is less complex.

2. The priestesses of the Ga sometimes speak in Twi (= Akan), sometimes in their native Ga, and sometimes in "Tserepon," which is probably a mixture of Twi, Ga, and Guan and corresponds to the "Ashanti" employed by the female shamans of the Anyi (personal communication from Marion Kilson).

Chapter 7

1. As far as we know, the Anyi have not a taboo, but a custom that forbids younger or socially inferior persons from speaking without being asked for their opinions in the presence of older or socially higher-ranking individuals.

2. We use the term "transference reaction" to refer to those attitudes of the subject toward the analyst that have been shaped by earlier experience and experience modalities, but for which it is not (yet) clear just which experiences

are being transferred to the analyst in the form of which objects (contact persons).

3. The difficulty experienced by many African schoolchildren in finding proper oral expression for the actually very clear thoughts that they are able to express in writing has been attributed to the fact that in school they are continually forced to speak before a person of authority, the teacher, and in public, before their schoolmates (1).

Chapter 8

1. Following a suggestion made in a letter from René A. Spitz, we should like to state our view that the unusually early appearance of intellectual independence is not characteristic of all children, but that a selective principle in line with the survival of the fittest comes into play. It can be assumed that those children who are poorly equipped to cope with the highly traumatic separation from the mother—either because of innate predispositions or because of their prior development—simply perish, and that only those survive who already possess a certain intellectual faculty. We have no statistical data, however, that might substantiate this assumption.

2. The authors were allowed by the medical staff of the state psychiatric hospital, Bingerville, to examine all hospitalized psychotic Anyi patients (four men and four women) during one day. We report the results of these psychiatric examinations in the original version of this book (pp. 387–88).

3. This is an expression we coined during our first studies of African peoples, and it has become firmly established in the meantime (75). Our original description of the phenomenon applies to the Dogon, the Anyi, and other African peoples as well. We have had to revise our original metapsychological explanation, however. What is referred to as "clan conscience" must be studied metapsychologically in each of its culture-specific manifestations, since its origins and its functions are not uniform.

Chapter 9

1. Ethnopsychoanalysis is a branch of cultural anthropology. The special aspects and the various goals and methods of research in the latter field cannot be dealt with in detail here. For a comprehensive account, refer to M. Harris (144).

2. The fundamental points of view, "paradigms" according to Kuhn (147), that find application here are primarily those of Freudian psychoanalysis and secondarily those of the social sciences (98, 110, 147). In our opinion, the field of cultural anthropology does not yet possess a generally applicable terminology of its own.

3. This statement is based in part on earlier investigations (14, 25) and in part on later impressions, which, however, are only symptomatic in character. Further verification is required.

References

The Anyi and Other Akan Peoples

1. Abraham, W. E. 1962. *The mind of Africa*. London: Weidenfeld and Nicolson.
2. Amon d'Aby, F. J. 1951. *La Côte d'Ivoire dans la cité africaine*. Paris: Larose.
3. ———. 1960. *Croyances religieuses et coutumes juridiques des Agni de la Côte d'Ivoire*. Paris: Larose.
4. Basehart, H. W. 1962. Ashanti. In *Matrilineal kinship*, ed. D. M. Schneider and Kathleen Gough. Berkeley: University of California Press.
5. Boutillier, J. L. 1960. *Bongouanou: Côte d'Ivoire*. Paris: Berger-Levrault.
6. Busia, K. A. 1951. *The position of the chief in the modern political system of Ashanti*. London: Oxford University Press.
7. Chéruy, P. 1911/12. Monographie du Cercle de l'Indénié. Manuscript.
8. Christensen, J. B. 1958. The role of proverb in Fante culture. *Africa*, vol. 28, no. 3.

9. Clignet, R. 1961. Première esquisse d'une psychologie de la femme en Côte d'Ivoire. *Bull. Inter-Afr. Labour Inst.*, vol. 8, no. 1.
10. Clozel, F. J. 1906. *Dix ans à la Côte d'Ivoire*. Paris.
11. Danquah, J. B. 1968. *The Akan doctrine of God*. London: F. Cass. Originally published 1944.
12. Debrunner, H. 1959. *Witchcraft in Ghana*. Accra: Presbyterian Book Depot.
13. Delafosse, M. 1900. *Essai de manuel (de langue) Agni*. Paris.
14. Dupire, Marguerite. 1960. Planteurs autochtones et étrangers en Basse-Côte d'Ivoire orientale. *Et. Eburnéennes*, vol. 8.
15. Field, M. J. 1948. *Akim-Kotoku*. London and Accra: Crown Agents Colonies.
16. ———. 1960. *Search for security*. London: Faber and Faber.
17. Fortes, M. 1953. Parenté et mariage chez les Ashantis. In *Systèmes familiaux et matrimoniaux en Afrique*, ed. A. R. Radcliffe-Brown and D. Forde. Paris: Presses Universitaires de France. Originally published 1950.
18. Fortes, M., and Evans-Pritchard, E. E. 1964. *African political systems*. London: Oxford University Press. Originally published 1941.
19. Fortes, M., and Dieterlen, Germaine. 1965. *African systems of thought*. London: Oxford University Press.
20. Fuller, F. 1968. *A vanished dynasty: Ashanti*. London: F. Cass. Originally published 1921.
21. Holas, B. 1961. *Changements sociaux en Côte d'Ivoire*. Paris: Presses Universitaires de France.
22. ———. 1963. *La Côte d'Ivoire: Passé-présent-perspectives*. Paris: Geuthner.
23. ———. 1965. *Le séparatisme religieux en Afrique Noire*. Paris: Presses Universitaires de France.
24. Kilson, Marion. 1968. Possession in Ga-ritual. *Transcult. Psychiat. Res.*, vol. 5, and personal communication.
25. Köbben, A. J. 1956. Le planteur noir. *Et. Eburnéennes*, vol. 5.
26. ———. 1964. Social change and political structure. In *Afrika im Wandel seiner Gesellschaftsformen*, ed. W. Fröhlich. Leiden: E. J. Brill.
27. Kyerematen, A. 1969. The royal stools of Ashanti. *Africa*, vol. 39, no. 1.
28. Manoukian, Madeleine. 1950. *Akan and Ga-Adangme peoples*. London: Oxford University Press.
29. Meyerowitz, Eva. 1951. *The sacred state of Akan*. London: Faber and Faber.
30. Mouëzy, H. 1953. *Assinie et le royaume de Krinjabo*. Paris: Larose.
31. Rattray, R. S. 1916. *Ashanti proverbs*. Oxford: Clarendon Press.
32. ———. 1923. *Ashanti*. Oxford: Clarendon Press.
33. ———. 1927. *Religion and art in Ashanti*. Oxford: Clarendon Press.
34. ———. 1933. The African child in proverb, folklore, and fact. *Africa*, vol. 4, no. 4.

35. ———. 1965. Prières des Ashanti. In *Textes sacrés d'Afrique Noire*, ed. Germaine Dieterlen. Paris: Gallimard.
36. Reindorf, C. C. 1966. *The history of the Gold Coast and Asante*. London: Oxford University Press. Originally published 1889.
37. Riis, H. N. 1854. *Grammatical outline and vocabulary in the Oji-language together with a collection of proverbs of the natives*. Basel.
38. Roehric, V. 1938. Douze contes du pays Agni. *Educ. Afr.*, vol. 101.
39. Rouch, J. 1963. Introduction à l'étude de la communauté de Bregbo. *J. Soc. Africanistes*, vol. 33, no. 1.
40. ———. 1965. Cantiques harristes. In *Textes sacrés d'Afrique Noire*, ed. Germaine Dieterlen. Paris: Gallimard.
41. Rougerie, G. 1957. Le pays Agni du sud-est de la Côte d'Ivoire forestière. *Et. Eburnéennes*, vol. 6.
42. Tauxier, L. 1932. *Religion, moeurs et coutumes des Agnis de la Côte d'Ivoire (Indénié et Sanwi)*. Paris: Geuthner.
43. Wilks, J. 1967. Ashanti government. In *West African kingdoms in the nineteenth century*, ed. D. Forde and P. M. Kaberry. London: International African Institute.

Other African References (Including Transcultural Psychiatry)

44. Adamson-Hoebel, E. 1968. *Das Recht der Naturvölker*. Olten: Walter. Originally published 1954.
45. Amiel, R. 1963. Rapport d'expertise. *O.M.S., AFR, MH*, vol. 1.
46. *Annuaire national de la Côte d' Ivoire*. 1965. Abidjan.
47. Baumann, H., and Westermann, D. 1957. *Les peuples et les civilisations de l'Afrique*. Paris: Payot. Originally published 1947.
48. Bertaux, P. 1966. *Afrika: Von der Vorgeschichte bis zu den Staaten der Gegenwart*. Frankfurt am Main: Fischer.
49. Boroffka, A., and Marinho, A. 1963. Psychoneurotic syndromes in urbanized Nigerians. *Transcult. Psychiat. Res.*, vol. 15.
50. Collomb, H. 1965. Bouffées délirantes en psychiatrie africaine. *Psychopathol. Afr.* (Dakar), vol. 1, no. 2.
51. Crowder, M. 1968. *West Africa under colonial rule*. London: Hutchinson.
52. Herskowits, M. J. 1962. *The human factor in changing Africa*. New York: Knopf.
53. Kiev, A. 1964. *Magic, faith and healing*. Glencoe, Ill.: Free Press.
54. Lambo, T. A. 1961. *Growth of African children*. Report of the First Pan-African Psychiatric Conference, Abeokuta.
55. Lamy, R. 1932. Enquête sur l'enfant noir en Afrique occidentale française. *Bull. Enseign. AOF*, vol. 21, no. 80.
56. Le Guerinel, N. 1968. Etude de cas à Bingerville (Côte d'Ivoire). *Psychopathol. Afr.* (Dakar), vol. 4, no. 1.
57. Leighton, A., and Lambo, T. A. 1963. *Psychiatric disorders among the Yoruba*. Ithaca, N.Y.: Cornell University Press.

58. Marinho, A. A. 1968. Une reévaluation du syndrome de "surmen-age." *Psychopathol. Afr.* (Dakar), vol. 4, no. 1.
59. Memel, F. 1966. Un guérrisseur de la Basse Côte d'Ivoire, Edjro Josué. Manuscript.
60. Neki, J., and Marinho, A. 1968. *A reappraisal of the "brain fag" syndrome.* Report of the Second Pan-African Psychiatric Conference, Dakar.
61. Ortigues, Marie-Cécile, and Ortigues, E. 1966. *Oedipe africain.* Paris: Plon.
62. Paulme, Denise. 1962. Une religion syncrétique en Côte d'Ivoire. *Cah. Etudes Afr.*, vol. 3 (9), no. 1.
63. Philipps, E. A. 1953. *Survey of African marriage and family life.* London: Oxford University Press.
64. Potehin, J. J. 1960. O feodalizme u Ašanti. *Sovetsk. Etnograf.*, vol. 6.
65. Powdermaker, Hortense. 1962. *Copper town: Changing Africa.* New York: Harper and Row.
66. Prince, R. 1960. The "brain fag" syndrome in Nigerian students. *J. Ment. Sci.*, vol. 106.
67. Radcliffe-Brown, A. R., and Forde, D. 1950. *African systems of kinship and marriage.* London: Oxford University Press.
68. Savage, C., and Prince, R. 1967. *Depression among the Yoruba.* Psychoanalytic Study of Society, no. 4. New York: International Universities Press.
69. Seligman, C. G. 1930. *Races of Africa.* London: Butterworth.
70. Wintrob, R. M. 1966. La relation entre psychoses et possession par les génies au Libéria. *Psychopathol. Afr.* (Dakar), vol. 2, no. 2.
71. Wittkower, E., and Weidmann, H. 1968. A combined psychoanalytical and anthropological approach to magic, witchcraft and sorcery. *Psychopathol. Afr.* (Dakar), vol. 4, no. 2.
72. Zempleni, A., and Rabin, J. 1965. L'enfant Nit-ku-bon. *Psychopathol. Afr.* (Dakar), vol. 1, no. 3.
73. Ziegler, J. 1964. *Sociologie de la nouvelle Afrique.* Paris: Gallimard.
74. Zolberg, A. R. 1964. *One-party government in the Ivory Coast.* Princeton: Princeton University Press.

Ethnopsychoanalytical Works by the Authors (to the Year 1969)

75. 1957. Charakteranalytischer Deutungsversuch am Verhalten "primitiver" Afrikaner. *Psyche* (Heidelberg), vol. 10, no. 5. Translated in *Man and his culture*, ed. W. Muensterberger. London: Rapp and Whiting, 1969.
76. 1958. Einige Charakterzüge "primitiver" Afrikaner. *Psyche* (Heidelberg), vol. 11, no. 11.
77. 1961. Die Anwendung der psychoanalytischen Methode auf Beobachtungen in Westafrika. *Acta Tropica* (Basel), vol. 18, no. 2.
78. 1962. Feldanthropologische Untersuchungen in Westafrika. *Schweiz. Z. Psychol.*, vol. 21, no. 1.

79. 1963. Eine scheinbare "Schamkultur." *Köln. Z. Soziol.*, vol. 15, no. 1.

80. 1963. *Die Weissen denken zuviel: Psychoanalytische Untersuchungen bei den Dogon in Westafrika.* Zurich: Atlantis. 2d ed., Munich: Kindler; French ed., *Les blancs pensent trop.* Paris: Payot, 1966.

81. 1964. Typical forms of transference among West Africans. *Int. J. Psycho-anal.*, vol. 45, nos. 2–3.

82. 1964. *Ego and orality in the analysis of West Africans.* Psychoanalytic Study of Society, no. 3. New York: International Universities Press.

83. 1963. Il complesso edipico nei Dogon dell'Africa Occidentale. *Rivista Psicoanalisi*, vol. 9, no. 2.

84. 1964. Anthropologie und psychoanalytische Rekonstruktion. *Schweiz. Z. Psychol.*, vol. 23, no. 2.

85. 1967. Observations sur la genèse du moi chez les Dogon. *Rev. Franç. Psychoanal.*, vol. 31, no. 1.

86. 1967. Zur Bedeutung von Mythus, Ritual und Brauch für die vergleichende Psychiatrie. In *Beiträge zur vergleichenden Psychiatrie*, ed. N. Petrilowitsch, vol. 2. Basel: Karger.

87. 1967. Considérations psychanalytiques sur le moi de groupe. *Psychopathol. Afr.* (Dakar), vol. 3, no. 2.

88. 1968. Aspekte des Gruppenich (Katamnese bei den Dogon). *Schweiz. Z. Psychol.*, vol. 27, no. 2.

89. 1969. Ist die Verinnerlichung der Aggression für die soziale Anpassung notwendig? In *Bis hierher und nicht weiter*, ed. A. Mitscherlich. Munich: Piper.

Psychoanalysis and Psychology

90. Arlow, J. A. 1961. Ego psychology and the study of mythology. *J. Am. Psychoanal. Ass.*, vol. 9.

91. Bally, G. 1945. *Vom Ursprung und von den Grenzen der Freiheit.* Basel.

92. Balint, M. 1957/58. Die drei seelischen Bereiche. *Psyche* (Heidelberg), vol. 11, no. 6.

93. Boyer, L. B., and Giovacchini, P. L. 1967. *Psychoanalytic treatment of schizophrenic and characterological disorders.* New York: Science House.

94. Boyer, L. B., and Boyer, Ruth. 1968. A combined anthropological and psychoanalytical contribution to folklore. Manuscript.

95. Devereux, G. 1967. Greek pseudo-homosexuality and the "Greek miracle." *Symbolae* (Oslo), vol. 42.

96. Eicke-Spengler, Martha. 1969. Psychoanalytische Beobachtungen und Überlegungen zum Syndrom der Hypochondrie. Unpublished paper submitted to *Schweiz. Ges. Psychoanalyse.*

97. Eisnitz, A. J. 1969. Narcissistic object choice, self representation. *Int. J. Psycho-anal.*, vol. 50, no. 1.

98. Eissler, K. R. 1968. The relation of explaining and understanding

in psychoanalysis. In *Psychoanalytic study of the child*, vol. 23. New York: International Universities Press.

99. Eirkson, E. H. 1950. *Childhood and society*. New York: Norton.

100. ———. 1959. *Identity and the life cycle*. New York: International Universities Press.

101. ———. 1966. The ontogeny of ritualization in man. In *Psychoanalysis: A general psychology*, ed. R. M. Loewenstein. New York: International Universities Press.

102. Federn, P. 1952. *Ego psychology and the psychoses*, ed. E. Weiss. New York: Basic Books.

103. Freud, Anna. 1960. Adolescence. In *Psychoanalytic study of the child*, vol. 13. New York: International Universities Press.

104. ———. 1965. *Normality and pathology in childhood*. New York: International Universities Press.

105. Freud, Sigmund. 1913. Totem und Tabu. *Imago* (London), vol. 9. English translation, Totem and taboo, in *Standard edition*, ed. J. Strachey, vol. 13. London: Hogarth Press.

106. ———. 1916. Trauer und Melancholie. *Imago* (London), vol. 10. English translation, Mourning and melancholia, in *Standard edition*, ed. J. Strachey, vol. 14. London: Hogarth Press.

107. ———. 1921. Massenpsychologie und Ichanalyse. *Imago* (London), vol. 13. English translation, Group psychology and the analysis of the ego, in *Standard edition*, ed. J. Strachey, vol. 18. London: Hogarth Press.

108. ———. 1922. Über einige neurotische Mechanismen bei Eifersucht, Paranoia und Homosexualität. *Imago* (London), vol. 13. English translation, Some neurotic mechanisms in jealousy, paranoia and homosexuality, in *Standard edition*, ed. J. Strachey, vol. 18. London: Hogarth Press.

109. ———. 1939. Der Mann Moses und die monotheistische Religion. *Imago* (London), vol. 16. English translation, Moses and monotheism: Three essays, in *Standard edition*, ed. J. Strachey, vol. 23. London: Hogarth Press.

110. Gitelson, M. 1964. On the identity crisis in American psychoanalysis. *J. Am. Psychoanal. Ass.*, vol. 12, no. 3.

111. Gressot, M. 1967. L'interdit de l'inceste précurseur et noyau du surmoi oedipien. *Rev. Franç. Psychanal.*, vol. 31, nos. 5–6.

112. Grunberger, B. 1964. Über das Phallische. *Psyche* (Heidelberg), vol. 17.

113. Hartmann, H. 1964. Understanding and explanation. In *Essays on ego psychology*. New York: International Universities Press. Originally published 1927.

114. Hartmann, H. 1960/61. Ich-Psychologie und Anpassungsproblem. *Psyche* (Heidelberg), vol. 14. Originally published 1939. English translation by D. Rapaport, *Ego psychology and the problem of adaptation*, J. Am. Psychoanal. Ass. Monogr. 1. New York: International Universities Press, 1958.

115. ———. 1964. Psychoanalysis and sociology. In *Essays on ego psychology*. New York: International Universities Press. Originally published 1944.

116. ———. 1964. The application of psychoanalytic concepts to social science. In *Essays on ego psychology*. New York: International Universities Press. Originally published 1950.

117. ———. 1964. Notes on the reality principle. In *Essays on ego psychology*. New York: International Universities Press. Originally published 1956.

118. Hartmann, H., and Loewenstein, R. 1962. Notes on the superego. In *Psychoanalytic study of the child*, vol. 17. New York: International Universities Press.

119. Haynal, A. 1968. Le syndrome de couvade. *Ann. Médico-Psychol.* (Paris), vol. 126, no. 4.

120. Joffe, W. G., and Sandler, J. 1965. Notes on pain, depression, and individuation. In *Psychoanalytic study of the child*, vol. 20. New York: International Universities Press.

121. Kris, E. 1953. *Psychoanalytic explorations in art*. London: Allen and Unwin.

122. Lincke, H. 1972. Das Überich. In *Lexicon Psychiatricum*. Berlin: Springer.

123. Loewenstein, R. M. 1951. *Christians and Jews*. New York: International Universities Press.

124. Mahler, Margaret. 1969. *On human symbiosis and the vicissitudes of individuation*. London: Hogarth Press.

125. Mitscherlich, A. 1969. *Die Idee des Friedens und die menschliche Aggressivität*. Frankfurt am Main: Suhrkamp.

126. Morgenthaler, F. 1969. Introduction to the panel on disturbances of male and female identity. *Int. J. Psycho-anal.*, vol. 50.

127. Moser, U. 1967. Die Entwicklung der Objektbesetzung. *Psyche* (Heidelberg), vol. 21.

128. Muensterberger, W. 1962. *The creative process: Its relation to object loss and fetishism*. Psychoanalytic Study of Society, no. 2. New York: International Universities Press.

129. ———. 1968. *Psyche und Milieu*. Jahrb. Psychoanal., no. 5. Bern: Huber.

130. Rapaport, D. 1967. The autonomy of the ego. In *Collected papers*. New York: Basic Books. Originally published 1951.

131. ———. 1967. The theory of ego autonomy: A generalization. In *Collected papers*. New York: Basic Books. Originally published 1957.

132. Richter, H. E. 1968. *Probleme der Familientherapie*. Jahrb. Psychoanal., no. 5. Bern: Huber.

133. Róheim, G. 1967. *Psychanalyse et anthropologie*. Paris: Gallimard. Originally published 1950.

134. Sandler, J., and Joffe, W. G. 1966. On skill and sublimation. *J. Am. Psychoanal. Ass.*, vol. 14.

135. Shentoub, S. A. 1964. Psychanalyse, ethnologie et ethnologie psychanalytique. *Rev. Franç. Psychanal.*, vol. 28, no. 3.
136. Spitz, R. A. 1957. *No and yes: On the genesis of human communication.* New York: International Universities Press.
137. ———. 1965. The evolution of dialogue. In *Drives, affects and behaviour,* ed. M. Schur, vol. 2. New York: International Universities Press. Originally published 1963.
138. ———. 1965. *The first year of life.* New York: International Universities Press.

The Social Sciences and the Arts

139. Balandier, G. 1955. *Sociologie actuelle de l'Afrique Noire.* Paris.
140. Boyer, Ruth. 1962. Social structure and socialization among the Apaches of the Mescalero reservation. Ph.D. diss., University of California.
141. Bühler, A. 1964. Die Messianischen Bewegungen der Naturvölker und ihre Bedeutung für Probleme der Entwicklungsländer. *Acta Tropica,* vol. 21, no. 4.
142. Camus, A. 1958. *Caligula.* Paris: Gallimard.
143. Cohen, Y. 1958. Some aspects of ritualized behaviour in interpersonal relationships. *Human Relations,* vol. 11, no. 3.
144. Harris, M. 1968. *The rise of anthropological theory.* New York: Cromwell.
145. Horn, K. 1968. Fragen einer psychoanalytischen Sozialpsychologie. *Psyche* (Heidelberg), vol. 22.
146. Kaplan, B. 1961. *Studying personality cross-culturally.* New York: Harper and Row.
147. Kuhn, T. C. 1970. *The structure of scientific revolutions.* 2d ed. Chicago: University of Chicago Press.
148. Lévi-Strauss, C. 1962. *Le totémisme d'aujourd'hui.* Paris: Presses Universitaires de France.
149. Mauss, M. 1968. Essai sur de don. In *Sociologie et anthropologie.* Paris: Presses Universitaires de France. Originally published 1924.
150. Schneider, D. M. 1962. The distinctive features of matrilineal descent groups. In *Matrilineal kinship,* ed. D. M. Schneider and Kathleen Gough. Berkeley: University of California Press.
151. Simmel, O., and Stählin, R. 1961. *Christliche Religion.* Frankfurt am Main: Fischer.
152. Tutuola, A. 1963. *The palm-wine drunkard.* London: Faber and Faber.
153. Whiting, J.; Kimball, R.; and Whiting, Beatrice. 1965. Field manual for the cross cultural study of child rearing. Rough draft, Harvard University.

Appendix: Ethnopsychoanalytically Oriented Works by the Authors, 1969–79

154. 1970. Personality traits susceptible to deterioration under the impact of cultural change. *Psychopathol. Afr.* (Dakar), vol. 6, no. 1.
155. 1971. *Fürchte deinen Nächsten wie dich selbst: Psychoanalyse und Gesellschaft am Modell der Agni in Westafrika.* Frankfurt am Main: Suhrkamp. 2d ed., Frankfurt am Main: Suhrkamp T. B. Wissenschaft, 1978 (original version of this book).
156. 1971. *Die Weissen denken zuviel.* Munich: Kindler (condensed version of #80).
157. 1972. Der Ausgang des oedipalen Konflikts in drei verschiedenen Kulturen. *Kursbuch* (Berlin) 29:179–201.
158. 1972. A contribution of ethno-psychoanalytic investigation to the theory of aggression. *Int. J. Psycho-anal.*, vol. 53, no. 2; German version 1973 in *Psyche* (Stuttgart), vol. 27, no. 3.
159. Morgenthaler, F. 1974. Die Stellung der Perversionen in Metapsychologie und Technik. *Psyche* (Stuttgart), vol. 28, no. 12.
160. 1975. Moi et oralité dans l'analyse des Dogon. *Connexions* (Paris) 15:43–48.
161. 1975. La méthode psychanalytique au service de la recherche ethnologique. *Connexions* (Paris) 15:25–42.
162. 1975. Is psychoanalysis a social science? In *The annual of psychoanalysis,* 3:371–93. New York: International Universities Press.
163. 1976. Anthropologie et psychiatrie. *Psychopathol. Afr.* (Dakar), vol. 12, no. 1.
164. 1978. The Swiss and southern German lower middle class: An ethno-psychoanalytic study. *J. Psychol. Anthropol.*, vol. 1, no. 1; originally published 1976 in *Psyche* (Stuttgart), vol. 30, no. 11.
165. 1978. The microscope of comparative psychoanalysis and the macrosociety. *J. Psychol. Anthropol.*, vol. 1, no. 2; originally published 1977 in *Psyche* (Stuttgart), vol. 30, no. 1.
166. 1977. Das Ich und die Anpassungs-Mechanismen. *Psyche* (Stuttgart), vol. 31, no. 6.
167. 1978. Der Widerspruch im Subjekt: Die Anpassungsmechanismen des Ich und die Psychoanalyse gesellschaftlicher Prozesse. In *Provokation und Toleranz: Festschrift für Alexander Mitscherlich.* Frankfurt am Main: Suhrkamp.
168. Morgenthaler, F. 1978. *Technik: Zur Dialektik der psychoanalytischen Praxis.* Frankfurt am Main: Syndikat.
169. 1978. *Der Widerspruch im Subjekt: Ethnopsychoanalytische Studien.* Frankfurt am Main: Syndikat.

Index

DATE DUE			
NO 16 '87			